IMMIGRATION AND THE LAW

EDITED BY
SOFÍA ESPINOZA ÁLVAREZ AND
MARTIN GUEVARA URBINA

IMMIGRATION AND THE LAW

———

Race, Citizenship, and Social Control

THE UNIVERSITY OF
ARIZONA PRESS
TUCSON

The University of Arizona Press
www.uapress.arizona.edu

ISBN-13: 978-0-8165-3762-4 (paper)

Cover design by Lisa Force

We thank the Empower Global Foundation for partially funding this book. Without its vital and generous support, these efforts would not be possible.

Agradecemos a la Fundación Empower Global por patrocinar parcialmente este libro. Sin su apoyo vital y generoso, este proyecto no sería posible.

Library of Congress Cataloging-in-Publication Data
Names: Álvarez, Sofía Espinoza, editor. | Urbina, Martin G. (Martin Guevara), 1972–
Title: Immigration and the law : race, citizenship, and social control / edited by Sofía Espinoza Álvarez and
    Martin Guevara Urbina.
Description: Tucson : The University of Arizona Press, 2018. | Includes bibliographical references and index.
Identifiers: LCCN 2017035689 | ISBN 9780816537624 (pbk. : alk. paper)
Subjects: LCSH: Emigration and immigration law—Social aspects—United States. | United States—
    Emigration and immigration—Government policy. | Immigration enforcement—United States.
Classification: LCC KF4819 .I47135 2018 | DDC 342.7308/2—dc23 LC record available at https://lccn.loc
    .gov/2017035689

Printed in the United States of America
♾ This paper meets the requirements of ANSI/NISO Z39.48-1992 (Permanence of Paper).

In memory of Dr. Mary C. Sengstock, who passed away before this book was published, but whose contribution enriches this book—leaving us a lasting legacy.

———

A LOS IMIGRANTES, GENTE DE BIEN

A ti hombre y mujer de bien que te has convertido en un ser honrado y trabajador, que al no tener lo esperado en tu tierra te has aventurado a encontrar un mejor mañana en tierras desconocidas.

Al aun no nacido que se ensaña en el vientre de su madre inmigrante y aguerrida, que con esfuerzo y dedicación criaría a su hijo/hija para ser un hombre/mujer de bien.

A todos aquellos hombres y mujeres tenaces que aguantan frio, tristeza, hambre y humillaciones por creer y aventurarse a alcanzar el tan popular "Sueño Americano."

A todos nosotros que hemos despertado de tal sueño para encontrarnos con una trama de envidia, rencor, racismo y discriminación.

A quienes de la estafa del "Sueño Americano" hemos sido afortunados de sobrevivir y despertar.

A ustedes hombres y mujeres que llenos de coraje están al pie del cañón revolucionando y luchando contra toda injusta realidad.

TO IMMIGRANTS, GOOD PEOPLE

To the good, honest, and hardworking men and women who have ventured out to find a better life in unfamiliar lands.

To all those tenacious men and women who endured cold, sadness, hunger, and humiliation in the hope of achieving the much popularized one-dimensional "American Dream."

To all of us immigrants who have awakened from the scam dream to find a story of envy, resentment, racism, and discrimination.

To the courageous men and women who have struggled, soldiered, and revolutionized against all unjust reality.

S.E.A.

M.G.U.

CONTENTS

List of Tables　　　　　　　　　　　　　　　　　　　　　*xi*

Preface　　　　　　　　　　　　　　　　　　　　　　　*xiii*

Acknowledgments　　　　　　　　　　　　　　　　　　*xxv*

Introduction. U.S. Immigration Laws: The Changing Dynamics of Immigration　　　　　　　　　　　　　　　　　　　　　**3**

SOFÍA ESPINOZA ÁLVAREZ AND MARTIN GUEVARA URBINA

1.　**Beyond the Wall: Race and Immigration Discourse**　　　**30**

ARNOLDO DE LEÓN

2.　**Exposing Immigration Laws: The Legal Contours of Belonging and Exclusion**　　　　　　　　　　　　　　　　　　**46**

STEVEN W. BENDER

3.　**Divided Lines: The Politics of Immigration Control in the United States**　　　　　　　　　　　　　　　　　　　**61**

ROXANNE LYNN DOTY

4.　**Immigration, Illegality, and the Law: Governance, Equality, and Justice**　　　　　　　　　　　　　　　　　　　**80**

CLAUDIO G. VERA SÁNCHEZ

5. Building America: Immigrant Labor and the U.S. Economy   100

RUTH GOMBERG-MUÑOZ

6. Always Running: La Migra, Detentions, Deportations, and
    Human Rights   120

LUPE S. SALINAS

7. Challenges to Integration: The Children of Immigrants and
    Direct and Indirect Experiences with the Law   169

LEO R. CHÁVEZ

8. Borders and Dreams: Immigration, Diversity, and
    Multiculturalism in the New Millennium   203

BRENDA I. GILL AND MARY C. SENGSTOCK

9. Five Myths About Immigration: Immigrant Discourse, Locating
    White Supremacy, and the Racialization of Latino Immigrants
    in the United States   235

DANIEL JUSTINO DELGADO

10. Covering the Immigrant Story: Immigration Through the Lens
    of the American Media   268

PETER LAUFER

11. Immigration, Criminalization, and Militarization in the Age of
    Globalization   281

SOFÍA ESPINOZA ÁLVAREZ AND MARTIN GUEVARA URBINA

Conclusion: Immigration Laws and Social Control Movements:
Situating the Realities of Immigration in the Twenty-First Century   301

MARTIN GUEVARA URBINA AND SOFÍA ESPINOZA ÁLVAREZ

Contributors   *343*
Index   *349*

TABLES

7.1 Characteristics of Adult Children of Latin American and Asian
     Immigrants in the Study   174

7.2 Immigration Status at Time of Entry and at Time of Interview,
     Respondent and Parents   177

7.3 Neighborhood Crime   179

7.4 Number of Neighborhood Crime Problems   180

7.5 Arrest/Incarceration   182

7.6 Prejudice/Discrimination   184

7.7 Logistic Regression Analysis of Years of Schooling, Latino and
     Asian American 1.5- and 2nd-Generation Children of Immigrants
     in the Greater Los Angeles Metropolitan Area   190

7.8 Logistic Regression Analysis of Personal Income, Latino and Asian
     American 1.5- and 2nd-Generation Children of Immigrants in the
     Greater Los Angeles Metropolitan Area   193

PREFACE

ITH SHIFTING DEMOGRAPHICS in the United States, along with national economic crises, national security propaganda, and questionable international relations, some people feel that the "face of America" has been drastically changing, with devastating implications in the midst of globalization. During the 2016 presidential campaign, some politicians, government officials, pundits, bigots, immigration hawks, intellectual racists, and the conservative media joined in Donald Trump's call to "make America great again." In reality, while the face of the United States has been changing, particularly since the latter part of the twentieth century, and more visibly in the early years of the new millennium, America has been changing from its inception. In his *Letters from an American Farmer*, J. Hector St. John de Crèvecoeur described America at its founding as a "mixture of English, Scotch, Irish, French, Dutch, Germans, and Swedes. From this promiscuous breed, that race now called Americans have [*sic*] arisen."

In what seems to be a calculated move, he left out the Sephardic (Spanish) Jews who were among the first settlers in New York when it was New Amsterdam founded by the Dutch, and he also left out the black slaves. Blacks and Latinos aside, he concisely summed up "the American character" at the beginning of the nation, a characterization that held sway for U.S. immigration during the nineteenth century and up to the end of World War II in 1946—establishing an *institutionalized racial ideology of a white nation*. What was less noticed at the time was the increased "browning" of America starting in 1848 after the Treaty of Guadalupe Hidalgo, with the five hundred million acres of land the United States severed and appropriated from Mexico (and the people thereon) as loot from the U.S. expansionist war with Mexico (1846–48)—part of an expansionist movement under the imperialist doctrine of Manifest Destiny that continued with the appropriation of the Philippines, Puerto Rico, and sundry islands in the Pacific (with the inhabitants) as a result of the U.S. war with Spain (1898). Thus, the United States began the twentieth century with a much browner face than it started with in 1776; though, while the brownness was viewed and treated in negative light (e.g., rampant prejudice, racism, exploitation, and violence), it was yet to be perceived as a major cultural, economic, or political threat. The expanded "browning" was then abetted by an exodus of 1.5 million Mexicans migrating "north from Mexico" between 1910 and 1930 (McWilliams 1990; Urbina, Vela, and Sanchez 2014), an exodus that could be characterized as *returned migration*. They were, after all, returning in a sense to an area of land that was once their homeland, browning the face of the United States even more, with subsequent demographic shifts (and corresponding brownness) in the later twentieth century and early twenty-first century. Since 2014, for instance, we have been facing a complex of immigration brought on by an exodus of children from Central America seeking asylum from critical conditions in their countries, together with the Syrian refugee "crisis" in 2015. Indeed, in 2016, centuries after the European colonization of North America, we were told we faced an immigration crisis, and heard presidential candidates "debate" immigration laws, immigration enforcement, and national security. With highly charged political rhetoric and an attitude of "it's either now or never," some politicians and other anti-immigration critics conveniently declared a *war on immigrants*, along with a *war on drugs* and a *war on terrorism*—passionately and aggressively demanding that a wall be built between the United States and Mexico to stop Mexican immigrants (and others) from entering the United States.

A closer analysis of immigration over time, as delineated in this book, reveals that immigration laws, border enforcement, and discourse are more reflective of economic cycles, political will, cultural phobias, and ideological motives than the realities of immigration. Broadly, in a country of immigrants, to which people continue to migrate from all over the world, there has been a highly selective pattern for defining and categorizing who is included and who is excluded. For instance, while immigration has been a topic of discourse for several decades, the focus, in all dimensions, has been on brown immigrants, particularly people of Mexican heritage. Yet, in recent years, Mexican immigration leveled off at zero, and most recently we have witnessed "reverse migration," as more Mexican immigrants are leaving the United States than are migrating north. As for the latest so-called immigration crises, child migration, like adult migration, results from the kinds of conditions that have spurred human migrations globally since time immemorial. To be sure, Syrian refugees (children and adults) are being processed through the "cultural lens" of the gatekeepers, and the migration of Central American children seeking *socorro* (help) or *asilo* (asylum) in the United States is colored by the perceived color of their skin, not the actual content of their vulnerable and uncertain plight.

In a society where laws have been used as a strategic mechanism to define, categorize, criminalize, and *conquer* selected segments of society, immigration laws have been used as a formal, official, and "legal" avenue for building, maintaining, and expanding power, dominance, and control. Like criminal laws, immigration laws (and their agents—police officers, correctional officers, attorneys, and judges) have governed the confines of *belonging* and *exclusion*—shaping and reshaping the "immigrant" experience and overall American experience through the lens of (almost exclusively) white male ideology, under the notion of "it's the law" of this great nation, with the Constitution often being cited. In truth, immigration laws, like criminal laws, are not synonymous with equality or justice, as what is "legal" is not always about equality, legitimacy, or justice. As associate justice of the U.S. Supreme Court Oliver Wendell Holmes once declared, "This is a court of law, young man, not a court of justice," and in the words of Professor Paul J. Kaplan, "Courts talk like upper-class white men and subordinate those who do not," suggesting that throughout American history legality has not always favored marginalized, indigent, powerless, or colored people.

The United States has historically characterized itself as a country grounded in democratic principles, like freedom, equality, civil liberties, voting rights, representation, opportunity, and justice, with the Statue of Liberty (in New York City) welcoming new immigrants to the "land of opportunity." In truth, the United States has more often been a scene of political, economic, and social chaos, as well as selective and oppressive immigration laws and enforcement in the historical fight for expansion, wealth, power, control, and dominance, than showing a unified movement for equality in its main institutions or universal freedom, justice, and opportunity for people migrating to or residing in the mainland. In effect, while there has been gross inequality and injustice in all major U.S. institutions, some of the greatest discontinuities, inefficiencies, inequalities, and injustices have been generated and maintained by the American legal system, along with other components of the criminal justice system that have been designed to create order, manage populations, and silence certain segments of society through intimidation, arrest, incarceration, deportation, execution, and disenfranchisement. Worse, in the very arena where the machinery of justice is operating and so where efficiency, equality, and justice are supposed to prevail, some of the most catastrophic events and movements, including abuse, violence, and violations of civil liberties, are taking place, with certain segments of society strategically targeted, particularly the most vulnerable—undocumented immigrants.

After centuries of supposed "liberation," people tend to blindly accept immigration laws and other criminal justice polices without truly questioning (or challenging) the essence of American laws, as recently documented by Joe R. Feagin in *White Party, White Government: Race, Class, and U.S. Politics* (2012), Alfonso Gonzales in *Reform Without Justice: Latino Migrant Politics and the Homeland Security State* (2014), and Steven W. Bender in *Mea Culpa: Lessons on Law and Regret from U.S. History* (2015). Most notably, in the context of race and ethnicity, which color the parameters of immigration, as early as 1740 (years before the Declaration of Independence), the South Carolina Slave Code, for example, declared that "the people commonly called negroes, Indians, mulattos and mestizos have [been] deemed absolute slaves, and the subjects of property in the hands of particular persons the extent of whose power over slaves ought to be settled and limited by positive laws so that the slaves may be kept in due subjection and obedience" (cited in Hall, Wiecek, and Finkelman 1996, 37). This resulted in a centuries-long legacy of racism, manipulation, exploitation, marginalization, oppression, and silencing of racial minorities and immigrants, with undocumented people having to live in fear and in the shadows. Starting with the Declaration of Independence (1776), race has played a central role in defining U.S. laws and how criminal justice policies are applied to blacks, brown people, and undocumented people. As for ethnic minorities in the United States, normally left out of the pages of history, Latinos, like blacks, have suffered the indignities of conquest and de jure segregation. In the case of Mexican Americans, who by 2013 constituted about 10.9 percent (34.6 million) of the U.S. population and about 64.1 percent of all Latinos in the country, under the rationale of Anglo-Saxon expansion and Manifest Destiny, premised on the ideology of the racial, ethnic, religious, and cultural superiority of white Americans, the Treaty of Guadalupe Hidalgo that ended the Mexican-American War in 1848 granted the United States 55 percent of Mexico's territory, an area that now constitutes about one-third of the continental United States. The conquest, however, set in motion an anti-Mexican legacy of hate that continues today. In fact, soon after, policies like the 1855 "Greaser Act," an anti-vagrancy law enacted in California defining vagrants as "all persons who are commonly known as 'Greasers' or the issue [children] of Spanish and Indian blood," was a deliberate use of U.S. law to target Mexicans based on race and ethnicity (Morín 2009, 16). As José Luis Morín (2009, 15) declares: "This history is instructive as to how Latinas/os would be regarded in later years, since persons of mixed racial backgrounds, as many Latinas/os are, have been and often continue to be viewed with disdain, and subject to discrimination by the dominant 'White' social structure."

Immigration laws, enforcement, and discourse have to be analyzed within a broader context, beginning with law and order. Toward the end of the twentieth century, with America's social control movement (including the war on drugs and the war on immigrants) gaining momentum, Jonathan Simon (1997, 173) proposed that advanced industrial societies are actually "governed through crime," with the overdeveloped societies of the West and North Atlantic "experiencing not a crisis of crime and punishment but a crisis of governance that has led [them] to prioritize crime and punishment as the preferred contexts of governance," redefining the limits of immigration and criminal laws and police roles, practices, and ideologies, while socially reconstructing the parameters of race and ethnicity and by extension immigration enforcement and social control in general. Then, at the turn of the century, Tony Fitzpatrick (2001, 220) argued that as "global capital becomes apparently unmanageable" and "as the polity and the economic detached after a century of alignment," the state must give itself, particularly its agents, like the police and court officials, something to do, and so the state "socially and discursively constructs threats that only it can address through . . . punitive responses to the chaos it has [helped facilitate]," as in the case of the war on immigrants, the war on drugs, the war on terrorism, and various other aggressive social control movements—movements that have culminated in the militarization of the southern border and police departments around the country—not to mention the billions in funding for additional equipment and salaries for thousands of immigration agents. In the twenty-first century, with migration, crime, and criminal justice systems becoming increasingly transnational (Ruddell and Urbina 2004, 2007), combined with a militarized immigration police force and assisted by advanced surveillance technology and a highly charged American media, "at once totalizing and individualizing," such strategies cohere in appealing political formations that can govern "all and each" with stealthy precision (Gordon 1991, 3; Urbina and Álvarez 2015, 2016, 2017; Welch 2006; Whitehead 2013), giving the state a *means* of absolute power, control, and dominance, and to a feared and mal-informed society an appearance of objectivity, legitimacy, justice, and global unity and solidarity.

As documented in the chapters of this book, from the early conquest of Native Americans, to slavery, to the conquest of Mexicans, to the conquest and colonization of Puerto Ricans, to the war on terrorism, with its corresponding elements (like racial profiling, public space housing sweeps, police surveillance cameras, drug/prostitution-free zones, immigration raids, and "zero-tolerance" anti-immigrants operations), such movements clearly reveal that the U.S. obsession with law and order is just as much about race and ethnicity as it is about safety, equality, and justice. As for the anti-immigrants movement, while we often hear about the Arizona anti-immigrants movement, Arizona is not alone in its crusade to banish Latino immigrants, using the law and the police as an apparatus to stop people who appear Latino for questioning. Policies such as Nebraska 5165, Florida H.B. 7089, Alabama H.B. 56, and Georgia H.B. 87, what some scholars have coined as *crimmigration*, along with policies of twenty-two other states, are *racially coded policies* that often target immigrants and revive the specter of a racialized past. For example, Nebraska 5165, which prohibits renting to immigrants, bears remarkable similarities to Jim Crow laws and restrictive covenants that once prevented renting apartments or selling homes to blacks in white areas. Or, consider H.B. 56 in Birmingham, Alabama, which targets immigrant children with the objective of expelling them from public schools: the law resonates with the policies of the South that maintained educational exclusion for African Americans. Arizona S.B. 1070, which requires police officers to stop any person suspected of being undocumented ("Mexican looking" people), and H.B. 7089 in Florida, which punishes a person with twenty days of jail for failure to present documentation, resemble the slave codes of the South, which required slave patrols to apprehend anyone in the countryside who was suspected of not having their freedom papers or still being a slave. Just as slave patrols were once required to distinguish between black freedmen and slaves, officers must differentiate between undocumented Latinos and documented ethnic minorities. Nationally, too, Latino communities categorized as undocumented become susceptible to aggressive anti-immigrant policies. Consider, for instance, the criminalization of immigrations through various net-widening "operations" (like Operation Gatekeeper, Operation Hold the Line, Operation Jobs, Operation Repatriation, Operation Return to Sender, Operation Safeguard, Operation Streamline, and Operation Wetback), resulting in thousands of Latino deportations and thousands of Latino immigrants incarcerated around the country in facilities operated by private for-profit companies. In a recent study, Yolanda Vásquez (2011) documents that although Latinos represented just 53.1 percent of immigrants residing in the United States, they accounted for 94 percent of the total number of noncitizens deported. Racially coded policies are often justified through verbose political rhetoric and inflammatory charges that immigrants are taxing the economy, appropriating all the jobs, and undermining educational opportunities of U.S. citizens.

Beyond the anti-immigrants movement, the war on drugs and the war on terrorism have also fueled the anti-Mexican and anti-Latino sentiment. As reported by law professor David Cole (2001, 248), "Racial profiling studies . . . make clear that the war on drugs has largely been a war on minorities. It is, after all, drug enforcement that motivates most racial profiling." Similarly, like the war on drugs, according to the American Civil Liberties Union, "the war on terror has quickly turned into a war on immigrants." Contrary to the notion that laws are color-blind and that ethnicity/race (combined with skin color) does not influence final outcomes, the redefining of race, ethnicity, crime, and punishment shown in imprisonment rates (including immigration facilities for adults and children), as reported by University of California, Berkeley professor Loïc Wacquant (2001, 82), "turning over from 70 percent white at the mid-century point to nearly 70 percent black and Latino today, although the ethnic patterns of criminal activity have not been fundamentally altered during that period."

What is going on? This broad question will be addressed throughout this book. To begin the dialogue, though, we will note that during the last two decades, with shifting demographic trends, possibly in no other time in U.S. history has the dominant majority experienced a more significant "cultural crisis." After centuries of their being in *total control* in all facets of life, their ideas about race, ethnicity, gender, immigration, citizenship, and social life, and about other essential issues like representation and voting are under attack by the intertwining forces of diversity and multiculturalism as well as political and economic uncertainty, as recently documented by Martin Guevara Urbina in *Twenty-First Century Dynamics of Multiculturalism: Beyond Post-Racial America* (2014). For instance, in the late twentieth century, Harvard's leading political scientist, Samuel P. Huntington (1996, 204), added to the anti-Mexican immigration propaganda by passionately commenting about the growing Latino population and the inevitable "clash of civilizations," charging that "while Muslims pose the immediate problem to Europe, Mexicans pose the problem for the United States." Then, in the twenty-first century, Professor Huntington (2004, 32), who taught at Harvard University for more than a half century, charged that "the single most immediate and most serious challenge to America's traditional identity comes from the immense and continuing immigration from Latin America, especially from Mexico." For Americans to ignore the question of whether the United States will "remain a country with a single national language and a core Anglo-Protestant culture," says Huntington, is to "acquiesce to their eventual transformation into two peoples with two cultures (Anglo and Hispanic) and two languages (English and Spanish)." And "the possibility of a de facto split between a predominantly Spanish-speaking United States and an English-speaking United States" would represent "a major potential threat to the country's cultural and political integrity." To trace the historical roots of immigration laws, enforcement, and discourse is to see that the immigration debate is more about culture than it is about legality—the fear of losing a historically cultivated white identity (the idea of a white nation) with its established domains of power, control, and dominance. In part "because the United States considers itself a 'moral' and 'law-and-order' society, the US has a phobia of the *outsider*, the *different*, and the *stranger*. As an institutionalized state of feeling and thinking, such phobia has manifested itself into ignorance, which in turn has resulted in viciousness and vindictiveness . . . [and] fear of those who threaten our interests or the status quo has manifested itself into low levels of tolerance" (Nieling and Urbina 2008, 233), making the criminal justice system, which includes immigration laws, enforcement, deportations, and incarceration, the prime apparatus for suppression, control, and silencing of those who threaten the dominant social structure. Consequently, those who wish to reform the immigration system, the legal system, or the criminal justice system as a whole, or simply join a criminal justice profession, like the judicial system, face a severe challenge, and once on the job must survive in an almost all-white environment, as until recently institutions have been composed mostly of white men. As a friend recently observed during a trip to a federal courthouse, "Did you notice? Everyone in the court was white, except the defendants [undocumented immigrants and others for drug charges] . . . and they call it a court of justice. *Porque no* (why not) a court of injustice. . . . There they are, looking at the defendants with disdain, yet that's how they get their paycheck, wow, the system on payroll."

The historical record reveals that as the United States strives for positive social transformation, the historically troubled immigration laws and enforcement represent some of the most deeply rooted social problems in society. Immigration officers at the ports of entry and border patrol agents are the frontline agents of immigration laws and thus the most visible upholders of national security, democracy, freedom, and public safety. Fundamentally, "at the heart of the American paradigm is the perception that law and its agents . . . are colorblind and thus justice is impartial, objective, and seeks *la verdad* (the truth). But, *la realidad* (reality) differs . . . decision makers are often more guided by their environment than by objectivity" (Urbina 2003, 124). The historical and contemporary dynamics of interacting forces, like conquest, colonialism, slavery, identity, and citizenship, continue to influence the everyday experience of undocumented people, legal residents, and U.S. citizens and, in the area of law and order, how immigrants and other defendants are processed and treated by immigration agents and American police and subsequently the judicial and penal systems—including the thousands of immigrants processed for deportation or incarceration.

The rapidly shifting immigration trends, diversity, multiculturalism, and demographics across the country in the twenty-first century, in the midst of globalization (including globalized migration), merit a newly energized research agenda to analyze immigration in its totality, delineating the interaction of historical and contemporary forces driving immigration laws, enforcement, and discourse. For instance, while the immigration debate continues to revolve around Latino immigrants, particularly Mexican immigrants, Asians have already surpassed Latinos as the largest group of new immigrants to the United States. They are now the fastest-growing *racial* group in the country, and they are projected to surpass Latinos as the largest group of immigrants by 2065 (Pew Research Center 2013). Evidently, the time has come to explore the ways in which ethnicity and race shape immigration laws, enforcement practices, and discourse, in order to gain insight into the *future of America*. With shifting demographics, it is crucial to better understand the experience of the already largest immigrant group (Asians), the largest minority group (Latinos), and the largest ethnic minority group (Mexicans) in the United States, which, according to predictions, will soon constitute the two largest ethnic/racial groups in the country (Latinos and Asians) and represent *the emerging new face of America and the upcoming majority*.

The central mission of this project was to bring together a group of prominent scholars from around the country to closely analyze the contours of immigration laws, enforcement, and discourse. First, broadly, the focus will be primarily on examining a series of interconnected issues, including how U.S. immigration laws have changed over time; how immigration laws have governed *belonging* and *exclusion*; the "politics" of immigration; the parameters of legality, criminalization, and civil rights; immigrant labor and the American economy; raids, detentions, and deportations; challenges to integration; myths about immigration; militarization of the southern border; social control movements; cultural diversity and multiculturalism; immigration through the lens of the American media; and governance, equality, and justice. Second, while many aspects of immigration have been well documented, much less analyzed are the *mechanisms, beliefs,* and *ideologies* that govern immigration laws, enforcement, and discourse, and by extension the immigrant experience, the minority experience, and the American experience. Notably, understanding the historical roots of ideologies governing immigration and social control in general is not only vital to better understand immigrants, U.S. minorities, and the American society, but essential for analyzing the dynamics of legal decision-makers (government officials, politicians, and others) over the years as well as the immigration agents who are involved in the day-to-day administration of the law. Contributing authors seek to examine not only the historical manipulation, prejudice, racism, exploitation, oppression, violence, and brutality that are evident, but also the cultural, structural, financial, political, and ideological forces that have influenced and continue to perpetuate the current state of immigration in the United States. In analyzing historical and contemporary forces that have impacted the immigrant experience in everyday life, public sentiment, and immigration policy, we seek to expose how anti-immigrants movements and other social control movements, enforcement practices, and immigration laws need particular ideas about ethnicity, race, culture, and legality not only to exist but to legitimize their existence and practice. These are issues that will ultimately influence the role of immigration agents in their everyday interaction with immigrants (undocumented and documented) and ethnic/racial minorities residing in the country. Lastly, in addressing various essential issues in this book, the contributing authors demonstrate that the lack of knowledge on immigration is not inevitable, and thus the book details policy and research recommendations to help fill voids in the immigration discourse and so lead to *comprehensive, equitable, and humane immigration reform and sound policies for the twenty-first century.*

SOFÍA ESPINOZA ÁLVAREZ

MARTIN GUEVARA URBINA

REFERENCES

Bender, S. W. 2015. *Mea Culpa: Lessons on Law and Regret from U.S. History.* New York: New York University Press.

Cole, D. 2001. "Formalism, Realism, and the War on Drugs." *Suffolk University Law Review* 35: 241–55.

Feagin, J. R. 2012. *White Party, White Government: Race, Class, and U.S. Politics.* New York: Routledge.

Fitzpatrick, T. 2001. "New Agenda for Social Policy and Criminology: Globalization, Urbanization, and the Emerging Post-Social Security State." *Social Policy and Administration* 35: 212–29.

Gonzales, A. 2014. *Reform Without Justice: Latino Migrant Politics and the Homeland Security State.* New York: Oxford University Press.

Gordon, C. 1991. "Governmental Rationality: An Introduction." In *The Foucault Effect: Studies in Governmentality*, edited by G. Burchell, C. Gordon, and P. Miller, 1–52. Chicago: University of Chicago Press.

Hall, K., W. Wiecek, and P. Finkelman. 1996. *American Legal History: Cases and Materials.* 2nd ed. New York: Oxford University Press.

Huntington, S. 1996. *The Clash of Civilizations? The Debate.* New York: Foreign Affairs.

———. 2004. "The Hispanic Challenge." *Foreign Policy*, March/April, 30–45.

McWilliams, C. 1990. *North from Mexico: The Spanish-Speaking People of the United States.* New York: Praeger.

Morín, J. L. 2009. *Latino/a Rights and Justice in the United States: Perspectives and Approaches.* 2nd ed. Durham, N.C.: Carolina Academic Press.

Nieling, S., and M. G. Urbina. 2008. "Thoughts for the Future." In *A Comprehensive Study of Female Offenders: Life Before, During, and After Incarceration*, by M. G. Urbina, 223–34. Springfield, Ill.: Charles C Thomas.

Pew Research Center. 2013. *The Rise of Asian Americans.* Washington, D.C.: Pew Research Center. http://www.pewsocialtrends.org/files/2013/04/Asian-Americans-new-full-report-04-2013.pdf.

Ruddell, R., and M. G. Urbina. 2004. "Minority Threat and Punishment: A Cross-National Analysis." *Justice Quarterly* 21: 903–31.

———. 2007. "Weak Nations, Political Repression, and Punishment." *International Criminal Justice Review* 17: 84–107.

Simon, J. 1997. "Governing Through Crime." In *The Crime Conundrum*, edited by L. Friedman and G. Fisher, 171–90. Oxford: Oxford University Press.

Urbina, M. G. 2003. "The Quest and Application of Historical Knowledge in Modern Times: A Critical View." *Criminal Justice Studies: A Critical Journal of Crime, Law, and Society* 16: 113–29.

——, ed. 2014. *Twenty-First Century Dynamics of Multiculturalism: Beyond Post-racial America.* Springfield, Ill.: Charles C Thomas.

Urbina, M. G., and S. E. Álvarez, eds. 2015. *Latino Police Officers in the United States: An Examination of Emerging Trends and Issues.* Springfield, Ill.: Charles C Thomas.

——. 2016. "Neoliberalism, Criminal Justice, and Latinos: The Contours of Neoliberal Economic Thought and Policy on Criminalization." *Latino Studies* 14: 33–58.

——. 2017. *Ethnicity and Criminal Justice in the Era of Mass Incarceration: A Critical Reader on the Latino Experience.* Springfield, Ill.: Charles C Thomas.

Urbina, M. G., J. E. Vela, and J. O. Sánchez. 2014. *Ethnic Realities of Mexican Americans: From Colonialism to 21st Century Globalization.* Springfield, Ill.: Charles C Thomas.

Vasquez, J. M. 2011. *Mexican Americans Across Generations: Immigrant Families, Racial Realities.* New York: New York University Press.

Wacquant, L. 2001. "Deadly Symbiosis: When Ghetto and Prison Meet and Mesh." In *Mass Incarceration: Social Causes and Consequences,* edited by D. Garland, 82–120. London: Sage.

Welch, M. 2006. *Scapegoats of September 11th: Hate Crimes and State Crimes in the War on Terror.* New Brunswick, N.J.: Rutgers University Press.

Whitehead, J. 2013. *A Government of Wolves: The Emerging American Police State.* New York: SelectBooks.

ACKNOWLEDGMENTS

I T WOULD HAVE been impossible to conduct this project and edit this book without the everlasting patience, advice, and unconditional support of many highly talented, sincere, loyal, and dedicated people. To begin, our most profound appreciation goes to the contributing authors for not only participating in this project but also being vested in producing provoking, refreshing, and captivating original chapters. We are honored to have had their patience, encouragement, and support during the lengthy process. This book never would have come to fruition without their assistance, perseverance, and advice throughout the various stages of the project.

We would like to acknowledge Dr. Adalberto Aguirre Jr. (University of California–Riverside), Dr. Tomas Almaguer (San Francisco State University), Dr. David V. Baker (University of South Carolina at Wilmington), Dr. David E. Barlow (Fayetteville State University), Dr. Melissa H. Barlow (Fayetteville State University), Professor Steven W. Bender (Seattle University School of Law), Dr. Charles Ramirez Berg (University of Texas at Austin), Dr. Leo R. Chávez (University of California–Irvine), Dr. Charles Crawford (Western Michigan University), Dr. Arnoldo De León (Angelo State University), Dr. Joe R. Feagin (Texas A&M University, College Station), Dr. Ruth Gomberg-Muñoz (Loyola University, Chicago), Dr. Ramon A. Gutierrez (University of Chicago), Dr. Peter Laufer (University of Oregon), Dr. Rubén Martínez (Michigan State University), Dr. Alfredo Mirandé (University of California–Riverside), Dr. Felipe de Ortego y Gasca (Western New Mexico University), Dr. Marcos Pizarro (San Jose State University), Dr. Mary Romero (Arizona State University), Dr. Rick Ruddell (University of Regina, Saskatchewan), Professor Lupe S. Salinas (Thurgood Marshall School of Law), and Dr. L. Thomas Winfree (Arizona State University) for their words of wisdom, compassion, and support during difficult, uncertain, or tearful moments. We are forever indebted to you for never losing confidence in us and encouraging us to continue with our research and publications.

Much love and respect to Dr. Jorge Castañeda Gutman (New York University) for his motivation and encouragement. We also extend our profound gratitude to Professor Francisco Roberto Ramírez (Universidad de Guanajuato, México) for his guidance and assistance in academic and legal endeavors. We thank María Aurora Ramírez Padrón, law school director/career coordinator (Universidad de León, San Miguel de Allende, Guanajuato, México), for her kindness, support, and advice. Also, a word of acknowledgment and appreciation goes to Jonathan Stefanonni for his friendship, affection, and everlasting support.

Demonstrating its active role in social reform and transformation and human rights through discovery and knowledge, the Empower Global Foundation provided funding for the early stages of this project as well as the final stage (publication), ensuring that the project would become a reality. Vested in the betterment of our communities, Empower Global creates, designs, supports, and encourages the development of social programs, schemes, proposals, and research-based projects to contribute to, habilitate, and influence the empowerment of all individuals without distinction—at all levels of social strata and in all geographic locations. In addition, the foundation promotes education, discovery, knowledge, and cultural sensibility holistically. Considering that globalization represents a cornerstone for the growth of society, a central mission of the Empower Global Foundation is to implement progressive actions with international impact.

We would like to say a special thanks to our publisher, the University of Arizona Press, including the publications committee, Kristen Buckles (editor-in-chief), Stacey A. Wujcik, and the staff for being extremely patient, supportive, helpful, and understanding throughout the entire publishing process. Their patience, guidance, encouragement, and professionalism have been a real blessing. And, of course, we extend our profound gratitude to the external viewers for reviewing the manuscript and providing us suggestions for improving and enriching the volume. Lastly, we would like to acknowledge the heroic and, at times, magical efforts of all the people who contributed to the making of this book in one way or another. Seldom do we have the honor and privilege to work with such highly talented, honest, and loyal individuals—crusaders for discovery, equality, and justice.

S.E.A.

M.G.U.

IMMIGRATION AND THE LAW

Introduction

U.S. IMMIGRATION LAWS

The Changing Dynamics of Immigration

SOFÍA ESPINOZA ÁLVAREZ AND MARTIN GUEVARA URBINA

> Unless US citizens acknowledge and understand their country's
> imperial past, they will not be able to understand its present or
> future. Much of the recent and current Hispanic resettlement
> of parts of the United States is a consequence of empire. . . .
> Countercolonization follows colonization, and the waves of
> migrants always flow back like returning tides.

—FELIPE FERNÁNDEZ-ARMESTO

WHEN THE FOUNDING fathers of America signed a Declaration of Independence (1776) that stated that "all men are created equal," it was quite obvious to them that women, eventually about half of the population, were not equal to men, and it was also quite obvious that by *law* "all men" meant "white men," not black men, brown men, red men, yellow men, or men of any other color. When Patrick Henry, a slaveholder himself, supposedly declared, "Give me liberty, or give me death," liberty in actuality was reserved for white men, particularly wealthy white men. Paradoxically, one of America's most sacred official documents, the Declaration of Independence, asserts that human beings are endowed with "unalienable rights," and that if a government deprives people of such rights, "it is the right of the people to alter or abolish it." Emblazoned across the front of the U.S. Supreme Court Building, the most visible icon of the American legal system, is the principle on which our system is based—"Equal Justice Under Law." An exploration of the American experience, though, reveals that from the very founding of the United States, the idea that "all men are created equal," a phrase used by Thomas Jefferson, has coexisted with some of the most heinous, vicious, and vindictive atrocities, injustices, and inequalities in the country's history (Acuña 2014; Almaguer 2008; Bender 2003, 2015; De León 1983; Feagin 2006, 2013, 2014; McWilliams 1990; Urbina, Vela, and Sánchez 2014).

With pressing changes in diversity, multiculturalism, and demographics across the country in the twenty-first century (Urbina 2014), the historically *narrow* way in which research and publication have been conducted, along with public discussion and government policy, must be changed to be more inclusive if we are to understand "immigration" in its totality so as to design and implement immigration reform that will yield positive, effective, and just results. With the globalization of knowledge, technology, and social control, if the United States is going to be the country of the future, a truly democratic country, with equality, justice, and "representation" not only for whites but also for Asians, blacks, Latinos, Native Americans, other ethnic/racial groups, and, yes, immigrants, the country must not only acknowledge the historical significance of immigrants and pass comprehensive reforms to address the undocumented status of immigrants currently residing in the country, but also implement mechanisms to prevent the continued marginalization, exploitation, and criminalization of undocumented (and documented) immigrants in the United States.

The book has three goals. First, to better understand the centuries-old immigrant discourse, multiple historical and contemporary facets of immigration will be delineated, from the arrival of the first "immigrants" in what became the United States, to the exodus of Central American children on the U.S.-Mexico border in 2014, to the Syrian refugee "crisis" in September of 2015. Second, given that the immigration debate has revolved around Latinos (particularly Mexicans) for almost two hundred years, and given the fact that they are now the largest minority group in the country and projected to be one of two largest ethnic/racial groups, the contributing authors reveal the Latino immigrants' story over the years, showing the implications and ramifications of working/living undocumented in the United States, while situating their experiences within the Latino community as well as within the overall American society. Third, while immigration has been debated, analyzed, and documented from various angles, much less analyzed are the *mechanisms, beliefs, motives, and ideology* that have historically governed (to this day) the immigration discourse, immigration laws, and enforcement. The contributing authors examine not only the historical manipulation, prejudice, discrimination, exploitation, oppression, and brutality, but also the structural, political, cultural, and ideological forces that have influenced and continue to perpetuate the current situation for immigrants in the United States. In analyzing historical and contemporary forces that have impacted the immigrants' experience in everyday life, public sentiment, and immigration policy, we seek to reveal how anti-immigrants movements, police enforcement practices, and immigration laws need particular ideas about ethnicity/race not only to exist but also to legitimize their existence and practice.

THE CHANGING DYNAMICS OF IMMIGRATION OVER THE YEARS

Since the early days of the country, the immigration dilemma has been widely debated and, while at times highly symbolic, always has crucial implications and ramifications. With significant shifts in demographics during the last few years, though, immigration, particularly immigration reform, has become a controversial issue being debated across the United States, from the floor of the Capitol to state legislatures to city streets. Amplified by the media, anti-immigrant sentiments have multiplied along with efforts to rid the country of "illegal" (and some legal) immigrants, particularly after the September 11, 2001, attacks (Welch 2006, 2007, 2009). While there has always been an anti-immigrants movement, since the advent of the war on terrorism, along with the war on drugs, the movement has become more aggressive, including stepped-up deportations, workplace raids, and the passage of more than three hundred state laws and local ordinances restricting access to employment, housing, driver's licenses, education, hospitals, public assistance (like food stamps), and even library cards (Rumbaut 2008), along with actions like racial profiling, violence, and violations of civil rights (Dunn 2009; Johnson 2000; Posadas and Medina 2012; Romero 2006; Romero and Serag 2004). During the last several years, for instance, we have witnessed federal immigration authorities staging factory raids across the country, resulting in arrests, deportations, and separated families (Golash-Boza 2015; Román 2013; Salinas 2015; Tichenor 2002), while leaving employers scrambling to fill "immigrant jobs" to avoid economic ruin.

Highly governed by economic cycles, so-called immigration crises, viciously erupting like long-dormant volcanoes every few years, have defined and redefined what "immigrants" mean to politicians, government officials, law enforcement officials, and the American public. The latest eruption, according to some critics, struck Americans like a tidal wave in 2014, with thousands of children from Central America arriving at the U.S.-Mexico border, looking for protection, shelter, food, and an opportunity to stay in the country. Media coverage characterized the migration as a "child immigrant crisis," sparking passionate and at times aggressive protests across the country. When immigrants are Latino (or, more precisely, *brown* or *black*), Americans worry a little more. Redefining the *image* of immigrants, the right-wing media has stirred up moral panic over job stealing, criminality, "anchor babies," welfare dependence, bilingualism, drug traffickers, Mexican "narco-terrorists," al-Qaeda terrorists disguised as Mexicans, and even a conspiracy by Mexicans to "retake" the Southwest, the region that once belonged to Mexico.

In 2015, the illegal immigration discourse was elevated to the highest point of the political spectrum, as presidential candidates strategically targeted immigrants as a winning issue. Even DREAMers (high school graduates brought to the United States as minors) have been under attack by anti-immigrant critics. In a country of immigrants, what is going on? In *Dream Chasers: Immigration and the American Backlash* (2015), John Tirman documents that the hostile resistance to immigration in the United States is more cultural than political, and that although strategically coded in language about job stealing, secure borders, and national security, the cultural resistance to immigration expresses a fear that new immigrants are significantly changing the historically dominant white, Protestant, "real American" culture. Exploring the immigration discourse over time, its twists and turns, though, we find that the immigration debate is governed not only by culture, economic cycles, politics, or the American media, but by the interactions of historical and contemporary forces, with targeted, underlying motives, some of which are not easy to observe or delineate, as illustrated in the following chapters.

IMMIGRATION TRENDS IN THE TWENTY-FIRST CENTURY

For several decades, the immigration debate has revolved around Latino immigrants, particularly immigrants of Mexican heritage. In the new millennium, though, shifting demographic trends are not only reshaping the American landscape, but also the many facets of immigration and everyday life in the United States. Seeking to situate the immigration discourse within a broader context, we now delineate immigration trends in the twenty-first century. Reportedly, about 1.4 million Mexicans immigrated to the United States between 2005 and 2010, which is about the same number of Mexicans who left the country during the same time frame. Some figures show that only 100,000 undocumented immigrants from Mexico, including visa violators, came to the United States in 2010, down from the 525,000 who came over each year between 2000 and 2004. Nationally, the number of undocumented immigrants from Mexico dropped from 7 million in 2007 to 6.1 million in 2011 (Passel, Cohn, and Gonzalez-Barrera 2012). In 2005, 35,000 Brazilians were detained trying to enter the country illegally. Between October 2009 and March 2011, about 2,600 undocumented immigrants from India were also detained, a sharp increase from the typical 150–300 apprehensions per year. As the number of immigrants from Central America has gone up, though, the number of undocumented immigrants from Mexico (who still make up the majority of apprehensions nationwide) has been steadily declining. In fact, undocumented immigration from Mexico is at its lowest level in decades. Data analysis by the Pew Center, "Net Migration from Mexico Falls to Zero—and Perhaps

Less," finds that "there is net zero migration taking place from Mexico to the United States" (Passel, Cohn, and Gonzalez-Barrera 2012, 1).

Asians have surpassed Latinos as the largest group of new immigrants to the United States, according to the Pew Research Center. China was the country of origin for 147,000 U.S. immigrants in 2013, while Mexico accounted for just 125,000, according to U.S. Census Bureau researchers. India, with 129,000 immigrants, also accounted for more immigrants than Mexico (Jensen et al. 2015). The year before, 2012, Mexico and China were basically tied as the "top-sending countries," Mexico at 125,000 and China at 124,000. In fact, for a decade, immigration from China and India, which boast the world's largest populations, has been rising. In recent years, though, it's not just China and India; several other countries accounted for a high amount of immigrants in 2013, including Japan, South Korea, and the Philippines.

Combined, about 430,000 Asians (36 percent of all new immigrants) arrived in the United States in 2010, and about 370,000 (31 percent) new immigrants were Latino, according to U.S. Census data. The wave of incoming Asians pushed the total number of Asian Americans to a record of 18.2 million, about 5.8 percent of the total U.S. population. By comparison, non-Latino whites (197.5 million) accounted for 63.3 percent, while Latinos (52 million) and non-Latino blacks (38.3 million) accounted for 16.7 percent and 12.3 percent, respectively. The study "The Rise of Asian Americans" (Pew Research Center 2013) reveals that Asian Americans also have the highest income, are the best educated, and are the fastest-growing *racial* group in the United States. Data released by the U.S. Census Bureau in May 2012 also showed that there were more minority children born in the United States than white children for the first time in history, signaling an era in which whites will no longer be the majority (Urbina 2014). According to the census report, 50.4 percent of children born in a twelve-month period that ended July 2011 were Asian American, black, Latino, or from other minority groups, while non-Latino whites accounted for 49.6 percent of all births during the same period. In fact, in the first decade of the twenty-first century minority babies accounted for 49.5 percent of all births.

Latinos are still the biggest ethnic/racial minority group in the United States. However, about two-thirds of them are now native-born, not recent immigrants. Among the U.S. Asian population, two-thirds (65 percent) are foreign-born. As detailed in subsequent chapters, the earliest immigrant waves to the United States came from northern and western Europe, then southern and eastern Europe, then Latin America, and finally from China and India. However, in recent years a significant (comparatively) number of new immigrants have not come from China, India, or Mexico, but other Asian countries. Once combined, recent immigrants from those countries accounted for about a third of the roughly 1.2 million immigrants in 2013, according to census figures. Considering continued shifts in demographics, the question becomes, how big is the Asian wave going to be? Do these new trends signal a distinct wave of immigrants yet to be seen, further remapping America's multiethnic, multiracial, and multicultural society?

While figures vary depending on "classification" and reporting sources, census data show a slowing of immigrants moving north, particularly immigrants from Mexico, who have been the main target of resistance for decades. Notably, immigration from Mexico has been declining due to improvements in the Mexican economy, a drastic decline in birthrates in Mexico, and the increasingly dangerous passage across the border during the last decade. This trend is also partly attributable to the sluggish U.S. economy, beginning with the Great Recession; fewer job opportunities, particularly in the housing and construction industries; increased border enforcement; punitive sanctions for those apprehended; and the militarization of the border. Rosendo Hinojosa, chief of the Rio Grande Valley Border Patrol Sector, for instance, attributes the overall increase in apprehensions, resulting in increased sanctions, to more agents in his sector, from 1,850 in 2007 to 2,500 in 2012 (Lozano 2012; see also Urbina and Álvarez 2015, 2017).

Other figures show that the number of undocumented immigrants fell to 11.1 million, down from a high of some 12 million in 2007, following more than a decade of increases. Reportedly, about 2.5 million undocumented immigrants, 400,000 per year on average, have come to the United States since 2009 when President Barack Obama took office, according to the Center for Immigration Studies, an ultra-conservative anti-immigrants organization. Typically, the number of immigrants that leave the country offsets the number of people entering the country, but following Obama's executive order in June 2012, in which he allowed some young undocumented immigrants to stay in the country under certain conditions, immigration numbers started to increase from mid-2013 to about May 2015, when 790,000 came into the country, according to the Center for Immigration Studies. To be sure, whether immigration numbers have been "up or down" during the first part of the twenty-first century, some politicians, along with immigration hawks, pundits, bigots, and even intellectual racists, have been quick to demonize undocumented immigrants, notably Donald Trump during his presidential campaign.

TWO HISTORICAL FORCES DRIVING IMMIGRATION: THE ECONOMY AND POLITICS

Historically, two primary factors have governed the immigration debate, policy, and practice—American politics and the economy. In fact, contrary to the perceived notion that the current anti-immigrants political climate is a new era of debate, politics and economic cycles have shaped and reshaped immigration. For instance, long before Arizona, which has been on the forefront of the immigration debate, Alabama and other states pursued anti-immigrant measures, and measures like Proposition 187 in California proved that it was politically possible to remap immigration laws in modern times. A generation before the Tea Party, conservative anti-immigrant politicians sent the public into a statewide frenzy to pass Proposition 187 under "Save Our State" propaganda, proposed during a time when California was experiencing a deep recession and needed a convenient scapegoat. In this case, as many times before, the easy target was undocumented (and documented) immigrants, mostly Latinos, who were significantly shifting the demographics of California to the resentment and antagonism of the old *gabacho* guard, who for centuries were in total control. In fact, the issue of "illegal" immigration was just a smoke screen to achieve a California Jim Crow—a convincing excuse and justification to adopt state-sanctioned xenophobia in the most draconian ways imaginable. Underneath the formal language, the aim of Proposition 187 was to create an atmosphere of fear, rejection, and a moral panic, and thus drive all immigrants out of California. For example, one section would deny public benefits (from public schooling to health care and food assistance) to undocumented immigrants and their children, foreign-born or U.S. citizens. Other provisions were designed to forced public employees (like teachers), doctors, and even clergy members to report anyone they suspected of being in the country "illegally" to La Migra (the Border Patrol). A federal judge eventually ruled it unconstitutional in 1999, and "the proposition's success unwittingly became the Waterloo of the far-right in California" (Arellano 2014, 1). Twenty years before Republicans nationwide tried to gain national attention, and more importantly, votes, by railing about undocumented immigration, the California GOP used this historical initiative to win seats in the state capitol. Not only do the economy and political environment govern the immigration discourse, but they interact with multiple intertwining factors to shape and reshape the immigration discourse, laws, and enforcement, with, of course, vested motives underneath it all, as detailed in the following chapters.

REDEFINING THE DEPORTATION MOVEMENT

During the last few years, immigrant deportations have been a focal point of the anti-immigrants movement, widely debated across the country and widely publicized by the media. However, there seems to be much confusion regarding the legal parameters of immigrant deportations because of changes in immigration laws, terminology, and classification. To begin, the term "deportation" has been widely used in virtually all media reporting—receiving much publicity during the Obama administration—creating a skewed image in the minds of the American public. In actuality, the "deportation" category has been obsolete in U.S. immigration laws since 1996 (Law 2014). Prior to 1996, U.S. immigration laws distinguished between immigrants who were "excluded," that is, apprehended and prevented from entering the country, and those who were "deported," that is, expelled from the country after they had made their way into the United States. After 1996, both "exclusion" and "deportation" were grouped into one legal procedure called "removal." Since then, the term "deportation" has had no formal meaning within the official immigration statistics. However, it has continued to be used by the media, creating confusion among the public.

As for the actual legal application, the immigrants who were apprehended (usually along the two-thousand-mile border) and prevented from entering the country were part of another category, "voluntary departure," before 2006. This category was then renamed "return," which also includes the subcategory of "reinstatement." There is also another category of "expedited removals," which refers to immigrants who do not appear before an immigration judge, including a procedure carrying sanctions if a judge ordered "removal." These immigrants accept a sanction that forgoes a court appearance before an immigration judge because *formal removal* (where the U.S. government processes them through legal proceedings and pays for their return to their country of origin) would result in a multiyear ban (five to twenty years) on their eligibility to *legally* reenter the United States. As such, this policy has been characterized as "catch and release" enforcement. The legal ramifications of a return are less harsh than those for a formal removal because returned immigrants could come back legally (and presumably illegally) at any time after being returned to their country of origin.

Therefore, comparing deportation statistics across different eras or, as commonly cited, across presidential administrations, is suspect because it's often unclear what categories of immigrants are being counted, included, or excluded. For instance, Nixon's war on drugs, Reagan's war on drugs, and the Merida Initiative in 2008 (a pact between Mexico and the United States to fight organized crime) were designed with targeted motives and objectives, often utilizing strategically selected terminology to rationalize their goals. Further, different presidential administrations (and law enforcement agencies) choose to emphasize certain statistics, typically to justify expanding budgets (particularly for technology and payroll), but of course with underlying motives (Urbina and Álvarez 2016). As for presidential administrations, some critics state that the George W. Bush administration appears to have reported *removals* and *returns* together, while the Obama administration emphasized the number of *removals*. The confusion enables politicians to "play" the media and the public, while allowing them to carve out their own political legacy. For instance, if we want to portray Barack Obama as weak on immigration enforcement, we can use the *removal* numbers, which compared to his predecessors, are lower; and if we want to make Obama look tough on border enforcement, we can combine the *return* and *removal* numbers, as George W. Bush apparently did. Or, we could use the now meaningless "deportation" figures. Both options would conflate return and removal, and increase the overall number of expulsions. However, these nuances are unlikely to make it into the political immigration discourse anytime soon. In 1987, the U.S. Court of Appeals for the Seventh Circuit described immigration laws as "second in complexity only to the internal revenue code."

DEPORTATIONS: HISTORICAL TRENDS

While deportations have been a popular topic of discussion during the last several years, they are part of the long history of immigration. During the last several decades the focus has been on Latino immigrants. In fact, as detailed in the following chapters, the history of U.S. deportations is deeply intertwined with the history of Mexican migration (Castañeda 2007; Gutiérrez 1997; Urbina, Vela, and Sánchez 2014). The number of removals, returns, and total deportations was negligible until 1942, a major year in American history and the year unauthorized (and authorized) Mexican migration spiked at the advent of the popular Bracero Program, a binational government agreement that brought 4.5 million Mexican laborers to the United States over a twenty-two-year span. The termination of the Bracero Program coincided with the 1965 Hart-Celler Act, which for the first time in history placed numerical limits on immigration from the Western Hemisphere. This shift in immigration policies resulted in a sharp increase in the number of migrants classified as "illegal," which in turn led to unprecedented numbers of apprehensions and deportations. Still, from 1965 to 1996 there were never more than a handful of removals for every one hundred returns, with the latter closely matching the total number of deportations (Goodman 2014). However, changes in immigration laws starting in 1996 have extended the number of offenses that result in removal and allow "expedited removal" by immigration officials rather than immigration judges. These changes in immigration laws, along with an increasing enforcement budget and a decline in Mexican migration over the last few years, have meant an increasing number of removals and greater parity between removals and returns—reshaping immigration trends. According to some figures, in fiscal year 2011, removals outnumbered returns for the first time since 1941, the year before the start of the Bracero Program.

ARE MORE IMMIGRANTS BEING "DEPORTED" FROM THE UNITED STATES THAN EVER BEFORE?

During the Obama presidency, activists, the news media, and others stressed that his administration had removed nearly two million undocumented immigrants, and was on track to deport more immigrants than any other presidential administration in U.S. history—earning him the title of "Deporter-in-Chief." However, some figures indicate that the United States is actually deporting *fewer* people than it did before, but the process has become more punitive. As noted above, there are two main ways in which immigrants can be forced to leave the country: by *removal*, which the federal government defines as "the compulsory and confirmed movement of an inadmissible or deportable alien out of the United States based on an order of removal," and by *return*, "the confirmed movement of an inadmissible or deportable alien out of the United States not based on an order of removal," which was formerly referred to as a "voluntary departure." In fiscal year 2013, the U.S. government removed 368,644 people who were in the country without documentation, down from a record 419,384 the year before. In 2012, according to federal statistics for both removals and returns, the United States deported a total of 649,352 people, also down from President Bill Clinton's all-time high of 1,864,343 in fiscal year 2000 (Goodman 2014). Reportedly, deportations are not at an all-time high level, but removals are. Therefore, while the Obama administration removed a record number of immigrants during the last few years, it did not "deport" a record number. Granted, the distinctions between the two might not seem of critical importance, as they both result in immigrants leaving the country, mostly against their will; however, there are some critical differences. Removal carries an automatic five- or ten-year ban on applying to reenter the country, and if apprehended a second time, immigrants could face incarceration and a twenty-year or lifetime ban on applying to reenter. The repercussions of return (or voluntary departure) are less punitive. In some cases immigrants are allowed to remain in the country for a brief period to prepare for their departure, giving them time to organize employment and family-related issues. Voluntary departure also carries a shorter ban on reentry (or no ban) if immigrants have been in the country for less than 180 days. Though, of course, both removal and return require individuals to leave the country as ordered by federal authorities, and thus both need to be counted in the total number of "deportations."

However, according to the Immigration Policy Center (Ewing 2014), if we analyze the anti-immigration movement from another angle, there has been no decline in immigration enforcement in the United States, but simply deportation by another name. The deportation movement has been growing for decades under Republican and Democratic administrations and congresses, and supported by law enforcement officials, along with many other anti-immigrant critics, from media personalities to academics. In part, the drive for this growth resulted from a section of the Immigration Reform and Control Act of 1986 (IRCA), known as the MacKay amendment, encouraging deportation proceedings against immigrants convicted of deportable offenses, followed by additional punitive anti-immigrant legislation. Subsequently, since the mid-1990s, the number of "removals" (deportations) quickly increased. At the same time, the number of apprehensions began to fluctuate widely, highly influenced by shifting economic conditions in the United States and Mexico, taking a drastic downturn when the 2007 recession hit the country. Further, while the number of "voluntary returns" has tracked apprehensions closely, since 2005 voluntary returns have been made available to fewer and fewer apprehended immigrants, as deportation (with criminal sanctions for reentry into the United States) became the preferred option for processing immigrants by U.S. immigration authorities (Ewing 2014).

Therefore, analyzed from this angle, contrary to claims that there has been greater leniency, the U.S. deportation machine has grown larger in recent years, targeting criminals and noncriminals, whether they are undocumented immigrants, longtime legal residents, and, in the case of Latinos, even U.S. citizens. The deportation frenzy began long before Obama took office, as federal and state authorities have been, for about two decades, following an enforcement approach to immigration that favors mandatory detention and deportation over the traditional reliance on the discretion of immigration judges who consider the unique circumstances of individual cases. Subsequently, the "soft" immigration approach has resulted in a passionate and aggressive campaign of imprisonment and expulsion of noncitizens, a strategically political campaign authorized by Congress and implemented by the executive branch, carried out by the thousands of federal immigration agents along the two-thousand-mile U.S.-Mexico border and across the country (Urbina and Álvarez 2015). To be sure, while the current anti-immigrants campaign preceded the Obama administration by decades, it grew dramatically during that time. Further, while this has been a result of laws placing deportations on *automatic*, the continued increase in deportations also reflects policy changes by the Obama administration. That is, "rather than putting the brakes on this non-stop drive to deport more and more people, the administration chose to add fuel to the fire" (Ewing 2014, 1).

In sum, like his predecessors, President Obama responded to the presumed immigration crisis with additional laws, increased border enforcement, more detention beds, more immigration judges, and pressure on political leaders in Latin American countries. However, to understand the contours of deportation we must look beyond the numbers and analyze what the increase in removals means for the people who are being deported. To begin, the criminalization of undocumented immigrants has turned repeat immigration violations into felony offenses, punishable in some cases by years of imprisonment in immigration facilities across the country. Also, contrary to the criminality argument by anti-immigrant critics, most immigrants being deported are not dangerous criminals. According to statistics by U.S. Immigration and Customs Enforcement (ICE), four-fifths of all deportations processed by the agency in fiscal year 2013 did *not* fit ICE's definition of a "Level 1" priority (Ewing 2014). Numbers aside, what has drastically changed is the manner in which people are being deported.

Today deportations are more severe and permanent, carrying short- and long-term consequences for deportees, their families, and even the economic system and by extension the American society (Goodman 2014). Consider, for instance, that immigration officials deported more than 200,000 parents of U.S.-born children between 2010 and 2012, and a recent report estimates that 5,000 children have been placed in foster care after one or both of their parents were deported to their country of origin. Deportation, of course, is only one fuel that keeps the immigration wheels turning, as a congressional mandate requires Immigration and Customs Enforcement to detain a historically unprecedented 34,000 people in immigration facilities or private for-profit prisons each day, further fueling the immigration machine. Lastly, as delineated in subsequent chapters, more than ever, the U.S.-Mexico border has been militarized, making the "American dream" more expensive, difficult, and dangerous than ever before, requiring a deadly journey that for many immigrants begins thousands of miles before they even reach the U.S.-Mexico border.

PLAN FRONTERA SUR (SOUTHERN BORDER PLAN)

When the exodus of Central American children occurred in the summer of 2014, the U.S. media immediately focused on the arrival of more than sixty thousand children, characterizing it as a "child immigrant crisis." Anti-immigrant hawks, political pundits, and other bigots were quick to passionately pontificate about the supposed porosity and insecurity of the U.S.-Mexico border, suggesting the construction of a type of Berlin Wall, armed with immigration officers and military personnel with shoot-to-kill orders to protect us from the influx of immigrant children. The Department of Homeland Security detained thousands of immigrant children in warehouses and air force bases (Miller 2014), further propagating the myth of an unsecured border. In truth, parts of the U.S.-Mexico boundary already have massive walls where guards have detained thousands of men, women, and children, intimidated and harassed immigrants, and even shot and killed across the international line. And this is only part of the story, as most media coverage has reported only the U.S. side of the *border battle* with the refugee children from Central America.

Thousands of miles to the south, the Mexican government has been taking action to prevent immigrant children and adults from moving north toward the United States, essentially performing the job of the U.S. Border Patrol. In the midst of the globalization of the national security propaganda (Bacon 2009; Chossudovsky 2015; Fitzpatrick 2001), the U.S. border enforcement operation has been extended south to the Guatemala border, in what Border Patrol chief Mike Fisher characterized as a "layered approach" (Miller 2014, 1). Now, undocumented Central American immigrants are confronted with a highly "layered" border in southern Mexico, before beginning a thousand-mile journey through Mexico to the U.S.-Mexico border. Of course, the transnationalization of border enforcement has also been coordinated with the Mexican government. Showing his solidarity with the U.S. government, on July 7, 2014, Mexican president Enrique Peña Nieto announced the country's Plan Frontera Sur (Southern Border Plan). While seldom mentioned in the news media, what started with a U.S.-sponsored deportation movement known as Plan Sur in 2000 was transformed within a decade into what officials in 2010 characterized as the "twenty-first-century border." Subsequently, during the first fifteen years of the twenty-first century the U.S. border enforcement regime has been expanding and has gone beyond patrolling the U.S.-Mexico boundary to policing the Mexico-Guatemala border, even expanding into Central American and targeting men, women, and children seeking employment or refuge *en el norte* (in the north), that is, the United States.

The layered approach effectively and quickly yielded results for the border enforcement regime. Mexican deportations of Central Americans increased to unprecedented levels, surpassing deportations by the United States. In 2014, Mexico deported 107,814 immigrants, the vast majority from Central America (Hootsen 2015). Between October 2014 and April 2015, Mexico apprehended 92,889 Central Americans, while the United States apprehended 70,226 "other than Mexican" immigrants, compared to the previous year (October 2013 to April 2014) when the United States detained 159,103 "other than Mexicans," three times the 49,893 immigrants from Central America detained by Mexico (Stevenson and Arce 2015). In fact, Plan Frontera Sur has been so effective that Mexico's arrest totals far exceeded the 70,226 immigrants apprehended by U.S. border agents during the first six months of 2015 who were classified as "other than Mexican," the majority being from El Salvador, Guatemala, and Honduras (Miroff 2015). These figures mark a major shift from the previous year, when U.S. immigration agents detained 159,103 non-Mexican immigrants.

As for immigrant children, the flow of child immigrants sharply slowed at Mexico's northern border. In 2014, more than 46,000 unaccompanied minors from Central America crossed into the United States (Stevenson and Arce 2015), but the trend quickly shifted. According to U.S. official figures, about 23,000 unaccompanied minors were detained from October 2014 to the end of May 2015, about half as many as during the same period the previous fiscal year (Sole 2015). By June 2015, the number of detained immigrants registered as "unaccompanied children" was down by 51 percent (to 22,869), about the same as the number of "family units" (minors accompanied by a family member) apprehended crossing "illegally" (Miroff 2015), showing that "family unit" apprehensions were also down along the U.S. border during the same period, by 47 percent (Associated Press 2015). While the wave of child immigrants has declined along the U.S.-Mexico border, detentions of Central American minors have increased sharply in Mexico. Some figures also show that 6,113 minors traveling alone were detained by Mexican authorities between January and May 2015, 20 percent more than the previous year (Sole 2015). Mexico's National Immigration Institute reported in June 2015 that Mexican officials had been detaining 49 percent more minors from Central America in the first five months of 2015 than during the same period in 2014, with about half of the 11,893 immigrant minors detained between January and May 2015 traveling alone or with a smuggler, compared to 8,003 in 2014 and 3,496 in 2013. Of those detained during the first five months of 2015, two-thirds were between the ages of twelve and seventeen and one-third were eleven or younger, with the great majority coming from El Salvador, Guatemala, and Honduras. Reportedly, child migrant deportations by Mexican authorities have increased to the point that they are now almost on par with U.S. deportations, and shelters in Mexico now report far fewer immigrants from Central America than in previous years (Hootsen 2015), revealing that the southern border is preventing many immigrants from even crossing into Mexico or moving beyond the border.

Clearly, the Southern Border Plan is preventing many Central American adults and minors from reaching the U.S. border. Reportedly, Plan Frontera Sur included five thousand federal agents to intercept northbound immigrants along the Guatemala border, increased enforcement at highways and railway checkpoints, the establishment of more border, highway, and railway checkpoints, increased raids on immigrant shelters and other facilities, and an increased focus on keeping immigrants off the "famous" freight train known as La Bestia (The Beast), El Tren de la Muerte (the Death Train), and El Tren de los Desconocidos (the Train of the Unknowns). Some critics also charge that the "official message" that Plan Frontera Sur is only focused on Mexico's southern border is false, as it applies to all corridors used by Central American immigrants. Reportedly, the plan involves a joining of the Federal Police, SEDENA (the Secretariat of National Defense), and the National Immigration Institute, yielding massive detentions of Central Americans.

Then, in another layer of supposed defense from immigrants, Central American countries have presented their own plan to deal with America's immigration crisis. First, Mexican president Enrique Peña Nieto and Guatemalan president Otto Pérez Molina took action on July 2014 by enacting Plan Frontera Sur to detain immigrants from crossing into Mexico. To be sure, this is not the first time Mexico has increased border enforcement; however, while in the past increased enforcement was viewed more as a favor to the United States, with few Central Americans staying in Mexico, today it's a combination of intense pressure from Washington and the fact that Mexican immigration to the United States has leveled out to zero (the number of Mexicans leaving the United States, deported or for other reasons, is now about equal to the number of new immigrants who make the journey north), encouraging Mexico to redefine immigration enforcement and its relationship with the United States. Then, pressured by Washington, Central American countries (El Salvador, Guatemala, and Honduras) designed their own plan, "The Plan of the Alliance for Prosperity in the Northern Triangle," to focus on economic development, job creation, and strengthening institutions to address the leading causes of northern migration—unemployment, poverty, and violence. Announced in November 2014, their new anti-immigrants initiative is too new to assess, but the plan has yet to produce significant results, since savage poverty and grave violence continue forcing people to migrate north, pulled by the illusion of the American dream.

As for those detained, they experience a "turned-around journey." In most cases, Mexico holds immigrants only long enough to verify their nationalities, and quickly sends them back to their home countries. According to Mexico's National Immigration Institute, "The time that foreigners are in immigration (detention) centers depends only on the speed with which the authorities of their (home) countries confirm their nationality." By comparison, when immigrants are detained crossing the border into the United States "illegally," the process to send them home can take anywhere from hours to years. While Mexican nationals are often returned quickly (sometimes the same day they are detained), due to geographical distance, immigrants from other countries normally spend at least a few days in U.S. custody before being returned to their country of origin, which is even more complicated when immigrants are children, especially if they are traveling alone. The U.S. deportation process can take much longer if immigrants are seeking asylum, as they are also processed by immigration judges. For immigrants who make a legal attempt to stay in the United States, the wait for a court date and a final decision on their case can last several years; there was a backlog of more than 449,000 cases pending in U.S. immigration courts in 2014. According to the U.S. Department of Justice, there were about 41,920 requests for asylum in 2014, including the ones from Central Americans, and about 49 percent of requests processed in 2014 were granted. Mexico, though, grants only a very small number of asylum requests (Stevenson and Arce 2015). As for those who manage to enter into the paradise of *el norte*, their journey in search of the American dream unfolds as documented in the following chapters.

MEXICAN IMMIGRANTS: FROM MIGRANTS TO IMMIGRANTS, TO ILLEGAL ALIENS, TO NARCO-TERRORISTS

Of all the people who have migrated to the United States, perhaps no other group has experienced the constant hostilities that Latino immigrants, particularly Mexicans after 1848, have endured over the years. During the early part of the twentieth century, for instance, Mexicans were required to strip naked and be disinfected with various chemical agents, including gasoline, kerosene, sodium cyanide, cyanogens, sulfuric acid, and Zyklon B before gaining entry (Romo 2005; Urbina, Vela, and Sánchez 2014). The risks of the fumigation process included the possibility of death, such as occurred in 1916 when fifty individuals in the El Paso, Texas, jail were stripped of their clothing, bathed in gasoline, and caught on fire, killing twenty-seven. Zyklon B, the fumigation of choice, was later used in Nazi Germany in gas chambers. Further, police officers were accused of taking pictures of naked Mexican women and sharing the photos. Such unequal and brutal treatment led to the 1917 Bath Riots, where several thousand individuals protested this practice as dehumanizing and deadly (Romo 2005).

Once in the United States, as Paul Warnshius (1931) discovered, Mexican immigrants were stereotyped and arrested in disproportionate numbers for public disorder crimes as a means to keep them in check, and were subjected to routine dragnets and brutal field tactics by the police. As an example of early ethnic and racial stereotypes, a Chicago police sergeant asserted that "Indian and Negro blood does not mix very well. That is the trouble with the Mexican, he has too much Negro blood" (Warnshius 1931, 39). In retrospect, the police felt justified in heightening their aggression against Mexicans, other Latinos, and blacks. As noted by Adalberto Aguirre and Jonathan Turner (2007, 2), "When people associate superficial biological differences with variations in psychological, intellectual, and behavioral makeup, they may feel justified in treating members of a distinctive group in discriminatory ways."

In 1954 Congress authorized Operation Wetback, giving Border Patrol agents blanket authority to stop and search "Mexican-looking" people to check their residence status. Between 1954 and 1959 the Border Patrol deported approximately 3.8 million (though figures vary) undocumented persons and U.S. citizens of Mexican descent to Mexico (Gutiérrez 1997; Salinas 2015). Two decades later, contradicting the notion that U.S. immigration laws are color-blind, in *United States v. Brignoni-Ponce* (1975) the Supreme Court ruled that the Fourth Amendment allows police officers to use "Mexican appearance" as a legitimate consideration when making an immigration stop or questioning people about their citizenship or immigration status, as long as *racial profiling* is not the sole factor. Then, in *United States v. Martínez-Fuerte* (1976), the Supreme Court ruled that the Fourth Amendment was not violated by the Border Patrol when they routinely stopped vehicles at checkpoints, largely on the basis of the occupants' appearance of Mexican ancestry (Sullivan 2008). These decisions impacted police practices and police-community relations, as detailed by Alfredo Mirandé in "Latinos and Fourth Amendment Protection Against Unreasonable Search and Seizures" (2012).

In the first decade of the twenty-first century, researchers Cecilia Menjívar and Cynthia Bejarano (2004, 122) conducted interviews with immigrants from Cuba, El Salvador, Guatemala, and Mexico in Phoenix, Arizona, and concluded that "not all immigrants, not even all Latinos, share the same experiences." Their home country influenced how they were perceived in terms of crime, policing, and socioeconomic status in the United States, conceptualized by the authors as "bifocal lens." For instance, individuals from El Salvador and Guatemala were associated with political violence, Cubans were defined as "deserving" refugees, and Mexicans were categorized as undocumented ("illegal") immigrants, or to use the racist vernacular, "wetbacks." The bifocal lens shaped the daily lives of Latinos, especially their *mobility* in the neighborhood, forcing Central Americans and Mexicans to go to great lengths to avoid contacts with police for fear of being detected, arrested, or deported. In another study, Bejarano (2005) researched a border community in Arizona where youths reported fear of the Border Patrol due to immigration checks at schools. In fact, children were told to carry birth certificates or face deportation. Among various pressing issues were two detrimental ones for Latino youths: how being undocumented created a feeling of *no rights* in a supposedly democratic country; and how secondary knowledge of English was essential in establishing identity and status. Clearly, "the mastery of English is profoundly important in claims making and establishing legitimacy in the United States" (Bejarano 2005, 49). Outside the Southwest, researchers conducted a focus group in Mount Pleasant, D.C., with men and women from El Salvador, Columbia, Honduras, and the Dominican Republic (Hammer and Rogan 2002), where among various concerns respondents identified how their inability to speak English and officers' inability to speak Spanish posed great difficulty in interactions, ultimately impacting police-community relations.

With shifting demographic trends in an already highly diverse and multicultural society (Urbina 2014; Urbina and Álvarez 2015; Urbina and Wright 2016), monolingual English-speaking police officers seem to be unable to communicate with Spanish-speaking suspects and community members who speak only Spanish, and bilingual officers may not be fluent enough to speak clearly or fully comprehend regional dialects or localism. In fact, throughout the legal process, Latinos with limited English proficiency often lack interpreter assistance (Urbina 2004), which heightens their fear in dealing with police officers and makes the criminal justice system nearly incomprehensible (Lazos Vargas 2002; Urbina 2018; Urbina and Álvarez 2017; Walker et al. 2004). For instance, the lack of adequate interpreters throughout the entire police process, including the ability to correctly interpret 911 calls in Spanish, threatens the protection of Miranda rights for monolingual Spanish-speaking Latinos (Urbina and Álvarez 2015).

In sum, the hundreds of local ordinances, multiple state laws, and various federal legislative mandates have socially redefined undocumented workers. Over time, undocumented workers have been legally redefined, *from migrants to immigrants, from immigrants to illegal aliens, and most recently, from illegal aliens to narco-terrorists,* implying criminality and thus impacting the nature of immigration enforcement. *"The criminalization of immigrants, in turn, has resulted in the criminalization of non-criminals and, in essence, the criminalization of Mexicans and the whole Latina/o community"* (Castañeda 2007; Posadas and Medina 2012, 93; Romero 2000), creating "an underclass of people *locked down* and *invisible,* in fear of deportation and being separated from their families" (Posadas and Medina 2012, 89). One recent study found that the vulnerability to deportation or detention negatively impacts the well-being of Latino immigrants, including the stability of the family household, the mental and emotional state of children, and the children's academic achievement (Brabeck and Xu 2010).

CHAPTER OUTLINE

Considering the long-lasting and complicated history of U.S. immigration laws, enforcement, and discourse, the array of issues currently confronting both undocumented and documented communities, and the shifting trends in the ethnic/racial landscape, this book seeks to provide a comprehensive account of the interaction of historical and contemporary forces in shaping the immigrants' experience over time as well as to examine police-minority relations to better understand the current state of immigration and gain further insight into the future of immigration in a multiethnic, multiracial, and multicultural society. Delineating the spheres of immigration laws and border enforcement in a highly diverse society in the twenty-first century, this book combines historical, theoretical, and empirical research—placing immigration within a broader police, community, and international context.

In chapter 1, "Beyond the Wall: Race and Immigration Discourse," Arnoldo De León uses the Mexican experience as a point of reference to detail the historical influence of race on the immigration discourse, establishing a baseline for subsequent chapters, which will expand and supplement the immigration discourse with historical, theoretical, philosophical, and empirical studies and analysis. By detailing how ethnicity/race has been defined and redefined over time, influencing immigration laws, enforcement, and discourse, the author provides a foundation for understanding not only the central mission of this volume but also the American experience. In chapter 2, "Exposing Immigration Laws: The Legal Contours of Belonging and Exclusion," Steven W. Bender explores the scope and nature of immigration laws over time, documenting how the interactions of race, ethnicity, class, and national origin, among other forces, have historically governed the legal and social parameters of immigration laws, illegality, and immigrants—defining belonging and exclusion in the United States. Providing the legal analysis often missing in discourse regarding *belonging* and *exclusion*, which are central to the immigration debate, the author buttresses the volume with the legal rationality to understand immigration in its totality. In chapter 3, "Divided Lines: The Politics of Immigration Control in the United States," Roxanne Lynn Doty illustrates that a comprehensive understanding of the *politics* of immigration control requires a broadened understanding of "the political" (versus "politics"), an understanding that goes beyond a focus on political parties, elections, campaigns, the passing of laws, and other activities engaged in by the government. Such an understanding also illustrates that the ways immigration has been transformed into a highly politicized issue are intricately connected to a broadened conceptualization of "the political," where the very possibility of conventional politics depends on a broader realm in which social spaces, meanings, identities, and political subjects are created and recreated. As seldom seen in academic discourse, the author exposes the *centrality* of "the political" and "politics" of immigration, revealing one of the most timely and relevant forces governing immigration. In chapter 4, "Immigration, Illegality, and the Law: Governance, Equality, and Justice," Claudio G. Vera Sánchez charges that the term "illegal" carries detrimental implications, and asserts that terms like "unauthorized" should be used instead. Vera Sánchez describes several pressing national issues within our contemporary era of social control and globalization—including crime and drugs in communities, the labor market, taxes and social services, federal regulation of immigration, and America's culture—and delineates how unauthorized immigrants are identified as the root cause of these problems, which prompts regulation, surveillance, criminalization, and punishment of unauthorized immigrants. Moving beyond what some critics identify as the central focus of immigration, illegality, this chapter extends the discourse to key universal principles, equality and justice, enriching the volume with provoking analyses of what constitutes immigration from a humanistic standpoint. In chapter 5, "Building America: Immigrant Labor and the U.S. Economy," Ruth Gomberg-Muñoz challenges the historically manipulated *idea* of immigrant labor and explores how U.S. immigration policies have actively promoted and maintained a foreign-born labor force for more than two hundred years. The author also shows that immigrant labor is not just any labor, but has historically provided a particular type of labor for certain sectors of the U.S. economy. Gomberg-Muñoz also documents that immigrant workers are not passive in the face of exploitative policies, but active participants in labor struggles that have profoundly shaped work conditions. In a sophisticated analysis, the author examines immigrant labor and the American economy in their totality. In chapter 6, "Always Running: La Migra, Detentions,

Deportations, and Human Rights," Lupe S. Salinas examines America's immigration policy as it relates to the nation's labor needs during the century before the attacks on New York City and Washington, D.C., in 2001, then addresses U.S. immigration and border enforcement in the post-9/11 era. He includes sections on enforcement raids and racial profiling, detentions, deportations, and human rights violations that result from these official actions. He specifically addresses the dilemmas posed by the migration of refugees and the arrival of unaccompanied children and asks whether the U.S. government is meeting its obligations under the U.N. Declaration of Human Rights as they relate to the treatment and detention of children and adults. He also critiques governmental policies that permit removals based on relatively minor crimes, thus raising serious concerns about the arbitrariness of granting residence under the law and violation of one's due process right not to be repatriated and not be subjected to an unconscionable loss of residence in one's new country. With regard to the detention of undocumented persons, Salinas reviews legislative policy that effectively results in a detentions quota. With vivid detail and provoking legal analysis, Judge Salinas gives the volume great authority with a masterful discussion of a fundamental but often neglected element in immigration discourse, human rights. In chapter 7, "Challenges to Integration: The Children of Immigrants and Direct and Indirect Experiences with the Law," Leo R. Chávez examines the possible implications of experiences with the legal system for two key indicators of how children of immigrants are integrating into U.S. society (years of schooling and personal income). The author claims that integration is influenced by how one perceives being welcomed by the larger society—that is, their sense of belonging. Thus, perceptions of prejudice and discrimination are also part of how children of immigrants view their social environment. To examine these issues, the author relies on survey data collected on adult children of Chinese, Filipino, Guatemalan, Korean, Mexican, Salvadoran, Taiwanese, and Vietnamese immigrants in the greater Los Angeles area. Moving beyond the historical focus of adult integration, the author ventures into the lives of those who have received limited attention in the immigration debate, children, enriching the volume by incorporating the stories of the most disadvantaged. In chapter 8, "Borders and Dreams: Immigration, Diversity, and Multiculturalism in the New Millennium," Brenda I. Gill and Mary C. Sengstock analyze the historical *evolution* of immigration and its influence on diversity and multiculturalism. The authors report that contrary to the popular imagination, America has been a diverse nation since its earliest colonial days, and management of the varying races, ethnicities, and cultures has been problematic—normally seen as threatening by the dominant majority. Demystifying the notion of social integration, the authors situate immigration within a historical multicultural context, giving the volume historical and contemporary relevance. In chapter 9, "Five Myths About Immigration: Immigrant Discourse, Locating White Supremacy, and the Racialization of Latino Immigrants in the United States," Daniel Justino Delgado documents that anti-Latino immigrant discourse has existed in the United States since its inception, and its effects have shaped the experiences of Latinos in ways seldom acknowledged. The author documents that all immigrant deaths, as an example, and the discourse about Latino immigrants in the borderland can be understood as directly tied to the racialized narratives on immigration. The author also argues that human rights violations are fundamental to the functioning of social systems in the United States (and other nations), and are ultimately the result of a history of white European settler colonialism and white supremacy. The consequences of these racial histories have led to the normalization of everyday white supremacy, belief in white virtuousness, and a focus on immigrants as the racial Other. The author charges that because of these racial histories the biggest myth surrounding immigration is that immigration is not about *race*; in reality, race *is* the central factor organizing these various discourses, myths, and narratives on immigration. The author vividly dismantles and exposes a series of myths about immigration for what they really are. In chapter 10, "Covering the Immigrant Story: Immigration Through the Lens of the American Media," Peter Laufer tells the story of Juana María Rodriguez as a "provoking" grassroots example of the emotional costs (along with the lovely successes) that can occur when individuals take immigration law into their own hands—illustrating, with vivid detail, the everyday experience of thousands of immigrants. Laufer delineates how the legal and social *construction* of immigration "illegality" is rooted in a group's access to privilege, wealth, and power—the small segment of society that controls the American media. The media continues formulating and propagating centuries-old ethnic/racial stereotypes and repressive practices by the dominant group against immigrants, which must be deconstructed if we are to achieve a post-racial America. Giving *voice* to those who have been marginalized, oppressed, and silenced, the author grants immigrants a human face, giving the volume strategic techniques for resistance and empowerment. In chapter 11, "Immigration, Criminalization, and Militarization in the Age of Globalization," Sofía Espinoza Álvarez and Martin Guevara Urbina document that globalization has evolved into *a new form of slavery* for society's most vulnerable, particularly undocumented people. It has redefined immigration laws, enforcement, and discourse, shifting immigration trends, exacerbating criminalization, and, for the first time in American history, militarizing U.S. borders, even to our neighborhoods. As Americans view walls, fences, and war zones around the world with indignation, do they see what is going on in America, in our own backyards? We envision war in foreign lands, but not in America and certainly not in our neighborhoods. Exploring the contemporary criminalization of immigrants and the aggressive militarization of the border, the authors situate immigration within a social (community) context, giving the volume a societal framework for discourse. In the conclusion, "Immigration Laws and Social Control Movements: Situating the Realities of Immigration in the Twenty-First Century," Martin Guevara Urbina and Sofía Espinoza Álvarez situate immigration laws, enforcement, and discourse within a broader international context. They show that the anti-immigrants movement must be seen in relation to other social control movements, like the *war on drugs* and the *war on terrorism*, in the midst of globalization to fully capture the realities of immigration—what the authors characterize as *underneath it all*. Clearly, according to the authors, the anti-immigration movement goes far beyond apprehensions and deportations. For instance, at the same time that Mexican immigration has zeroed out, and more recently has undergone *reverse* Mexican migration, why is the United States, supposedly the most powerful country in the world, declaring a multibillion dollar war to ward off approximately 3 percent of the population, the undocumented laborers who are among the most vulnerable, exploited, oppressed, and marginalized segments of society? Demonstrating the historical, contemporary, and transnational connectivity of the multiple forces governing immigration over time, the authors make a case for the volume as a must-read book.

SUMMARY

Analyzing the twists and turns of immigration over time reveals that immigrants are confronted not only by a long, complicated, and dangerous journey, but also by a mixture of powerful and intertwining historical and contemporary forces (like language, citizenship, and culture), issues that influence not only immigrants' everyday experience once they reach the United States, including their interaction with immigration officials and other law enforcement agents, but also border enforcement practices. Obtaining a more inclusive picture of immigration laws, enforcement practice, and discourse from the early days in the Americas to the new millennium enables us to better understand the current state of immigration and the ethnic and racial realities of immigrants, and gives us insight into the future of immigration in the United States and abroad. With shifting demographic trends, understanding the emerging new face of America and the upcoming majority—Asians and Latinos—is vital if we wish to move beyond post-racial America and be the country of the future, reflective of a truly democratic society.

Similarly, understanding the historical roots and ideology that have shaped and governed immigration laws, enforcement, and discourse is not only vital to better understand the immigrant experience and overall American experience, but essential for analyzing the dynamics of immigration over the years, and, by extension, how new immigrants are being situated within immigrant communities, minority communities, and society at large. Considering the rapid shift in demographic trends, this book provides a conceptual framework for better understanding the needs, experiences, and future of immigrants in the workforce (as one example) throughout the country. The issues highlighted in this introduction, like deportations, criminality, citizenship, and ethnic/racial profiling—which challenge our quest for social economic policies, safety, equality, justice, and due process—will be further examined in the following chapters, supplemented with historical, social, theoretical, philosophical, and legal analysis, along with empirical studies. Immigration laws, enforcement, and discourse are investigated within a broader context—immigrant communities, society at large, and the international community. Clearly, the rapidly shifting landscape merits a newly energized research agenda to explore the ways in which immigration shapes policies, enforcement, and dialogue, and, by extension, all facets of social life, from the economic system to the political system. Lastly, the contributing authors demonstrate that ignorance of the many "faces" of immigration is not inevitable, and thus the book provides policy and research recommendations to help bridge long-neglected gaps in the immigration discourse, and ultimately to create *comprehensive, equitable, and humane immigration policies and reform for the twenty-first century*, while providing context for further empirical studies, analysis, documentation, and dialogue.

REFERENCES

Acuña, R. 2014. *Occupied America: A History of Chicanos*. 8th ed. Boston: Pearson.

Aguirre, A., and J. Turner. 2007. *American Ethnicity: The Dynamics and Consequences of Discrimination*. 5th ed. New York: McGraw-Hill.

Almaguer, T. 2008. *Racial Fault Lines: The Historical Origins of White Supremacy in California*. Berkeley: University of California Press.

Arellano, G. 2014. "Republicans Used California's 'Juan Crow' Law as a Model for Other States. Now It's Dead, and So Is the Far-Right." *Guardian*, September 18. http://www.theguardian .com/commentisfree/2014/sep/18/republicans-california-juan-crow-law-repealed.

Associated Press. 2015. "Mexico Deports 49 Percent More Central American Minors in First 5 Months of 2015." *Fox News*, June 22. http://www.startribune.com/mexico-deports-49 -percent-more-minors-in-first-5-months/309047741/.

Bacon, D. 2009. *Illegal People: How Globalization Creates Migration and Criminalizes Immigrants*. Boston: Beacon Press.

Bejarano, C. L. 2005. *¿Que Onda? Urban Youth Culture and Border Identity*. Tucson: University of Arizona Press.

Bender, S. W. 2003. *Greasers and Gringos: Latinos, Law, and the American Imagination*. New York: New York University Press.

———. 2015. *Mea Culpa: Lessons on Law and Regret from U.S. History*. New York: New York University Press.

Brabeck, K., and Q. Xu. 2010. "The Impact of Detention and Deportation on Latino Immigrant Children and Families: A Quantitative Exploration." *Hispanic Journal of Behavioral Sciences* 32: 341–61.

Castañeda, J. 2007. *Ex Mex: From Migrants to Immigrants*. New York: New Press.

Chossudovsky, M. 2015. *The Globalization of War: America's "Long War" Against Humanity*. Montreal: Global Research.

De León, A. 1983. *They Called Them Greasers: Anglo Attitudes Toward Mexicans in Texas, 1821–1900*. Austin: University of Texas Press.

Dunn, T. J. 2009. *Blockading the Border and Human Rights: The El Paso Operation That Remade Immigration Enforcement*. Austin: University of Texas Press.

Ewing, W. A. 2014. "The Growth of the U.S. Deportation Machine." *American Immigration Council*. http://www.immigrationpolicy.org/just-facts/growth-us-deportation-machine.

Feagin, J. R. 2006. *Systemic Racism: A Theory of Oppression*. New York: Routledge.

———. 2013. *The White Racial Frame: Centuries of Racial Framing and Counter-Framing*. 2nd ed. New York: Routledge.

———. 2014. *Racist America: Roots, Current Realities, and Future Reparations*. New York: Routledge.

Fitzpatrick, T. 2001. "New Agenda for Social Policy and Criminology: Globalization, Urbanization, and the Emerging Post-Social Security State." *Social Policy and Administration* 35: 212–29.

Golash-Boza, T. M. 2015. *Deported: Policing Immigrants, Disposable Labor, and Global Capitalism*. New York: New York University Press.

Goodman, A. 2014. "How the Deportation Numbers Mislead." *Al Jazerra America*, January 24. http://america.aljazeera.com/opinions/2014/1/what-the-deportationnumbersdonattell.html.

Gutiérrez, D., ed. 1997. *Between Two Worlds: Mexican Immigrants in the United States*. Wilmington, Del.: Jaguar Books.

Hammer, M., and R. Rogan. 2002. "Latino and Indochinese Interpretive Frames in Negotiating Conflict with Law Enforcement: A Focus Group Analysis." *International Journal of Intercultural Relations* 26: 551–75.

Hootsen, J. 2015. "The Border Surge, a Year Later: The Perilous Corridor to the U.S. Slowly Clearing Out." *Fox News*, June 9. http://latino.foxnews.com/latino/politics/2015/06/09/border-surge-year-later-perilous-corridor-to-us-slowly-clearing-out/.

Jensen, E., A. Knapp, C. Borsella, and K. Nestor. 2015. "The Place-of-Birth Compositions of Immigrants to the United States: 2000–2013." *U.S. Census Bureau*. http://www.census.gov/content/dam/Census/newsroom/press-kits/2015/china_paa_v14.pdf.

Johnson, K. R. 2000. "The Case Against Race Profiling in Immigration Enforcement." *Washington University Law Quarterly* 78: 675–736.

Law, A. O. 2014. *The Immigration Battle in American Courts.* New York: Cambridge University Press.

Lazos Vargas, S. 2002. " 'Latina/o-ization' of the Midwest: Cambio de Colores (Change of Colors) as Agromaquilas Expand into the Heartland." *Berkeley La Raza Law Journal* 13: 343–68.

Lozano, J. 2012. "Officials: More Illegal Immigrants from C. America." *Christian Science Monitor,* December 21. http://www.csmonitor.com/USA/Latest-News-Wires/2012/1221/Illegal-immigration-from-C.-America-on-the-rise.

McWilliams, C. 1990. *North from Mexico: The Spanish-Speaking People of the United States.* New York: Praeger.

Menjívar, C., and C. Bejarano. 2004. "Latino Immigrants' Perceptions of Crime and Police Authorities in the United States: A Case Study from the Phoenix Metropolitan Area." *Ethnic and Racial Studies* 27: 120–48.

Miller, T. 2014. "Mexico: The U.S. Border Patrol's Newest Hire." *Al Jazerra America*, October 4. http://america.aljazeera.com/opinions/2014/10/mexico-us-borderpatrolsecurity immigrants.html.

Mirandé, A. 2012. "Latinos and Fourth Amendment Protection Against Unreasonable Search and Seizures." In *Hispanics in the U.S. Criminal Justice System*, edited by M. G. Urbina, 145–61. Springfield, Ill.: Charles C Thomas.

Miroff, N. 2015. "Donald Trump Wants a Border Wall. These Statistics Show Mexico Is a Step Ahead of Him." *Washington Post*, June 22. https://www.washingtonpost.com/news/worldviews/wp/2015/06/22/donald-trump-wants-a-border-wall-these-statistics-show-mexico-is-a-step-ahead-of-him/.

Passel, J., D. Cohn, and A. Gonzalez-Barrera. 2012. "Net Migration from Mexico Falls to Zero—and Perhaps Less." Washington, D.C.: Pew Research Center. http://www.pewhispanic.org/2012/04/23/net-migration-from-mexico-falls-to-zero-and-perhaps-less/.

Pew Research Center. 2013. "The Rise of Asian Americans." Washington, D.C.: Pew Research Center. http://www.pewsocialtrends.org/files/2013/04/Asian-Americans-new-full-report-04-2013.pdf.

Posadas, C., and C. Medina. 2012. "Immigration Lockdown: The Exclusion of Mexican Immigrants Through Legislation." In *Hispanics in the U.S. Criminal Justice System*, edited by M. G. Urbina, 80–93. Springfield, Ill.: Charles C Thomas.

Román, E. 2013. *Those Damned Immigrants: America's Hysteria over Undocumented Immigration.* New York: New York University Press.

Romero, M. 2000. "State Violence and the Social and Legal Construction of Latino Criminality: From El Bandido to Gang Member." *Denver University Law Review* 78: 1089–1127.

———. 2006. "Racial Profiling and Immigration Enforcement: Rounding Up of Usual Suspects in the Latino Community." *Critical Sociology* 32: 447–72.

Romero, M., and M. Serag. 2004. "Violation of Latino Civil Rights Resulting from INS and Local Police Use of Race, Culture, and Class Profiling: The Case of Chandler Roundup in Arizona." *Cleveland State Law Review* 52: 75–96.

Romo, D. D. 2005. *Ringside Seat to a Revolution: An Underground Cultural History of El Paso and Juárez: 1893 to 1923*. El Paso, Tex: Cinco Puntos Press.

Rumbaut, R. G. 2008. "The Coming of the Second Generation: Immigration and Ethnic Mobility in Southern California." *Annals of the American Academy of Political and Social Science* 196: 196–236.

Salinas, L. S. 2015. *U.S. Latinos and Criminal Injustice*. East Lansing: Michigan State University Press.

Sole, C. 2015. "Child Migrant Crisis Endures on Mexico's South Border." *Yahoo! News*, June 26. http://news.yahoo.com/child-migrant-crisis-endures-mexicos-south-border-043413823 .html.

Stevenson, M., and A. Arce. 2015. "Mexico Deports More Central Americans Than the United States." *American Renaissance*, June 18. https://www.amren.com/news/2015/06/mexico -deports-more-central-americans-than-the-united-states/.

Sullivan, A. 2008. "On Thin ICE: Cracking Down on the Racial Profiling of Immigrants and Implementing a Compassionate Enforcement Policy. *Hastings Race and Poverty Law Journal* 6: 101–44.

Tichenor, D. 2002. *Dividing Lines: The Politics of Immigration Control in America*. Princeton, N.J.: Princeton University Press.

Tirman, J. 2015. *Dream Chasers: Immigration and the American Backlash*. Cambridge, Mass.: MIT Press.

Urbina, M. G. 2004. "Language Barriers in the Wisconsin Court System: The Latino/a Experience." *Journal of Ethnicity in Criminal Justice* 2: 91–118.

———, ed. 2014. *Twenty-First Century Dynamics of Multiculturalism: Beyond Post-racial America*. Springfield, Ill.: Charles C Thomas.

———. 2018. *Hispanics in the U.S. Criminal Justice System: Ethnicity, Ideology, and Social Control*. 2nd ed. Springfield, Ill.: Charles C Thomas.

Urbina, M. G., and S. E. Álvarez, eds. 2015. *Latino Police Officers in the United States: An Examination of Emerging Trends and Issues*. Springfield, Ill.: Charles C Thomas.

———. 2016. "Neoliberalism, Criminal Justice, and Latinos: The Contours of Neoliberal Economic Thought and Policy on Criminalization." *Latino Studies* 14: 33–58.

———. 2017. *Ethnicity and Criminal Justice in the Era of Mass Incarceration: A Critical Reader on the Latino Experience*. Springfield, Ill.: Charles C Thomas.

Urbina, M. G., J. E. Vela, and J. O. Sánchez. 2014. *Ethnic Realities of Mexican Americans: From Colonialism to 21st Century Globalization*. Springfield, Ill.: Charles C Thomas.

Urbina, M. G., and C. R. Wright. 2016. *Latino Access to Higher Education: Ethnic Realities and New Directions for the Twenty-First Century*. Springfield, Ill.: Charles C Thomas.

Vásquez, Y. 2011. "Perpetuating the Marginalization of Latinos: A Collateral Consequence of Immigration Law into the Criminal Justice System." *Howard Law Journal* 54: 11–20.

Walker, N., J. Senger, F. Villarruel, and A. Arboleda. 2004. *Lost Opportunities: The Realities of Latinos in the U.S. Criminal Justice System*. Washington, D.C.: National Council of La Raza.

Warnshius, P. 1931. "Crime and Criminal Justice Among Mexicans in Illinois." In *National Commission on Law Observance and Enforcement Report, Crime and the Foreign Born*, 265–329. Washington, D.C.: Government Printing Office.

Welch, M. 2006. *Scapegoats of September 11: Hate Crimes and State Crimes in the War on Terror*. New Brunswick, N.J.: Rutgers University Press.

———. 2007. "Immigration Lockdown Before and After 9/11: Ethnic Constructions and Their Consequences." In *Race, Gender, and Punishment: From Colonialism to the War on Terror*, edited by M. Bosworth and J. Flavin, 149–63. Piscataway, N.J.: Rutgers University Press.

———. 2009. *Crimes of Power and States of Impunity: The U.S. Response to Terror*. New Brunswick, N.J.: Rutgers University Press.

Chapter 1

BEYOND THE WALL

Race and Immigration Discourse

ARNOLDO DE LEÓN

The way Americans most understand the history of Latinos in
this country, a lot of it is being told now through the lens of
what's happening with the immigration debate. While that's an
important debate that has security and moral implications, in my
view, there's also a huge history of Latinos in the United States
that's never been told.

—KEN SALAZAR

IMMIGRANTS HAVE COME to the United States from all over the world at various
times, moving freely, as there were no borders. At the same time, the immigration
discourse *focused on and targeted* people who were viewed as nonwhite, undesirable,
or "outsiders." Quickly, the immigration debate revolved around people of color, particularly people of Mexican heritage and eventually the entire Latino community in
the United States. In this chapter, then, the central objective is to use the Mexican
experience to delineate the historical influence of race on the immigration discourse.
Subsequent chapters will expand and supplement with historical, theoretical, philosophical, and empirical studies and analysis, while situating the experience of colored
minorities within a broader context.

Since the time Anglos acquired Mexico's Far North, first with Texas in 1836 and
then the rest of what became the U.S. Southwest in 1848, white Americans have
engaged in a *discourse* concerning the categorization of Mexican-origin people.
Throughout U.S. history Americans have racialized people from Mexico (whether
foreign- or U.S.-born) and have questioned their fitness for a place in the American
mainstream. Historians have advanced a number of explanations for this racialization.
During the 1840s, a long-standing interpretation holds, Manifest Destiny portrayed
Mexicans as biologically inferior to the Anglo-Saxon, and the occupation of the U.S.
Southwest and the domination of those living in the conquered regions (as well as

immigrants) after the War with Mexico increasingly racialized Mexicans (Almaguer 2008; De León 1983; Gómez 2007; Horsman 1981; Menchaca 2001; Mitchell 2005; Ngai 2004). Most recently, Natalia Molina in *How Race Is Made in America* (2013) proposes that behind such images dwelt the "construction" of what she labels "racial scripts," a process by which characteristics attributed to some racialized groups are then projected onto other peoples considered similarly genetically backward. Therefore, Anglo Americans imputed to Mexicans traits they had already imputed to Native Americans and African American slaves before the 1820s (Molina 2010, 2013). Was there a place, then, in U.S. life for people regarded as mixed-blood, indolent, immoral, and seemingly unassimilable?

Beginning in the early years of the 1900s, Americans engaged in more salient conversations as to how Mexicans fit into their society. In New Mexico and Arizona, the statehood debate brought the question of race to the fore. Views among some Anglo elements about racially mixed Mexicans—who constituted more than one-third of the total population in the two territories—delayed statehood until 1912. There and elsewhere, a vast influx from Mexico due to the Mexican Revolution of 1910, to labor shortages during World War I (1914–18), and to the passage of the National Origins Act of 1924 (which reduced immigration from Europe) raised during the 1920s the question of what to do about the waves of Mexicans crossing into the United States. Did their presence augur well for the country's well-being, or were they seen as foreigners and un-American by habits and therefore a blight on the nation (Dobkin 2009; Molina 2013; Noel 2014; Reimers 1998)? Then, as now, Americans inclined to propose anti-immigrant legislation and to initiate anti-immigrant drives against those whom they saw as not meriting acceptance into society.

A healthy debate has developed in recent decades among scholars searching for an explanation of the hostility toward people from Mexico who have sought new beginnings in the United States, toward immigrants who have long held residence in the United States, and, for that matter, toward those born in the United States of parents of Mexican nationality, who continue to be considered foreigners. Mae M. Ngai in *Impossible Subjects: Illegal Aliens and the Making of Modern America* (2004) finds that perceptions of Mexicans (both native- and foreign-born) as "racial others"— and by extension, as "illegal aliens"—explains this impulse. At present, she explains, long-extant racialization has come to designate Mexicans "as a caste, unambiguously situated outside the boundaries of formal membership and social legitimacy" (Ngai 2004, 2). In agreement with Ngai, Leo R. Chávez in *The Latino Threat: Constructing Immigrants, Citizens, and the Nation* (2013) adds that Americans through the decades attributed to Mexicans biological deficiencies that disqualified them from citizenship. Such racialization swayed Anglos into distinguishing Mexicans from other immigrant groups and to scornfully label the former as "illegals" (Chávez 2013). Other scholars offer similar explanations (Dobkin 2009; Gutiérrez 1995; Molina 2010, 2013; Navarro 2009; Noel 2014).

RACE, IMMIGRATION, AND MEXICANS

The National Origins Act of 1924 favoring northern European countries left the door open to immigration from Western Hemisphere nations. Lobbyists speaking for agricultural and industrial interests had convinced Congress that their operations would fail without the availability of cheap labor, which Latin American countries and Mexico in particular could supply (Dobkin 2009; Hernández 2010). However, in certain segments of the population, the presence of large numbers of Mexicans caused anxiety, and the distress felt by so many generated a sustained public discourse on the perils of immigration throughout the remainder of the 1920s. A squad of eugenicists, nativists, government officials, health specialists, social workers, academicians, journalists, union organizers, and others went before congressional committees to depict Mexicans as mongrels, low-class, and criminals. Witnesses considered Mexicans intellectually deficient, unhygienic, apolitical, culturally backward, and prone to becoming public charges. Those continuing to insist on the need for cheap labor assured alarmists that there was no reason to worry, defending the Mexicans on *similar* racist logic: immigrant workers were biologically inferior, docile, compliant, and harbored an innate instinct for returning to the homeland at the end of the harvest cycle. They were people easily controlled (Cardoso 1980; Divine 1957; García 2001; Gutiérrez 1995; Henderson 2011; Hernández 2010; Ngai 2004; Noel 2014; Reisler 1976; Sheridan 2002).

In the end, the several congressional hearings of the era produced no specific laws that halted or slowed the flow of immigrants from Mexico. However, the strident stance taken by anti-immigration advocates did have the effect of affirming the racial identity of Mexican immigrants. Government agencies now closely adhered to provisions in existing laws, discriminating against those crossing the border by subjecting them to a regimen that included humiliating acts such as mass bathing, delousing, and medical checkups, as well as the levying of fees that many could barely afford. The majority of the immigrants avoided the procedure required for lawful entry, and so in the mind of many Americans, "the undocumented Mexican laborer who crossed the border to work in the burgeoning industry of commercial agriculture emerged as a prototypical illegal alien" (Ngai 2004, 71). The Border Patrol, established in 1924, stood vigil along a dividing line that by this time acted as a *racial boundary*, separating those who belonged (whites) from those who did not (people of color), though targeting Mexicans (Hernández 2010; Molina 2013; Noel 2014).

The matter of citizenship and belonging had been discussed to such lengths during the immigration debates of the 1920s that the label "Mexican" came to be associated with racial foreignness. Then during the Depression era (1929–39), any discussion about qualifications for the citizenship became moot because of concerns that aliens would take the limited jobs. Still, barring immigrants from working in the United States did not satisfy exclusionists, and thus deportation and repatriation movements—to include even U.S.-born Mexicans—became the order of the day. Ngai (2004, 75) interprets the repatriation of Mexicans as "a racial expulsion program exceeded in scale only by the Native American Indian removals of the nineteenth century" (see also Gutiérrez 1995; Noel 2014).

But not long after, in the World War II years (1939–45), the United States negotiated with Mexico for a labor contract that would provide the agricultural and industrial sectors with the labor needed to support the war effort. Segments of the population, however, found themselves conflicted about what came to be called the Bracero Program, an agreement between the United States and Mexico (in effect from 1942 to 1964) for use of huge numbers of guest workers to tend the fields seasonally. While the braceros served a purpose, in the racialized mind of others they represented a foreign, temporary, and dispensable element (Gutiérrez 1995; Ngai 2004; Noel 2014).

In the end, braceros proved insufficient to meet labor requirements, and by the latter 1940s and continuing into the 1950s, "wetbacks" filled the deficiency. The presence of these undocumented laborers, deemed law violators and criminals, racialized Mexicans further, and the slur "wetbacks" came to be applied to U.S.-born Mexican Americans as well. As Natalia Molina (2013, 114) puts it, "From the 1950s to the 1980s, the term taught the public what *Mexican* meant in this new immigration regime." Indeed, U.S.-born Mexicans came under surveillance when in 1954 the government launched Operation Wetback, a massive program to deport Mexican nationals residing in the United States illegally. Already conditioned to think in racialized ways, Immigration and Naturalization Service (INS) agents on numerous occasions freely used racial profiling in conducting sweeps in Mexican American communities (Molina 2013).

Pressing issues of the 1960s deflected American attention from immigration. The Immigration and Naturalization Act (also known as the Hart-Celler Act) passed in 1965 contributed further to this lull. In that civil rights era (1954–68), as liberals appealed for racial equality, Congress responded by eliminating the restrictionist policy established under the National Origins Act of 1924. The 1965 act, however, troubled many Americans, as thousands still crossed from Mexico in defiance of the quota placed on Latin American countries. Those who arrived to meet labor demands did so outside the law, and thus the term "Mexican" continued to have odious racial connotations, associated with foreignness, illegality, and criminality (Ngai 2004; Romero 2000).

Congress sought to enact further immigration legislation to address the renewed anxiety. Two bills in the 1970s proposed solutions: the Peter Rodino bill of 1972 and the Jimmy Carter bill of 1977. The bills similarly proposed an identification system of national scope, sanctions against employers who set out to hire undocumented workers, more funding for the INS, and other measures necessary to secure the border. Neither bill became law (Gutiérrez 1995). However, continued agitation against what some viewed as an enemy army invading the country, terrorists threatening national security, and an undesirable lot that could not be Americanized led Congress to pass the Immigration Reform and Control Act of 1986 (IRCA). The act included provisions granting amnesty to almost three million foreign-born Mexicans living in the United States, penalizing employers who hired undocumented workers, and strengthening the Border Patrol by allocating increased funds for border enforcement. Because some of IRCA's provisions proved unenforceable, because Mexico faced perennial economic woes, and because the U.S. economy still craved cheap labor, immigration continued unremittingly (Chávez 2013; Massey, Durand, and Malone 2002; Ngai 2004).

By the end of the twentieth century, immigration opponents hesitated to voice their concern about Mexicans in racist terms. Still, a white supremacist mindset nourished vile feelings about immigrants just as it had since the 1920s (Dobkin 2009; Muller 1997). Critics depicted the immigrants as part of Mexico's criminal element, associated with drug-smuggling rings; as opportunists arriving with the intent of having babies so that later (at age twenty-one) these "anchor babies" would be entitled to sponsor their families and bring them to the United States as part of a reunification procedure allowed by law; as people coming to use the country's welfare services; and as a horde arriving to reconquer the territory Mexico lost to the United States in 1848. Such charges resulted in congressional acts in the 1990s, Immigration and Naturalization Service measures—among them Operation Gatekeeper in California, Operation Safeguard in Arizona, and Operation Hold the Line in Texas—and state referenda such as California's Proposition 187 (passed in 1994, this law denied immigrants public services), all in an effort to curb immigration (Chávez 2013; Dunn 2009; Foley 2004; Massey, Durand, and Malone 2002; Navarro 2009; Nevins 2001). One scholar concludes, "The U.S. has rejected color-based discrimination in many other areas, and yet vestiges of historical racism continue to prevail in modern immigration policy" (Dobkin 2009, 40; see also Johnson 2007).

While not directly citing race mixture as a specter jeopardizing the American fabric, opponents (including pundits, opinion writers, media personalities, and others) after the 1990s still depicted Mexican immigrants and Mexican Americans as foreigners unable to assimilate, as illegals, and as "others" who either imperiled established cultural tenets or, worse, could fragment the United States and in a seceded region erect their own sovereign domain (Chávez 2013; Gutiérrez 1995). Such descriptions stoked further anti-immigrant actions. Individuals such as rancher Roger Barnett and his brothers in southern Arizona in 1999 organized a campaign to hunt down border violators and "protect" private property and America. Barnett, supported by some other local ranchers, claimed the right to use weapons to execute his group's purpose even if it involved killing immigrants (Navarro 2009). Another response to this supposed immigration crisis was the passage in 2005 of H.R. 4437, the Border Protection, Antiterrorism, and Illegal Immigration Control Act. H.R. 4437 contained provisions that made it a criminal offense (actually a felony) to be living in the country in violation of immigration laws. Those aware of Mexicans residing in the United States illegally would also be subject to prosecution. The bill further made funds available for a seven-hundred-mile-long fence along parts of the U.S.-Mexico border. Plans to erect such a government-financed obstacle harked back to the 1950s, and now for those committed to halting immigrants such goals had been realized (Chávez 2013; Molina 2013; Navarro 2009).

TO ACQUIESCE OR DEFEND?

The discourse on Mexican immigration produced only muffled resistance from Mexican American communities. Careful response to the sensitive issue remained the accepted mode until about the 1960s, when Latino sentiment toward those from Mexico hardened. During the 1920s, to be sure, there did exist advocates (called "marginalizationists" by Linda C. Noel) who took steps to defend the immigrants—to try and mollify exclusionists. Before the 1920s, marginalizationists confidently maintained that Mexicans would not harm the country, so long as they remained relegated to the fringes of the mainstream. By the 1920s, amid the influx from Mexico and the rising tide of resistance against Mexican immigration, however, these supporters changed their minds and accepted the general stereotypes of Mexicans as being "of mixed heritage, dependent, lacking in aspiration, and overall a people with an inferior culture" (Noel 2014, 120). The question, though, was how to meet the needs of southwestern agriculturalists. The marginalizationists rationalized that Mexicans possessed an instinct for returning home once their seasonal sojourn to the United States ended—thus they posed no threat. Should the immigrants stay, they could be effectively controlled and silenced. As Kelly Lytle Hernández documents in *Migra: A History of the U.S. Border Patrol* (2010, 29), "Highly racialized practices of social segregation, political repression, and community violence accompanied the patterns of economic exploitation that locked the region's large Mexicano population into low-wage work."

While these advocates of marginalization (which included Mexican Americans such as members of the League of United Latin American Citizens, or LULAC) had during the 1920s sympathized with the immigrants—arguing that they would be in the country only temporarily or could be controlled if they stayed—during the Depression these erstwhile defenders endorsed campaigns of deportation and repatriation. Ironically, when labor shortages during World War II called for new workers, marginalization proponents resurfaced to speak of the good character of the immigrants, albeit portraying them as sojourners. Noel (2014, 18) observes keenly, "Marginalization remains the core of American immigration policy and incorporation to this day."

Until about the 1970s, Mexican Americans refrained from taking potentially risky positions on the immigration question. David G. Gutiérrez, author of one of the most comprehensive overviews of Mexican immigration history, found numerous reasons why U.S.-born Mexican Americans delayed voicing a defense of the immigrants. First, Mexican Americans believed immigrants displaced the native-born from jobs and undermined efforts at unionization. Second, the immigrants reinforced for Anglos the negative image white society already held of Mexicans. Like white Americans, native-born Mexican Americans viewed the newcomers as uncouth and backward and so did not merit protection (the immigrants, on the other hand, referred to Mexican Americans as "*pochos*"). Further, Mexican Americans, among them 1920s civic leaders and 1930s LULACers, considered the immigrants detrimental to community development. Into the post–World War II years, LULAC and the newly formed American G.I. Forum (AGIF 1948) continued adhering to old stands, opposing the Bracero Program and bitterly decrying the presence of "wetbacks" (Blanton 2009; Gutiérrez 1995).

There was, to be sure, a minority position taken on behalf of immigrants during the late 1930s and through the mid-1950s. Labor union activists, mainly, contended that Mexican Americans should look after immigrant interests, maintaining that immigrants had earned citizenship rights by virtue of their contributions to the American labor system, by their display of commitment to the American way of life, and by their long residence in the United States. Labor unionists argued further that immigrants with extended settlement in the country should be hired in the World War II defense industry because of labor shortages (Gutiérrez 1995).

The McCarthy-era hunt for immigrant subversives also roused Mexican Americans into defending the undocumented. Union men condemned the 1952 McCarran-Walter Act that decreed deportations of law-abiding immigrants. Older organizations such as LULAC, dismayed over the red scare's intrusion on Mexican American rights, began to question its historical lack of concern for the immigrants' well-being. During the last half of the 1950s, the LULAC and other groups adopted a more sympathetic outlook toward immigrants, believing they deserved a place in the broader Latino community (Gutiérrez 1995; Vargas 2005).

In the 1960s and after, the Chicano Movement redirected attention to the immigration issue (which national problems of that era had interrupted) and in so doing forcefully pushed for a review of earlier anti-Latino immigration policies. Behind this 1970s reassessment lay a spike in media reporting of rising immigration from Mexico (and fears that this new wave threatened the nation's order), congressional deliberations on the perils of immigration, and intensified activity on the part of the INS to round up illegals. Drawn now to the plight of the victimized immigrants and into the pro-immigrant ranks were older organizations such as LULAC, the AGIF, the Mexican American Political Association of California, and even the United Farm Workers Union (Gutiérrez 1995).

Thus, during the late 1970s Mexican American attitudes on immigration shifted from pre-Chicano-era assumptions, so that almost all national Latino organizations and activists came to reject congressional immigration legislation. They opposed both the Rodino bill and the Jimmy Carter bill and, at the National Chicano/Latino Conference on Immigration and Public Policy held in San Antonio in 1977, representatives from various Latino organizations targeted the Jimmy Carter bill and denounced it as infringing on the civil rights of Mexicanos (both native- and foreign-born). Latinos of this generation took immigrant bashing as a personal affront, and the defense of their rights now embraced immigrant rights as well (Gutiérrez 1995).

The positions taken during the 1970s persisted into the 1980s and 1990s. Starting in the year 2000, according to Armando Navarro's (2009) exhaustive historical study of the "immigration crisis," pro-immigrant groups escalated their attacks on 1990s immigration-control initiatives such as Operation Gatekeeper and Operation Safeguard. Meanwhile, during the summer of 2000, Navarro and others concerned with widening attacks on immigrants (and Mexican Americans) founded in California the National Alliance for Human Rights (NAHR). NAHR sought to respond more forcefully to anti-immigration offensives and during the first years of the 2000s took stands against nativist stirrings, including Roger Barnett's activities in Arizona. Then, in 2006 it was drawn into the fray created by the passage of H.R. 4437. H.R. 4437 had galvanized pro-immigrant forces (and immigrants themselves) that had arisen in response to expanding anti-immigrant campaigns since the late 1990s (Navarro 2009).

The enactment of the bill in the House—as well as troubles in Arizona, the proliferation of hate groups nationwide, and the advancement of nativist legislation at the state level—inaugurated a social movement called by Professor Navarro (University of California at Riverside) the Movimiento Pro-Migrante. The hostile climate of the period portended for immigrants an unpromising future in the United States, and they felt the need for some sort of public demonstration to still the anti-immigrant mood (Molina 2013; Navarro 2009). Pro-immigrant organizations at this point prepared to muster their resources, contest the anti-immigrant frenzy, and display immigrant power.

To demonstrate disapproval of H.R. 4437, organizers for immigrant rights throughout the country (between January and April 2006) held news conferences, met with political figures, and coordinated public outcries that included marches and rallies. In February 2006 delegates attending a NAHR meeting in Riverside, California, proposed (among several recommendations) a nationwide public remonstrance against H.R. 4437. Preludes to what would become a major demonstration of immigrant indignation in May included marches, absentee campaigns at schools, and walkouts at some businesses, all coordinated by pro-immigrant advocates and their immigrant supporters (Navarro 2009).

On May 1, 2006, more than two million people across the United States participated in what came to be dubbed the "Great American Boycott 2006: A Day Without an Immigrant." Marchers assailed H.R. 4437 and demanded that Congress reassess immigration policy. In some 150 cities throughout the United States, immigrants (many of whom did not attend school or go to work that day) and Mexican Americans alike joined the demonstrations, for organizers, among them NAHR members, had long viewed immigrant bashing as an attack on the entire Latino community. This sweeping expression of unity on May 1, 2006, displayed the potential for Latino political and economic power (Navarro 2009; see also Chávez 2013).

The Movimiento Pro-Migrante proved to be short-lived. Navarro offers causes, both external and internal, for the movement's dissipation. On the one hand, opposition forces hunkered down and refused to give ground to the movement. On the other hand, the Movimiento lacked authoritative leadership, efficient organization, a concise and enticing ideology, an adequate strategy for reaching its aims, and a workable means to wield effective power. Support for H.R. 4437 eroded by that summer, so that the bill no longer acted as a rallying cry for the immigrants and their supporters (Navarro 2009).

COMBATING RACISM

Just as they had earlier raised no common voice in defense of immigrant rights, Mexican Americans did not act vigorously—at least not until the 1970s—to contest the racist ideas that exclusionists harbored about "Mexicans" in general. Mexican Americans either silently assented to stereotyping, found ways to circumvent perverse characterizations, or declared themselves white people with citizenship rights. In New Mexico and California, Mexican Americans took a defensive posture to evade racist depictions of Mexicans. Many fell back on a "fantasy" forged during the latter decades of the nineteenth century and by so doing hoped to invalidate the many traits exclusionists attributed to them. During the 1920s and 1930s, native-born Mexicans in parts of the Southwest insisted that they were of Spanish heritage and able to trace their lineage to the Europeans who had settled New Spain's Far North long before Anglos arrived there (Spickard 2007).

Mexican Americans further shielded themselves from racist portrayals by asserting title to Caucasian status. Such a classification, they argued, made them citizens with all the rights and privileges of bona fide Americans. By claiming whiteness, they sought to neutralize the racist idea advanced by exclusionists that immigrants—supposedly of a different racial constitution and residing in the United States only seasonally—lacked such protections. For LULAC during the 1930s, belonging to the Caucasian race (as opposed to the immigrants whom society considered "others" undeserving of rights) included the right to integration, the right to vote, and the right to serve on juries (Ngai 2004; Noel 2014; Overmyer-Velásquez 2013).

As noted earlier, Mexican American leaders during the 1950s became dismayed over possible repercussions for Mexican American communities in light of McCarthy-era anti-immigrant legislation, reaction by white society to the "wetback" problem, and government-sponsored programs such as the aforementioned Operation Wetback. Executing Operation Wetback often produced civil rights intrusions interpreted by Mexican American communities as part of "a much larger system of race and class exploitation" (Gutiérrez 1995, 153). So too did INS campaigns into cotton fields, workplaces, and barrios appear as encroachments on the personal lives and civil liberties of constitutionally protected citizens of Mexican descent. Still, during the first half of the 1950s organizations such as the AGIF and LULAC responded to such violations in a manner reminiscent of the weak stands they had taken during the 1930s (Gutiérrez 1995; Navarro 2009).

Criticisms of what spokespersons for Mexican American communities saw as racist attacks on immigrants—but affecting all people of Mexican descent—became more numerous during the late 1960s and into the 1970s. In 1972, for example, a coalition of Denver Chicanos issued a statement maintaining that the Rodino plan, specifically, appeared to be an effort to "perpetuate racism" against all Mexicans, regardless of their citizenship status (Gutiérrez 1995).

In the latter decades of the twentieth century the denouncing of anti-immigrant prejudice continued and embraced more "mainstream" organizations, such as the National Council of La Raza and the Mexican American Legal Defense and Education Fund, which viewed immigrant bashing as undisguised racism extending to all people of Mexican origin. Segments of the Mexican American leadership expressed similar beliefs about aspects of Proposition 187. The proposition, it seemed to many Latino voters, targeted them as much as it did undocumented residents. Even after a federal court decision declared Proposition 187 unconstitutional, pro-immigrant advocates in the Golden State (taking the nativist assault on Latino immigrants as an attack on all Latinos) continued to confront the onslaught by staging rallies and marches, by meeting with politicians, and by displaying umbrage in other ways (Gutiérrez 1995; Navarro 2009; Reimers 1998).

As anti-immigrant campaigns during the early 2000s did not let up, Mexican American pro-immigrant forces broadened their involvement in the immigrant discourse. In 2003, the previously discussed NAHR embarked on more direct action in confronting Arizona rancher vigilantism and militia expansion. NAHR further joined other immigrant defenders throughout the country in pushing back against unrelenting immigrant bashing, the swelling racist support for curbing immigration, the formation of the Minuteman Project in Arizona during the years between 2004 and 2005, and Border Patrol raids in California. Border Patrol searches in the summer of 2004 especially irked Latino Californians, as La Migra engaged in racial profiling and in enforcing its duties violated the citizen rights of the native-born. NAHR activists in particular referred to the drives as "rogue raids" executed in a "Gestapo like manner" (Navarro 2009).

The Minuteman Project's racism particularly incensed pro-immigrant groups such as NAHR. The Minuteman unit consisted of nativists who authorized themselves to reconnoiter the border in militia style to identify migrant transgressors. NAHR saw the group as consisting of Mexican haters and, to monitor its activities, in late March/early April 2005 it sent representatives to the Arizona-Sonora border to thwart Minuteman Project activities, expose Minuteman volunteers as "racist and domestic terrorists," and prevent them from abusing undocumented migrants. Soon after this excursion, however, NAHR, burdened by numerous other commitments, scaled back on the Arizona venture. In any case, internecine conflict weakened the Minuteman Project by 2007 (Navarro 2009; see also Chávez 2013).

Into the 2010s, in many parts of the country racism was driving anti-immigrant actions and attitudes. In 2010, for example, the Arizona legislature passed a bill (and other states followed) that permitted (in the eyes of its critics) flagrant racial profiling. In the course of executing their duties, law enforcement officers could inquire as to the legal status of individuals if they felt "reasonably suspicious" that such persons lacked appropriate documents (Foley 2004; see also Magaña 2013). Perhaps the need for maintaining white racial supremacy still accounted for these anti-immigrant directives. As one historian states, "While certainly not all anti-immigrant activists are racists, it seems fair to say that racial anxiety plays a large part in their worldview. They especially fear the so-called 'browning of America'" (Henderson 2011, 146–47).

IMMIGRATION DISCOURSE IN THE
NEW MILLENNIUM

Presently, there is an ongoing discussion of the potential perils of immigration versus its harmless and even beneficial nature. The defense of immigrants has remained fierce, as indicated by political scientist Armando Navarro's recap of rebuttals by academicians to alarmists' familiar tropes. Nativists maintain that Mexican nationals become a burden on the economy, but studies show that through hard work and tax contributions immigrants add billions of dollars to the country's economic system. Alarmists posit that immigrants displace native workers, when in fact most new arrivals occupy low-skilled jobs that help some industries (such as construction) prosper. Moreover, immigrants with business acumen set up establishments (e.g., restaurants) that engender economic growth. Enemies of the immigrants assert that the undocumented burden the health and public service systems, but such is not the case. Actually, immigrants do not rely on these networks to the same extent that citizens do, yet they add monetarily to those old-age and health plans. Critics also claim the immigrants do not contribute to the tax structure. This too is erroneous, as the immigrants pay salary, sales, and property taxes but then do not benefit from their contributions because of their undocumented status. The accusation that immigrants engage in criminal activity is belied by the record that shows that they avoid encounters with law enforcement agencies (Morín 2009; Salinas 2015; Urbina 2018; Urbina and Álvarez 2015, 2017). High rates of English proficiency and acceptance of American cultural tenets (while remaining bicultural) among immigrant children dispel the myth that immigrants do not assimilate (Foley 2004; Navarro 2009).

Sympathy for immigrants has not been confined to academic circles or spokespersons for the Latino community. Some church groups are involved, as are civil liberties organizations and local government officials. Numerous sanctuary cities throughout the country offer refuge to the undocumented. These cities protect immigrants from being interrogated by police or city government officials regarding their citizenship standing (Foley 2004; Nicholls 2013; Reimers 1998).

More recently, the children of the immigrants have taken up the cause of the DREAMers. This cohort petitions Congress to pass the DREAM Act (the Development, Relief, and Education for Alien Minors Act), first considered in 2001 (but still not enacted), allowing for those brought to the United States at a young age to follow a legal course to residency (Motomura 2012). Through marches, lobbying efforts, use of social media, and articulate public pleas for an understanding of their predicament, DREAMers have since around 2010 publicized their cause nationwide. Simply put, they argue that they have resided in the United States almost all their lives, they owe allegiance to no other country, are significant contributors to society, and thus should be recognized as fully protected Americans (Foley 2004; Nicholls 2013).

However, immigrant opponents make just as sincere a case against people who come illegally or prolong their stay in the United States. Ann Coulter's recent *Adios, America* (2015) again raises the prospect of America being inundated by undesirables from Mexico who can only fracture the nation. Politicians still speak of completing the border fence mandated under the Secure Fence Act of October 2006 in the wake of the H.R. 4437's defeat. Recent efforts to further extend the wall along the two-thousand-mile U.S.-Mexico line have faltered, as Congress cannot obtain the money to support the enterprise (Navarro 2009; NBC News 2013). Republicans raised the issue as they campaigned in the 2015–16 presidential race. Donald Trump promised to build an impenetrable *wall* and to deprive DREAMers of their right to citizenship guaranteed under the Fourteenth Amendment.

In the aftermath of 2015–16 political events and highly charged political rhetoric, like "Build the Wall," a "big beautiful wall," to stop Mexicans, other Latinos, Syrians, Muslims, and anyone trying to enter the country through Mexico, there have been significant barriers and a frightening environment for immigrants (undocumented and documented), particularly Mexicans and Muslims. Since taking office on January 20, 2017, the Trump administration, with its anti-immigrants movement, has redefined immigration laws, immigration enforcement, political discourse (and discourse in general), and public sentiment. Consider, for instance, Trump's highly controversial travel ban through executive orders, or what some critics have characterized as a "Muslim ban," in that the ban included seven predominantly Muslim countries (Iran, Iraq, Libya, Somalia, Sudan, Syria, and Yemen), excluding the countries that, reportedly, pose the most danger to the United States. Internally, Trump quickly *threatened* to block federal funding for sanctuary cities and states, like California, who challenged his order to collaborate with immigration officials, *shaming* cities and states and their officials for presumably protecting "immigrant criminals." In fact, in March 2017, U.S. Magistrate Judge Andrew Austin declared that an ICE raid in Austin, Texas, was direct retribution for a new policy instituted by Travis County Sheriff Sally Hernandez that limited her department's cooperation with immigration agents—creating a divided, uncertain, vindictive, and hostile environment not only for people traveling to the United States, but also in communities across the country, including places of employment, hospitals, churches, and even schools. Challenging Trump's immigration policies, the California Senate passed S.B. 54 to limit state and local police cooperation with federal immigration authorities, characterized by its author, Senate President Pro Tem Kevin de León, as "a rejection of President Trump's false and cynical portrayal of undocumented residents as a lawless community." If it passes at the California State Assembly, the bill would then go to Governor Jerry Brown to be signed into law.

CONCLUSION

Clearly, beyond the river, beyond the fence, and beyond the recently proposed wall, the immigration discourse has been highly governed by the forces of race, along with the interaction of multiple historical and contemporary issues, principally economics and politics. The historical record also reveals that while immigrants have migrated to the United States from all over the world, forming a country of immigrants, the immigration debate has *focused* on people of color, particularly people of Mexican origin during the last two centuries. Worse, from its inception, immigration discourse, immigration laws, and immigration enforcement have been shaped and reshaped by the twists and turns of prejudice, racism, oppression, dominance, and control. After almost two centuries, the discourse on immigration and the undercurrents of these forces, including racism, that have historically imbued them, continues.

REFERENCES

Almaguer, T. 2008. *Racial Fault Lines: The Historical Origins of White Supremacy in California.* Berkeley: University of California Press.

Blanton, C. K. 2009. "The Citizenship Sacrifice: Mexican Americans, the Saunders-Leonard Report, and the Politics of Immigration, 1951–1952." *Western Historical Quarterly* 40: 299–320.

Cardoso, L. 1980. *Mexican Emigration to the United States, 1897–1931.* Tucson: University of Arizona Press.

Chávez, L. R. 2013. *The Latino Threat: Constructing Immigrants, Citizens, and the Nation.* Stanford, Calif.: Stanford University Press.

Coulter, A. 2015. *Adios America: The Left's Plan to Turn Our Country into a Third World Hellhole.* Washington, D.C.: Regnery.

De León, A. 1983. *They Called Them Greasers: Anglo Attitudes Toward Mexicans in Texas, 1821– 1900.* Austin: University of Texas Press.

Divine, R. A. 1957. *American Immigration Policy, 1925–1951.* New Haven, Conn.: Yale University Press.

Dobkin, D. S. 2009. "Race and the Shaping of U.S. Immigration Policy." *Chicana/o-Latina/o Law Review* 28: 19–42.

Dunn, T. J. 2009. *Blockading the Border and Human Rights: The El Paso Operation That Remade Immigration Enforcement.* Austin: University of Texas Press.

Foley, N. 2004. *Mexicans in the Making of America.* Cambridge, Mass.: Belknap Press of Harvard University Press.

García, M. 2001. *A World of Its Own: Race, Labor, and Citrus in the Making of Greater Los Angeles, 1900–1970.* Chapel Hill: University of North Carolina Press.

Gómez, L. E. 2007. *Manifest Destinies: The Making of the Mexican American Race.* New York: New York University Press.

Gutiérrez, D. 1995. *Walls and Mirrors: Mexican Americans, Mexican Immigrants, and the Politics of Ethnicity.* Berkeley: University of California Press.

Henderson, T. J. 2011. *Beyond Borders: A History of Mexican Migration to the United States.* Madison: Wiley-Blackwell.

Hernández, K. L. 2010. *Migra: A History of the U.S. Border Patrol.* Berkeley: University of California Press.

Horsman, R. 1981. *Race and Manifest Destiny: The Origins of American Racial Anglo-Saxonism.* Cambridge, Mass.: Harvard University Press.

Johnson, K. R. 2007. *Opening the Floodgates: Why America Needs to Rethink Its Borders and Immigration Laws.* New York: New York University Press.

Magaña, L. 2013. "SB1070 and Negative Social Construction of Latino Immigrants in Arizona." *Aztlán: A Journal of Chicano Studies* 38: 157–58.

Massey, D., J. Durand, and N. Malone. 2002. *Beyond Smoke and Mirrors: Mexican Immigration in an Era of Economic Integration.* New York: Russell Sage.

Menchaca, M. 2001. *Recovering History, Constructing Race: The Indian, Black, and White Roots of Mexican Americans.* Austin: University of Texas Press.

Mitchell, P. 2005. *Coyote Nation: Sexuality, Race, and Conquest in Modernizing New Mexico, 1880–1920.* Chicago: University of Chicago Press.

Molina, N. 2010. "The Power of Racial Scripts: What the History of Mexican Immigration to the United States Teaches Us About Relational Notions of Race." *Latino Studies* 8: 156–75.

———. 2013. *How Race Is Made in America: Immigration, Citizenship, and the Historical Power of Racial Scripts.* Berkeley: University of California Press.

Morín, J. L. 2009. *Latino/a Rights and Justice in the United States: Perspectives and Approaches.* 2nd ed. Durham, N.C.: Carolina Academic Press.

Motomura, H. 2012. "Making Legal: The DREAM Act, Birthright Citizenship, and Broad-Scale Legalization." *Lewis and Clark Law Review* 16: 1127–48.

Muller, T. 1997. "Nativism in the Mid-1990s: Why Now?" In *Immigrants Out: The New Nativism and the Anti-immigrant Impulse in the United States,* edited by J. F. Perea, 105–18. New York: New York University Press.

Navarro, A. 2009. *The Immigration Crisis: Nativism, Armed Vigilantism, and the Rise of a Countervailing Movement.* Lanham, Md.: Altamira Press.

NBC News. 2013. "Price Tag for 700 Miles of Border Fencing: High and Hard to Pin Down." *NBC News,* June 21. https://usnews.newsvine.com/_news/2013/06/21/19062298-price-tag-for-700-miles-of-border-fencing-high-and-hard-to-pin-down?lite.

Nevins, J. 2001. *Operation Gatekeeper: The Rise of the "Illegal Alien" and the Making of the U.S.-Mexico Boundary*. New York: Routledge.

Ngai, M. 2004. *Impossible Subjects: Illegal Aliens and the Making of Modern America*. Princeton, N.J.: Princeton University Press.

Nicholls, W. J. 2013. *The DREAMers: How the Undocumented Youth Movement Transformed the Immigrant Rights Debate*. Stanford, Calif.: Stanford University Press.

Noel, L. C. 2014. *Debating American Identity: Southwestern Statehood and Mexican Immigration*. Tucson: University of Arizona Press.

Overmyer-Velásquez, M. 2013. "Good Neighbors and White Mexicans: Constructing Race and Nation on the Mexico-U.S. Border." *Journal of American Ethnic History* 33: 5–34.

Reimers, D. 1998. *Unwelcomed Strangers: American Identity and the Turn Against Immigration*. New York: Columbia University Press.

Reisler, M. 1976. *By the Sweat of Their Brow: Mexican Immigrant Labor in the U.S., 1900–1940*. Westport, Conn.: Greenwood Press.

Romero, M. 2000. "State Violence, and the Social and Legal Construction of Latino Criminality: From El Bandido to Gang Member." *Denver University Law Review* 78: 1089–1127.

Salinas, L. S. 2015. *U.S. Latinos and Criminal Injustice*. East Lansing: Michigan State University Press.

Sheridan, C. 2002. "Contested Citizenship: National Identity and the Mexican Immigration Debates of the 1920s." *Journal of American Ethnic History* 21: 9–18.

Spickard, P. R. 2007. *Almost All Aliens: Immigration, Race, and Colonialism in American History and Identity*. New York: Routledge.

Urbina, M. G., ed. 2018. *Hispanics in the U.S. Criminal Justice System: Ethnicity, Ideology, and Social Control*. 2nd ed. Springfield, Ill.: Charles C Thomas.

Urbina, M. G., and S. E. Álvarez, eds. 2015. *Latino Police Officers in the United States: An Examination of Emerging Trends and Issues*. Springfield, Ill.: Charles C Thomas.

———. 2017. *Ethnicity and Criminal Justice in the Era of Mass Incarceration: A Critical Reader on the Latino Experience*. Springfield, Ill.: Charles C Thomas.

Vargas, Z. 2005. *Labor Rights Are Civil Rights: Mexican American Workers in Twentieth-Century America*. Princeton, N.J.: Princeton University Press.

Chapter 2

EXPOSING IMMIGRATION LAWS
The Legal Contours of Belonging and Exclusion

STEVEN W. BENDER

No Statue of Liberty ever greeted our arrival in this country. . . .
We did not, in fact, come to the United States at all. The United
States came to us.

—LUIS VALDEZ

ESPITE THE "NEW Colossus" poem on the Statue of Liberty, which welcomes masses of poor migrants seeking economic opportunity and survival, a review of U.S. immigration laws reveals a troubled legacy of *exclusion* of various groups of immigrants on the basis of race and other discriminatory grounds. Although cyclical in the intensity of the exclusions depending on labor demand, the upshot of the history of U.S. immigration laws is that minorities and other vulnerable groups often fall victim to restrictive policies that reinforce and ensure that these groups never fully "belong" in the Anglo-centric vision of U.S. culture and economic power.

As detailed in this chapter, U.S. immigration policies have especially targeted for exclusion those groups seen as nonwhite, such as Chinese once barred from entry under the Chinese Exclusion Act and, most recently, child refugees fleeing violence in Central America and attempting to enter the United States as undocumented immigrants. However, even some white immigrants have been excluded by our immigration policies, if they were seen as nonwhite, as were southern and eastern Europeans in the early twentieth century, or if they were gay, poor, or perceived to be Communists. U.S. states beat the same racialized drum in their own history of exclusions based on race and ethnicity. For instance, Oregon's constitution once excluded blacks from entering the state, and during the Great Depression Colorado took up arms to exclude Mexicans and Mexican Americans seeking to enter the state from New Mexico in search of jobs. These exclusions are mirrored today by such discriminatory state laws as Arizona's S.B. 1070, the "show me your papers" law targeting undocumented Mexican immigrants.

Intertwined with race and ethnicity, class-based immigration exclusions, such as those barring migrants who could become public charges, also define the history of our federal immigration policies. State laws too once restricted the entry of poor people from other states (Motomura 2006). Oftentimes, class-based restrictions have intersected with racialized policies, as when U.S. immigration officials would invoke federal restrictions against the entry of people likely to utilize public resources, and thus exclude immigrants of color from the developing world (Johnson and Trujillo 2011). The interactions of race, ethnicity, class, and national origin, among other forces, have historically governed the legal and social parameters of immigration laws, illegality, and immigrants—ultimately defining belonging and exclusion in the United States.

ASIAN EXCLUSIONS

Chinese migrated in large numbers to the United States in the mid-1800s during the Gold Rush and were initially welcomed. For example, in 1852 the governor of the freshly minted state of California praised Chinese migrants as a vital workforce: "one of the most worthy classes of our newly adopted citizens—to whom the climate and character of these lands are peculiarly suited" (Takaki 1998, 81). However, derogatory attitudes toward Chinese soon swept the region and the greater United States, as evidenced first at the local level with the 1852 foreign miner's tax in California aimed at Chinese (and Mexicans). At the time, two-thirds of the U.S. Chinese population labored in the California gold mines—about 24,000 workers (Takaki 1998). Chinese workers arriving by steamship soon supplied the backbone of the labor force in the equally dangerous industry of transcontinental railroad construction, and ex-miners supplied labor in a variety of San Francisco industries and in California agriculture.

The race factor, though, soon came to the surface. An inflammatory *New York Tribune* article charged that the "Chinese Problem" was more serious than what African Americans posed given perceptions of Chinese "in-assimilability." Chinese at the time were ineligible for U.S. citizenship, as were any other persons defined as nonwhite, under a 1790 law reserving citizenship for white people only—a law that was kept in place until 1952 though not enforced. Notably, from this citizenship restriction came the accusation in the *Tribune* that Chinese workers were "reared in China, expecting to return to China, living while here in a little China[town] of its own, and without the slightest attachment to the country—utter heathens, treacherous, sensual, cowardly and cruel" (Takaki 1998, 109). Placing the constitutional stamp on selected exclusion and in a sense legitimizing selective immigration control and discourse, the California Supreme Court stated in 1854 that Chinese immigrants were "a race of people who nature has marked as inferior, and who are incapable of progress or intellectual development beyond a certain point, as their history has shown; differing in language, opinions, color, and physical conformation; between whom and ourselves nature has placed an impassable difference."[1] In short, they did not "belong." In 1882, Congress, embracing the anti-Chinese sentiment and the scapegoating of Chinese workers during economic downturns (Motomura 2006), with negative attitudes prevailing even in U.S. regions with few or no Chinese residents, denied entry of "all persons of the Chinese race," except for a small number of Chinese teachers, students, tourists, merchants, and officials, declaring that "the coming of Chinese laborers to this country endangers the good order of certain localities." Reflecting the sentiment of mainstream society across the country, the U.S. Supreme Court upheld the Chinese exclusion law in 1889, giving Congress carte blanche to protect the United States from "vast hordes of [a foreign nation's] people crowding in upon us."[2] In fact, in 1904 Congress extended the ban indefinitely, but decades later, in 1943, strategic alliances with China during World War II removed the *legal racial barrier*, as political imperatives trumped this blatantly racist exclusion.

With the Chinese excluded from entry, California agriculture turned to another group of Asian immigrants, the Japanese, as did Hawaiian sugar plantations. The Japanese experience was similar to that of the Chinese. Unable to gain citizenship because they were categorized as nonwhite,[3] Japanese immigrant workers were first welcomed, then vilified, culminating in the so-called Gentlemen's Agreement procured by the United States from Japan in the early 1900s, under which the Japanese government would not issue travel documents to its citizens bound for the United States to work, effectively excluding them (Johnson et al. 2009). With the anti-Chinese and anti-Japanese sentiment spreading rapidly, prejudice soon encompassed all Asians, and Congress extended the Chinese exclusion laws in 1917 to all Asians in the "Asiatic barred zone," including India, Thailand, and other Asian countries, aside from Filipinos and Guam residents who were under U.S. control at the time (Johnson et al. 2009).[4]

NATIONAL QUOTAS UNDER 1924 LAW: EXCLUDING UNDESIRABLE EUROPEANS

Evident in the history of U.S. immigration laws and the racial/ethnic experience is the fluidity of undesirable groups or, more precisely, the classification and categorization of "undesirable" groups. As one observer summarized, "At different historical moments, German, Irish, Jewish, and Italian immigrants all were deemed to be of different and inferior racial stock. Benjamin Franklin, for example, decried the settling of German immigrants in Pennsylvania and considered them to be of a different 'race' than the English" (Johnson 2002, 1486). In the early 1900s, restrictionists sounded the alarm about entry of southern and eastern Europeans, thought to be reluctant to assimilate, particularly because of their perceived unwillingness to learn and embrace the English language. Culminating in the 1924 National Origins Act, which evolved from a 1921 law and dominated U.S. immigration policy until 1965, this exclusionary mindset targeted southern and eastern Europeans who had come to the United States in significant numbers in the first decades of the 1900s. By 1920, for instance, one-fifth of California's population was Italian. In relation to the Asian laws that were still effective at the time, the design of the 1924 law was a step forward from outright exclusion of a *selective racialized group*, but no less discriminatory in its intent and design to preserve a cultural vision of the United States as northern and western European in orientation.

The national origin formula supplied a quota (cap) for each nationality (e.g., Italian) based on the number of foreign-born residents from that country living in the United States in 1890—conveniently before the advent of significant southern and eastern European immigration. By design, the formula aimed to halt "the tendency toward a change in the fundamental composition of the American stock" (Johnson et al. 2009). Succeeding in its aim, the 1924 national origin quota, at a time when Asian immigration was even more overtly curtailed, limited immigration of European Jews, Italians, Slavs, and Greeks (Johnson et al. 2009), whose early 1900s population surge was halted. Illustrating the gross inequality of immigration control, under the 1924 act the annual quota for Italian immigrants allowed 5,800 people, but the *same law* allowed an annual entry of nearly 66,000 immigrants from Great Britain (Feagin 1997). The formula allowed for a combined 70,000 plus immigrants from Italy and Great Britain, along with thousands of other Europeans; however, these figures are often excluded from immigration discourse.

BRING ON THE MEXICANS: THE BRACERO PROGRAM

Unlike all other immigrants, Mexicans lived in a substantial portion of what is now the United States before the U.S. conquest of the Southwest in the U.S.-Mexican War. At the war's end in 1848, some 75,000 Mexicans resided in what is now the U.S. Southwest. The first substantial postwar migration of Mexicans to the United States occurred during the 1910s when U.S. immigration laws excluded Asians and labor shortages existed during World War I (1914–18). Industries such as agriculture, railroads, meat packing, steel mills near Chicago, and mining all drew Mexicans north at the same time the Mexican Revolution (1910–20) pushed many residents in the same direction.

As early evidence of the schizophrenic invitation-and-exile cycle of Mexican immigrant labor in the U.S. immigration experience, during economic downturns in 1921–22 U.S. government officials and private citizens combined forces to physically oust Mexicans. However, despite this ouster, southwestern agricultural and transportation industries, among other labor interests, lobbied to keep Mexicans freed from the national origin quota restrictions of the Immigration Act of 1924. As enacted, the 1924 immigration law focused its discriminatory design on southern and eastern European immigrants (e.g., Jews from the Russian Empire, Romania, and Austria-Hungry), while in a broad stroke entirely exempting the Western Hemisphere from these restrictive immigration limits. In theory, at least, Mexicans, Canadians, and other Latin Americans could emigrate to the United States in search of economic opportunity without numerical restrictions. In practice, however, Mexican immigration was strategically exploited, manipulated, and tightly controlled. A raft of discretionary administrative restrictions allowed regulators to shut off or allow Mexican immigration depending on the prevailing economy and labor needs; after all, it was much easier to deport a Mexican across the river than to deport a European across the globe. Aware of the indigent status of most Mexicans migrating north, restrictions included a head tax levied on each immigrant, set at eight dollars a person in 1917 and supplemented in 1924 by a ten-dollar visa fee. The 1917 Immigration Act also imposed a literacy test on immigrants (Tichenor 2002), and federal immigration laws forbade admission to those likely to become a public charge reliant on social services. Conveniently, this exclusion was particularly susceptible to manipulation based on labor needs: in times of economic distress Mexican immigrants could be turned away under the rationale that employers were not hiring, and therefore, without the prospect of a job, migrants could not manage to feed and house themselves. At the same time, these restrictions could be lifted to usher in Mexican migrants in times of labor demand, as was done in 1917 when the U.S. Department of Labor waived the head tax and literacy test for incoming Mexican workers, although not without dousing them with dangerous pesticides supposedly to ensure they did not harbor pests harmful to U.S. agriculture. In reality, this brutal and humiliating practice was more reflective of "let's break them down upon arrival" to ensure a process of manipulation, exploitation, oppression, control, and dominance from the onset than of real concerns for diseases (Urbina, Vela, and Sánchez 2014).

When the Great Depression (1929–39) began to unfold, Mexican immigrants and anyone, even U.S. citizens, who appeared to be Mexican, were scapegoated and aggressively ousted from the United States. Vigilantes did their part by threatening to burn Mexican residents out of their homes, not only in border states but also in places like Oklahoma, and signs in Texas warned Mexicans to leave town or face burnings, lynching, or executions (Acuña 2014; Almaguer 2008; De León 1983; De León and

Del Castillo 2012; Urbina, Vela, and Sánchez 2014). Local governments denied Mexican Americans welfare benefits and sometimes arranged their transport south of the border, while federal immigration officials in the fledgling immigration enforcement infrastructure raided U.S. cities to sweep up Mexicans suspected of having entered outside of official immigration channels under the lax or nonexistent border enforcement. In a movement that seemed to have an "it's either now or never" mentality, Colorado's governor, caught up in the anti-Mexican sentiment, declared martial law in 1936 to seal the Colorado–New Mexico border with National Guard troops to "prevent and repel the further invasion of . . . aliens, indigent persons, or invaders," a directive not only targeting Mexican workers but the entire Mexican community (Bender n.d.). In fact, even U.S.-citizen children of Mexican immigrants were caught up in the frenzy, which removed some 20 percent of the U.S. Mexican population during the Great Depression era (Bender 2012).

With the start of World War II (1939–45), Mexican immigrants returned. Their labor was essential in the midst of war. The forcible internment of Japanese farmers and workers made it imperative to have a cheap mobile labor force in the fields and factories, as did the desire of growers for abundant immigrant labor as a means of resisting the spread of unions in agriculture. As white workers fled the fields toward unionized urban jobs, Mexican immigrants filled the shortage of exploitable agricultural labor. However, it was not enough to simply open the administrative faucet to allow unfettered Mexican entry. Rather, the labor recruitment tool formally known as the Bracero Program was quickly orchestrated. The program became so successful for American employers (and the building and survival of the United States) that it was kept in various forms from its inception in 1942 to its demise in late 1964 when Congress was convinced that it led to oppressive and slavery-type conditions for workers.

As negotiated by the Mexican and U.S. governments, the Bracero Program specified the terms of employment for Mexican workers, including wages, housing, and transportation, thereby minimizing the potential for dreaded collective bargaining in the fields. Despite sidestepping the few administrative hurdles to immigration for Mexicans at the time, such as the head tax and literacy test, the bracero system ensured that Mexican migrant workers would not overstay their term if the need for labor fell. Since their spouses and children stayed behind in Mexico, and they were not fed, housed, or transported, bracero workers tended to be men traveling alone, and deductions were made from their paychecks and retained by the U.S. government, to be paid as a pension fund only after their return to Mexico—although these funds disappeared (Bender 2012). During its two-decade operation, the Bracero Program brought 4.8 million Mexican laborers into the United States, most of them working in the southwestern agricultural industry and generally for the largest agribusiness operations. Nationally, braceros worked in twenty-six states and reached their peak in

1959 when 450,000 Mexican migrants entered the United States under the program (Román 2013).

However, despite the seemingly broad invitation of the Bracero Program, Mexican workers remained welcome only in times of economic prosperity, as illustrated by the so-called Operation Wetback mass deportation campaign. The title itself was offensive and racist. Operating from 1953 to 1955, this federal campaign deported some 3.7 million Latinos, most of them Mexicans and some of them U.S. citizens wrongly deported in the sweep for undocumented immigrants.

LET'S EXCLUDE THE MEXICANS: THE POST-1965 ERA OF EXCLUSIONS

Some might see Donald Trump's anti-Mexican comments as new or unaligned with the sentiment of American politicians, government officials, and mainstream America, not to mention bigots, immigration hawks, political pundits, and intellectual racists. However, the Depression-era repatriations and Operation Wetback, as two examples, are stark reminders of the historically uneasy relationship between U.S. labor, U.S. society, and Mexican workers coming north for grueling and dangerous work for abysmal pay. In fact, a decade after Operation Wetback, a new cycle was set in motion; that is, 1965 brought a new era of vulnerability during which Mexican (and other Latin American immigrant) workers needed to immigrate as undocumented immigrants regardless of the intensity of demand for their labor, because rigid and restrictive legal limits on Mexican immigration were imposed for the first time that year, almost immediately after Congress allowed the bracero labor importation program to end.

Responding to criticisms by John F. Kennedy (Kennedy 1964) and others of the discriminatory national origin immigration system in place since the 1920s, in the heyday of the civil rights movement Congress enacted the Immigration and Nationality Act in 1965. The act intended to replace the national origin quotas with an immigration structure prioritizing family reunifications and imposing a uniform per-country maximum of 20,000 immigrants annually from Eastern Hemisphere countries and an overall hemispheric total of 170,000 visas. Most of the Eastern Hemisphere visas were designated for relatives of U.S. citizens or lawful permanent residents seeking reunification with family members, and by the late 1980s, 90 percent of lawful immigration to the United States (the vast majority from Asia and Latin America) invoked these kinship categories (Hing 2006), though other figures report family ties at 63 percent (Motomura 2006).[5] For the first time, however, under the 1965 act Congress imposed limits on Western Hemisphere immigration—initially specified as 120,000 immigrants annually without individual country limits, presumably recognizing the dominance of immigration from Mexico and Canada. Senator Robert Kennedy spoke against the restriction to no avail, arguing that the 1965 act would impose rigid limits on immigration from Latin America and Canada for the first time in U.S. history, and abandon the "special relationship" recognized in the hemisphere's exclusion from the 1924 national origin structure. Kennedy warned: "In a world which is searching for increased cooperation and closeness between nations, the relationships of the United States with Canada and Latin America could serve as a goal and a model for others. We should not go backward now" (Bender 2008, 106). Further, under the new 1965 immigration regime migrants had to show that they were not *displacing* U.S. workers. Worse from the perspective of Mexican immigrants, ten years later, in 1976, Congress imposed a per-country limit of just 20,000 immigrants from each Western Hemisphere country,[6] abandoning the flexibility of the hemispheric-wide limit of 120,000 migrants with no per-country limits. As one commentator summed up the dramatic shift in Mexican migrant policy after the 1960s and 1970s, "Mexico went from enjoying access to 450,000 annual guest worker visas [under the Bracero Program] and an unlimited number of residence visas to having no guest worker visas at all and just 20,000 visas for permanent residence" (Bender 2012, 126).

Soon, backlogs of requests for Mexican migrant entry grew and rendered the lawful immigration "line" (as in the familiar politician directive to undocumented immigrants to "get in the line like everyone else") an unfeasible way to gain admission to the United States. While there were limited employment visas that favored high-skilled employment, for immigrants with advanced degrees or those with so-called extraordinary ability, this new restrictive regime ignored labor needs in construction, assembly lines, housekeeping, and landscaping, among other vital jobs. Mexican laborers were forced to enter outside the legal process to fill the jobs that often beckoned them, if they could survive their undocumented entry. At the same time, the post-1965 exclusionary era became marked by a hyper-intensive emphasis on *border security and domestic immigration enforcement*, with Mexican migrants becoming the *face* of undocumented migrants in the eyes of the public and immigration officials. Further, under the new terminology of the 1965 act and other immigration laws, immigrants were redefined as "aliens," suggesting illegality and exclusion, in contrast to citizens who belong here. Quickly, the new terminology helped situate immigrants, particularly Mexican immigrants, as being outside the law and undeserving of the extensive rights and benefits accorded to U.S. citizens (Johnson and Trujillo 2011) and, from the perspective of many anti-immigrant voices, as lesser humans who fall outside the U.S. Anglo-Protestant cultural narrative.

Reacting to this anti-Mexican migrant phobia that swept both political parties in the wake of these immigration law changes, presidents from both parties have participated in the hyper-securitization of the border but also its occasional relaxing to allow for regularizing the status of millions of undocumented migrants, most of them from Mexico. The cycle of invitation and exile consistent with economic growth and decline now takes place against a backdrop of dangerous border crossings and limited allowances of legal authorization to enter and remain in the United States. The debate continues to this day, as illustrated by the discourse of various candidates during the 2016 presidential election cycle, and intensified by Donald Trump's anti-Mexican comments in June 2015.

In the two decades after the 1965 act, undocumented immigration from Mexico increased almost by design as employers kept demanding immigrants for low-wage labor despite restrictive entry limits. Growing hysteria over undocumented immigration, but recognition of the needs of labor and agribusiness, resulted in the compromise legislation of 1986—the Immigration Reform and Control Act signed by President Reagan, which offered legalization to millions of undocumented workers, while at the same time supposing naively that it could halt future undocumented entries by imposing, as a major feature of the reform, sanctions on employers who hire undocumented immigrants. With great profits to be made by exploiting Mexican immigrants, these sanctions proved ineffective. Forgery mills produced false papers and employers looked the other way given the inconsistent enforcement of sanctions and their ability to shift responsibility by delegating the hiring of workers to thinly capitalized labor contractors. Broadly, legalization under the 1986 act in the form of permanent residence status benefited two groups—undocumented immigrants who had resided in the United States since before 1982 and, more generously, agricultural workers who had worked for at least ninety days in the prior year (from May 1985 to May 1986). Ultimately, between 2.7 and 3.1 million undocumented workers, about 90 percent of them from Mexico, took advantage of the legalization process to secure legal residence.

As evidence of the failure of employer sanctions, the undocumented migrant population soared, and by the 2000s it amounted to an estimated eleven to twelve million people. As in the past, the anti-immigrant sentiment shifted the contours of immigration policy and enforcement. After the terrorist bombing of the World Trade Center in 1993, immigration policy focused on the U.S.-Mexico border, despite the reality that many undocumented entrants entered lawfully and simply overstayed their visas rather than crossed the border surreptitiously. Yet, the attention on the U.S.-Mexico border, and workplace raids in the U.S. interior carried out by the INS (Immigration and Naturalization Service) and its successor, ICE (Immigration and Customs Enforcement), are the current reality of U.S. immigration policy and dominate political debate, which tends to focus, as a condition of any discussion of additional pathways to citizenship, on first securing the border.

During the Clinton administration of the mid-1990s, Congress enacted the Illegal Immigration Reform and Immigrant Responsibility Act of 1996, which armed the border with additional Border Patrol agents, fences, walls, and technology to detect unlawful crossings. Obviously directed at Mexican entrants, the new strategy of border buildup also resulted in the Operation Gatekeeper strategy of "control through deterrence" (Johnson et al. 2009), leading to the deaths of thousands of migrant crossers in subsequent years. By concentrating border security in urban areas such as Tijuana, where most undocumented immigrants had previously entered, the border infrastructure that sprouted in the mid-1990s acted to push migrant crossers toward longer and far more treacherous routes in desolate areas, resulting in countless deaths and making migrants more dependent on trafficking networks and cartels for their survival.

At the turn of the century, the September 11, 2001, terrorist attacks gave additional impetus to the border-buildup frenzy, criminalization, and imprisonment (Welch 2002, 2007, 2009), notwithstanding that all of the terrorists arrived in the United States legally, most using six-month tourist visas, with two who overstayed, as documented by Michael Welch in *Scapegoats of September 11th: Hate Crimes and State Crimes in the War on Terror* (2006). Fears that al-Qaeda could use the Mexican coyote network to smuggle in terrorists kept attention on our southern border as politicians traded ideas on how best to secure the border, culminating in Republican presidential candidate Herman Cain's suggestion in 2011 that a lethal electrified border fence would help stop undocumented migrants, an idea that reappeared in different form in 2015 with Republication presidential candidate Donald Trump's promise to build a wall along the entire border to keep Mexicans out. As in previous anti-Mexican movements, with the unspoken sentiment of "it's either now or never," Congress adopted the Secure Fence Act in 2006, signed by President Bush, authorizing the construction of seven hundred miles of double-reinforced fencing along the two-thousand-mile U.S.-Mexico border. Augmenting these security measures, immigration officials in the border zones could also engage in racial profiling of Mexican-appearing persons when stopping travelers, which the U.S. Supreme Court "blessed" in the interest of immigration enforcement.[7] Buoyed by this ruling, immigration enforcement efforts, whether carried out by the federal government, or at the margins by vigilantes and state/local government officials, have tended to concentrate on Mexican-appearing people, and more generally on those of Latino appearance, despite the reality that Puerto Ricans are U.S. citizens and most U.S. residents of Latino appearance are citizens or lawfully admitted residents.

As the anti-Mexican sentiment gained further momentum across the country, within the U.S. interior vigilantes and state/local governments assumed the role of immigration law enforcers, often resorting to racial profiling to target suspected undocumented immigrants for scrutiny (Urbina 2018; Urbina and Álvarez 2015, 2017). Consider, for instance, two well-known local anti-immigrant control efforts,

California's Proposition 187 and Arizona's S.B. 1070, which were both gutted by subsequent court challenges. Approved by voters in 1994, Proposition 187 denied the state's public benefits, such as prenatal health care, education, and welfare, to persons not verified to be U.S. citizens or lawfully admitted immigrants. Left partially in force by the U.S. Supreme Court, Arizona's "show me your papers" law allows police to determine the immigration status of people they stop or arrest, if they have reason to believe, presumably through racial profiling, that the person is an undocumented immigrant.

President Obama's administration offers perhaps the best example of the executive role in the cyclical tolerance of and exile of migrants, in this case directed at undocumented migrants from Mexico. In his first term, his administration chose to deport more immigrants annually than did the preceding "enforcement-friendly" Bush administration. At the same time, in 2012, Obama embraced so-called DREAMers—undocumented persons who were brought as children without authorization, many of whom went on to college or military service—and by executive order blocked the deportation of certain productive young immigrants, under his Deferred Action for Childhood Arrivals (DACA) directive. In 2014, Obama flexed executive power again by expanding the childhood deferred action category to encompass additional undocumented child migrants who arrived before age sixteen, and to include in the deferred action program undocumented parents of U.S. citizens and lawful permanent residents (known as Deferred Action for Parents of Americans and Lawful Permanent Residents) and also undocumented persons who are the children of U.S. residents or lawful permanent residents. Established through executive order, however, these immigration allowances are vulnerable to contrary action by Congress, courts, or a subsequent president. For example, as of late 2015, Deferred Action for Parents was stalled in its implementation by legal action. As the heated controversy continued, some of Obama's executive actions were put on hold by a federal district court judge in Texas in February 2015.

OTHER DISFAVORED IMMIGRANTS

Encompassing gay persons and those suspected as Communists, U.S. immigration policies have operated to exclude various disfavored groups on grounds distinct (in theory) from race and ethnicity. Still, these categories, often indeterminate, have also been wielded against racial and ethnic minorities, based on identifiers like national origin, skin color, language, and culture. Status-based exclusionary standards in U.S. immigration history include the barring of "immoral" persons, those with diseases, disabled persons, persons of "psychopathic inferiority," vagrants, and the illiterate (Feagin 1997). Reflecting the prevailing prejudice against gay people, the exclusion of migrants of "psychopathic inferiority," as mandated under the federal Immigration Act of 1917, was intended by Congress to bar "homosexuals and sex perverts" from entry and U.S. citizenship. Although Congress finally removed the bar in 1990, same-sex partners were nonetheless excluded from participating in family reunification allowances until the 2013 invalidation of the Defense of Marriage Act, by which Congress had refused to recognize the legitimacy of gay marriage or unions.

Religious prejudices led to the discriminatory 1924 national origin structure that helped exclude European Jews from entry. More recently, in the aftermath of the September 11, 2001, attacks, Muslims and those appearing to be Muslim or Arab were subjected to heightened immigration scrutiny, such as under the Alien Absconder Initiative, which sought to locate noncitizens with unexecuted removal orders, with its focus on men of the Islamic faith or of Arab ethnicity, as well as through use of voluntary interview programs and special registration programs targeting immigrants from Muslim countries (Bender 2015).

Fear of certain political affiliations is also embedded in U.S. immigration laws. Enacted during the height of the Cold War, the Immigration and Nationality Act of 1952 provided for the exclusion of members of the following classes: anarchists, members of organizations that advocate opposition to organized government, members of the Communist Party, those who advocate the economic or governmental doctrines of world communism or the establishment of a totalitarian dictatorship, or those who advocate in writing for the overthrow of the U.S. government by force or other unconstitutional means (Johnson et al. 2009). Any suspicion of Communist sympathy was also a ticket to deportation of a non-U.S. citizen (Johnson et al. 2009). Clearly, while anti-immigrant movements might appear, on the surface, to focus on supposed illegality, irrespective of race and ethnicity, anti-immigrant sentiment is highly influenced by race and ethnicity, which intertwine with multiple identifiers (like national origin, skin color, and language), which also interact with other indicators, like religion.

CONCLUSION

As detailed herein, while there is a notion that immigration has recently become a problem or out of control, American immigration laws have a long history of shifting the terms of belonging and exclusion. Perhaps no one knows this better than American Indians, who originally occupied the entire country, and later Mexicans, who lost 55 percent of their territory (including Arizona, California, New Mexico, Nevada, Texas, and Utah) to the United States in 1848. As Mexicans sometimes say, "We didn't cross the border, the border crossed us." Today, instead of accepting Trump's highly charged political slogans, which became his *winning political slogans*, we need to distinguish the politics from the political (see Doty, this volume), resisting his anti-immigrant movement, while empowering people so that they can confront injustice and fight for human rights, equality, and representation. Strategically disguised under sensitive notions like "national security," "America first," and "criminal illegal aliens," Trump's presidential proclamations on immigration law and enforcement have been more "political weapons" to raise the passions of his voting base and mobilize his supporters than pragmatic or humane approaches for immigration reform, public safety, national security, or positive economic and social transformation.

From a progressive standpoint, as a country that identifies itself as a nation of immigrants, and that was built on the backs of immigrant labor, the United States should aspire to move beyond its history of discriminatory immigration policies and practices. While Congress eventually apologized for the Chinese Exclusion Act (the Senate in 2011 and the House in 2012), there is much more to confront and question in the legacy of our immigration laws and the cycle of disposable people these laws encourage within the model of invitation and exile, which still demarcates our problematic relationship with migrants. One fact to acknowledge is that Europeans, whether they were defined or categorized as "undesirable," were and continue to be, by most accounts, "white." Beyond the twists and turns of immigration laws over the years, other questions have lingered. For instance, how has the experience, numerically and socially, of Europeans (including the "undesirables") compared with the experience of people of "color," who, in addition to being classified as undesirable, are also classified as nonwhite and suffer other disadvantages, like the stigma of being "illegal" and the ramifications of poverty?

NOTES

1. People v. Hall, 4 Cal. 399, 404 (1854).
2. Chae Chan Ping v. United States, 130 U.S. 581, 606 (1889).
3. Takao Ozawa v. United States, 260 U.S. 178 (1922). "White person" means someone from Europe, not Japanese.
4. These racially restrictive exclusions ended for Chinese in 1943 during World War II, for Filipinos and Indians in 1946, and for other Asians in 1952 (Bender 2015).
5. Motomura (2006) identifies another 16 percent of lawful immigration recipients as falling under job-related immigration allowances and an additional 12 percent qualifying as refugees.
6. A similar per-country cap still applies, but certain classifications of immigrants, such as immigrant spouses of U.S. citizens, are exempt from the cap (Johnson and Trujillo 2011).

7. United States v. Brignoni-Ponce, 422 U.S. 873 (1975). "The likelihood that any given person of Mexican ancestry is an alien is high enough to make Mexican appearance a relevant factor [in an immigration stop]."

REFERENCES

Acuña, R. 2014. *Occupied America: A History of Chicanos.* 8th ed. Boston: Pearson.

Almaguer, T. 2008. *Racial Fault Lines: The Historical Origins of White Supremacy in California.* Berkeley: University of California Press.

Bender, S. W. 2008. *One Night in America: Robert Kennedy, César Chávez, and the Dream of Dignity.* Boulder, Colo.: Paradigm Publishers.

———. 2012. *Run for the Border: Vice and Virtue in U.S.-Mexico Border Crossings.* New York: New York University Press.

———. 2015. *Mea Culpa: Lessons on Law and Regret from U.S. History.* New York: New York University Press.

———. n.d. *How the West Was Juan: Reimagining the U.S.-Mexico Border.* Unpublished manuscript.

De León, A. 1983. *They Called Them Greasers: Anglo Attitudes Toward Mexicans in Texas, 1821–1900.* Austin: University of Texas Press.

De León, A., and R. Del Castillo. 2012. *North to Aztlán: A History of Mexican Americans in the United States.* 2nd ed. Hoboken, N.J.: Wiley-Blackwell.

Feagin, J. R. 1997. "Old Poison in New Bottles: The Deep Roots of Modern Nativism." In *Immigrants Out! The New Nativism and the Anti-immigrant Impulse in the United States,* edited by J. F. Perea, 13–43. New York: New York University Press.

Hing, B. O. 2006. *Deporting Our Souls: Values, Morality, and Immigration Policy.* New York: Cambridge University Press.

Johnson, K. R. 2002. "The End of 'Civil Rights' As We Know It?: Immigration and Civil Rights in the New Millennium. *UCLA Law Review* 49: 1481–1511.

Johnson, K. R., and B. Trujillo. 2011. *Immigration Law and the US-Mexico border: ¿Sí Se Puede?* Tucson: University of Arizona Press.

Johnson, K. R., R. Aldana, B. O. Hing, L. Saucedo, and E. F. Trucios-Haynes. 2009. *Understanding Immigration Law.* Newark, N.J.: LexisNexis.

Kennedy, J. F. 1964. *A Nation of Immigrants.* New York: Harper and Row.

Motomura, H. 2006. *Americans in Waiting: The Lost Story of Immigration and Citizenship in the United States.* New York: Oxford University Press.

Román, E. 2013. *Those Damned Immigrants: America's Hysteria over Undocumented Immigration.* New York: New York University Press.

Takaki, R. 1998. *Strangers from a Different Shore: A History of Asian Americans*. New York: Back Bay Books.

Tichenor, D. 2002. *Dividing Lines: The Politics of Immigration Control in America*. Princeton, N.J.: Princeton University Press.

Urbina, M. G., ed. 2018. *Hispanics in the U.S. Criminal Justice System: Ethnicity, Ideology, and Social Control*. 2nd ed. Springfield, Ill.: Charles C Thomas.

Urbina, M. G., and S. E. Álvarez, eds. 2015. *Latino Police Officers in the United States: An Examination of Emerging Trends and Issues*. Springfield, Ill.: Charles C Thomas.

———. 2017. *Ethnicity and Criminal Justice in the Era of Mass Incarceration: A Critical Reader on the Latino Experience*. Springfield, Ill.: Charles C Thomas.

Urbina, M. G., J. E. Vela, and J. O. Sánchez. 2014. *Ethnic Realities of Mexican Americans: From Colonialism to 21st Century Globalization*. Springfield, Ill.: Charles C Thomas.

Welch, M. 2002. *Detained: Immigration Laws and the Expanding I.N.S. Jail Complex*. Philadelphia: Temple University Press.

———. 2006. *Scapegoats of September 11th: Hate Crimes and State Crimes in the War on Terror*. New Brunswick, N.J.: Rutgers University Press.

———. 2007. "Immigration Lockdown Before and After 9/11: Ethnic Constructions and Their Consequences." In *Race, Gender, and Punishment: From Colonialism to the War on Terror*, edited by M. Bosworth and J. Flavin, 149–63. Piscataway, N.J.: Rutgers University Press.

———. 2009. *Crimes of Power and States of Impunity: The U.S. Response to Terror*. New Brunswick, N.J.: Rutgers University Press.

Chapter 3

DIVIDED LINES

The Politics of Immigration Control in the United States

ROXANNE LYNN DOTY

> We have a strange immigration policy for a nation of immigrants. And it's a policy unfit for today's world.

—MARK ZUCKERBERG

T O SPEAK IN a comprehensive and meaningful way of the *politics* of immigration control, one must engage a broadened understanding of "the political," an understanding that goes beyond a focus on political parties, elections, campaigns, the passing of laws, and other activities involving the government. This is not, of course, to suggest that these things are of minor significance or irrelevant and should be ignored. They are certainly of key importance in immigration discourse. Understanding the "political," however, suggests that "politics" is much more than what conventionally comes to mind and what is typically portrayed in the media. It is also an avenue for illustrating that the ways in which immigration has been transformed into a highly politicized issue are intricately connected to a broadened conceptualization of "the political." The very possibility of conventional politics depends on a broader realm wherein social spaces, meanings, identities, and political subjects are created and recreated.

"POLITICS" AND "THE POLITICAL"

Informed by of the work of several critical theorists, Jenny Edkins (1999) outlines the distinctions between "politics" and "the political" in a way that is useful for better understanding contemporary immigration control. "Politics" is the realm that is generally thought of when the term is used by the media, political parties, government figures, and mainstream political scientists. It includes the activities of the government, the president, the House of Representatives, the Senate, various branches of the state, diplomacy, foreign policy-making, electing leaders, and passing laws. Obviously it is essential to understand these things in order to speak of the politics of immigration control. However, to remain in this realm is to miss many important factors that are implicated in controlling borders and those who are granted permission to cross them. Therefore, for a broadened view one must consider the realm of "the political," which refers to all that is associated with and plays a role in the construction of the social order, the meanings that give *legitimacy* to a country's borders and the identities of those who are deemed to "belong" and those who are characterized as "not belonging," as well as the justifications for including some and excluding others—divided lines. As Edkins (1999, 3) points out, the power at work in the political "establishes a social order and a corresponding form of legitimacy."

Considering the polemical, passionate, and sometimes aggressive immigration discourse, this broadened understanding of politics is key to understanding the politics of immigration control both historically and in contemporary times. In the following sections I examine key points in contemporary U.S. immigration and border control policies. I then analyze the connections between immigration and two highly influential and interrelated issues that have been connected to immigration in multiple ways: (1) race and immigration control, and (2) national security and the criminalization of unauthorized immigrants.

CONTEMPORARY IMMIGRATION POLICY IN THE UNITED STATES

Certainly the legal realm is significant when speaking of the politics of immigration control. The law is a key instrument of the state as well as an arena of debate. It is the arena in which the sovereign state exercises authority in the domestic realm and also the arena in which the territorial boundaries and policies pertaining to the protection of those boundaries are delineated. Significantly, only in an imaginary world is the legal realm devoid of politics. In fact, especially when it comes to immigration, law and politics are inextricably linked to each other. This is glaringly clear from simply noting the location of the Border Patrol within the federal government bureaucracy. The Border Patrol has gone from being originally housed within the Labor Department in 1924 to its move to the Justice Department in 1993 to its current location as part of Customs and Border Protection within the Department of Homeland Security. Implicit in these bureaucratic organizational moves is the *redefinition of immigration from a labor issue to a justice issue to one of national security*. Politics is implicated in these definitions and redefinitions of immigration and in the laws that control it. Of course, the "lines" between labor and justice and national security, like most lines, are themselves quite fluid. It should be noted, though, that well before September 11, 2001, and the subsequent move of the Border Patrol to the Department of Homeland Security, immigration had been linked with security issues, as discussed below.

Ostensibly in an effort to halt further undocumented immigration, the Immigration Reform and Control Act (IRCA), which introduced employer sanctions for the first time, offered a legalization program, and authorized expansion of the Border Patrol, was passed in 1986. The arguments were that the newly legalized immigrants would halt demand for undocumented immigrant workers, the employer sanctions would deter companies from hiring those in the United States without authorization, and the expanded Border Patrol would halt future illegal immigration (Andreas 2000). That none of these things happened provided the context for the anti-immigrant backlash of the early 1990s, which eventually resulted in the passage of two pieces of legislation in 1996 that at the time represented the harshest crackdown on immigrant rights in recent years (Doty 2003).

The Illegal Immigration Reform and Immigrant Responsibility Act (IIRIRA) of 1996 departed from previous legislation in its overwhelming exclusionary nature, its diminution of the rights of immigrants, and the hardening of lines between citizens and noncitizens. Physical boundaries between the United States and Mexico were fortified. Judicial review was sharply curtailed, and through a process of "expedited removal," immigration officials were authorized to quickly deport asylum seekers and undocumented immigrations at entry points and airports. In addition, with the stroke of a pen, the act also expanded the definition of deportable crimes, along with revising other agreements and arrangements. Significantly, for instance, Section 133 of IIRIRA ushered in the infamous 287(g) program, which allowed the INS (Immigration and Naturalization Service) to enter into agreements, through a memorandum of agreement, with local and state police to enforce federal immigration laws (Provine and Doty 2011).[1] This program was used extensively after September 11, 2001, in the anti-immigrant hysteria that followed that attack, especially in places like Arizona. Logically, it led to a drastic increase in detentions of persons charged with immigration violations (Provine and Doty 2011). Highly criticized, the program was terminated in 2012.

Reviewing the social and political climate during this time frame, we can see that the passing of IIRIRA in 1996 took place within the political context of major welfare reform and the downsizing of social services. Clearly, the Personal Responsibility and Work Opportunity Act, which was also passed in 1996, was a cornerstone of the Republican Contract with America, a Republican Party document outlining its platform were it to become the dominant political party in power. In fact, many of the contract's policy ideas originated at the Heritage Foundation, a conservative think tank (Gayner 1995). This act had significant ramifications for immigrants. For the first time, for example, legal immigrants were barred from receiving various public benefits. Reportedly, nearly half of the $54 billion in estimated savings from the welfare reform instituted in the act was expected to come from immigrant exclusions (Doty 2003).

However, the intensification of immigration control actually began before the 1996 laws came into being. Proposition 187, a ballot initiative passed in California in 1994, would have excluded undocumented children from public schools and blocked them and their parents from nearly all public services had it not been stuck down later by federal courts on the grounds that it was unconstitutional (Cornelius 2005). Of course, the fact that the proposition was eventually declared unconstitutional does not mean it was without effect. With the resounding passage of Proposition 187, President Bill Clinton's advisors believed a ramped-up show of force along the U.S.-Mexico border would neutralize Republican criticism leading up to the 1996 presidential election. Subsequently, the Clinton administration began spending large amounts of money on border enforcement (Cornelius 2005).

The stepped-up enforcement efforts, which included various "operations," including Operation Hold the Line in El Paso (1993), Operation Gatekeeper in San Diego (1994), Operation Safeguard in central Arizona (1995), and numerous others in Arizona, California, New Mexico, and Texas, constituted what came to be known as "prevention through deterrence." Prevention through deterrence was a major departure from the previous practice of border enforcement, which pursued and apprehended immigrants shortly *after* they had crossed into the United States. Further, in stepping up enforcement at key crossing points, this strategy redirected unauthorized border crossings away from urban areas to ever more remote and dangerous places. The policy, which continues today, is directly responsible for the skyrocketing number of border-crossing deaths that have ensued (Doty 2011). In 1994, for example, 23 migrants died along the California-Mexico border, but in 1998 this number had increased to 147 (Hing 2015). From 1997 to 2013 over 6,000 known migrant deaths occurred along the Arizona-Mexico border (Hing 2015), alarming figures for just two of the states along the two-thousand-mile border. A similar trend is shown by other figures. While in 1994, fewer than 30 migrants had died along the border, this increased to 147 in 1998, 387 in 2001, and 409 in 2007 (Jimenez 2009; No More Deaths 2011). It should be kept in mind that all death statistics are usually undercounts, as bodies are not always found.

Reviewing the shifts in immigration policies and enforcement, although the 287(g) program was ushered in with IIRIRA in 1996, it was not until the early 2000s that it began to be used in full force, with local communities taking it upon themselves to enforce federal immigration laws. In April 2002 U.S. Attorney General John Ashcroft issued a classified memo arguing that state and local police had the inherent authority to make arrests for violations of civil immigration laws (Provine and Doty 2011).

In addition, the Justice Department began to enter immigration-related information, including outstanding deportation orders, into databases used by local police departments (Provine and Doty 2011). This resulted in civil immigration offenses becoming part of the nationwide criminal-justice database, the National Criminal Information Center, contributing to the phenomenon that has come to be referred to as "crimmigration," the criminalization of unauthorized immigrants, discussed in greater detail below.

RACE AND IMMIGRATION CONTROL

Policy makers generally do not like to speak of race and immigration in the same breath, but there are good reasons why the centuries-old ghost of race is not easily put to rest when it comes to immigration. Key concepts that are intricately connected to immigration and the laws that control it surface in debates over the control of borders and are bound up with a complex history in which racialized identities circulate in different guises. The concepts of nation, sovereignty, cultural integrity, national security, and criminality orbit around constructions of race in a complex way (Doty 2010; Romero 2000). In a sound and holistic discourse, one cannot speak of citizenship and issues of inclusion and exclusion while ignoring race.

Along with ethnicity and religion, race has been a key element in constructing and reconstructing the nation-state, the political community, and the identities that are deemed part of that community (Provine and Doty 2011). Immigration policies are often responses to popular racialized anxieties about immigrants. Recognizing this, though, requires a sophisticated understanding of racism and its insidious effects. Racism today is often not overt, but rather subtle and built into the structures of society, including laws and policies. From a law and society context, Michael Omi and Howard Winant (1994) offer the concept of "racial project" as a set of practices or structures that help form ideas about difference, which are then used to justify harsh treatment (Provine and Doty 2011; Urbina 2018; Urbina and Álvarez 2015, 2017). This is clearly evident in U.S. immigration control policies and laws, both historically and in contemporary times. In theory immigration laws apply to all immigrants, but in practice current border enforcement and interior policies have been directed primarily at migrants from Mexico and Central America, while those who have overstayed their visas, who account for about 40 percent of the unauthorized population, have not been a primary source of concern (Provine and Doty 2011).

Scholars have asked whether the organized assault on immigrants comes from them being largely persons of color (Dobkin 2009). In this vein, drawing on the "white supremacist order model" of Desmond King and Rogers Smith, Donald Dobkin (2009) suggests that current immigration control policies continue to be highly shaped by race, though race is seldom mentioned in formal or official immigration discourse. Drawing on the racial formation thesis of Omi and Winant (1994), King and Smith (2005) critique previous studies of U.S. immigration policies for not including recognition of the "racial orders" thesis, which rejects claims that racial injustices are aberrations in America. Dobkin (2009) points out, as an example, that while the Immigration and Nationality Act of 1965 was largely sold as legislation that would end national-origin-based quotas and thus help terminate discrimination against people of color, the impact was just the opposite. That is, while the law did away with the national origins quota system and the remnants of Asian exclusion laws, it placed a 20,000 annual limit on immigrants from any single country, and established an overall limit of 120,000 immigrants from the Western Hemisphere. This resulted in expanding immigration from many countries, but the numerical restrictions for Mexico and the Western Hemisphere resulted in Mexico quickly exceeding its limit, pushing that country to the frontline of immigration control and placing Mexican immigrants in a vulnerable and exploitable situation.

Race also enters the picture in more local "happenings" related to immigration, though disguised under a different pretext. For example, the Department of Homeland Security planned to build a fence along the U.S.-Mexico border in 2008. This received a great deal of attention owing to environmental, social, and political issues. However, the proposed fence was not to be a continuous barrier; lengths of open space would remain along various sections. Researchers found, though, that the wall-designated areas were more prevalent in lower-income areas containing large Latino (mostly Mexican) populations. Thus there were significant disparities in the demographics of groups that would be affected directly by the border fence and those not directly affected (Wilson et al. 2008).

In fact, the connection between immigration and race is nowhere more prominent than in the relationship between the anti-immigrant movement and white supremacist individuals and organizations in the United States. While civilian border patrol groups that had their "fifteen minutes of fame" in the mid-2000s claimed to vet their volunteers and warn that racists were not welcome, the connections cannot be denied.[2] There is overwhelming evidence that the widespread anti-immigrant sentiments provided fertile ground for those who promoted racist, white supremacist ideologies (Doty 2009). Well-known white-supremacist groups such as Stormfront, White Revolution, the National Alliance, New Saxon, and even the Ku Klux Klan have promoted the anti-immigrant cause and often publicize civilian border patrol events on their websites. In addition to the more obvious groups, author Carol Swain points to the "new white nationalism," whose adherents are more educated and often pass as mainstream conservatives. They focus on "a preference for people of one's own group," claiming such sentiments are "natural, normal, and healthy" (Doty 2009, 61).

This, of course, raises the question of what determines "one's own group." Clearly, race lurks not too far from the surface here.

In fact, in the twenty-first century, after centuries of supposed social transformation and decades of declarations that race no longer matters, racism continues to rear its head in overt ways as well, as was clearly evident in the summer of 2014 when unaccompanied migrant children arrived at the U.S.-Mexico border in larger numbers. A North Carolina Ku Klux Klan leader called for the shooting of immigrant children, declaring, "If we pop a couple of 'em off and leave the corpses laying on the border, maybe they'll see we're serious about stopping immigrants" (Hing 2015; see also Savan 2014). While some people now argue that the times of lynching, hanging, and burning blacks and Mexicans alive are long gone (Delgado 2009; Harris and Sadler 2007; McLemore 2004; McWilliams 1990; Samora, Bernal, and Peña 1979; Urbina and Álvarez 2015, 2017; Urbina, Vela, and Sánchez 2014), words such as these should not be regarded simply as idle threats, especially given the 2015 murder of nine African Americans in South Carolina in a racially motivated act of domestic terrorism (Apuzzo, Schmidt, and Perez-Pena 2015).

IMMIGRATION AND NATIONAL SECURITY

Immigration control is intrinsically connected to the issue of security, whether the "threat" is real, imagined, exaggerated, or fabricated. This is especially the case since the attack on the United States on September 11, 2001. This connection is evident in the transfer of the Border Patrol into the Department of Homeland Security. However, the connection between immigration control and security can be seen to go back much further. Throughout U.S. history immigrants have been demonized and constructed as invaders and threats, with the U.S. border, especially the U.S.-Mexico border, seen as under siege. Among the many charges by U.S. politicians, government officials, scholars, and others, in 1975 the U.S. Commissioner of Immigration, Leonard Chapman, warned of a "vast and silent invasion of illegal aliens," and in 1978 former CIA director William Colby, asserting that Mexico was a greater threat than the Soviet Union, said that by the end of the century the Border Patrol would "not have enough bullets to stop them." In one of the biggest U.S. cities, Dallas Mayor Pro Tem Jim Hart cautioned voters in 1985 that illegal aliens had "no moral values" and that they were destroying the city's neighborhoods and threatening the security of Dallas. Worse, according to Hart, women in Dallas could be "robbed, raped or killed" (Cockcroft 1982, 58; Maxon 1985). Even former president George W. Bush, a wealthy Texas rancher and former governor of Texas, noted in a speech on May 2006 that illegal immigration "strains state and local budgets and brings crime to our communities." Security concerns revolving around immigration, of course, are not limited to "territorial security" but include fears of cultural pollution, the loss of a coherent national identity, and a general devaluation of "our" way of life—all of which have been, and continue to be, evident in the statements of extremist anti-immigrant activists and ostensibly more mainstream political leaders who oppose any comprehensive immigration reform.

Broadly, fear of threats to national and cultural identity highlights another way that race and immigration are linked, though race is typically not mentioned. Scholars have used the concept of the "new racism" or "neo-racism" or racism without race, as documented by Eduardo Bonilla-Silva in *Racism Without Racists: Color-Blind Racism and the Persistence of Racial Inequality in the United States* (2006). Martin Barker (1981, 21) used the term "new racism" to refer to the promotion of the idea there is some inherent naturalness to nations and their identities and that "feelings of antagonism will be aroused if outsiders are admitted." Etienne Balibar (1991) defines "neo-racism" as a racism of the reversal of population movements—that is, movements from the less economically well-off countries to the richer industrialized countries, a phenomenon that is only intensified in contemporary times of accelerated globalization, as documented by David Bacon in *Illegal People: How Globalization Creates Migration and Criminalizes Immigrants* (2009).

Another contemporary practice related to immigration and security is the dramatic uptick in detaining unauthorized immigrants. A third law passed in 1996 was the Antiterrorism and Effective Death Penalty Act of 1996 (AEDP), which contained a number of immigration-related provisions, including a limit on judicial review of various removal orders. This law was in part a consequence of the 1995 bombing of the Alfred P. Murrah Federal Building in Oklahoma City, despite the fact that this was an act of domestic terrorism (Johnson 2015). Nationally, the presumed or constructed linkages between immigration and national security can be seen in two contemporary manifestations: (1) the militarization of the U.S.-Mexico border, and (2) the criminalization and incarceration of unauthorized immigrants, a phenomenon some scholars characterize as *crimmigration*.

The rapid growth of the U.S. Border Patrol in recent years presents clear evidence of how the border between the United States and Mexico has become militarized (Urbina and Álvarez 2015, 2017; Whitehead 2013). The Border Patrol is now the nation's largest law enforcement agency, with an annual budget of $12.4 billion and 46,000 gun-carrying customs officers and border patrol agents (Graff 2014; Urbina and Álvarez 2015). Today the Border Patrol is part of Customs and Border Protection (CBP), which itself is the largest law enforcement air force in the world and roughly the size of Brazil's entire combat air force (Graff 2014). A hiring surge by CBP, which is part of the Department of Homeland Security, has resulted in the increased use of deadly force by Border Patrol agents as well as numerous investigations of corruption and criminal activity (Graff 2014; Urbina 2018; Urbina and Álvarez 2015). Further, this drastic increase in size is also clearly implicated in the militarization of the U.S.-Mexico border.

Another area that illustrates the consequences of defining unauthorized immigration as a security issue is the dramatic increase in raids and "targeted immigration enforcement operations," with a corresponding increase in immigrant detention. As documented by various critics, "targeted enforcement operations" conducted by ICE focus on single homes, apartment buildings, businesses, and individuals. In fact, in many cases those who were not part of the initial "target" are, nonetheless, rounded up and either deported or sent to detention (Hing 2015). One striking example is the 2007 raids in New Bedford, Massachusetts, where over three hundred ICE agents raided the Michael Bianco factory. Immigration agents handcuffed and manacled 362 immigrant workers from Guatemala, El Salvador, and other Central American countries (Tirman 2015). This was one of several dozen raids conducted by ICE around the same time.

The 1996 IIRIRA included a major mandatory detention provision for several classes of immigrants who are not criminal immigrants. This includes asylum seekers in the expedited removal process until they can demonstrate a credible fear of persecution, persons ordered removed for at least ninety days following their final removal order, and aliens inadmissible or deportable on national security grounds (Longeuvan 2015). Mark Krikorian (2006) of the Center for Immigration Studies, ostensibly a research-oriented think tank but with strong links to the anti-immigrant movement, suggested a "third way" of dealing with unauthorized immigrants that would not entail massive roundups or pathways to citizenship. This "third way" was a policy of "attrition through enforcement," which would "prevent illegals from being able to embed themselves in our society. That would involve denying them access to jobs, identification, housing, and in general making it as difficult as possible for an illegal immigrant to live a normal life" (Krikorian 2006, 1; see also Doty 2009; Johnson 2007).

Over the past several years this has become the de facto enforcement strategy in the United States, as illustrated in the dramatic increase in the number of unauthorized immigrants held in detention, not on criminal charges but civil immigration offenses; the increased rate of deportations; raids on homes, workplaces, and communities in which migrants reside; as well as the use of local law enforcement to carry out much of this strategy. For instance, as of 2016 the migrant detainee population in the United States was over 30,000. The number of migrants removed by ICE in fiscal year 2016 was 240,255, up from 235,413 in 2015 but a decrease from 409,849 in 2012. A recent study by the Urban Institute and the National Council of La Raza reports that, besides adult immigrants, there are approximately five million children in the United States with at least one undocumented parent.

Beyond the border region, interior enforcement practices have resulted in the separation of families, economic hardship, and psychological trauma. In one incident, ICE officials with weapons drawn pulled over a school bus full of children, some of whose parents were being taken into custody. This overall situation creates tremendous tension between the values we profess to hold near and dear, like family, community, compassion, equality of opportunity, and fairness, and life on the ground as it is lived and experienced daily. It is a striking example of society structured along the lines of the exception, as suggested by theorists Carl Schmidt (1996) and Giorgio Agamben (2005). Exceptionalism refers to situations where individuals or groups become "exceptions" through the exercise of sovereign state power—resulting in various exclusions, like the denial of rights and opportunities, along with respect, that are generally accorded to others. Exceptionalism can be enacted at various official levels as well as by ordinary citizens (see Doty 2009).

In fact, exceptionalism is nowhere more evident than in the current U.S. system of detaining unauthorized immigrants. The contemporary U.S. detention system relies on a confusing array of county and local prisons, ICE facilities, and private prison corporations to house migrants awaiting deportation. Immigrant deportation and detention has skyrocketed in recent years, with a significant portion of detainees being held by private contractors. As reported by various observers, immigrants are now the fastest-growing population in federal custody and a growth market for prison corporations (Greene and Patel 2007; see also National Public Radio 2011). A recent report issued by the Migration Policy Institute reports that since 1996 immigrant detention has increased geometrically, with the most recent spike occurring after 9/11 (Meissner and Kerwin 2009). In fiscal year 1994 the average daily population in custody was 6,785, but by fiscal year 2007 this figure increased to over 30,000, with almost 35,000 immigrants in custody in 2016. Between fiscal year 2003 and fiscal year 2007, the total number of noncitizens detained by ICE per year increased from 231,500 to 311,213 (Meissner and Kerwin 2009). According to the Department of Homeland Security (DHS), in fiscal year 2016 the agency apprehended 530,250 individuals nationwide, and conducted a total of 450,954 removals and returns. The Border Patrol reported 415,816 apprehensions nationwide, compared to 337,117 in fiscal year 2015, and ICE arrested 114, 434 individuals, compared to 125,211 in fiscal year 2015. Corresponding with increased deportation and detention figures, more than half of ICE's fiscal year 2009 appropriated revenues, nearly $2.5 billion, support its Detention and Removal Operations (DRO, now called ERO), with $1.7 billion for custody operations (Meissner and Kerwin 2009). The figure for fiscal year 2010 was virtually unchanged, with $2.55 billion allocated to DRO (U.S. Department of Homeland Security 2010). In fact, the Border Patrol's annual budget increased from $263 million in 1990 to more than $3.8 billion in 2016, the budget of CBP has more than doubled from $5.9 billion in 2003 to $13.2 billion in 2016, and ICE spending has grown 85 percent, from $3.3 billion in 2003 to $6.1 billion in 2016.

Illustrating the symbiotic relationship between the political economy and immigration control (Urbina 2018; Urbina and Álvarez 2015), 17 percent of ICE's detainees are held in privately owned "contract detention facilities" (CDFs), though the involvement of private corporations in immigrant detention is much more extensive (Meissner and Kerwin 2009).[3] Reportedly, the two largest private prison operators in the United States each receive over 10 percent of their revenue directly from ICE (National Immigration Forum 2009). During a conference call with investors in June of 2009, Corrections Corporation of America's (CCA) president Damon Hininger remarked, "We believe this suggests that ICE will continue providing meaningful opportunity for the industry for the foreseeable future" (cited in Feltz and Baksh 2009, 1). The CEO of Geo Group, CCA's major competitor, expressed a similar sentiment to investors in February 2009, declaring, "My personal view is that Homeland Security and the detention beds necessary to detain illegal aliens will increasingly be seen as a national imperative to protect U.S. workers and their jobs" (cited in Feltz and Baksh 2009, 1).

Observers report that ICE quickly began contracting with seven different CDFs, and, in addition to these facilities, detainees have been held in seven service processing centers (SPCs), which are owned by ICE and operated by private contractors (Salinas 2015; Schriro 2009). Other facilities that hold detainees are county jails dedicated solely to housing ICE detainees and shared-use county jails (Salinas 2015; Schriro 2009). As further evidence of the "twisted" relationship between immigration officials and private corporations, ICE's budget proposal for fiscal year 2010 included a request for the complete privatization of the immigrant detention system (National Immigration Forum 2009). The U.S. Senate approved the request, but the U.S. House rejected it, stating that a move to an exclusively private system would be premature until ICE could show that it can adequately provide oversight to ensure medical care and detention standards at existing CDFs (National Immigration Forum 2009; see also Department of Homeland Security Appropriation Bill 2009).

A new investigation provides a glimpse into privatization, economics, and the conditions in privatized, for-profit immigrant detention centers in the United States. The report, "Imprisoned Justice," documents how migrants are forced to eat rotten food, drink contaminated water, endure arbitrary solitary confinement, have little or no access to medical care, and are denied their rights to legal counsel. As noted herein, under the Obama administration there was a significant increase in the number of people deported and detained, as nearly three million immigrants were deported and the number of people in migrant detention facilities increased to 34,000. Discussing the study, which lasted from April 2016 to March 2017, Azadeh Shahshahani, legal and advocacy director for the Georgia-based nonprofit organization Project South, reports that "given Trump's fondness for private prison corporations and his plans for a large-scale crackdown on immigrants, I think we can expect the overall situation to get even worse for immigrants." In fact, the United States already has the largest immigration detention operation in the world. ICE detained more than 352,000 people in 2016 alone, an average of 31,000 to 34,000 people per day, at an average cost of $127 per person per day. Much of the high cost of immigration detention is tied to privatization. Corrections Corporation of America (now known as CoreCivic), the largest detention contractor with ICE, owned or controlled 66 facilities and managed another 11, with a total of 88,500 beds in twenty states, as of the end of 2015, and nearly three-fourths (72 percent) of beds in U.S. immigration detention facilities in 2015 were operated by for-profit prison corporations.

Another "force multiplier" in the legal apparatus of immigration enforcement is the Criminal Alien Program (CAP), whose purpose is to identify non-U.S. citizens in jails and prisons throughout the United States and secure a final order of removal before they are released (Criminal Alien Factsheet 2011).[4] The result has been a series of "criminal alien requirements" (CARs) issued by the Federal Bureau of Prisons, which solicit private prison companies to hold low-security foreign nationals serving criminal sentences prior to deportation (Raher 2009). An example of this is the $400,948,418 contract awarded to CCA (the largest for-profit private prison corporation in the United States) on October 28, 2011, to house approximately 1,750 "low security, adult male inmates that are primarily criminal aliens."[5] In fact, 48 percent of noncitizens detained by ICE in 2009 were detained through the Criminal Alien Program (Shahshahani 2012; Schriro 2009). These contracts are not with ICE, and the detainees are held on criminal charges, which is not the case in immigration detention centers. CARs, however, are important to the private prison industry and can be considered part of the immigration industrial complex. In other words, after serving their criminal sentences these same prisoners are generally transferred to immigration detention centers, where they are held until they are deported. This has been characterized as an "inverted double jeopardy," where an individual can be "tried once but punished twice" (Bosworth and Kaufman 2011, B110). This also allows private prison companies to benefit twice in that the same companies often run the private prisons and the private immigrant detention centers. Stephen Raher (2009) has suggested that CARs have perhaps been the "single greatest salvation" of the private detention industry, notably for CCA (see also Feltz 2009; Wood 2011).

In addition, in 2005 the Department of Homeland Security (DHS) in conjunction with the Department of Justice (DOJ) began Operation Streamline, which mandates that in areas where it is in effect all migrants crossing the border without documents be detained while awaiting trial, prosecuted with a misdemeanor or felony charge, and eventually deported (Buentello et al. 2010; see also Operation Streamline Policy Brief 2010).[6] Operation Streamline was launched in a 210-mile section of the Texas–New Mexico border near Del Rio, Texas, and eventually was in force in the major border patrol sectors in Arizona, California, New Mexico, and Texas. By December 2014, only the Del Rio, Laredo, and Tucson sectors continued to participate in Streamline. Before Operation Streamline was in place, those first-time border crossers who chose to return voluntarily were transported by the Border Patrol to their home countries; otherwise, they were formally removed through the civil immigration system (Operation Streamline Policy Brief 2010). With immigration control being redefined from various angles, Operation Streamline rapidly created unprecedented caseloads in eight of the eleven federal district courts along the U.S.-Mexico border (Operation Streamline Policy Brief 2010). It is highly significant that acts previously handled through the civil immigration system are now considered criminal, thus contributing to the skyrocketing rates of detention of undocumented migrants and the need for even more detention space. Here too, by creating more demand for detention beds, Operation Streamline benefits the private prison industry. For instance, Grassroots Leadership reports that the growth of Operation Streamline–related immigration detention centers in Texas alone has been significant. Since the beginning of Operation Streamline, more than five thousand U.S. Marshals–contracted private prison beds have been constructed in Texas. Nationally, the private contractors for these beds have been GEO and MTC (Management Training Corporation) (Buentello et al. 2010).

Lastly, one of the most egregious contemporary immigration-related enforcement practices is the detention of families. A recent report tells the story of twenty-eight-year-old Rosa, who fled gang violence in Honduras with her seven-year-old daughter, Ana. According to the Lutheran Immigration and Refugee Service and the Women's Refugee Commission (2014), they were held for three months at the Artesia, New Mexico, family detention center. In Texas, mothers held with their children at another family detention center in Karnes County went on a five-day hunger strike the week before Easter 2015, resulting in some being placed in isolation for a day along with their children.[7] Not only are these not isolated incidents, but the situation has become more detrimental. In December 2014 the largest family detention center for immigrants opened in Dilley, Texas. The center, South Texas Family Residential Center, is a former camp for oil-field workers located one hundred miles north of the U.S.-Mexico border, between Laredo and San Antonio, Texas. It is designed to hold about twenty-four hundred detainees, most of whom are women and children. The fifty-acre site is being managed by CCA. While CCA describes its mission in Dilley as simply "to provide an open, safe environment with residential housing as well as educational opportunities for women and children who are awaiting their due process," others have described the site as "standing on a dirt road lined with cabins in a barren compound enclosed by fencing" (Preston 2014).

Further complicating the child migrant situation, between October 2013 and September 2014 the U.S. government apprehended 68,334 family members at the U.S.'s southwest border, a 361 percent increase from the previous year, according to the Lutheran Immigration and Refugee Service and the Women's Refugee Commission (2014), and increased to 77,674 in fiscal year 2016. On June 24, 2015, Homeland Security Secretary Jeh Johnson announced that there would be "substantial changes" to the department's family detention policies and that they will seek to end long-term family detention (U.S. Department of Homeland Security 2015). However, as of 2017 details have not been released, and the American Immigration Council (2015) reports that even before the Trump administration, the Obama administration believed that family detention could be justified and reformed. In fact, Trump's executive orders could expand family detention centers, without proper reforms (Knefel 2017).

CONCLUSION

The historical record clearly reveals that immigration and immigration laws have always been a focal point of discourse. However, as detailed herein, to provide a comprehensive and meaningful analysis of contemporary immigration policies and enforcement in the United States, we must first delineate the contours of the related "politics" and "political" of immigration control, which tend to function as the global force governing the confines of immigration—which resulted in *divided lines*. Once we illustrate how immigrant subjects are defined, redefined, created, and recreated, we can begin the complicated task of delineating the historical and contemporary effects of race and national security on immigration control, allowing us to situate the immigration discourse within a broader context. Ultimately, by exposing the political, legal, and social twists and turns of immigration over time, we can propose and hopefully implement an effective and just immigration reform. This is the challenge of our times, as illustrated during the 2015–16 presidential election, when the anti-immigrant sentiment was exploited by Donald Trump and his sixteen fellow Republican presidential candidates, and quickly increased after Trump took office on January 20, 2017.

Along with Trump's highly charged political rhetoric, the Trump administration has been focusing more on immigration enforcement than effective and humane immigration reform. For instance, instead of designing and proposing comprehensive immigration reform in the best interest of immigrants and the American society, he has focused on his proposed "big, beautiful wall," travel bans through executive orders, which have been blocked by federal judges (indicating Trump's irrationality), hiring additional federal immigration agents, requesting federal funding for local and state police agencies to collaborate with the Department of Homeland Security (Border

Patrol and ICE), and threatening and shaming sanctuary cities and states for protecting immigrants, including "criminal illegal aliens." From a pragmatic standpoint, Trump's focus on immigration enforcement, without designing humane comprehensive reform, has grave implications and consequences not only for immigrants but the entire American society, including some of Trump's supporters who seem to be more motivated by racism, rage, hate, fear, and ideology than the actual truths and realities of immigration.

NOTES

1. On December 21, 2012, ICE announced its decision "not to renew any of its agreements with state and local law enforcement agencies that operate task forces under the 287(g) program."

2. The phrase "fifteen minutes of fame" is credited to Andy Warhol, who included it in a 1968 exhibition of his work at the Moderna Museet in Stockholm, Sweden: "In the future, everyone will be world-famous for 15 minutes."

3. This 17 percent does not represent the total detainee population in facilities run by private corporations, only those in CDFs. Private contracts are often awarded to corporations to provide guard and other services to ICE-owned SPC facilities, as is the case with the Florence Service Processing Center.

4. ERO was formerly called the Office of Detention and Removal (DRO). ICE's Office of Enforcement and Removal (ERO) assumed responsibility for the Office of Investigations Alien Criminal Apprehension Program on June 1, 2007.

5. Criminal Alien Requirement 12, Solicitation Number: RFP-PCC-0017, Contract Award Number: DJB1PC-0016. Copy on file with authors.

6. Prior to Operation Streamline, judges could exercise "prosecutorial discretion" and consider the circumstances of individual migrants. Operation Streamline removed this.

7. One detainee, Kenia, and her two-year-old son were released on bond in April after spending five months in the Karnes family detention center.

REFERENCES

Agamben, G. 2005. *State of Exception.* Chicago: University of Chicago Press.

American Immigration Council. 2015. "Homeland Security Secretary Announces Changes to Family Detention Policies." E-mail to author, June 24, on file with author.

Andreas, P. 2000. *Border Games: Policing the U.S.-Mexico Divide.* Ithaca, N.Y.: Cornell University Press.

Apuzzo, M., M. S. Schmidt, and R. Perez-Pena. 2015. "Federal Hate Crime Charges Likely in South Carolina Church Shooting." *New York Times*, June 25, A17.

Bacon, D. 2009. *Illegal People: How Globalization Creates Migration and Criminalizes Immigrants*. Boston: Beacon Press.

Balibar, E. 1991. "Is There a Neo-racism?" In *Race, Nation, Class-Ambiguous Identities*, edited by E. Balibar and I. Wallerstein, 59–60. London: Verso.

Barker, M. 1981. *The New Racism*. London: Routledge.

Bonilla-Silva, E. 2006. *Racism Without Racists: Color-Blind Racism and the Persistence of Racial Inequality in the United States*. Lanham, Md.: Rowman and Littlefield.

Bosworth, M., and E. Kaufman. 2011. "Foreigners in a Carceral Age: Immigration and Imprisonment in the United States." *Stanford Law and Policy Review* 22, no. 2: 429–54.

Buentello, T., S. Carswell, N. Hudson, and B. Libal. 2010. "Operation Streamline: Drowning Justice and Draining Dollars Along the Rio Grande." *Grassroots Leadership*. blibal @grassrootsleadership.org.

Cockcroft, J. 1982. "Mexican Migration, Economic Crisis, and the International Labor Struggle." In *The New Nomads: From Immigrant Labor to Transnational Working Class*, edited by M. Dixon and S. Jonas, 48–61. San Francisco: Synthesis Publications.

Cornelius, W. 2005. "Controlling 'Unwanted' Immigration: Lessons from the United States, 1993–2004." *Journal of Ethnic and Migration Studies* 31: 775–94.

Criminal Alien Factsheet. 2011. http://www.dhs.gov/index.shtm.

Delgado, R. 2009. "The Law of the Noose: A History of Latino Lynching." *Harvard Civil Rights–Civil Liberties Law Review* 44: 297–312.

Department of Homeland Security Appropriation Bill. 2009. H.R. Report 110-862. 110th Cong., 2d Sess.

Dobkin, D. S. 2009. "Race and the Shaping of U.S. Immigration Policy." *Chicana/o-Latina/o Law Review* 28: 19–42.

Doty, R. L. 2003. *Anti-immigrantism in Western Democracies: Statecraft, Desire, and the Politics of Exclusion*. London: Taylor and Francis.

———. 2009. *The Law into Their Own Hands: Immigration and the Politics of Exceptionalism*. Tucson: University of Arizona Press.

———. 2010. "SB1070 and the Banality of Evil." *Z Magazine*. http://www.zcommunications .org/contents/172695.

———. 2011. "Bare Life: Border-Crossing Deaths and Spaces of Moral Alibi." *Environment and Planning D: Society and Space* 29: 599–612.

Edkins, J. 1999. *Poststructuralism and International Relations: Bringing the Political Back In*. Boulder, Colo.: Lynne Rienner.

Feltz, R. 2009. "Focus on 'Criminal Aliens' Increases Demand for Immigrant Detention Business." *Huffington Post*. http://www.huffingtonpost.com/reneee-feltz/focus-on-criminal-aliens.

Feltz, R., and S. Baksh. 2009. "Detention Retention." *American Prospect*, June 2. http://prospect.org/cs/articles?article=detention_retention.

Gayner, J. 1995. "The Contract with America: Implementing New Ideas in the U.S." *Heritage Foundation*, October 12. http://www.heritage.org/research/lecture/the-contract-with-america-implementing-new-ideas-in-the-us.

Graff, G. M. 2014. "The Green Monster: How the Border Patrol Became America's Most Out of Control Law Enforcement Agency." *Politico*, November–December. http://www.politico.com/magazine/story/2014/10/border-patrol-the-green-monster-112220.html.

Greene J., and S. Patel. 2007. "The Immigrant Gold Rush: The Profit Motive Behind Immigrant Detention." A report submitted to the U.N. Special Rapporteur on the Rights of Migrants. http://209-.85.173.132/search?.

Harris, C., and L. Sadler. 2007. *The Texas Rangers and the Mexican Revolution: The Bloodiest Decade, 1910–1920*. Albuquerque: University of New Mexico Press.

Hing, B. O. 2015. "Ethics, Morality, and Disruption of U.S. Immigration Laws. *Kansas Law Review* 63: 981–1044.

Jimenez, T. 2009. *Replenished Ethnicity: Mexican Americans, Immigration, and Identity*. Berkeley: University of California Press.

Johnson, K. R. 2007. *Opening the Floodgates: Why America Needs to Rethink Its Borders and Immigration Laws*. New York: New York University Press.

———. 2015. "20 Years Ago: Oklahoma City Bombing Rocked the Nation, Changed Immigration Law." *ImmigrationProf Blog*. http://lawprofessors.typepad.com/immigration/2015/04/20-years-ago-oklahoma-city-bombing-rocked-the-nation.html.

King, D. S., and R. M. Smith. 2005. "Racial Orders in American Political Development." *American Political Science Review* 99: 75–92.

Knefel, J. 2017. "Trump's Executive Orders Could Drastically Expand Family Detention Centers." *Truthout*, February 5. http://www.truth-out.org/news/item/39339-trump-s-executive-orders-could-drastically-expand-family-detention-centers.

Krikorian, M. 2006. "A Third Way." *Palm Beach Post*. http://cis.org/node/419.

Longeuvan, B. 2015. "Mandatory Detention and the Commodification of Immigrants." Guest blogger, immigration professor blog. http://lawprofessors.typepad.com/immigration/2015/05/mandatory-detention-and-the-commodification-of-immigrants.html.

Lutheran Immigration and Refugee Service and the Women's Refugee Commission. 2014. *Locking Up Family Values, Again*. http://lirs.org/wp-content/uploads/2014/11/LIRSWRC_LockingUpFamilyValuesAgain_Report_141114.pdf.

Lydgate, J. 2010. "Assembly-Line Justice: A Review of Operation Streamline." Policy Brief. January. The Chief Justice Earl Warren Institute on Race, Ethnicity, and Diversity. Berkeley Law Center, University of California, Berkeley. https://www.law.berkeley.edu/files/Operation_Streamline_Policy_Brief.pdf.

Maxon, T. 1985. "Hart Angers Hispanics with Letter on Aliens." *Dallas Morning News*, February 5.

McLemore, D. 2004. "The Forgotten Carnage 89 Years Ago: Rangers Singled Out Hispanics, and Thousands Died." *Dallas Morning News*, November 28.

McWilliams, C. 1990. *North from Mexico: The Spanish-Speaking People of the United States.* New York: Praeger.

Meissner, D., and D. Kerwin. 2009. *DHS and Immigration: Taking Stock and Correcting Course.* Migration Policy Institute. http://www.migrationpolicy.org/research/dhs-and -immigration-taking-stock-and-correcting-course.

National Immigration Forum. 2009. "The Math of Immigration Detention." *National Immigration Forum.* http://immigrationforum.org/blog/themathofimmigrationdetention/.

National Public Radio. 2011. "Who Benefits When a Private Prison Comes to Town?" *All Things Considered*, November 5.

No More Deaths. 2011. *A Culture of Cruelty: Abuse and Impunity in Short-Term U.S. Border Patrol Custody.* http://forms.nomoredeaths.org/wp-content/uploads/2014/10/ CultureOfCruelty-full.compressed.pdf.

Omi, M., and H. Winant. 1994. *Racial Formation in the United States: From the 1960s to the 1990s.* New York: Routledge.

Preston, J. 2014. "Detention Center Presented as Deterrent to Border Crossings." *New York Times*, December 15, A18.

Provine, D. M., and R. L. Doty. 2011. "The Criminalization of Immigrants as a Racial Project." *Journal of Contemporary Criminal Justice* 27: 261–77.

Raher, S. 2009. "The Prison-Keeper's Dilemma: Unsustainable and Undesirable Business Practices in Privatized Corrections." http://bepress.com/stephen_raher/2.

Romero, M. 2000. "State Violence, and the Social and Legal Construction of Latino Criminality: From El Bandido to Gang Member." *Denver University Law Review* 78: 1089–1127.

Samora, J., J. Bernal, and A. Peña. 1979. *Gunpowder Justice: A Reassessment of the Texas Rangers.* Notre Dame, Ind.: University of Notre Dame Press.

Savan, L. 2014. "The KKK Wants a 'Shoot to Kill' Policy to Include Migrant Children." *The Nation.* http://www.thenation.com/blog/180840/kkk-wants-shoot-kill-policy-aimed -immigrant-children#.

Schmidt, C. 1996. *The Concept of the Political.* Chicago: University of Chicago Press.

Schriro, D. 2009. *Immigration Detention Overview and Recommendations.* Homeland Security, Immigration and Customs Enforcement. https://www.ice.gov/doclib/about/offices/odpp/ pdf/ice-detention-rpt.pdf.

Shahshahani, A. 2012. "Prisoners of Profit: Immigrants and Detention in Georgia." *ACLU.* https://www.aclu.org/blog/prisoners-profit-immigrants-and-detention-georgia.

Tirman, J. 2015. *Dream Chasers: Immigration and the American Backlash.* Cambridge, Mass.: MIT Press.

Urbina, M. G., ed. 2018. *Hispanics in the U.S. Criminal Justice System: Ethnicity, Ideology, and Social Control.* 2nd ed. Springfield, Ill.: Charles C Thomas.

Urbina, M. G., and S. E. Álvarez, eds. 2015. *Latino Police Officers in the United States: An Examination of Emerging Trends and Issues.* Springfield, Ill.: Charles C Thomas.

———. 2017. *Ethnicity and Criminal Justice in the Era of Mass Incarceration: A Critical Reader on the Latino Experience.* Springfield, Ill.: Charles C Thomas.

Urbina, M. G., J. E. Vela, and J. O. Sánchez. 2014. *Ethnic Realities of Mexican Americans: From Colonialism to 21st Century Globalization.* Springfield, Ill.: Charles C Thomas.

U.S. Department of Homeland Security. 2010. "Fact Sheet, ICE Fiscal Year 2010 Enacted Budget." https://www.scribd.com/document/24704564/ICE-Fact-Sheet-FY2010-Budget-11-5 -09.

———. 2015. "Statement by Secretary Jeh Johnson on Family Residential Centers." https://www .dhs.gov/news/2015/06/24/statement-secretary-jeh-c-johnson-family-residential-centers.

Whitehead, J. 2013. *A Government of Wolves: The Emerging American Police State.* New York: SelectBooks.

Wilson, J. G., J. Benavides, A. Reisinger, J. Lemen, Z. Hurwitz, J. Spangler, and K. Engle. 2008. "An Analysis of Demographic Disparities Associated with the Proposed U.S.-Mexico Border Fence in Cameron County, Texas." Briefing paper to the Inter-American Commission on Human Rights of the Organization of American States. http://www.academia.edu/ 12512717/An_analysis_of_demographic_disparities_associated_with_the_proposed_U.S .Mexico_border_fence_in_Cameron_County_Texas.

Wood, G. 2011. "A Boom Behind Bars: Private Jail Operators Are Making Millions Off the Crackdown on Illegal Aliens." http://www.msnbc.com/id/42197813/ns/business-us .business.

Chapter 4

IMMIGRATION, ILLEGALITY, AND THE LAW

Governance, Equality, and Justice

CLAUDIO G. VERA SÁNCHEZ

> Like other discriminatory legislation in our country's history,
> immigration laws define and differentiate legal status on the
> basis of arbitrary attributes. Immigration laws create unequal
> rights. People who break immigration laws don't cause harm
> or even potential harm (unlike, for example, drunk driving,
> which creates the potential for harm even if no accident occurs).
> Rather, people who break immigration laws do things that are
> perfectly legal for others, but denied to them—like crossing a
> border or, even more commonly, simply exist.
>
> —AVIVA CHOMSKY

IN 2015, DONALD Trump, during his campaign for president, went on a tirade about immigrants, "When Mexico sends its people, they're not sending their best. . . . They're sending people that have lots of problems, and they're bringing those problems with us. They're bringing drugs. They're bringing crime. They're rapists." These comments reflect a longstanding sentiment when it comes to immigration, one that has historically targeted various groups, like the Irish, Chinese, Japanese, and Mexicans (Hernández 2006; Moehling and Piehl 2009). In the twenty-first century, though, according to Henry Giroux (2015, 1), "rather than viewing Trump's comments as a political virus that has deep roots in nativist apoplexy and a long legacy of racism and state violence, his despicable remarks are reduced to an uncivil rant by a bullying member of the billionaire class." These remarks are therefore not confined to Trump alone, but rather reflect a campaign against unauthorized immigrants (Chacon 2012), a transnational crusade situated within an age of globalization and its accompanying crises within several political, social, and economic domains, including education, health care, social services, and social control.

Today, in a highly competitive, technological, and global society, Americans face a myriad of challenges, such as skyrocketing costs for education and health care, lack of affordable housing, as well as high crime in their neighborhoods, and are offered unfounded explanations and solutions.[1] For instance, after carefully considering the political and economic issues, which is more difficult: subsidizing education for all Americans, as well as restructuring zoning laws prohibiting underprivileged students from attending better schools, or blaming immigrant children for being a burden on the educational system? Is it more daunting to guarantee a living wage for Americans, and to reintroduce the jobs that America has lost to deindustrialization, or to vilify unauthorized immigrants for taking *all* the jobs? Is it more difficult to figure out how to publicly fund and make social services attainable, like health care for needy families, or to condemn unauthorized immigrants for draining the economy? The seemingly insurmountable obstacles that Americans face help individuals like Trump achieve celebrity status, offer hope that the government may finally offer sound solutions, and legitimize unmitigated campaigns against unauthorized immigrants. These politicians often have not solved a single problem, or mitigated a single social ill, but have helped to criminalize unauthorized immigrants. The purpose of this chapter is to describe several national crises (including crime and drugs in communities, the labor market, taxes and social services, federal regulation of immigration, and America's culture) that are pressing issues within our contemporary era of social control in the midst of globalization, and to discuss how unauthorized immigrants are identified as the root cause of these problems, which prompts regulation, surveillance, criminalization, and punishment of unauthorized immigrants.

In this chapter, the labels "unauthorized immigrants" and "authorized immigrants" will be used as opposed to "illegal immigrant" and "legal immigrant." "Illegal immigrant" is often preferred by states and cities that seek to criminalize immigrants. Under federal law, however, unauthorized immigration is considered a civil offense as opposed to a criminal offense—in essence, immigration law is not criminal law (Chacon 2009; Macdonald 2014; Sweeney 2010). Civil offenses—like staying in the country past the expiration date of a visa, coming into the country without documentation, failure to pay child support, or breaking a lease—are often defined as matters of administration. Such civil offenses are indeed cumbersome to states and localities; yet politicians and the public are mistaken in their attempts to treat unauthorized immigration like a class-one felony. Therefore, the term "unauthorized immigrant" better captures that a rule of administration or a rule in administrative matters has been broken and hence falls within the parameters of civil law. Therefore, these individuals have not engaged in conduct that is criminally illegal under federal law; they are simply not authorized to reside in the United States.

AN AMERICAN CRISIS OF THE INTRACTABLE CRIME PROBLEM: THE MYTH OF THE DRUG-SMUGGLING IMMIGRANT

Despite the fact that crime rates have plummeted in the United States since the 1990s, alarm over gun-toting Mexican cartels is alive and well in public discourse (Sohoni and Sohoni 2013). Although crime has declined precipitously across the country, some states and localities report heightened levels of serious crime. The tasks of figuring out how to make high-crime neighborhoods secure and stable for families and how to reduce the insatiable demand for drugs in the Unites States and its accompanying violence are challenging. As a result, a common "solution" is to blame unauthorized immigrants for their perceived contribution to these social ills.

Both the flow of immigration from Mexico and the correlation between immigration and crime are often overestimated. Studies reveal that immigration has been diminishing since the year 2000 (Contreras 2014). Figures show, for instance, that the number of Mexicans migrating to the United States decreased by 60 percent from 2006 to 2010 (Correra-Cabrera 2013). Studies suggest that the declining U.S. economy and stricter border controls are partly responsible for an overall reduction in immigration (Correa-Cabrera 2013). Still, border towns are notorious for fearmongering about spillover from organized crime and drug cartels in Mexico. However, the most frequently found spillover is a positive one, and lies in the highly skilled immigrants from Mexico, a trend that increased by 20 percent in 2007 and 38 percent in 2009 (Correa-Cabrera 2013). For example, the border town of El Paso, Texas, which has received an unprecedented level of *authorized* immigration, reported recovering from the U.S. recession at a faster rate than the rest of the country (Correa-Cabrera 2013). Adam Isacson and Maureen Meyer (2012, 6) find that "the U.S. side of the border displays a marked *lack* of spillover violence from Mexico. Even as Mexican border states and municipalities exhibit some of the world's highest homicide and violent crime rates, most U.S. jurisdictions directly across the border are experiencing fifty-year lows."

Contrary to mainstream discourse, immigration may actually be responsible for stabilization or reductions in crime and delinquency in neighborhoods, states, and localities (Becerra et al. 2012; Dinovitzer, Hagan, and Levi 2009; Griswold 2009; Harris and Feldmeyer 2013; Jennings et al. 2013; Lyons, Velez, and Santoro 2013; Martinez 2014; Ramey 2013; Reid et al. 2005; Wadsworth 2010). Cross-cultural studies also conclude that despite the unwavering myth about the connection between immigration and crime, the data do not substantiate these beliefs (Figgou et al. 2011; Koff 2009). The Hamilton Project, for instance, shows that immigrants are five times less likely to be housed in correctional supervision than U.S.-born individuals (Greenstone and Looney 2010). Of course, while the anti-immigrants rhetoric has been a focal point of debate, the campaign to criminalize immigrants, or to assume that an immigration and crime connection exists, is not new. Jennifer Chacon (2007, 1841) documents that in the early 1990s, in their mission to defend Proposition 187, politicians claimed that "illegal-alien gangs roam our streets, dealing drugs and searching for innocent victims to rob, rape and, in many cases, murder those who dare violate their turf [and] . . . nearly 90% of all illicit drugs are brought here by illegals." Yet these fearmongers have not cited any evidence. Daniel Griswold (2009, 43) concludes that despite the recent economic recession, "the past 15 years have seen the most rapid drop in crime rates in the nation's history. . . . The social instability that has beset the United States since the 1960s has either stabilized or begun, happily, to reverse itself. The two [immigration and crime] should not be happening simultaneously if the critics [of immigration] are to be believed. And yet they are."

Out of a deep-rooted hysteria and paranoia, vigilante groups are working tirelessly to purge unauthorized immigrants from the American society. Sang Kil (2011) argues that the metaphor of the "body politic" is useful in anti-immigrants discourse for describing immigrants as a disease, an attack on American conservatives, or an invasion of the nation. The Tea Party, for example, is infamous for supporting anti-immigration movements and policies like Arizona's S.B. 1070, promoting them under the banner of American nationalism and protectionism, as illustrated on their website: "There is a domestic war heading our way. We must defuse it with our votes and our positive actions or America, as we know it, will be dissolved." These groups often erroneously assume that immigrants are admitted to the country without highly enforced regulation, and question the value and contributions of immigrants currently residing in the United States, despite the fact that many American citizens, other than being procreated in the states, have done little, if anything, to earn privileges. Charging that "your citizenship is given to unworthy illegal aliens," these conservatives have duped vulnerable populations of marginalized whites and U.S.-born minorities who are disappointed by the broken promise of upward mobility traditionally provided by American institutions. Chris Hedges (2013, 1) maintains that this movement "stokes the anger of many Americans, mostly White and economically disadvantaged, and encourages them to lash back at those who, they are told, seek to destroy them." In a 2005 speech, as one example, Barbara Coe referred to unauthorized workers as "illegal barbarians who are cutting off [the] heads and appendages of blind, White disabled gringos" (Chacon 2007, 1841). In truth, despite alarmist claims about immigrants' predisposition to crime, the strongest propensity the immigrant community appears to have is an unrelenting insistence on working hard. Most reports centering on unauthorized immigrants show low criminal involvement and high participation in the workforce (Gomberg-Muñoz 2011; Martinez 2014; Román 2013).

AN AMERICAN CRISIS IN THE LABOR MARKET: IMMIGRANTS ARE TAKING ALL THE JOBS

In an era of globalization, consisting of a society that has radically transformed from industrialization to highly skilled labor, many Americans struggle to find decent jobs. Further, a conversion from an industrialized nation to a service-oriented society also marks a significant shift in the U.S. economy. However, U.S. labor within this new paradigm is not globally competitive. American workers, for example, require health care, equitable wages, and a host of benefits that are not guaranteed in many parts of the world. In addition, according to some critics, high tax brackets make it very expensive to conduct business in the United States. Offering American companies adequate economic incentives, along with reasonable tax breaks, may be a starting point for reversing this trend. Politicians, though, resist this type of strategizing. It is much easier to center public discourse on how unauthorized immigrants take all the jobs, although data show the real reasons why low-skilled Americans are suffering from limited job opportunities—for example, deindustrialization. Prior to 1986, it was not illegal to work in the United States without authorization or to hire unauthorized workers. In 1986, though, with the Immigration Reform and Control Act, Congress decided to make employers part of immigration enforcement, in a sense, criminalizing "labor"—Mexican labor and Latino labor—of unauthorized immigrants (Saucedo 2010).

Almost two decades into the twenty-first century, politicians have yet to supply evidence that immigrants are taking over even a small proportion of working-class to middle-class occupations, like those of teachers, counselors, or police officers. The obstinate belief that immigrants negatively impact the labor market is exacerbated by the fact that today a college degree is no longer a guarantee of *success* and is linked to large amounts of debt, debt that keeps graduates in a subjugated position for many years (Giroux 2006). For instance, Rutgers University found that three years after graduation only 50 percent of graduates held a full-time job (Stone, Van Horn, and Zukin 2012). Consequently, the insistence on attributing labor shortages and fluctuations to immigrants (Sohoni and Sohoni 2013), as opposed to deindustrialization and other factors that have transformed the U.S. economy, criminalizes the work of unauthorized immigrants without considering that they are employed in occupations (like agriculture, restaurants, and gardening) that are viewed as undesirable by most Americans.

Still, in the face of serious exploitation, the labor contributions of immigrants are becoming too obvious to be ignored (Gomberg-Muñoz 2011; Hinojosa-Ojeda 2012; Massey, Durand, and Malone 2002; Nadadur 2009). Kelly Hernández (2006, 425) finds that Mexican immigration has benefited the United States and has hurt Mexico because it has "drained the country of one of its greatest natural resources, a cheap and flexible labor supply." Griswold (2009) reports that an increase in low-skilled immigrants would boost the U.S. economy by $180 billion a year. Further, analysts argue that low-skilled immigrants actually benefit even low-skilled U.S. workers, allowing them to avoid the lowest rung of the occupational ladder. In reality, immigrants and U.S. workers are not in competition for the same jobs (Catanzarite 2002). Michael Greenstone and Adam Looney (2010) find that immigrants benefit the economy because they boost wages and lower prices. In addition, immigrants enhance the purchasing power of Americans by lowering the prices of "immigrant-intensive" services like babysitting, gardening, dry cleaning, housekeeping, and other cleaning services. Patricia Cortes (2008) documents that unauthorized immigrants impact the wages of low-skilled immigrants but not low-skilled U.S. natives, and have a beneficial impact on prices for immigrant-intensive services. Cortes (2008, 414) maintains that a person's purchasing power depends not only on wages but prices, and concludes that "through lower prices, low-skilled immigration brings positive net benefits to the U.S. economy."

Lastly, contrary to the notion that immigrants do not contribute to our communities beyond their labor, immigrants also contribute to the U.S. economy via job generation. Greenstone and Looney (2010) document that immigrants are 30 percent more likely to open a business, and immigrant college graduates are more likely to file patents than U.S.-born individuals. Studies clearly show that instead of stealing all the jobs, immigrants create jobs and introduce innovation into the U.S. economy. All in all, immigrants and U.S.-born individuals are rarely in competition for the same jobs, immigrants help lower prices, and immigrants create jobs, which enhances the standard of living for Americans.

SOCIAL SERVICES HAVE DWINDLED AND MY TAXES HAVE GONE UP: WHY SHOULD I SPEND MY MONEY ON UNAUTHORIZED IMMIGRANTS?

In this age of globalized capitalism, undue attention is paid to the expenditures and fiscal burdens of states and localities for what they view as an intractable immigration problem. Hard-working Americans, the argument goes, are "footing" the bill for education, social services, and other related expenditures, which overburden the economic system. The argument centers on the supposed lack of tax contributions from immigrants, and rarely on mega-corporations (or wealthy individuals) who easily circumvent tax codes. For example, it is well documented that many American companies do not pay their proportionate share of taxes, including companies like Apple, Google, and Microsoft (Helman 2014). There is no apoplectic response to the billions of dollars that are withheld from the U.S. economy by masterful tax accountants, yet there is national indignation at the thought of an immigrant child receiving a "free education" with subsidized tax dollars.

The contention that immigrants fail to pay taxes is not supported by the IRS code, which allows unauthorized immigrants to file taxes (Internal Revenue Service 2015; see also Lipman 2006). Unauthorized immigrants not only pay taxes, but they also contribute at a higher tax rate than similarly situated individuals who are authorized to work in the United States. When a person pays taxes and receives no refund in return, this puts them in a higher tax bracket. Secondly, those who use inaccurate Social Security numbers also pay taxes. The Social Security office has the Earnings Suspense File, which is generated from all the Social Security numbers that cannot be matched to a person. In 2010 alone, $70.3 billion went into the Suspense File, monies that are then invested in trust funds. For instance, $2 billion is allocated to Medicare's Hospital Insurance Trust Fund and $8.7 billion toward Social Security, according to the Medicare NewsGroup website. Although some of the income can be traced to clerical errors, the majority of funds originates from Social Security numbers of unauthorized workers (Porter 2005) and disproportionately from certain labor sectors, like restaurants, construction, and farming. In fact, in its 2013 report, the Social Security Administration reported: "We estimate that earnings by unauthorized immigrants result in a net positive effect on Social Security financial status generally, and that this effect contributed roughly $12 billion to the cash flow of the program for 2010. We estimate that future years will experience a continuation of this positive impact on the trust funds" (Goss et al. 2013, 3; see also Lipman 2006). These figures are similar to those in other reports, such as the one by the Institute on Taxation and Economic Policy (2013), which shows that immigrants pay approximately $10.3 billion annually in state and local taxes, and if legalized their contributions would increase by another $2 billion a year. Although the public is often alarmed at the thought of immigrants using "false" Social Security numbers, despite the fact that taxes are accrued, few seem bothered by others who often forgo their tax responsibilities, like math and English tutors who tutor at places like Starbucks or people's homes and are paid cash, contractors who repair people's homes, and businesses that accept only cash.

Worse, despite immigrants' fiscal contributions to public services, steps have been taken to prevent unauthorized immigrants from receiving public services. Proposition 187, the Illegal Immigration Reform and Immigrant Responsibility Act of 1996 signed by President William (Bill) Clinton, and the 1996 welfare reform act (Personal Responsibility and Work Opportunity Reconciliation Act) were designed to curtail the benefits that go to unauthorized immigrants (Chacon 2007; Cianciarulo 2012). These policies make most unauthorized individuals ineligible for federal public benefits, including but not limited to loans, licenses, food and housing assistance, and public education (Chacon 2007; Rocha et al. 2014). Naturally, immigrant children do incur costs (Román 2013), but no more than American children, simply because of expenses like education and health care. Immigrants do add expenses to states and localities (Nadadur 2009; Román 2013), but the initial losses are made up in tax revenue by contributions from unauthorized immigrants (Greenstone and Looney 2010). Further, as noted above, not only do immigrants pay taxes, but they also pay for services used by Americans (e.g., Medicare, Social Security) that they are ineligible to receive (Crowley 2013; Lipman 2006).

THE FEDERAL GOVERNMENT IS TOO SOFT ON ILLEGALS: THE STATE'S QUEST TO CRIMINALIZE UNAUTHORIZED IMMIGRANTS THROUGH PUBLIC POLICY

It has long been established that only the federal government can regulate immigration and that states can implement policies only if they complement federal regulation (Chacon 2012). However, federal control of immigration regulation has been challenged by states. Consider, for example, Hazleton, Pennsylvania, where local officials prohibited landlords from renting to unauthorized immigrants and revoked the licenses of business owners who hired such immigrants. Other localities have banned the soliciting of work in public places (Chacon 2012; Cianciarulo 2012). Chacon reported in 2012 that during the previous five years, lawmakers had proposed over seven thousand state immigration proposals, such as the Legal Arizona Workers Act (LAWA), which denies business licenses to those who hire unauthorized workers, and Arizona's S.B. 1070, which criminalizes actions that are neither civil nor criminal offenses under federal law (Cianciarulo 2012). In fact, despite controversial legal challenges, the U.S. Supreme Court has upheld some provisions of Arizona's S.B. 1070. Justice John T. Noonan of the U.S. Court of Appeals for the Ninth Circuit declared: "The Arizona statute before us has become a symbol. For those sympathetic to immigrants to the United States, it is a challenge and a chilling foretaste of what other states might attempt" (Jonsson 2011).

Anti-immigration policies are fueled by the feeling that the federal government is not doing enough to curb unauthorized immigration (Cianciarulo 2012), despite the fact that the U.S. government spent over $15 billion on border enforcement alone in 2012, compared to the $3.5 billion budget in 1998 (Chacon 2012). Further, according to Daniel Morales (2014), by 2013 there was a significant increase in the prosecution of immigrants (close to 100,000) at the federal level for entering the country without authorization. Despite the fact that immigration rates are declining precipitously, in national polls 65 percent of those surveyed identified immigration to be a "very serious problem" (Chapin 2011, 130). Ninety-five percent of those who have committed immigration violations are detained after being arrested for nonviolent infractions or misdemeanors; nevertheless, these numbers skyrocketed from 81,000 detainees per day in 1994 to 380,000 in 2008, and deportations increased from 18,000 in 1980 to 392,000 in 2011 (Chacon 2012). As reported by Chacon (2012, 639), "the past fifteen years have witnessed a massive expansion of federal resources dedicated to immigration enforcement, an unprecedented militarization of the southern border, an exponential increase in the number of noncitizens held in detention, and a more than twelvefold increase in the number of criminal immigration prosecutions. Yet, the mantra that the federal government is not enforcing immigration law is still frequently invoked in the national dialogue concerning immigration."

Not surprisingly, Justice Noonan's prediction that other states would copycat Arizona's S.B. 1070 quickly became a reality. Alabama's H.B. 56 is considered one of the nation's toughest anti-immigration laws. It includes but is not limited to police officers stopping immigrants based on reasonable suspicion, prohibiting immigrants from receiving any benefits at the state or local level, preventing immigrants from attending public state colleges or universities, demanding that public primary schools identify and report immigrant student children, forbidding the renting of dwellings to immigrants, restricting hiring practices, and nullifying contracts with unauthorized immigrants (Chacon 2012). Some aspects of H.B. 56 have been challenged as being unconstitutional by the courts, but this has not prevented various other states from drafting anti-immigration legislation.

Immigration regulation and expansion is also taking place at the local police level, given the latitude in federal law allowing officers to perform duties reserved for federal officials (Quereshi 2010). Although immigration advocates challenged parts of Arizona's S.B. 1070, which required police to act as immigration officers, police organizations can easily circumvent those regulations by cross-deputizing officers. Critics, for instance, charge that section 287(g) of the Illegal Immigration Reform and Immigrant Responsibility Act of 1996 deputizes local law enforcement to carry out the duties of immigration officers. As a result, unauthorized immigrants are unlikely to call the police, and hence these policies undermine public safety and relationships with the police (Chapin 2011; Urbina 2018; Urbina and Álvarez 2015, 2017). In fact, studies suggest that immigrant women are deterred from reporting domestic violence for fear that ICE (Immigration and Customs Enforcement) may be called (Quereshi 2010). Allison Hartry (2012), for instance, found that in cases where immigrant women invoked the assistance of authorities, they lost their families and children to deportations or foster care. There too, Arizona's S.B. 1070 places immigrants at great peril by forcing officers to investigate immigration status based on physical appearance. Clearly, the federal government is not only regulating unauthorized immigration in a highly questionable fashion, but nationally authorizing and legitimizing racial profiling. For example, although many officers oppose the targeting of immigrants, others such as Sheriff Joe Arpaio of Maricopa County, Arizona, have made cities/counties a battleground for discriminatory behavior and civil rights violations. Maricopa County registers an abnormally high rate of deportations, despite the fact that ICE's own data reveal that 79 percent of people deported are noncriminals or were detained for minor offenses (Chapin 2011). According to Violeta Chapin (2011), various local law enforcement agencies have opposed the cross-deputization of officers on three accounts: (1) public safety will suffer from unauthorized immigrants being fearful to report crimes; (2) cross-deputization will prompt racial profiling of Latino residents; and (3) the financial burden of immigration regulation will have an adverse impact on state and local budgets. It is estimated that the indirect cost of the 287(g) program in Arkansas alone was $7.9 million annually, from training officers, foster care for children of those arrested, litigation and legal liability, and police education campaigns, along with higher prices owing to a scarcity of labor from unauthorized immigrants (Chapin 2011). In addition, officers who refuse to enforce this law can be sued for failure to adhere to state immigration regulations. Broadly, policies like Arizona's S.B. 1070 prevent immigrants from having meaningful relationships with governmental entities or mainstream America.

Another area of federal expansion, highly active in regulating unauthorized immigration, involves the accelerated militarization of the U.S.-Mexico border (Hernández 2012; Kil 2011; Romero 2008; Stowell et al. 2013). In justifying the militarization of the border, officials invoke the specter of immigrant criminality, as when Senator Orrin Hatch stated: "We can no longer afford to allow our borders to be just overrun by illegal aliens. . . . Frankly, a lot of our criminality in this country today happens to be coming from criminal, illegal aliens who are ripping our country apart. A lot of the drugs are coming from these people" (Chacon 2007, 1843). The appropriation of federal funds for border enforcement has increased in less than a decade from $1 billion to $10 billion annually (Stowell et al. 2013). As part of this anti-immigration movement (included in the funding), Congress once agreed to build a 700-mile fence between the two countries, and the Pentagon's 1033 Program turns over leftover weapons from Afghanistan and Iraq to U.S. police departments (Giroux 2013). However, in many cases, police organizations are not trained to use high-tech weaponry, and do not have anyone who can properly fly Black Hawk helicopters. President Barrack Obama also contributed to this monumental effort, and was manipulated into framing immigration as an issue of criminality, aggressively asserting that he was committed to deporting immigrants "who are criminals, gang bangers, people who are hurting the community" (Hing 2014, 142; Romero 2000). In November 2014, Obama helped stop the deportations of over four million individuals and yet at the same time increased the militarization of border communities (Nakamura, Costa, and Fahrenthold 2014)—without, however, addressing the realities of immigration.

In sum, immigration laws like Arizona's S.B. 1070 and Hazleton, Pennsylvania's Illegal Immigration Relief Act Ordinance are grounded in the notion that the federal government has not acted to effectively regulate unauthorized immigration and criminalize unauthorized immigrants and sanction employers. The consequences for business owners, such as revoked business licenses and heavy fines, have been upheld by the Supreme Court under LAWA (the Legal Arizona Workers Act). Many of these policies are predicated on the deterrence-by-aversion assumption; that is, if unauthorized immigrants' lives are made miserable enough, they will be deterred from migrating to the United States and those who currently live in the states will self-deport. Studies, however, suggest that aggressive immigration enforcement has different impacts on behavior, for example, forcing immigrants to stay in the country longer for fear that they will not be able to return to their place of employment or see their family (Rocha et al. 2014). Lastly, contrary to state and federal officials who argue that the federal government has done little to curb immigration, there has been expanded federal regulation of unauthorized immigration that extends to states and localities across the United States.

A CRISIS IN AMERICAN IDEOLOGY AND THE CULTURE OF CRUELTY: THE DECIMATION OF IMMIGRANTS' RIGHTS

According to Giroux (2011), the American society is experiencing a crisis of culture, which he describes as a culture of cruelty that ignores immigrants' plight and promotes a callous disposition toward those who suffer human rights abuses at the hands of local police, immigration officers, and the American government. Further, this culture of cruelty also marks a transition from social investment to social containment. In a quest for increased regulation of immigration, the number of detainees has increased, but the ramifications are severe, including immigrant deaths when crossing the desert/border and mistreatment of those held in detention centers (Androff and Tavassoli 2012).

Then, as if the immigrants' journey was not harsh enough, some politicians continue to deny unauthorized immigrants basic rights and contend that no provision in the Constitution guarantees rights for foreign nationals, a claim disputed by legal scholars (Al-Khatib 2014; Lang 2015; Macdonald 2014; Sweeney 2010). Legal scholars argue that the Supreme Court in cases such as *INS v. López Mendoza* (1984) and *Padilla v. Kentucky* (2010) suggested that legal protections for unauthorized immigrants be considered. In practice, however, constitutional protections like habeas corpus are not triggered by the containment or ill treatment of unauthorized immigrants in immigration detention centers. Border detainees have experienced human rights violations (including withholding of food or water, pregnant women denied medical attention, bathroom facility denial) and even more extensively lack of due process, particularly in mass hearings for mass pleas to be convicted for crossing the border (Androff and Tavassoli 2012; Johns 2013), which also jeopardize the immigrants' ability to become legal residents. The withholding of these rights is very questionable, given that the Supreme Court in *Wong Wing v. United States* (1896) established that noncitizens are entitled to due process rights when punishment is involved. Citizens and noncitizens are entitled to protection against self-incrimination, double jeopardy, and due process as stipulated by the Fifth Amendment, and noncitizens are also entitled to trial by jury and the right to counsel under the Sixth Amendment.

The legal controversies become more pronounced because civil and criminal law are often conflated in the arena of unauthorized immigration. Technically, immigration offenses are civil offenses (Macdonald 2014), and thus while many use the term "illegal alien" to describe immigration offenses, a civil offense is a violation of administrative matters (being in the country without documentation), suggesting that "unauthorized immigrant" is a more appropriate term. The Supreme Court in *Wong Wing v. United States* (1896) concluded that immigration law is not criminal law: "The order of deportation *is not a punishment for crime*. . . . It is but a method of enforcing the return to his own country of an alien who has not complied with the conditions . . . which the Government of the nation . . . has determined that his continuing to reside here [United States] shall depend." As such, despite the continued insistence on treating immigration offenses as criminal violations, the protections in criminal law are virtually nonexistent in immigration law. Therefore, although the criminal label is often applied to unauthorized immigrants ("illegal immigrants" or "illegal aliens"), the constitutional protections (like entitlement to court-appointed counsel) are not afforded (Chacon 2009; Sweeney 2010). Katherine Beckett and Heather Evans (2015), for instance, document that immigrants are held for extended periods of time even if the charges are civil violations, and individuals are arrested and interrogated without *Miranda* warnings, thereby blurring the distinction between civil and criminal processes. Aarti Shahani (2010) found that immigrants in New York City flagged by ICE spent on average 73 days longer in detention than their counterparts, even after controlling for race and offense type. Beckett and Evans (2015) found that unauthorized immigrants spend 170 percent more days in jail than their similarly situated counterparts. Further, according to Beckett and Evans (2015, 266), although attorneys strive to treat people fairly and equally, unauthorized immigrants who are apprehended are likely not to plead guilty because of fear of deportation. "If they have more to lose they're less likely to [plead guilty]. They'll spend six months in jail when the recommendation was for thirty days, because they're afraid that they're going to be guaranteed to get kicked out, and they lose all their connections to whatever they have here."

Globally, as part of the transnational social control movement, the rate of immigrant detention is not an accident (Urbina 2018; Urbina and Álvarez 2016, 2017), but instead is compounded by the denial of legal protections, rigidly implemented policies, and Americans' apathy toward immigrants' plight. For instance, although Congress determined that immigration status should not be a factor in detaining people awaiting criminal trial, immigration officials have a "bed mandate" that requires them to detain a minimum of 34,000 unauthorized individuals per day, or risk losing funding from the Department of Homeland Security (Brickenstein 2015). Therefore, "crimmigration" involves the dialectical and symbiotic social control movement, with the intertwining of goals and procedural processes of the criminal legal system and the immigration enforcement system. The justification for these policies centers on the claim that unauthorized immigrants pose a threat to public safety, are a great flight risk, or pose a threat to national security. Consequently, laws have been significantly altered since 1996, increasing punishments for violations of immigrant laws to include deportation for status offenses, like minor drug offenses and drug addiction. However, available data from 2009 to 2011, for example, suggest that half of all ICE detainees had no criminal record, and those who did had been convicted of minor traffic violations (Brickenstein 2015). To be sure, since unlawful immigration rates have declined over the years and serious offenders have been deported, the only way ICE can maintain the "bed mandate" is by prosecuting and incarcerating unauthorized immigrants for minor offenses or with no criminal record.

CONCLUSION

This chapter opened with the attacks of Donald Trump during the presidential campaign, which he has continued after taking the Oval Office. He clearly is not alone in believing that unauthorized immigrants negatively impact the United States in terms of crime and delinquency, the labor market, social services, taxes, and in a sense all facets of social life. In a highly multiracial, multiethnic, and multicultural society, though, we must shift attention from Trump's discourse to a deep-rooted political virus with a longstanding legacy in American society (Giroux 2015). Instead of focusing narrowly on Trump's comments, we must consider historical and contemporary forces that "produce" a *Donald Trump*, who is in part a product of society. In effect, Trump cannot be Trump without the support of thousands if not millions of passionate and aggressive supporters, or established institutions and ideological forces. In the twenty-first century, American society is undergoing a radical transformation, coupled with a national crisis in the midst of globalization, which enables politicians who make hollow appeals to American nativism and nationalism to become overnight celebrities, because they offer long-awaited and logical, yet shortsighted, solutions to immense problems that afflict American institutions.

Because they see social and economic challenges as rooted in unauthorized immigration, states and localities have been working indefatigably to legislatively address the supposed shortcomings of the federal government. The militarization of the U.S.-Mexico border, the Supreme Court's decision about Arizona's S.B. 1070, legislation like 287(g) that extends the grasp of immigration federal enforcement at the local police level, along with human rights abuses in detention centers and absentee federal protections—all are a testament to federal regulation, surveillance, criminalization, and punishment of unauthorized immigrants.

If we examine the "twists and turns" of Trump's political discourse on immigration, with a focus on four crucial points during his political career—June 16, 2015, when he officially declared his candidacy for president; July 19, 2016, when he received the GOP presidential nomination; November 8, 2016, when he won the election; and January 20, 2017, when he was inaugurated as president—it is evident that his immigration discourse and behavior have significantly intensified since his election to the presidency. Reviewing his first one hundred days in office, it is evident that Trump is winning the "criminal immigrant" narrative. Consider, for instance, the long list of unprecedented actions, implications, and ramifications, including searching of cell phones at ports of entry, no use of technology (e.g., iPad and laptop) on certain airlines, ban of large electronics in cabins on certain flights, arrests of DREAMers, deportation of veterans, increased immigration raids, increased arrests and deportations, pressing border landowners to sell their property for the wall to be built or risk losing their land, and disregard for wildlife with the proposed wall. According to some critics (Wellman 2017), in a move "straight from Nazi playbook," the U.S. Immigration and Customs Enforcement has started publishing a weekly list of alleged criminal immigrants in "sanctuary" cities under Trump's executive order, "Enhancing Public Safety in the Interior of the United States." In targeting the most disadvantaged, the Trump administration continues to create fear of arrest or deportation, resulting in less crime being reported, children not going to school, children crying in school, immigrants not going to the doctor, and thousands of immigrants (undocumented and documented) not going to work or returning to their country of origin—creating a desperate labor shortage for U.S. employers, which will eventually impact the entire American society.

If mainstream America was exposed to the realities of immigration, and if unscrupulous politicians stopped baiting the American public, people would realize that the United States significantly benefits from immigrants, both authorized and unauthorized. Immigrants do create costs for state and local governments, such as education for immigrant children (Román 2013). However, inspect the evidence in its totality and the following patterns emerge, showing that immigrants (1) reduce or stabilize crime in communities (MacDonald, Hipp, and Gill 2013); (2) take jobs that nobody else wants; (3) generate jobs; (4) pay taxes for services that Americans utilize but immigrants are ineligible for; (5) improve the standard of living for Americans by reducing the cost of immigrant-intensive services; and (6) make a host of contributions in diverse areas of social life, culturally and intellectually. These benefits alone force us to question the *anti-Latino labor movement* as well as the aggressive national campaign to categorize, criminalize, apprehend, incarcerate, and deport immigrants.

NOTE

1.   The terms "America" and "Americans" are often used throughout the chapter. These words are imprecise in that they narrowly refer to individuals who reside in the United States, despite the fact that technically everyone who lives on the continent of America is an American. Irrespective of their accuracy, they often represent an ideology that encompasses U.S. nationalism and nativism. Therefore, they are useful to the extent that they help describe America as a body/country/ideology that is being invaded by unauthorized immigrants (Kil 2011).

REFERENCES

Al-Khatib, A. 2014. "Putting a Hold on Ice: Why Law Enforcement Should Refuse to Honor Immigration Detainers." *American University Law Review* 64: 109–68.

Androff, D. K., and K. Y. Tavassoli. 2012. "Deaths in the Desert: The Human Rights Crisis on the U.S.-Mexico Border." *Social Work* 57: 165–73.

Becerra, D., D. Androff, C. Ayon, and J. Castillo. 2012. "Fear vs. Facts: Examining the Economic Impact of Undocumented Immigrants in the U.S." *Journal of Sociology and Social Welfare* 39: 111–35.

Beckett, K., and H. Evans. 2015. "Crimmigration at the Local Level: Criminal Justice Processes in the Shadow of Deportation." *Law and Society Review* 49: 241–77.

Brickenstein, E. 2015. "Making Bail and Melting ICE." *Lewis and Clark Law Review* 19: 229–61.

Catanzarite, L. 2002. "Dynamics of Segregation and Earnings in Brown-Collar Occupations." *Work and Occupations* 29: 300–345.

Chacon, J. 2007. "Unsecured Borders: Immigration Restrictions, Crime Control, and National Security." *Connecticut Law Review* 39: 1827–91.

———. 2009. "Managing Migration Through Crime." *Columbia Law Review* 109: 135–48.

———. 2012. "Overcriminalizing Immigration." *Journal of Law and Criminology* 102: 613–52.

Chapin, V. R. 2011. "Silencio! Undocumented Immigrant Witnesses and the Right to Silence." *Michigan Journal of Race and Law* 17: 119–58.

Cianciarulo, M. S. 2012. "The 'Arizonification' of Immigration Law: Implications of *Chamber of Commerce v. Whiting* for State and Local Immigration Legislation." *Harvard Latino Law Review* 15: 85–128.

Contreras, V. R. 2014. "The Role of Drug-Related Violence and Extortion in Promoting Mexican Migration: Unexpected Consequences of a Drug War. *Latin American Research Review* 49: 199–217.

Correa-Cabrera, G. 2013. "Security, Migration, and the Economy in the Texas-Tamaulipas Border Region: The Real Effect of Mexico's Drug War." *Politics and Policy* 41: 65–81.

Cortes, P. 2008. "The Effect of Low-Skilled Immigration on U.S. Prices: Evidence from CPI Data." *Journal of Political Economy* 116: 381–422.

Crowley, N. C. 2013. "Naked Dishonesty: Misuse of Social Security Number for an Otherwise Legal Purpose May Not Be a Crime Involving Moral Turpitude After All." *San Diego International Law Journal* 15: 205–48.

Dinovitzer, R., J. Hagan, and R. Levi. 2009. "Immigration and Youthful Illegalities in a Global Edge City. *Social Forces* 88: 337–72.

Figgou, L., A. Sapountziz, N. Bozatzis, A. Gardikiotis, and P. Pantazis. 2011. "Criminality: Accounts of Fear and Risk in Talk About Immigration to Greece." *Journal of Community and Applied Social Psychology* 21: 164–77.

Giroux, H. A. 2006. "Higher Education Under Siege: Implications for Public Intellectuals." *Thought and Action*, Fall: 63–78. http://www.henryagiroux.com/links/higher%20edu%20under%20siege.pdf.

———. 2011. "America's Culture of Cruelty." *Truthout*, January 24. http://truth-out.org/archive/component/k2/item/94040:americas-culture-of-cruelty.

———. 2013. "Punishing Youth and Saturated Violence in the Era of Casino Capitalism." *Association of Mexican-American Educators Journal* 7: 10–16.

———. 2015. "Trumping America." *Truthout*, July 8. http://www.truth-out.org/news/item/31788-trumping-america.

Gomberg-Muñoz, R. 2011. *Labor and Legality: An Ethnography of a Mexican Immigrant Network*. New York: Oxford University Press.

Goss, S., A. Wade, J. P. Skirvin, M. Morris, K. M. Bye, and D. Huston. 2013. "Effects of Unauthorized Immigration on the Actuarial Status of the Social Security Trust Funds." April. https://www.socialsecurity.gov/oact/NOTES/pdf_notes/note151.pdf.

Greenstone, M., and A. Looney. 2010. "Ten Economic Facts About Immigration." *Hamilton Project*, September. http://www.brookings.edu/~/media/research/files/reports/2010/9/immigration-greenstone-looney/09_immigration.pdf.

Griswold, D. 2009. "Higher Immigration, Lower Crime: Today's 'Underclass' of Newcomers Seek a Day's Work, Not a Drug Deal." *Commentary*, December. http://object.cato.org/sites/cato.org/files/articles/Griswold-HigherImmigrationLowerCrime.pdf.

Harris, C. T., and B. Feldmeyer. 2013. "Latino Immigration and White, Black, and Latino Violent Crime: A Comparison of Traditional and Non-traditional Immigrant Destinations." *Social Science Research* 42: 202–16.

Hartry, A. S. 2012. "Gendering Crimmigration: The Intersection of Gender, Immigration, and the Criminal Justice System." *Berkeley Journal of Gender, Law and Justice* 27: 1–27.

Hedges, C. 2013. "The Radical Christian Right and the War on Government." *Truthdig*, October 6. http://www.truthdig.com/report/item/the_radical_christian_right_and_the_war_on_government_20131006.

Helman, C. 2014. "What America's 15 Most Profitable Companies Pay in Taxes." *Forbes*, April 15. http://www.forbes.com/sites/christopherhelman/2014/04/15/what-americas-most-profitable-companies-pay-in-taxes/.

Hernández, C. C. G. 2012. "Immigrant Outsider, Alien Invader: Immigration Policing Today." *California Western Law Review* 48: 231–44.

Hernández, K. L. 2006. "The Crimes and Consequences of Illegal Immigration: A Cross-Border Examination of Operation Wetback, 1943–1954." *Western Historical Quarterly* 37: 421–44.

Hing, B. O. 2014. "Re-examining the Zero-Tolerance Approach to Deporting Aggravated Felons: Restoring Discretionary Waivers and Developing New Tools." *Harvard Law and Policy Review* 8: 141–76.

Hinojosa-Ojeda, R. 2012. "The Economic Benefits of Comprehensive Immigration Reform." *Cato Journal: An Interdisciplinary Journal of Public Policy Analysis* 32: 175–99.

Institute on Taxation and Economic Policy. 2013. "Undocumented Immigrants' State and Local Tax Contributions." *ITEP*, July. http://www.itep.org/pdf/undocumentedtaxes.pdf.

Internal Revenue Service. 2015. Individual Taxpayer Identification Number. *IRS*. http://www.irs.gov/Individuals/Individual-Taxpayer-Identification-Number-ITIN.

Isacson, A., and M. Meyer. 2012. *Beyond the Border Buildup: Security and Migrants Along the U.S.-Mexico Border*. April. Washington, D.C.: Washington Office on Latin America. http://www.wola.org/files/Beyond_the_Border_Buildup_FINAL.pdf.

Jennings, W. G., K. M. Zgoba, A. R. Piquero, and J. M. Reingle. 2013. "Offending Trajectories Among Native-Born and Foreign-Born Hispanics to Late Middle Age." *Sociological Inquiry* 83: 622–47.

Johns, J. B. 2013. "Filling the Void: Incorporating International Human Rights Protections into United States Immigration Policy." *Rutgers Law Journal* 43: 541–71.

Jonsson, P. 2011. "Alabama Immigration Law Faces Legal Challenge: Can It Survive?" *Christian Science Monitor*, July 8. https://www.csmonitor.com/USA/Politics/2011/0708/Alabama-immigration-law-faces-legal-challenge-Can-it-survive/Arizona.

Kil, S. 2011. "Immigration and Operations: The Militarization (and Medicalization) of the USA-Mexico Border." In *Traversing Transnationalism: The Horizons of Literary and Cultural Studies*, edited by R. Frenkel, P. R. Frassinelli, and D. Watson, 75–94. Netherlands: Rodopi Press.

Koff, H. 2009. "Macro-lessons from Micro-crime: Understanding Migrant Crime Through the Comparative Examination of Local Markets. *Theoria: A Journal of Social and Political Theory* 56: 92–117.

Lang, A. 2015. "An Opportunity for Change? Aggravated Felonies in Immigration Proceedings and the Effect of *Moncrieffe v. Holder*." *Boston University International Law Journal* 33: 101–37.

Lipman, F. 2006. "The Taxation of Undocumented Immigrants: Separate, Unequal, and Without Representation." *Harvard Latino Law Review* 9: 1–58.

Lyons, C. J., M. B. Velez, and W. A. Santoro. 2013. "Neighborhood Immigration, Violence, and City-Level Immigrant Political Opportunities." *American Sociological Review* 78: 604–32.

MacDonald, J. M., J. R. Hipp, and C. Gill. 2013. "The Effects of Immigrant Concentration on Changes in Neighborhood Crime Rates." *Journal of Quantitative Criminology* 29: 191–215.

Macdonald, L. 2014. "Why the Rule of Law Dictates That the Exclusionary Rule Should Apply in Full Force to Immigration Proceedings. *University of Miami Law Review* 69: 291–319.

Martinez, R. 2014. *Latino Homicide: Immigration, Violence, and Community*. New York: Routledge.

Massey, D., J. Durand, and N. Malone. 2002. *Beyond Smoke and Mirrors: Mexican Immigration in an Era of Economic Integration*. New York: Russell Sage.

Moehling, C., and A. M. Piehl. 2009. "Immigration, Crime, and Incarceration in Early Twentieth-Century America." *Demography* 46: 739–63.

Morales, D. I. 2014. "Crimes of Migration." *Wake Forest Law Review* 49: 1257–1324.

Nadadur, R. 2009. "Illegal Immigration: A Positive Economic Contribution to the United States." *Journal of Ethnic and Migration Studies* 35: 1037–52.

Nakamura, D., R. Costa, and D. Fahrenthold. 2014. "Obama Announces Immigration Overhaul Shielding 4 Million from Deportation." *Washington Post*, November 20. https://www.washingtonpost.com/politics/obama-immigration-plan-will-shield-37-million-from-deportation/2014/11/20/3345d672-70dd-11e4-893f-86bd390a3340_story.html?utm_term=.6fab973766b7.

Porter, E. 2005. "Immigrants Are Bolstering Social Security with Billions." *New York Times*, April 5. http://www.nytimes.com/2005/04/05/business/illegal-immigrants-are-bolstering -social-security-with-billions.html?_r=2.

Quereshi, A. 2010. "287(g) and Women: The Family Values of Local Enforcement of Federal Immigration Law." *Wisconsin Journal of Law, Gender and Society* 25: 261–300.

Ramey, D. M. 2013. "Immigrant Revitalization and Neighborhood Violent Crime in Established and New Destination Cities." *Social Forces* 92: 597–629.

Reid, L. W., H. E. Weiss, R. M. Adelman, and C. Jaret. 2005. "The Immigration–Crime Relationship: Evidence Across US Metropolitan Areas." *Social Science Research* 34: 757–80.

Rocha, R. R., D. P. Hawes, A. H. Fryar, and R. D. Wrinkle. 2014. "Policy Climates, Enforcement Rates, Migrant Behavior: Is Self-Deportation a Viable Immigration Policy?" *Policy Studies Journal* 42: 79–100.

Román, E. 2013. *Those Damned Immigrants: America's Hysteria over Undocumented Immigration*. New York: New York University Press.

Romero, M. 2000. "State Violence, and the Social and Legal Construction of Latino Criminality: From El Bandido to Gang Member." *Denver University Law Review* 78: 1089–1127.

———. 2008. "Crossing the Immigration and Race Border: A Critical Race Theory Approach to Immigration Studies." *Contemporary Justice Review* 11: 23–37.

Saucedo, L. M. 2010. "Immigration Enforcement Versus Employment Law Enforcement: The Case for Integrated Protections in the Immigrant Workplace." *Fordham Urban Law Journal* 38: 303–25.

Shahani, A. 2010. "New York City Enforcement of Immigration Detainers: Preliminary Findings." *Justice Strategies*, November 12. http://www.justicestrategies.org/publications/2010/ new-york-city-enforcement-immigration-detainers.

Sohoni, D., and T. W. P. Sohoni. 2013. "Perceptions of Immigrant Criminality: Crime and Social Boundaries." *Sociological Quarterly* 55: 49–71.

Stone, C., C. Van Horn, and C. Zukin. 2012. "Chasing the American Dream: Recent College Graduates and the Recession." *WorkTrends*, May. http://www.heldrich.rutgers.edu/sites/ default/files/products/uploads/Chasing_American_Dream_Report.pdf.

Stowell, J. I., M. S. Barton, S. F. Messner, and L. E. Raffalovich. 2013. "Addition by Subtraction? A Longitudinal Analysis of the Impact of Deportation Efforts on Violent Crime." *Law and Society Review* 47: 909–42.

Sweeney, M. A. 2010. "Fact or Fiction; The Legal Construction of Immigration Removal for Crimes." *Yale Journal of Regulation* 27: 47–89.

Urbina, M. G., ed. 2018. *Hispanics in the U.S. Criminal Justice System: Ethnicity, Ideology, and Social Control*. 2nd ed. Springfield, Ill.: Charles C Thomas.

Urbina, M. G., and S. E. Álvarez, eds. 2015. *Latino Police Officers in the United States: An Examination of Emerging Trends and Issues*. Springfield, Ill.: Charles C Thomas.

———. 2016. "Neoliberalism, Criminal Justice, and Latinos: The Contours of Neoliberal Economic Thought and Policy on Criminalization." *Latino Studies* 14: 33–58.

———. 2017. *Ethnicity and Criminal Justice in the Era of Mass Incarceration: A Critical Reader on the Latino Experience*. Springfield, Ill.: Charles C Thomas.

Wadsworth, T. 2010. "Is Immigration Responsible for the Crime Drop? An Assessment of the Influence of Immigration on Changes in Violent Crime Between 1990 and 2000." *Social Science Quarterly* 91: 531–53.

Wellman, N. 2017. "Straight from Nazi Playbook, Trump Publishes List of Alleged Criminal Immigrants." *Resistance Report*, March 20. http://resistancereport.com/news/straight-nazi-playbook-trump-publishes-list-alleged-criminal/.

Chapter 5

BUILDING AMERICA

Immigrant Labor and the U.S. Economy

RUTH GOMBERG-MUÑOZ

Everywhere immigrants have enriched and strengthened the
fabric of American life.

—JOHN F. KENNEDY

EVERY TUESDAY EVENING, a labor center on Chicago's South Side holds "open clinic" night. Workers begin arriving sometime after 5:00 p.m., usually in groups of twos and threes. Most are still in their work clothes—the heavy boots and Dickies jeans favored by those who do manual labor in the cold Chicago winter. By 6:00 p.m., some twenty men and women sit in the folding chairs that line the perimeter of the room. The discussion begins. One worker describes how he hurt his back on the construction site where he works as a bricklayer, and he worries that the construction company will not cover his medical expenses. Two women angrily recount verbal harassment by the manager of the laundromat where they work. Several workers complain that their employers owe them overtime or back wages. The center's organizers, themselves immigrant workers, take notes on each case, asking questions and preparing paperwork to submit to the National Labor Relations Board. Above their heads, a poster hangs on the wall. "Immigrant Rights Are Labor Rights," it reads.

Most of the workers here tell their stories in Spanish, and the neighborhood where the center is located, Pilsen, is predominantly Mexican. Three generations ago, Pilsen was a neighborhood of eastern European immigrants; in fact, it was immigrants from the Czech Republic who gave Pilsen its name. Before them, German and Irish immigrants had settled the area. Each generation of immigrant workers arrived in Pilsen for the same basic reason: they were attracted to the concentration of industry on Chicago's South Side and the promise of jobs that industry provides.

In the United States, many people believe that immigrants "take jobs" from Americans. This claim appears straightforward, but it actually rests on a host of assumptions:

that there is job competition between immigrant and native-born "American" workers, that immigrants exercise power over hiring decisions, and that access to scarce resources like jobs should be determined by workers' national origins. Additionally, there is yet a deeper ideology that undergirds this claim—that the U.S. economy is strong because of the efforts of "American" workers. Thus, when immigrants "take American jobs," they undermine those efforts, usurping resources that are the rightful legacy of native-born U.S. citizens.

The purpose of this chapter is to challenge that idea and explore how U.S. immigration policies have actively promoted and maintained a foreign-born labor force for more than two hundred years. This labor force has not been incidental to the strength of the U.S. economy, but critical to it, providing fundamental labor in agricultural, industrial, and service sectors throughout U.S. history. This chapter also shows that immigrant labor is not just any labor, but has historically provided a particular type of labor that responds to certain sectors of the U.S. economy—in particular, persistent demand for low-cost and flexible workers. Finally, this chapter shows that immigrant workers are not passive recipients of exploitative policies, but active participants in labor struggles that have profoundly shaped conditions of work in the United States and beyond.

SLAVERY AND INDUSTRY IN THE REPUBLIC'S FIRST CENTURY

When the United States became a sovereign nation-state in the latter decades of the eighteenth century, the ruling elites were largely descended from European immigrants who had arrived in the Western Hemisphere decades earlier. The early "founders" of the republic—men such as George Washington and Thomas Jefferson—were wealthy landowners whose plantations produced valuable export crops, such as tobacco, cotton, and grain. Of course, men like Washington and Jefferson did not tend these crops themselves. For that, they had slaves.

Indeed, the U.S. economy was built on the foundations of a "forced migration": the transatlantic slave trade. The slave trade brought more than half a million African slaves to U.S. shores, where they were sold to the earliest European settlers at Jamestown and, with their descendants, cultivated untold wealth for the colony and, thus, the empire.[1] In the years following U.S. independence, both the scope and scale of slavery expanded. In the eight decades from the American Revolution (1765–83) to the Civil War (1861–65), the number of slaves in the United States increased five times over, until, by the outbreak of the Civil War, the U.S. South was home to some four million slaves (Baptist 2014). As the practice grew, so did its significance to a modernizing U.S. economy: far from being incidental, chattel slavery was a linchpin of U.S. development into a wealthy, industrialized, capitalist nation in the nineteenth century (Baptist 2014).

While slavery was the largest, most brutal, and longest-lasting system of unpaid, compulsory labor in the United States, it was not the only one. Many early European immigrants were indentured servants, who worked for a contracted period in exchange for their passage to the United States. By the Revolutionary period (1764–89), as many as half of newly arriving immigrants from England and Scotland were indentured servants (Glenn 2002). After the contracted period, European indentured servants were "freed" to become craftspeople or land owners and, eventually, U.S. citizens—entitlements that were largely denied to both slaves and free blacks until nearly a century later.

In the early decades of the nineteenth century, the United States embarked on a massive territorial expansion, breaking the boundaries of the Eastern Seaboard to seize what is now the U.S. Midwest by 1803 and, with the invasion and conquest of Mexican territories, the U.S. West and Southwest by midcentury. This geographic expansion, accompanied by rapid industrial development following the Civil War, transformed the socioeconomic landscape of the United States and greatly increased the need for industrial and agricultural workers in the latter half of the nineteenth century.

Fueled by steel, oil, iron, coal, cotton, and livestock production, post–Civil War industry underwent an "economic explosion" (Glenn 2002; Wyman 1996, 48) with voracious labor needs. By the end of the nineteenth century, Europeans were arriving by the millions to work in steel mills, coal mines, textile mills, slaughterhouses, and garment factories, and they were building the urban infrastructure of growing cities such as New York, Philadelphia, Chicago, and San Francisco (Wyman 1996). It would be hard to overestimate the significance of European immigrants to the spectacular growth of U.S. industry in this period. The "Gilded Age" (1870s–1900) set the stage for future fortunes for steel, auto, and oil magnates such as Andrew Carnegie, Henry Ford, and John D. Rockefeller, while the immigrant smelters, machinists, and miners who made such wealth possible lived in deplorable conditions in crowded urban slums.

In the West, Chinese indentured servants were brought to California by the thousands to work in the mines and build the railroad tracks that would eventually connect East with West (Glenn 2002). However, when the United States experienced an economic downturn in the 1870s, these workers were targeted for vigilante violence (Chacon and Davis 2006) and became subject to the first restrictive immigration policy in the United States: the 1882 Chinese Exclusion Act. The Chinese Exclusion Act both barred the immigration of Chinese laborers and made those who were already in the United States "racially ineligible" for U.S. citizenship. The persecution of Chinese workers quickly spread to include Japanese landowners and Filipino farmworkers, and in 1917 the Asian Exclusion Act extended the bar on immigration to all Asians, from China west to Afghanistan (Glenn 2002). The Immigration Act of 1917 also provided for the importation of temporary workers who might otherwise be denied the right to live and work in the United States (Griffith 2006).

CHANGING THE FACE OF IMMIGRANT LABOR

In spite of early anti-immigrant sentiment directed mostly at Irish, German, and Scandinavian immigrants, and bars on entry for Chinese workers, the United States did not have an immigration system per se until the early twentieth century. Before then, there was no numerical restriction on immigration, although new arrivals were personally inspected at Ellis and Angel Islands and could be denied entry for things like mental and physical "deficiency" (Gould 1981). Still, rates of exclusion of arriving immigrants were very low—only about 1 percent of the 25 million new immigrants who arrived between 1880 and World War I (1914–18) were turned away (Ngai 2004).

By the 1920s, though, the arrival of millions of working-poor immigrants from southern and eastern Europe was stirring great anxiety among U.S. policy makers. This anxiety led to the first general immigration policy in the United States. At the time, congressional debates on immigration were guided by the *ideology of eugenics*, which attributed human social and behavioral differences to genetic traits and grouped people into distinct "races" that could be hierarchically ordered from superior to inferior (Gould 1981). Eugenicists found that new immigrants from Italy, Poland, Hungary, and Russia were "defective stock" and unalterably inferior to the "Nordic races" of northern and western Europe (Gould 1981). Worse, their innate "feeble-mindedness" led to high rates of criminality and weak morality, culminating in dangerously high fertility levels likely to be mixed with "Negro" blood (Chávez 2013; Gould 1981). Congressman Albert Johnson, chair of the House Immigration Committee and head of the Eugenics Research Association, warned his congressional colleagues that "inassimilable . . . filthy, un-American, and often dangerous" Jews would overrun the United States if their immigration remained unchecked (Daniels and Graham 2001, 20).

Johnson's solution to this immigration "problem" was a bill that he chiefly authored: the Johnson-Reed Act of 1924. The 1924 act was a landmark immigration bill that placed widespread restrictions on U.S. immigration for the first time. The act restricted annual visa allotments to 2 percent of the "national origins" of the U.S. population of 1890, based on that year's census data (Ngai 2004). The *national origins quota system was designed to create immigration patterns that more closely reproduced the desired racial composition of the United States*, and the census data were manipulated accordingly. The 1890, and not 1920, census was selected because it preceded the height of immigration from southern and eastern Europe. Further, nonwhite populations—including "immigrants from the New World and their descendants [Latin Americans]; any Asians or their descendants; the descendants of 'slave immigrants' [African Americans]; and the descendants of 'American aborigines' [Native Americans]"—were omitted from the data altogether (Daniels and Graham 2001, 22). The end result of the 1924 act was that 84 percent of all U.S. immigrant visas were granted to northern and western Europeans, and racial bars on immigration and citizenship for Asians were left intact (Ngai 2004).

MIGRATION FROM THE SOUTH

By the 1920s industrial development had become more tied to technological advance, and U.S. industries were less reliant on a mass immigrant labor force from Europe (Ngai 2004). At the same time, commercial agriculture in the U.S. West and Southwest was poised for growth, buoyed by the invention of the refrigerated railcar and irrigation technologies (Ngai 2004). However, prohibitions on Asian immigration had created a shortage of agricultural labor, leading U.S. growers to turn to Mexican workers to fill their labor needs (Massey 2009).

Notably, Latin Americans were exempted from numerical restrictions under the 1924 act in order to satisfy demands for their labor in the U.S. Southwest (Gutiérrez 1995; Ngai 2004). Because Latin Americans were neither guaranteed visas by the 1924 act nor restricted by quotas, their migration could be promoted during periods of high labor demand, such as the harvest season, then restricted when it was no longer needed. To rationalize this practice, Mexicans were characterized as a labor force whose racial characteristics made them ideally suited for arduous and low-paying agricultural work (Gutiérrez 1995; Pedraza and Rumbaut 1996). Additionally, while the 1924 act established the U.S. Border Patrol as a small unit of the Bureau of Immigration, itself part of the Department of Labor, the function of the Border Patrol was not to stop migration but to "regulate" the migration of Mexican workers according to seasonal and periodic labor demands (De Genova and Ramos-Zayas 2003; Ngai 2004).

To tap Mexico's labor reserve, recruiters traveled deep into the heart of Mexico's populated north-central valleys, where they enlisted Mexicans to work in agriculture, construction, and industry across the U.S. Southwest and in cities such as Chicago, Cleveland, and Pittsburgh (De Genova and Ramos-Zayas 2003). The Mexican-born population in the United States, approximately 68,000 people in 1880, grew by about 10,000 between 1880 and 1890, and then surged by 50,000 over the following decade (Gutiérrez 1995). Between 1900 and 1910, over 100,000 Mexican migrants arrived in the United States to work in a variety of U.S. industries, including agriculture, mining, railroad construction, and auto and steel manufacture (Gutiérrez 1995). By the 1920s, Mexican workers (both migrants and Mexican Americans) made up as much as 75 percent of the agricultural workforce in California and unskilled construction workforce in Texas (Gutiérrez 1995).

In the 1930s, the U.S. economy plunged into the Great Depression (1929–39). The Depression virtually immobilized industrial growth and dried up jobs in all sectors of the U.S. economy. As a result, migration from Mexico came to a virtual halt, and Mexicans were being rounded up and deported from the U.S. Southwest en masse. During the Great Depression, some 500,000 people of Mexican descent were deported from the United States, as many as half of whom were native-born U.S. citizens (Daniels and Graham 2001).

When the United States entered World War II (1941–45), the U.S. economy found itself once again experiencing a labor shortage. Rapidly, U.S. involvement in the war changed domestic labor needs in at least two ways: first, it pulled working-age white men from factories and fields to place them in the ranks of soldiers fighting the war; and second, it increased the demand for production of war materials. That is, the war reduced the U.S. labor force at the same time that it increased the demand for labor. To expand the labor supply, three main streams of workers were recruited into the U.S. labor force in larger numbers. The first consisted of married white women (impoverished, nonwhite, and immigrant women were already deeply integrated in the U.S. workforce) who were called on to support the war effort abroad by contributing to industrial production at home (Kossoudji and Dresser 1992). The second stream consisted of southern blacks, mainly impoverished tenant farmers and sharecroppers, who were recruited to industrial work in northern cities such as New York, Philadelphia, Detroit, Chicago, Los Angeles, and the Bay Area (Wilkerson 2010). While this "great migration" of African Americans did not involve crossing international borders, these workers experienced significant dislocation and encountered myriad racial, cultural, and economic boundaries to well-being in their northern homes. The third labor stream involved millions of Mexican workers, and smaller but significant numbers of Filipinos and Central Americans, who were recruited to work in the agricultural fields of the U.S. Southwest, where they harvested the food that would sustain industrial workers and the families of soldiers abroad. To ensure an unhindered labor supply, the United States and Mexico entered into a binational treaty in 1942 that has come to be known as the "Bracero Program." The Bracero Program was a contract-labor, or "guest worker," program through which some five million Mexican nationals worked in the United States on a temporary basis, mostly in agriculture, construction, and railroad maintenance (Ngai 2004). Employers who participated in the program were obligated to provide specified wages and housing for Bracero workers. In exchange, braceros could not negotiate for higher wages or better conditions, nor could they change employers. Braceros were also required to leave the United States when their contract ended. The program was initially conceived as an emergency wartime measure, but it proved so popular with U.S. growers that it was extended a number of times before it was ended in 1964, twenty-two years after it began.

The Bracero Program was, and continues to be, fraught with controversy. The availability of Bracero workers gave U.S. growers leverage over Filipino and Mexican American agricultural workers who were organizing for higher wages and better working conditions at the time (Gutiérrez 1995). Braceros themselves were subject to widespread wage theft, mistreatment, substandard food and housing, and dangerous working conditions (Ngai 2004). Further, while the Bracero Program was devised as an alternative to large-scale undocumented migration, the program actually exacerbated undocumented migration, both at the time and in the decades that followed. Indeed, it is estimated that, for every bracero, as many as four Mexican workers entered outside of the auspices of the program, as employers and workers sought to evade its constraints (De Genova and Ramos Zayas 2003). In response, the United States launched a high-profile mass deportation campaign in 1954, called "Operation Wetback." The *motive of Operation Wetback was not to reduce Mexican migration but to funnel it through the Bracero Program*, creating pressure on the Mexican government to extend the program and giving the appearance to the U.S. public that the border was "under control." In a tag-team effort, immigration agents arrested undocumented workers and transported them across the border to Mexico, where Department of Labor officials were waiting to process the deportees and send them back to work as braceros (Gutiérrez 1995: Massey, Durand, and Malone 2002). In all, the Bracero Program encouraged the migration of millions of Mexican workers to the United States, establishing networks between jobs in the United States and workers in Mexico that allowed migratory flows to become self-sustaining in the decades to come (Massey, Durand, and Malone 2002).

Like Mexican workers, Filipinos had been exempted from the restrictions on immigration established by the 1924 act. This is because the Philippines was a colony of the United States until 1935, and Filipinos, as U.S. nationals, were not subject to the jurisdiction of U.S. immigration laws at the time (Ngai 2004). Filipinos were recruited as a strikebreaking sugarcane labor force in Hawaii, and during World War I they were sought for work on the U.S. mainland in agriculture, shipyards, canneries, and hotels and restaurants. However, amid racially fueled hysteria at the presence of a predominantly male Filipino workforce, some two thousand Filipino workers were "repatriated" to the Philippines following decolonization of the islands in 1935 (Ngai 2004). Thus, levels of Filipino immigration did not reach those of their Mexican counterparts.

The Bracero Program ended in 1964, and in 1965 the U.S. Congress passed the Immigration and Nationality Act (INA) of 1965. The 1965 INA equalized the national origins quota system so that every country in the world would be allotted the same number of visas. It also eliminated remaining racial bars to immigration and citizenship and, instead, established a preference system that gave priority to family reunification and U.S. labor needs. However, although it was immigration policy, the 1965 INA was considered an extension of civil rights policies that were being enacted at the time (Lee 1999).

Still, the 1965 INA altered the face of U.S. immigration yet again. For the first time in fifty years, Asians could immigrate to the United States, and immigration from the continent quadrupled between 1960 and 1980, as Asians took advantage of their new ability to get U.S. visas primarily through employment programs (Glenn 2002; Ngai 2004). African immigration also increased, but it remained a very small proportion of the total (Daniels and Graham 2001). While it is often claimed (e.g., Daniels and Graham 2001) that Mexican immigration dramatically increased following 1965, calculations of Mexican immigration rarely include the cyclical but long-standing migration of millions of braceros between 1942 and 1964. If one includes bracero workers in historical immigration trends, immigration enforcement substantially leveled the rate of Mexican immigration over time and changed the "dramatic" increase to a more modest one (Massey, Durand, and Malone 2002).

UNDOCUMENTED WORKERS

In spite of the economic and social ties formed during the Bracero Program, the 1965 INA did not expand the availability of visas for Latin Americans, but reduced it. This is because the INA put caps on migration from Mexico and other Latin American nations for the first time ever—just one year after the Bracero Program ended. Between 1965 and 1980, the number of visas available to Latin Americans was reduced from an unlimited number to just twenty thousand per country per year (Glenn 2002). These restrictions did not ultimately curb the migration of Latin Americans to the United States, but it did make it far more difficult for them to migrate legally (De Genova 2005; Massey 2009).

In the decades following the 1965 INA, though, the number of people who live and work in the United States without legal authorization has grown sharply. The undocumented population grew from about 500,000 people in the 1960s, to two million by 1980, then three million by 1990. Fueled by economic crises in Mexico and elsewhere, the undocumented population soared to a high of some twelve million people by 2005 (Passel 1986; Passel and Cohn 2009). Reportedly, about 75 percent of the U.S.

undocumented population is of Latin American origin, with Mexicans composing the highest share, at about 59 percent of the total (Passel and Cohn 2009). The rise in the U.S. undocumented population is due to a combination of factors, including blocked avenues to legal immigration and status adjustment, economic crises in Latin America, and persistent demand for Mexican labor in the United States (Gomberg-Muñoz 2015; Massey 2009).

Representing a turning point in the history of immigration, since the 1980s U.S. immigration policies have increasingly been aimed at undocumented workers. In 1986, the Immigration Reform and Control Act (IRCA) made the employment of undocumented workers illegal for the first time, though a loophole in the law exempts employers from prosecution unless it can be proven that they were "aware" of their employees' unlawful status. IRCA also doubled the Border Patrol and included an amnesty program through which nearly three million undocumented people legalized their status (Calavita 1994). A decade later, in 1996, Congress passed the Illegal Immigration Reform and Immigrant Responsibility Act (IIRAIRA), which is widely considered to be the most punitive U.S. immigration bill to date. The IIRAIRA put measures in place that blocked many undocumented people from ever changing their immigration status, and it facilitated the deportation of lawful permanent residents (Coutin 2007). The 1990s also marked a major shift toward militarization of the U.S.-Mexico border. Throughout the 1990s, the U.S. Border Patrol built miles of steel fencing, new roads, and lighting along the border that was guarded with hundreds of new agents and high-tech detection systems (Meyers 2005).

The timing of IIRAIRA and U.S. border militarization is especially relevant because the 1990s also ushered in a proliferation of free-trade agreements between the United States and Mexico. These agreements, such as GATT (entered into by Mexico in 1986) and NAFTA (1994), lifted restrictions on the movement of capital, goods, money, and businesses at the same time that IIRAIRA and border "operations" restricted the movement of Mexican migrant workers (Massey, Durand, and Malone 2002). Free-trade agreements devastated the working and living conditions of many Mexicans, as cheap, mass-produced U.S. grains and goods flooded Mexican markets, pushing millions of farmers off of their land and undermining the ability of Mexican craftspeople to sell their wares. The Mexican economy contracted in the 1980s and again, following NAFTA's passage, in the 1990s; and the Mexican peso fell to a fraction of its pre-1970 value, while unemployment, debt, and crime all rose precipitously (Greider 1997). After a hundred years of migration, Mexican workers faced historic restrictions on their movement at the very same time that free-trade agreements undermined their ability to stay home and make a living as workers, farmers, and small business owners. Subsequently, Mexican migration continued, but with legal avenues restricted, it became ever more characterized as "illegal."

In effect, in spite of punitive immigration policies, undocumented labor continues to be an important component of the U.S. economy. Comparing the rate of people in the labor force, more undocumented men are in the labor force than either U.S. citizens or lawful immigrants; and some 94 percent of undocumented men are working or seeking work, compared with 85 percent of legal immigrant men and 83 percent of U.S.-born men (Passel and Cohn 2009). Therefore, there is broad recognition that undocumented migration is primarily a labor migration, and that most undocumented people come to the United States to work, and thus widespread employment of undocumented workers is tacitly, if not overtly, permitted across the United States.

Undocumented workers are *critical* to the agricultural labor force: at least one in four U.S. farmworkers is undocumented (Passel and Cohn 2009). The low wages earned by agricultural and processing plant workers drive down prices on a wide range of basic foodstuffs, from produce to meat to dairy products (Holmes 2013; Striffler 2005). In urban areas of the United States, undocumented workers increasingly labor in an expanding low-end service economy, where they attend to middle-class industries such as hospitality, maintenance, and construction (Sassen 1988; Zlolniski 2006). Undocumented workers compose over 10 percent of the U.S. workforce in low-end service industries such as groundskeeping and building maintenance (19 percent), construction (17 percent), and food preparation and service (12 percent) (Passel 2006; Passel and Cohn 2009). While rates of undocumented women's participation in the formal economy are comparatively low (often because they are raising children), women are more likely to be doing informal work as live-in domestics, childcare providers, housecleaners, and food vendors (Chang 2000; Hondagneu-Sotelo 2007). Ironically, in spite of their elevated participation in the labor force, undocumented workers are more likely to live in poverty than U.S. citizens and are particularly vulnerable to exploitative working relations, poor and dangerous working conditions, and economic instability (De Genova and Ramos-Zayas 2003; Kochhar 2005; Mehta et al. 2002).

In all, the labor of undocumented workers benefits several sectors of the U.S. economy. Most obviously, it enhances the profit margin of employers who pay their undocumented employees low wages and, typically, also deny them health insurance, overtime wages, workers' compensation benefits, and unemployment benefits (Fussell 2011; Mehta et al. 2002). Because of their legal vulnerability, undocumented workers have little recourse against exploitative employers and, with no social safety nets, may even work "extra hard" to give themselves a competitive edge over other workers (Gomberg-Muñoz 2010; Waldinger and Lichter 2003). The firms that employ undocumented workers lobby legislators to maintain their access to an undocumented labor force. Even as immigration enforcement has dramatically intensified over the past several decades, workplace enforcement declined drastically during the 1990s and early 2000s (Porter 2006; see also Preston 2006). Additionally, recent workplace enforcement measures, such as E-Verify, appear to increase employers' control over undocumented workers without necessarily compromising their access to a low-paid workforce (Gomberg-Muñoz and Nussbaum-Barberena 2011).

Undocumented workers also pay billions of dollars into tax coffers for benefits that they typically cannot claim. Undocumented workers can pay income taxes in one of two ways: either by using the Social Security number (SSN) of a lawful U.S. worker or by obtaining an Individual Taxpayer Identification Number (ITIN), which is issued by the Social Security Administration to people who are ineligible for a SSN. A 2014 report by the Institute on Taxation and Economic Policy found that undocumented people paid nearly $12 billion in federal, state, and local taxes in 2012 alone, at an average effective tax rate of 8 percent, compared to the effective tax rate of 5.4 percent paid by the top 1 percent of U.S. taxpayers (Gardner, Johnson, and Wiehe 2015; see also Lipman 2006). In spite of these contributions, undocumented workers are ineligible for Social Security, Medicare, health care under the Affordable Care Act, unemployment benefits, federal housing programs, food stamps, Supplemental Security Income, Temporary Assistance for Needy Families, most Medicaid services, or the Earned Income Tax Credit. In fact, the only public services that undocumented people are eligible to use are emergency medical care under the Medicaid system and elementary and secondary public education.

As undocumented workers prop up the U.S. economy and subsidize middle-class lifestyles with artificially low prices on food, childcare, and other services, their immigration status largely blocks their path to higher education and better paying employment (Chávez 2013; Urbina and Wright 2016). That is, the current immigration system does not seem to prevent the migration of low-paid workers so much as it keeps certain workers low paid by foreclosing their possibilities for legal immigration and any opportunities for upward mobility that legality affords.

OTHER SOURCES OF FLEXIBLE LABOR

In addition to being generally low paid, undocumented labor offers another advantage to U.S. employers: it is considered "flexible," available to be called up and then laid off at a moment's notice. The availability of a flexible workforce is especially important in industries with seasonal or fluctuating labor needs, such as agriculture, construction, and tourism, and in certain "high-end" service industries, such as consulting and project-based work. A variety of strategies creates "flexibility" among the labor force, including piece-rate pay, subcontracting, adjuncting, and temporary work (Griffith 2006; Zlolniski 2006). Indeed, as U.S. policies toward undocumented workers have become more draconian, new categories of temporary visas for migrant agricultural workers (H2-A), seasonal nonagricultural workers (H2-B), and high-skill workers (H1-B) have been created and, in some cases, expanded (Griffith 2006; Leiden and Neal 1990).

The temporary importation of agricultural workers is rooted in the Bracero period and continues today—it is the longest-running labor importation program in U.S. history (Griffith 2006). Each year, more than a hundred thousand temporary workers shore up U.S. agriculture and food-processing industries, most of them migrant workers from Mexico and the West Indies (Griffith 2006). At the other end of the labor market, hundreds of thousands of temporary workers, mostly from India, China, Canada, the Philippines, and South Korea, fill "high skill" positions in information technology, science, and medicine (Banerjee 2010; Batalova 2010). Whether they are "high" or "low" skilled, today's temporary migrant workers share many of the vulnerabilities of their Bracero-era counterparts, including having their legal status tied to a particular employer, vulnerability to exploitative pay and working conditions, and a tenuous status that renders their work situations highly unpredictable and insecure over the long term. Thus, although temporary visa holders escape the criminalization that targets the undocumented, they remain "documented but marginalized" in their U.S. jobs (Banerjee 2010).

As U.S. immigration policies have become increasingly restrictive and punitive, more people have been deported from the United States than ever before. For most of the twentieth century, deportation rates fluctuated between 10,000 and 20,000 per year, reaching highs of 30,000 to 36,000 during the sweeps of the Great Depression (1924) and Operation Wetback (1954), based on figures from the U.S. Department of Homeland Security (2013). In 1997, one year after passage of IIRAIRA, deportation rates reached more than 100,000 for the first time, and they have gone up fairly steadily ever since. Between 1997 and 2012 alone, more than 4.2 million people, the overwhelming majority of them men of color, were deported from the United States—more than double the total number of all prior deportations in the history of the United States (Golash-Boza and Hondagneu-Sotelo 2013). The mass deportation of working-class men has led some scholars to conclude that their labor has been made "redundant and disposable" by declining labor needs (Golash-Boza 2015; Golash-Boza and Hondagneu-Sotelo 2013).

However, there is also evidence that detained and deported workers continue to provide valuable labor to sectors of the U.S. economy. Currently, some 34,000 immigrants are held in detention every day in the United States, two-thirds of them in privately owned detention camps that generate millions of dollars in profit annually (Selway and Newkirk 2013). In these centers, tens of thousands of detained immigrants continue to work, providing essential labor to the centers' operations for $1 a day or less. In 2013, more than 60,000 immigrants worked while they were detained, making the centers, together, the single largest employer of undocumented workers in the nation (Urbina 2014; Urbina and Álvarez 2017).

In effect, as documented by Urbina and Peña in "Policing Borders: Immigration, Criminalization, and Militarization in the Era of Social Control Profitability" (2018) and Urbina and Álvarez in "Neoliberalism, Criminal Justice, and Latinos: The Contours of Neoliberal Economic Thought and Policy on Criminalization" (2016), the "profitability" of prisons, including immigration facilities, has been serving as a driving force for correctional expansion (state and federal prisons) and, in the case of immigrants, incarcerating more immigrants and keeping them incarcerated for longer periods of time. Broadly, "with great profits to be made in human capital, an unspoken governmental strategy is to carefully monitor the 'investment potential' of human capital in unemployed people and inmates versus the investment potential of human capital in criminal justice personnel and services provided." But this neglects that "unemployment leads to more poverty, which in turn leads to more property crime, corruption, white-collar crime and subsequently imprisonment, while at the same time securing economic opportunity and stability for criminal justice personnel who are part of the voting class" (Urbina and Álvarez 2016, 40–41). Urbina and Álvarez (2016, 50) assert that "the overrepresentation of Latinos in jail, prison, on probation or parole is not a grave failure" of the neoliberal state, "but a deliberate feature of neoliberal penalty, achieving what it was designed to accomplish, human profitability or, more precisely, ethnic profitability." In exploiting the "benefits and profit of punitive criminal justice policies," over $260 billion (2010 annual criminal justice direct expenditures), the notion of failure is "used as a strategic political argument for even more punitive policies" (Urbina and Álvarez 2016, 42). Already in April 2017, the Trump administration awarded its first federal contract for a new 1,000-bed immigrant detention center to be built outside Houston, Texas. The $110 million contract was given to GEO Group, a private prison company that operates 143 facilities around the world, which according to GEO's news release will "generate approximately $44 million in annualized revenues and returns on investment."

Additionally, as the scale of U.S. deportations has increased, so too has the number of workers who find employment in U.S.-owned businesses following deportation. Many deportees are longtime U.S. residents with English-language fluency and U.S. cultural capital; thus, these workers offer valuable skills for companies, such as call centers, that have been outsourced from the United States but continue to serve a U.S. customer base (Rivas 2014; Skipper 2006). The mass deportation of longtime U.S. residents effectively allows offshored U.S. companies to tap into a labor force that has all the cultural capital of U.S. workers, but works at a fraction of the price (Rodkey 2016; see also Golash-Boza 2015).

IMMIGRANT RIGHTS ARE WORKER RIGHTS

As this history demonstrates, immigrant workers in the United States are especially vulnerable to exploitative labor practices. This vulnerability is not a given, but is promoted by immigration and citizenship policies that disempower migrant workers and deny them certain rights. Further, while the consequences of these practices are especially harmful for immigrants, they can also hurt nonimmigrant workers by undermining unionization efforts, as the Bracero Program did, and suppressing overall wages. Thus, it is not surprising that many people, on both the political "right" and "left," call for restricting immigration in order to boost job prospects and wages for "American" workers. However, calls to restrict immigration for the benefit of U.S. workers not only legitimizes the idea that national origin should determine access to work, it also disregards the potential of immigrant workers to advance labor rights more broadly. In effect, throughout U.S. history, immigrant workers have deeply shaped the nature of work, and many of the conditions that workers now take for granted, including the eight-hour workday and workplace safety regulations, are the result of protracted struggles led by immigrant workers.

Therefore, in this last section, I present some of the best-known examples of immigrant-led labor struggles in U.S. history. Chicago in the late nineteenth century was a burgeoning industrial city and home to tens of thousands of immigrant workers from Germany, the Czech Republic, Ireland, and Mexico, among many other places. Industrial workers organized by the Federation of Organized Trades and Labor Unions had been actively campaigning for better working conditions, higher wages, and a limit to the workday for several years when they called for a general strike and an eight-hour workday on May 1, 1886. Workers in cities across the United States walked off their job sites, including an estimated thirty to forty thousand workers in Chicago. When police killed two Chicago strikers, a mass rally was held in Haymarket Square the following day. Accounts of the Haymarket Rally vary widely, but what is known is that a bomb was thrown at police late in the evening, killing one officer. Gunfire was exchanged, and an unknown number of protesters were killed, along with at least seven police officers. Seven organizers of the rally, five of them German, were tried and convicted of accessory to murder, and four were subsequently executed. While the persecution of the Haymarket organizers was a temporary blow to labor organizing efforts, the struggle for the eight-hour work day persisted, led by Chicago immigrant workers and embraced by workers in cities all over the world (Adelman et al. 2017). In honor of the Haymarket organizers, the 1st of May, or May Day, has become an internationally recognized day of worker solidarity and protest. May Day continues to be celebrated today, and it took on new significance in Chicago during a record-breaking rally for immigrant rights on May 1, 2006.

Another well-known mobilization of urban immigrant workers took place in 1909 and 1910 in New York City, the heart of the U.S. garment industry at the time. Young women from Jewish and Italian families formed the backbone of a low-paid shirtwaist labor force, and they toiled under oppressive conditions for sixty or more hours per week. In 1909, women at the Triangle Shirtwaist factory voted to organize as part of the United Hebrew Trades and went on strike when the company retaliated by firing the vote organizers. The initial strike lasted for five weeks, during which time picketers were threatened and beaten by men the company sent to intimidate the mostly female strikers. In response, organizers called for a general strike of New York City shirtwaist workers. Some twenty thousand walked off their jobs, and hundreds of women strikers were beaten and jailed, inspiring broad sympathy and eventually forcing the company to negotiate with the workers. As the first major successful labor struggle of women workers in the United States, the New York shirtwaist strike marked a turning point in organizing efforts among immigrant industrial workers in cities throughout the North.

The rising population of undocumented workers since the 1970s has led to disagreement among labor organizers about whether and how to organize undocumented immigrants. Some organizers have considered undocumented workers "unorganizable" due to their heightened vulnerability to exploitation and deportation (Gutiérrez 1995). Others have embraced the call to organize undocumented workers, and some, such as the Service Employees International Union (SEIU) and UNITE HERE, have been especially active in recruiting and organizing undocumented workers, successfully waging campaigns for better wages and conditions for predominantly immigrant workforces. One such high-profile effort was SEIU's Justice for Janitors campaign that mobilized workers in several U.S. cities in a successful fight against the decline in wages and working conditions in the 1980s and 1990s (Zlolniski 2006). Undocumented immigrants themselves are increasingly among the vanguard of mass workers' mobilizations. For example, in 2006, proposed legislation targeting undocumented immigrants galvanized record-breaking marches in support of immigrant rights. Marchers explicitly linked the struggle for immigrant rights with labor rights by holding the march on May Day, chanting the United Farm Workers slogan "Si Se Puede!" and invoking their contribution to the U.S. economy as workers to make claims for legal rights as immigrants.

The organizers at the labor center in Pilsen draw on this history every Tuesday as they help immigrant workers respond to workplace abuses. In addition to providing practical assistance with filing claims with the National Labor Relations Board, center organizers also hold adult education workshops, in which they discuss immigrant labor history in the United States and the role of immigrant workers in global capitalism. Further, every May 1, center organizers and clients join hundreds of other workers' centers, immigrant organizations, and church groups to celebrate the legacy of immigrant workers in the United States and carry on the struggle to labor with dignity, regardless of immigration status.

CONCLUSION

This chapter has shown that the U.S. economy is not strong in spite of immigration, but because of it. Yet, since the colonial period, immigrants have been excluded from full rights and participation in the U.S. nation-state and funneled into low-paid and insecure work. Though often socially degraded, such work forms the backbone of the U.S. economy and has helped make modern capitalism both possible and profitable. Still, immigrant labor history in the United States is not a tale of celebration, but of contestation. The strength of the U.S. economy comes at a price, one underwritten by the underpaid and politically constrained labor of immigrants and nonimmigrants alike. As policies seek to both guarantee and control their labor, workers push back, organizing to demand higher wages and better working conditions. In the current period, those demands increasingly include immigration reform that would expand the rights of undocumented workers and enable them to work and organize with less fear and retaliation. As they advocate for immigration reform, today's migrant workers draw on a *legacy* of immigrant labor more than two centuries old—as old as the United States itself.

NOTE

1. The importance of slavery to the U.S. economy is often excluded from U.S. immigration histories, and understandably so, since by the nineteenth century, most slaves were neither "immigrants" nor "forced migrants," but born in the United States. Nevertheless, I include slave laborers here because, if not exactly immigrants, neither were slaves considered "Americans"; even free blacks were denied U.S. citizenship until passage of the Fourteenth Amendment to the U.S. Constitution. Their case illustrates not only the dependence of the U.S. economy on workers who were not considered Americans, but also how U.S. citizenship policies have been used to deny rights and subordinate specific groups of U.S. workers.

REFERENCES

Adelman, R., L. Reid, G. Markle, S. Weiss, and C. Jaret. 2017. "Urban Crime Rates and the Changing Face of Immigration: Evidence Across Four Decades." *Journal of Ethnicity in Criminal Justice* 15: 52–77.

Banerjee, P. 2010. "Transnational Subcontracting, Indian IT Workers, and the U.S. Visa System." *Women's Studies Quarterly* 38: 89–111.

Baptist, E. 2014. *The Half Has Never Been Told: Slavery and the Making of American Capitalism.* New York: Basic Books.

Batalova, J. 2010. "H-1B Temporary Skilled Worker Program." *Migration Policy Institute*. http://www.migrationpolicy.org/article/h-1b-temporary-skilled-worker-program.

Calavita, K. 1994. "U.S. Immigration and Policy Responses: The Limits of Legislation." In *Controlling Immigration*, edited by W. Cornelius, P. Martin, and J. Hollifield, 55–82. Stanford, Calif.: Stanford University Press.

Chacon, J., and M. Davis. 2006. *No One Is Illegal: Fighting Racism and State Violence on the U.S.-Mexico Border*. Chicago: Haymarket Books.

Chang, G. 2000. *Disposable Domestics: Immigrant Women Workers in the Global Economy*. Boston: South End Press.

Chávez, L. R. 2013. *The Latino Threat: Constructing Immigrants, Citizens, and the Nation*. Stanford, Calif.: Stanford University Press.

Coutin, S. 2007. *Nation of Emigrants: Shifting Boundaries of Citizenship in El Salvador and the United States*. Ithaca, N.Y.: Cornell University Press.

Daniels, R., and O. L. Graham. 2001. *Debating American Immigration, 1882–Present*. New York: Rowman and Littlefield.

De Genova, N. 2005. *Working the Boundaries: Race, Space, and "Illegality" in Mexican Chicago*. Durham, N.C.: Duke University Press.

De Genova, N., and A. Y. Ramos-Zayas. 2003. *Latino Crossings: Mexicans, Puerto Ricans, and the Politics of Race and Citizenship*. New York: Routledge.

Fussell, E. 2011. "The Deportation Threat Dynamic and Victimization of Latino Migrants: Wage Theft and Robbery. *Sociological Quarterly* 52: 593–615.

Gardner, M., S. Johnson, and M. Wiehe. 2015. *Undocumented Immigrants' State and Local Tax Contributions*. Washington, D.C.: Institute on Taxation and Economic Policy.

Glenn, E. N. 2002. *Unequal Freedom: How Race and Gender Shaped American Citizenship and Labor*. Cambridge, Mass.: Harvard University Press.

Golash-Boza, T. M. 2015. *Deported: Policing Immigrants, Disposable Labor, and Global Capitalism*. New York: New York University Press.

Golash-Boza, T. M., and P. Hondagneu-Sotelo. 2013. "Latino Immigrant Men and the Deportation Crisis: A Gendered Racial Removal Program." *Latino Studies* 11: 271–92.

Gomberg-Muñoz, R. 2010. "Willing to Work: Agency and Vulnerability in an Undocumented Immigrant Network." *American Anthropologist* 112: 295–307.

———. 2015. "The Punishment/El Castigo: Undocumented Latinos and U.S. Immigration Processing." *Journal of Ethnic and Migration Studies* 41: 1–18.

Gomberg-Muñoz, R., and L. Nussbaum-Barberena. 2011. "Is Immigration Policy Labor Policy? Immigration Enforcement, Undocumented Labor, and the State." *Human Organization* 70: 366–75.

Gould, S. 1981. *The Mismeasure of Man*. New York: W. W. Norton.

Greider, W. 1997. *One World, Ready or Not: The Manic Logic of Global Capitalism*. New York: Simon and Schuster.

Griffith, D. 2006. *American Guestworkers: Jamaicans and Mexicans in the U.S. Labor Market.* University Park: Pennsylvania State University Press.

Gutiérrez, D. 1995. *Walls and Mirrors: Mexican Americans, Mexican Immigrants, and the Politics of Ethnicity.* Berkeley: University of California Press.

Holmes, S. 2013. *Fresh Fruit, Broken Bodies: Migrant Farmworkers in the United States.* Berkeley: University of California Press.

Hondagneu-Sotelo, P. 2007. *Doméstica: Immigrant Workers Cleaning and Caring in the Shadows of Affluence.* Berkeley: University of California Press.

Kochhar, R. 2005. "Survey of Mexican Migrants, Part Three: The Economic Transition to America." Washington, D.C.: Pew Hispanic Center. http://pewhispanic.org/reports/report.php?ReportID=58.

Kossoudji, S., and L. Dresser. 1992. "Working Class Rosies: Women Industrial Workers During World War II." *Journal of Economic History* 52: 431–46.

Lee, E. 1999. "American Gatekeeping: Race and Immigration Law in the Twentieth Century." In *Not Just Black and White: Historical and Contemporary Perspectives on Immigration, Race, and Ethnicity in the United States,* edited by N. Foner and G. Fredrickson, 119–44. New York: Russell Sage Foundation.

Leiden, W., and D. Neal. 1990. "Highlights of the U.S. Immigration Act of 1990." *Fordham International Law Journal* 14: 328–39.

Lipman, F. 2006. "The Taxation of Undocumented Immigrants: Separate, Unequal, and Without Representation." *Harvard Latino Law Review* 9: 1–58.

Massey, D. 2009. "Racial Formation in Theory and Practice: The Case of Mexicans in the United States." *Race and Social Problems* 1: 12–26.

Massey, D., J. Durand, and N. Malone. 2002. *Beyond Smoke and Mirrors: Mexican Immigration in an Era of Economic Integration.* New York: Russell Sage Foundation.

Mehta, C., N. Theodore, I. Mora, and J. Wade. 2002. *Chicago's Undocumented Immigrants: An Analysis of Wages, Working Conditions, and Economic Contributions.* Chicago: UIC Center for Urban Economic Development.

Meyers, D. 2005. *US Border Enforcement: From Horseback to High-Tech.* Washington, D.C.: Migration Policy Institute.

Ngai, M. 2004. *Impossible Subjects: Illegal Aliens and the Making of Modern America.* Princeton, N.J.: Princeton University Press.

Passel, J. 1986. "Estimating the Number of Undocumented Aliens." *Bureau of Labor Statistics.* http://www.bls.gov/opub/mlr/1986/09/rpt2full.pdf.

———. 2006. "Size and Characteristics of the Unauthorized Migrant Population in the U.S.: Estimates Based on the March 2005 Current Population Survey." *Pew Hispanic Center,* March 6. http://pewhispanic.org/reports/report.php?ReportID=61.

Passel, J., and D. Cohn. 2009. "A Portrait of Unauthorized Immigration in the United States." *Pew Hispanic Center,* April 14. http://pewhispanic.org/files/reports/107.pdf.

Pedraza, S., and R. G. Rumbaut. 1996. *Origins and Destinies: Immigration, Race, and Ethnicity in America*. New York: Wadsworth.

Porter, E. 2006. "The Search for Illegal Immigrants Stops at the Workplace." *New York Times*, March 5. http://www.nytimes.com/2006/03/05/business/yourmoney/05view.html.

Preston, J. 2006. "Pickers Are Few, and Growers Blame Congress." *New York Times*, September 22. http://www.nytimes.com/2006/09/22/washington/22growers.html?_r=1& pagewanted=all&.

Rivas, C. M. 2014. *Salvadoran Imaginaries: Mediated Identities and Cultures of Consumption*. New Brunswick, N.J.: Rutgers University Press.

Rodkey, E. 2016. "Disposable Labor, Repurposed: Outsourcing Deportees in the Call Center Industry." *Anthropology of Work Review* 37: 34–43.

Sassen, S. 1988. *The Mobility of Labor and Capital: A Study in International Investment and Labor Flow*. Cambridge: Cambridge University Press.

Selway, W., and M. Newkirk. 2013. "Congress Mandates Jail Beds for 34,000 Immigrants as Private Prisons Profit." *Bloomberg News*, September 23. http://www.bloomberg.com/news/ articles/2013-09-24/congress-fuels-private-jails-detaining-34-000-immigrants.

Skipper, W. 2006. "Services Offshoring: An Overview." *Anthropology of Work Review* 27: 9–17.

Striffler, S. 2005. *Chicken: The Dangerous Transformation of America's Favorite Food*. New Haven, Conn.: Yale University Press.

Urbina, M. G., ed. 2014. *Twenty-First Century Dynamics of Multiculturalism: Beyond Post-racial America*. Springfield, Ill.: Charles C Thomas.

Urbina, M. G., and S. E. Álvarez. 2016. "Neoliberalism, Criminal Justice, and Latinos: The Contours of Neoliberal Economic Thought and Policy on Criminalization." *Latino Studies* 14: 33–58.

———. 2017. *Ethnicity and Criminal Justice in the Era of Mass Incarceration: A Critical Reader on the Latino Experience*. Springfield, Ill.: Charles C Thomas.

Urbina, M. G., and I. A. Peña. 2018. "Policing Borders: Immigration, Criminalization, and Militarization in the Era of Social Control Profitability." In *Spatial Policing: The Influence of Time, Space, and Geography on Law Enforcement Practices*, edited by C. Crawford. Durham, N.C.: Carolina Academic Press.

Urbina, M. G., and C. R. Wright. 2016. *Latino Access to Higher Education: Ethnic Realities and New Directions for the Twenty-First Century*. Springfield, Ill.: Charles C Thomas.

U.S. Department of Homeland Security. 2013. *Yearbook of Immigration Statistics: 2012*. Washington, D.C.: U.S. Department of Homeland Security, Office of Immigration Statistics.

Waldinger, R., and M. Lichter. 2003. *How the Other Half Works: Immigration and the Social Organization of Labor*. Berkeley: University of California Press.

Wilkerson, I. 2010. *The Warmth of Other Suns: The Epic Story of America's Great Migration*. New York: Vintage.

Wyman, M. 1996. *Round-Trip to America: The Immigrants Return to Europe, 1880–1930*. Ithaca, N.Y.: Cornell University Press.

Zlolniski, C. 2006. *Janitors, Street Vendors, and Activists: The Lives of Mexican Immigrants in Silicon Valley*. Berkeley: University of California Press.

Chapter 6

ALWAYS RUNNING

La Migra, Detentions, Deportations, and Human Rights

LUPE S. SALINAS

> What sets worlds in motion is the interplay of differences, their
> attractions and repulsions. Life is plurality, death is uniformity.
> By suppressing differences and peculiarities, by eliminating
> different civilizations and cultures, progress weakens life and
> favors death. The ideal of a single civilization for everyone,
> implicit in the cult of progress and technique, impoverishes and
> mutilates us. Every view of the world that becomes extinct, every
> culture that disappears, diminishes a possibility of life.
>
> —OCTAVIO PAZ

AFTER THE ATTACKS on the Twin Towers and the Pentagon on September 11, 2001, America necessarily changed its security focus. Unfortunately, in the panic and insecurity, the nation's leadership also relaxed its observance of the rule of law and constitutional rights. As a result, the area of legal practice and expertise now popularly referred to as "crimmigration" law, which began in the 1980s, along with changes to the deportation criteria in 1996, resulted in the emergence of criminal and immigration law (Hernandez 2015).[1] The former Immigration and Naturalization Service (INS) disappeared, and its functions were taken over by offices within the Department of Homeland Security. One thing that did not change was that U.S. Latino citizens and Latino immigrants, whether documented or not, continued looking over their shoulders. La Migra, as the INS had been referred to by immigrants, continued in all respects, living up to its notoriety with its new names: Customs and Border Protection (CBP) and Immigration and Customs Enforcement (ICE) of the Department of Homeland Security (DHS). The ICE acronym has even been referred to in slang to describe how "cold" and insensitive the enforcement agents can be when dealing with immigrants.

Agents from the various agencies carry out immigration enforcement actions that involve hundreds of thousands of aliens suspected of violating U.S. immigration laws. These enforcement actions include apprehension or arrest, detention, return, and removal for violations that include illegally entering the United States, failing to abide by the terms and conditions of admission, or committing crimes. CBP and ICE are the DHS agencies charged with the primary responsibility for enforcement. CBP performs immigration enforcement at and between the ports of entry, while ICE is generally responsible for interior enforcement and detention and removal operations.

The Office of Immigration Statistics (OIS) reports information on aliens determined to be inadmissible, or who were apprehended, arrested, detained, returned, or removed during each fiscal year. In 2013, for instance, OIS reported that CBP determined approximately 204,000 aliens to be inadmissible. Also, DHS agents apprehended approximately 662,000 aliens, with Mexicans accounting for 64 percent. Adding the numbers from three other Latin American countries, Guatemala (11 percent), Honduras (9.7 percent), and El Salvador (7.7 percent), these four countries accounted for 93 percent of all apprehensions. In addition, ICE detained nearly 441,000 aliens and returned about 178,000 aliens to their home countries through processes that did not require a removal order.

Further, during 2013, DHS removed an all-time high of 438,421 aliens. Of these, 72 percent were Mexican citizens. Mexico and the next three leading countries, Guatemala, Honduras, and El Salvador, accounted for 96 percent of all removals. These removals included approximately 198,000 known criminal aliens, whose most common offenses were immigration related or involved dangerous drugs, criminal traffic offenses, or assault (Simanski 2014). Based on these numbers, in this chapter, I focus on the U.S. migration experience of Latinos from Mexico, Central America, and the Caribbean.

There is no question that official action must be taken to control the border. The United States, the world's major drug consumer, has a severe drug problem (Warner 2008). A Mexican drug cartel leader does not become a billionaire without a customer willing to buy his product. However, as Americans know or at least learn in government high school courses, the rule of law does not permit abuses, arrests without probable cause, and excessive and cruel detentions. Unfortunately, these specific injustices occur regularly in immigration enforcement.

The failure to conduct an intelligent debate in Congress about immigration will be discussed in the history books in the not-too-distant future. It is the fault of the electorate on both sides of the partisan divide that we tolerate a do-nothing Congress. Various factors explain the immigration policy impasse. Even though international terrorists have significantly threatened America's national security from 2001 in New York City to San Bernardino in 2015, our national leadership, with Congress playing a major role, has not been able to do much more than build a partial fence. This symbolic physical gesture contradicts the cherished American values immortalized by Emma Lazarus's famous words on the pedestal of the Statue of Liberty, urging the acceptance of the poor and the homeless (Lazarus 1883). Today, these words apply to people in need of security from poverty, war, dictators, and organized crime.

Instead of creating comprehensive immigration reform, Congress in 2006 authorized billions of dollars for a fence to obstruct aliens from crossing our southern border.[2] Nonetheless, the desperate continue to cross, jeopardizing lives to cross into the United States and find jobs to send funds to assist their impoverished families in Mexico. The legislatively sanctioned construction of this monstrosity of a barrier sends an offensive message to Central and Latin America in general and to our Mexican ally of over 165 years in particular. This barrier on the southern border serves as an obnoxious reminder to U.S. Latinos of the anti-Latino governmental actions in the enforcement arena.

The fence on the U.S.-Mexico border is disturbing for another reason. American politicians applauded President Ronald Reagan for telling Soviet leader Mikhail Gorbachev to tear down the Berlin Wall. Years later conservative politicians contradicted themselves by voting to fund the construction of a wall between two peoples who historically have been more than just neighbors. Mexico served as an ally in World War II, providing not only much needed oil to our country but also a group of pilots who flew missions over the Philippines to assist American and Filipino combat forces in defeating the Japanese. More critically, Mexico provided agricultural workers during the war to compensate for the limited U.S. workforce. Finally, as official government statistics regarding undocumented entries reveal, the wall has been a dismal failure in curtailing the hungry, frightened, and despairing migrants.

The Latino historical migration led to a 2010 census report of 50.5 million U.S. Latinos, a total that gives our country the second highest number in the world. The officially reported U.S. Latino census does not include the 3.7 million people who reside in Puerto Rico (Lopez, Gonzalez-Barrera, and Cuddington 2013). Mexico, with 114 million inhabitants, has the largest number of Latinos, while Spain, in third place, has 47 million. Colombia follows closely with a population of almost 45 million (Liu 2012). Among the diverse U.S. Latino population, Mexicans dominate, with 33.5 million, or nearly two-thirds (64.6 percent) of all Latinos in the United States (Logan and Turner 2013; Lopez, Gonzalez-Barrera, and Cuddington 2013).

The numerical dominance of people of Mexican descent might partly explain why Donald Trump specifies "Mexicans" as an immigration problem. After his hateful comments in June 2015, two brothers attacked a homeless Latino in Boston in August 2015. The older brother told police, "Donald Trump was right, all these illegals need to be deported" (DiNatale and Sacchetti 2015). Similarly, before Trump shared his racist venom, radio talk show extremists incited hostile men in 2008 to commit hate-inspired homicides, the killers looking for "Mexicans" to attack. In these arbitrary attacks on "Mexicans," two Ecuadorians died (Fernandez 2010; Johnson and Ingram 2013; Reyes 2008).[3]

In this chapter, I begin by providing the background of America's immigration policy as it relates to the nation's labor needs during the century before the attacks on New York City and Washington, D.C., in 2001. Once an undocumented person finds refuge in the United States, another major challenge begins. The unauthorized person initiates a new life, one of dread and anxiety in which he or she hides and lives in a fashion necessary to avoid discovery by La Migra.

I then address U.S. immigration and border enforcement in the post-9/11 era. This section discusses the collaborative federal and state actions as well as unilateral state and federal programs that seek compliance with immigration-related laws. However, I deliberately do not discuss thoroughly the repugnant practices of the state of Arizona's conservative leadership that have made life miserable for Latinos. The history of the state's insensitive dealings with nonwhite persons has already been addressed by Jeff Biggers in *State Out of the Union: Arizona and the Final Showdown over the American Dream* (2012) and other scholars.

I include sections on enforcement raids and racial profiling, detentions, deportations, and human rights violations that result from these official actions. I specifically address the dilemmas posed by the migration of refugees and the arrival of unaccompanied children. These issues raise the question of whether the U.S. government is meeting its obligations under the U.N. Declaration of Human Rights as it relates to the treatment and detention of children and adults. I also critique governmental policies that permit removals based on relatively minor criminal grounds, thus raising serious concerns about the arbitrariness of granting residence under the law and then violating migrants' due process right not to be repatriated and not to be subjected to an unconscionable loss of residence in their new country of residence. In addition, with regard to the detention of undocumented persons, I critically review legislative policy that led in effect to a detentions quota. Although the courts view deportation as a civil matter, some administrators apparently believe this authorizes them to detain persons for unreasonably long periods while they are having their immigration appeals or issues heard. Obviously, such practices constitute denials of due process of law.

LATINO U.S.A.: A PRODUCT OF AMERICA'S DOMESTIC AND FOREIGN POLICY

A long-term historical review confirms that the U.S. government bears significant responsibility for the current dilemma of unauthorized immigration into the United

States. Students of this centuries-old migration pattern realize that the undocumented population growth, estimated in 2013 at 11 million persons (Passel, Cohn, and Gonzalez-Barrera 2013), cannot be attributed solely to these migrants disregarding and failing to respect the sovereignty of another nation. Hunger, extreme poverty, religious and political oppression, corruption, and violence drive any human being to carry out the unthinkable, even if it means putting his or her life in extreme danger. As with the early colonists who migrated to America, the desire for liberty and to live in a world without hunger and religious intolerance drive people to take life-threatening risks.

In order to better understand the Mexican and Latino immigration presence, one needs to realize that this ethnic group has been involved in the "Manifest Destiny" version of the United States. U.S. westward expansion exploded after 1848, as more Mexicans and Anglos began to migrate to new destinations. But Mexicans already resided in what is now California, Texas, Arizona, and New Mexico. The arrival of Anglos and their attitude of superiority immediately conflicted with the Latino population. For one, the adoption of Mexican persons as American citizens created tensions. Anglos continued to view Latinos scornfully as just "Mexicans," a mindset that endured for over a century. Even if the Latino happened to be a soldier in uniform immediately after the end of World War II, he was still a "Mexican" to racist Anglos (Perales 1974).

During the first 150-plus years of U.S. Mexican American citizenship, millions of Mexicans and other Latinos entered the country with and without inspection. Consequently, both the Anglo public and law enforcement agents had difficulty distinguishing between immigrants and legal residents and citizens of Latino descent. I necessarily address the policies and practices by which undocumented Latinos have been detained by police agents, since this process has contributed to the detention and/or deportation of resident aliens and U.S. citizens (Perez and Lutz 2010; Preston 2011; Stevens 2011). In the criminalization of immigration, these legal and constitutional abuses produced the extremely embarrassing Border Patrol action when agents detained Brownsville, Texas, U.S. District Court Judge Filemon Vela on two occasions in 2000 as he drove with his staff on a federal highway along the U.S.-Mexico border to serve as a visiting jurist in Laredo, Texas. The stops occurred despite there being no reasonable suspicion to justify a legal detention or articulable facts to indicate suspected criminal activity or even undocumented alien status as required by the courts (Yardley 2000).[4]

Among the millions of unauthorized aliens in the United States, Mexican Latinos account for 52 percent (six million people), with an unknown number of Latino migrants from other countries (Passel, Cohn, and Gonzalez-Barrera 2013). Along with the historical anti-Mexican phobia, these numbers might also explain why Republican Party candidate Donald Trump in the 2016 campaign capitalized on the historical stereotype of blaming "Mexican" immigrants for the nation's problems with drugs, robberies, rapes, and other ills.

In the process of carrying out the massive immigration enforcement efforts, ICE and local police have violated the civil liberties of many innocent people. Civil rights lawyers have litigated on several fronts, decrying the numerous arrests, detentions, and deportations of innocent American residents and citizens erroneously suspected of being undocumented aliens. The litigators have accused agents of racial profiling, targeting Americans solely on the basis of their ethnicities, language, or even their accents (*New York Times* 2009). Fortunately, various organizations like the Mexican American Legal Defense and Educational Fund (MALDEF), the Puerto Rican Legal Defense and Educational Fund (known today as LatinoJustice PRLDEF), and the American Civil Liberties Union (ACLU) assist U.S. Latinos with their legal battles.

A SALINAS FAMILY ACCOUNT: THE MIGRATION TO TEXAS FROM NUEVO LEÓN, MEXICO

Vast migrations from Mexico, precipitated by the decade-long 1910 Mexican Revolution, increased the Mexican presence in the United States. I believe a personal account will illustrate the migrations of Mexicans and their "acceptance" by ranchers with open arms. Anglo society, on the other hand, did not particularly want to associate with Mexicans. The whites did not want to pick cotton in the penetrating heat and preferred seeing the Mexicans do the picking and adeptly utilizing the farm tools needed to remove the brush to prepare the land for the crops. These business needs of Anglo landowners and ranchers created a wave of Mexican migrants between 1910 and 1930.

Two sources support this assertion. First, my paternal grandfather, Reyes Salinas López, began his migrant travel to Texas at the age of nineteen from the northern Mexican state of Nuevo León. A copy of a 1913 border-crossing card documents my grandfather's intent to migrate to Sinton, Texas, approximately 150 miles away from the border port of entry. Years later, the 1930 U.S. Census (dated April 28, 1930) includes information about my paternal grandparents. Even though Mexican American leaders asserted that Mexicans were members of the white race, Anglo society did not agree. In the section of the census form labeled "Color or Race," my light-complexioned and blue-eyed grandmother, Dolores Garcia Hinojosa de Salinas, is listed as of the "Mexican race" with a "Mx" abbreviation (U.S. Department of Commerce 1930). A second source showing the Anglo desire for Mexican labor is an excellent study by Berkeley sociologist Paul S. Taylor, who in 1929 began research in the Nueces County, Texas, area where my grandfather worked as a sharecropper. Stories I heard from my grandfather and my father corroborate many of Taylor's findings. My grandmother accompanied my grandfather on what developed into a fifteen-year journey to Texas. After an infant daughter died in Galveston, Texas, my grandparents returned to Robstown, Nueces County, Texas, where Taylor coincidentally focused his research and where my father was born on a ranch in 1921. Eight of my father's siblings were born in Texas between 1920 and 1933, the year when the federal government's so-called repatriation program effectively convinced my paternal grandparents to pack up and "voluntarily" return to Mexico before La Migra, in their deportation fervor, had the chance to separate them from their six surviving U.S.-citizen children.

"Repatriation" is a misnomer. During these years, federal, state, and local governments worked together to involuntarily remove many U.S. citizens of Mexican ancestry who could not be "repatriated" because Mexico was not their native land. What occurred in the 1930s would today be classified as an "arbitrary arrest, detention or exile," a crime against humanity, and a form of "ethnic cleansing" (Johnson 2005, 4–6; United Nations 1948).

This period in American history became the "decade of betrayal" in which basic human rights were violated by the conscious failure of agents to inform detainees of their constitutional rights. In addition, the "free" press generally did not have the courage to report or inquire about the human rights violations (Balderrama and Rodriguez 1995). Clearly, the interests of business owners trumped the laws against unauthorized entries during these years. Simultaneously, agricultural interests encouraged the federal government to admit Mexican labor and even sponsored a $1,000 advertising campaign for the importation of cotton pickers. Farmers wanted "cheap Mexican labor" to pick their cotton (Taylor 1934). The cotton business was so prosperous (for the farmers) and popular (for the needy workers) that the Robstown, Texas, school nickname became "The Cotton Pickers"!

Anti-alien fervor increased with the economic collapse in late 1929. The Departments of State and Labor began to restrict immigration from Mexico, and the federal government increased border patrols. In addition, the opposition took on a racist twist when Texas congressman John Box (1928) presented a bill seeking to protect "Americans," though this excluded American citizens of Mexican descent, described by Box as a "degenerate" race (Gottheimer 2003, 157).

Surprisingly, the Nueces County cotton business interests supported the continuation of Mexican labor (Taylor 1934), while the more conservative professional Mexican Americans wanted immigration restrictions. These Latino citizens feared that the continued migration of uneducated Mexicans would "handicap" the upward mobility of Mexican American citizens, since the "steady flow of immigration of the laboring-peon class" caused difficulties in distinguishing between citizens and immigrants.

These concerns prompted the leadership of the United Latin American League to object strongly to further migration (Taylor 1934). They wanted to concentrate on the citizens and to limit the number of resident aliens. LULAC membership, for example, included only citizens. U.S. Latino citizens wanted to be respected by Anglos, but the racist attitudes prevailed. To gain favor among Anglo whites, many prominent Latino citizens began to discriminate against other Latinos and resorted to derogatory labels. The new immigrants were called "wetbacks" and other unpleasant names. Even Gus C. Garcia, the highly respected civil rights lawyer who argued *Hernandez v. Texas* (1954),[5] the primary and seminal Latino civil rights case before the U.S. Supreme Court, used this offensive term while discussing the unauthorized immigration issue before a Senate subcommittee (Garcia 1952). Cesar Chavez, another highly respected Latino and farmworker labor leader, used the term to discuss undocumented Mexicans whom growers in California exploited by having them break the strike Chavez had orchestrated to attain decent work conditions for Mexican American and Filipino agricultural workers.

U.S. IMMIGRATION POLICY BEFORE 1981: A STUDY IN CONTRADICTIONS

Historically, U.S. immigration policy has been hypocritical and contradictory. Rutgers law professor Linda Bosniak, an expert on immigration and citizenship issues, describes this phenomenon in American history in terms of the development of "inclusionary" and "exclusionary" projects. The inclusionary project includes "laws, practices, and institutions that tend to protect the social and legal rights of undocumented immigrants." The exclusionary project involves those same laws, practices, and institutions that "treat undocumented immigrants primarily as deportable aliens." To be clear, the inclusionary institutions embrace supportive agencies such as the Department of Labor, public schools, and religious organizations. At times, the inclusionary is undermined by the exclusionary project, such as when an undocumented worker is not paid by his employer as required by law (inclusionary) and abstains from a formal complaint for fear the employer will inform ICE agents of his status (exclusionary) (Oboler and Gonzalez 2005a).

In great part, this problematic American policy arises from the development of the United States. The nation began as a country for free white people. Africans were permitted, but only to serve their masters. The slaves continued to be the property of whites unless they were given their freedom.[6] Native Americans were tolerated so long as they obeyed the white man's edicts and remained on reservations. The American drive to control the continent from coast to coast set off the violence of Manifest Destiny. White Americans encountered a conquered mestizo population of Mexico comprising Mexican Indians and Spaniards. These Mexican Latinos suffered the wrath and intolerance of the dominant Anglos, with many being lynched (Carrigan and Webb 2003, 2013; Delgado 2009; Salinas 2015; Urbina, Vela, and Sanchez 2014). Over this past century and a half, violent lynchings have diminished, but other harmful practices continue to keep persons of color "in their place."

THE MIGRATION PATTERNS OF MEXICAN CITIZENS IN EARLY AMERICAN HISTORY

Mexican citizens migrated to the United States after 1909 because of adverse economic conditions as well as the violence and political upheaval created by the Mexican Revolution. After a "warm" welcome, the Great Depression in 1929 and its hardships caused politicians, small farmers, and even President Herbert Hoover to blame "Mexicans" and unauthorized workers for the economic disaster and prompted federal and local law enforcement deportations. In the action known as Operation Repatriation, agents apprehended and deported American citizens, both adults and minors, and permanent resident aliens. These minors accounted for 60 percent of all deportees (Acuña 1972; Balderrama and Rodriguez 1995).

The removal of alien workers began at the local level with city, county, and state governments. Their primary goal was to save the costs of providing welfare benefits for families with citizen children (Johnson 2005). In the process, Latino families were torn apart, especially when the U.S.-born children were young adults who did not want to abandon the only home and country they had known. In many cases, the children rebelled and stayed or just ran away from the parents who did not want to leave them behind.

Another cost-reduction effort by the L.A. County General Hospital included shipping the elderly, crippled, and tubercular patients to Mexico. This prompted the Mexican press to complain that contributions of Mexicans to U.S. economic prosperity were being callously disregarded, considered not enough to gain them official residence or acceptance in their adopted country to the North or create any concern about their citizenship status, health needs, or age factors (Balderrama and Rodriguez 1995).

In 1954, after American business interests had profited from both authorized and undocumented Mexican labor for over a decade, President Dwight D. Eisenhower ungratefully approved the insensitively named Operation Wetback as a response to poor economic conditions and surplus labor. Mexicans became the usual economic scapegoats, provoking the U.S. attorney general to launch raids to expel Mexicans from the United States: "Assisted by federal, state, county and municipal authorities— including railroad police officers, custom officials, the FBI, and the Army and Navy— and supported by aircraft, watercraft, automobiles, radio units, special task forces, and, perhaps most important of all, public sentiment, including that of growers, the Border Patrol launched the greatest maximum peacetime offensive against a highly exploited, unorganized, and unstructured 'invading force' of Mexican migrants" (Samora 1971, 52). The federal government deemed the alien removal process a success (Salinas and Torres 1976).

So twenty years after the expulsions of the Depression era, history repeated itself, as federal and state agents deported persons of various residential classifications. Among those snared in the expulsion campaign were American citizens of Mexican descent (Rosales 2006). To ensure the effectiveness of the expulsion process, many of those apprehended were denied a hearing by government agents to assert their constitutional rights and to present evidence that would have prevented their deportation. The government banished more than one million persons of Mexican descent in 1954 during these military-style deportations (U.S. Commission on Civil Rights 1980; U.S. Department of Homeland Security 2014a).

THE BRACERO PROGRAM ERA, 1942–1964

Americans and their Anglo leaders have frequently engaged in schizophrenic (i.e., contradictory) actions. In times of economic necessity, such as when crops need to be picked in the hot sun, whites often relied on their Mexican amigos. For example, shortly after the deportations prompted by the Great Depression, Congress in 1942 initiated a "temporary" Bracero Program (the name *bracero*, meaning "arms," was given to the workers who provided labor in the fields) that ended up lasting twenty-two years.[7] The program's limited purpose was to import Mexican workers to replace Americans who went to fight in World War II, a war that ended in 1945. Thus, on the one hand, "they" (aliens) caused the 1930s financial crisis, while on the other hand, "they" (aliens) were appreciated since they provided the essential labor created by the wartime shortage of workers.

The bracero statute survived the economic recession of 1954, but the demise of the Bracero Program began with dissatisfaction among unions and laborers who asserted that imported labor displaced domestic labor (Galarza 1964). Upon the 1964 termination of the Bracero Program, Mexico warned American officials of future massive undocumented entries. As predicted, apprehensions of undocumented Mexicans increased by 820 percent to a total of 788,145 undocumented aliens in 1974 (U.S. Immigration and Naturalization Service 1964, 1974). This increase also resulted from the imposition by Congress of the Western Hemisphere quota,[8] a policy decision that limited official immigration from Latin American countries (Acuña 1972).

The increases in the undocumented population during various periods in American history resulted from what is referred to as the "push-pull" factor. American businesses "pull" (attract) lower-wage workers from other countries to perform duties generally considered unattractive by the domestic workforce. Simultaneously, the sending country's economic hardships "push" their usually large population to seek a means of feeding their families by going to another country. Once in the country, these immigrant families have U.S.-born children who, as American citizens, provide hope for a future permanence in the United States.

The Bracero Program initiated an increase in unauthorized Mexican entries because it suggested to other Mexicans that American businesses desperately needed their labor. An excessive number applied under the Bracero Program. A very high number of unauthorized entries occurred because the program included several obstacles to lawful admission and because the extreme racial discrimination against Mexicans in Texas led to Mexico's initial objection to sending braceros to that state. When Texas employers nonetheless demanded workers, this encouraged an influx of undocumented aliens (Acuña 1972). For instance, in 1950, the INS seized half a million undocumented Mexican aliens. During this same period, only 120,000 authorized Mexican contract laborers and 18,000 resident Mexican aliens entered the United States (Samora 1971).

THE LATINO GROWTH FROM CENTRAL AMERICA AND OTHER LATIN AMERICAN COUNTRIES

The Central American migration has both an interesting and a regrettable history. The business and national security concerns of the United States in this part of the hemisphere prompted its support for civilian tyrants and military dictatorships. American leaders supported the military junta in El Salvador and the Somoza family dictatorship in Nicaragua, governments that used extreme violence against their own people (Zinn 2005). An indirect and inevitable consequence of these policies has been the migration of refugees from these nations, with a large number seeking refuge in the United States, a fact corroborated by me during my tour of service as the U.S. attorney general's immigration advisor, when I saw the numerous refugees and heard the desperate pleas of many Nicaraguans in hearings held in Miami and New Orleans.

The United States specifically funded the government and/or military forces in El Salvador (Oboler and Gonzalez 2005b), Guatemala (Miller 2011), and Nicaragua under the direct encouragement of CIA chief William Casey. The Nicaraguan involvement lasted four decades, starting with the rise to power of dictator Anastasio Somoza Garcia in the 1930s during the administration of Franklin D. Roosevelt. It ended with President Jimmy Carter providing U.S. support for Somoza's two sons in the family dictatorship (Davis 2011; Zinn 2005). This action contributed to the passage of special American legislation for Nicaraguan refugees (Martin and Yankay 2014).[9]

In El Salvador, the civil war that lasted from 1980 to 1992 caused a significant exodus to cities across the United States after more than 75,000 Salvadorans died and thousands of persons disappeared, resulting in a current U.S. population of over 1.2 million foreign-born Salvadorans (Liu 2012). Similarly, Guatemala experienced U.S. intervention for decades. In 1954, the CIA reportedly intervened to overthrow the leftist-leaning president. From 1960 to 1996, the nation experienced insurgency and civil war, with casualties approximating nearly 200,000 dead or missing (Liu 2012).

The late 1970s and the year 1980 saw a rapid increase in immigration and refugee arrivals from Central America (Fry 2009). As a result, once Ronald Reagan assumed office, Congress continued debating the immigration bill. The review process ended with the eventual passage of the 1986 Immigration Reform and Control Act (IRCA). The effort leading to IRCA began during the Carter years when Congress established the Select Commission on Immigration and Refugee Policy (SCIRP). A year later, during 1979–80, I served as special assistant to U.S. Attorney General Benjamin R. Civiletti and collaborated with the aides of cabinet members, senators, and members of Congress to provide information to the SCIRP executive director in preparation of his final report on an immigration reform plan. Congress created SCIRP in 1978, a year after President Carter submitted a plan asking Congress to add two thousand additional border patrol agents.

SCIRP met during 1980 and developed amnesty and employer sanction proposals, two issues my coauthor and I analyzed in a law review article (Salinas and Torres 1976). In 1980, during SCIRP hearings in Miami and New Orleans, Nicaraguan refugees dominated the proceedings with understandable concerns about their future. Shortly after my return to work as a federal prosecutor in Houston, SCIRP submitted its 1981 report to President Reagan. In 1986 Reagan signed the Immigration Reform and Control Act (Chishti, Meissner, and Bergeron 2011), a law primarily known for granting amnesty[10] to undocumented aliens and for sanctioning employers who knowingly hire unauthorized workers.[11] Those Republicans who today oppose comprehensive immigration reform in the past praised Reagan as a model conservative politician. They ignore the reality that he agreed to amnesty for those whose lengthy but law-abiding undocumented existence made them acceptable candidates for residence. Reagan apparently considered not only their lack of a criminal record but the nation's need for immigrants to supplement the nation's dwindling workforce.

U.S. IMMIGRATION ENFORCEMENT IN THE REAGAN ERA AND AFTER

The election of Ronald Reagan in 1980 resulted in a strong conservative majority that began to change the immigration enforcement system. The government in 1981 denied federal aid access to immigrants who were not authorized permanent residents. The administration in 1982 began Operation Jobs, conducting INS raids at workplaces and seizing five thousand persons in the process. During the first few years of the Reagan administration, Congress fine-tuned the immigration control bill begun during the last years of the Carter administration. The need for domestic labor is also evident from the 1990 increase of immigration visas to 675,000. In 1994, when unauthorized immigration increased, the government's Operation Gatekeeper tightened up the unsupervised crossing points in the San Diego area with fencing, stadium lights, and increased Border Patrol activity, forcing aliens to cross at points near the Arizona desert, which resulted in an estimated five thousand fatalities in areas where temperatures hit extreme highs and lows (Androff and Tavassoli 2012; Chomsky 2007).

FEDERAL AND STATE IMMIGRATION ENFORCEMENT EFFORTS

The collaboration of the 1930s and 1950s between local and federal immigration officials continued into the Reagan era. The political and economic forces that drove more immigrants and refugees to the United States also continued. Notwithstanding passage of the IRCA, or some would argue as a result of it, migration continued from Mexico and other Latino regions farther south. While the hope of amnesty may have tempted some, the predominant factors were extreme poverty and continued U.S. employer needs in the agricultural sector.

Not surprisingly, hostile anti-alien politics prevailed during the 1994 congressional election. The hostility was provoked by the 1993 bombing attack on the World Trade Center and indirectly by the 1995 destruction of the Oklahoma City federal building and the murders of over 150 Americans. International terrorists carried out the first attack, but a domestic terrorist, an Anglo-American military veteran, perpetrated the vicious April 19, 1995, bombing. Unfortunately for Latino immigrants, the search for the Oklahoma bomber featured rumors of a dark-complected suspect, possibly Latino. A few years later, another terrorist entered from Canada at a port of entry near Seattle with enough material to kill hundreds. He was caught and later convicted in April 2001, half a year before the attacks on the towers (Gottlieb 1999). Even though those who harmed or threatened America entered by air or through the Canadian border, politicians and Congress spotlighted the nation's border with Mexico in their ranting and raving about our national security. I do not argue for ignoring the border; I only urge that the anti-terrorist wrath not be misdirected indiscriminately at a traditionally hardworking group that has often come to the aid of the United States during war or to fill industrial and agricultural demands.

The demagoguery of Speaker Newt Gingrich and other Republicans motivated conservative followers to support the so-called Contract with America in 1994, a shrewd pledge the GOP made to the nation. The politicians appealed to the emotions and prejudices of the voters and converted the 1996 session of Congress into a mean-spirited effort against immigrants. These negative sentiments controlled or became entwined with terrorism concerns. As has occurred periodically, the public vented their frustration on immigrants, particularly those from Mexico, and blamed them for the nation's social ills, such as a perceived increase in crime and unemployment. Sound studies revealed, however, that cities with high immigrant populations had lower unemployment rates and lower crime rates than those with smaller immigrant populations (Cook 2003; Salinas 2015; Weissman 2009). In spite of the reality, the immigrant bashing continues.

Based on this anger, adeptly exploited by Speaker Gingrich, Congress enacted two of the harshest anti-immigrant statutes ever.[12] Officially known as the Antiterrorism and Effective Death Penalty Act (AEDPA) and the Illegal Immigration Reform and Immigrant Responsibility Act (IIRIRA), this legislation, referred to as the 1996 Immigration Acts, extensively amended the Immigration and Nationality Act of 1952 (INA).[13] IIRIRA legislation, in classic Orwellian Newspeak, replaced the term "deportation" with "removal" and represents a statute that impacts not only retroactively but also punitively.[14] President Bill Clinton noted the inherent unfairness in the antiterrorism effort in its lashing out at regular hardworking immigrants.[15]

The INA historically provided that the attorney general could exercise discretion in deciding whether to waive deportation of an alien otherwise subject to deportation or removal.[16] The 1996 Immigration Acts changed aspects of this law by restricting the circumstances under which aliens could seek relief from the attorney general.[17] IIRIRA, enacted a few months after AEDPA, went further by repealing the discretion provision and replacing it with a new section excluding from relief those persons who had been removed for conviction of "any aggravated felony."[18]

Under current U.S. immigration law, lawful permanent residents convicted of a minor crime may be removed from the only home they have ever known, forcing them to leave their families. Once deported, a convicted aggravated felon can never return to the United States. These laws are "not only cruel, but also wildly inconsistent, meting out the same punishment to lawful permanent residents who commit a misdemeanor offense as they do to undocumented non-citizens who enter the country to commit a terrorist act" (Cook 2003, 327–28). As an example, a so-called aggravated felony that resulted from a minor injury assault in a self-defense fight with a "bully" in high school mandates the exclusion of a resident alien from the only country he has known since his youth.[19] Worse, Congress radically changed the sentencing and punishment aspects by retroactively treating a conviction for a misdemeanor as an aggravated felony if it included a theft, burglary, or a minor injury assault as a crime of violence.[20] In other words, Congress included conduct predating the 1996 law, in contradiction to the protections against ex post facto punishment (Salinas 2004).

Since 1989, the number of lawfully admitted permanent resident aliens has grown by an average of one million annually (U.S. Department of Homeland Security 2014a). The number of permanent resident aliens potentially affected by new congressional immigration initiatives is high. Recent tallies reflect that the U.S. foreign-born population (naturalized, resident alien, and unauthorized) is about 40.4 million, or 13 percent of the total U.S. population of 311.6 million in 2011. Thirty-one percent of all American resident aliens are permanent resident aliens (green card holders) and total approximately 12 million (Hipsman and Meissner 2013). Congress provided for removal of such persons on the basis of relatively minor offenses, sometimes dictated only by the potential sentence and not at all by the nature or severity of the act. Thus there are concerns that denial of substantive due process may result in banishing a permanent resident alien from his or her adopted country without an opportunity to mend a onetime wayward act that might be justifiable or pardonable.

As noted earlier, in 1987, in a speech regarded as President Reagan's best, he urged Russian leader Gorbachev to remove the Berlin Wall (Reagan 1987). Less than twenty years later, the U.S. Congress undermined the impact of this historic challenge by approving construction of a wall along the Mexican border. While the two situations are distinct, they both involve human and personal rights. As noted herein, I recognize the need to have security control over whom we as a nation admit for residency. But Americans will have to set aside partisan attitudes and the political aim to win votes by working together for the security of America. To state it emphatically, neither political party has any claim to the exclusive resolution of this multifaceted and complex issue known as "comprehensive immigration reform." All factions must meet diplomatically at the negotiating table.

I also do not question the authority of any sovereign nation to take appropriate action to control entries at its border. But I view the building of an 800-mile-long fence along the U.S.-Mexico border as not only contradictory to American values as expressed by President Reagan in Berlin but also disparaging to Mexican and other Americans of Latino descent. These citizens and resident aliens, who compose over 50.5 million of our U.S. population, have been loyal Americans, with many having served heroically in the U.S. military. During World War II fourteen soldiers from Texas received the coveted Congressional Medal of Honor. Six of the fourteen were of Latino descent (Garcia 1952). In other words, Latinos accounted for 43 percent of the medal recipients even though this ethnic group constituted only 11 percent of the entire Texas population at the time (Gibson and Jung 2002).

If the governmental goal in building the wall was to create a barrier to control unauthorized immigration, then the high detention and deportation numbers establish that this unsightly structure has been a dismal failure. *The 800 Mile Wall*, a film directed by John Carlos Frey (2010), addresses the construction of the wall as well as the adverse effects on migrants trying to cross into the United States. The film's trailer describes it as "an unflinching look at a failed U.S. border strategy that many believe has caused the death of thousands of migrants and violates fundamental human rights." Since the construction of the wall began, "over five thousand migrant bodies have been recovered in U.S. deserts, mountains and canals" as migrants have crossed treacherous deserts and territory hoping to find low-skill and low-paying jobs. *The 800 Mile Wall* documents the "ineffective and deadly results" of a futile border policy. In responding to the immigrant "invasion," the secretary of the Department of Homeland Security waived numerous critical and highly regarded statutes like the National Environmental Policy Act, Endangered Species Act, and the Native American Graves Protection and Repatriation Act in order to build the wall (Frey 2010). Finally, the wall project has been an expensive failure, costing an average of $2.8 million per mile (U.S. Government Accountability Office 2009).

About the same time as the fence project began, President George W. Bush initiated Operation Return to Sender (Flaccus 2007). Although described as a concerted effort to apprehend criminal aliens, over 75 percent of those apprehended in the five-year period prior to 2009 were noncriminal aliens with gainful employment (Bernstein 2009). With only limited resources, the federal government prioritized the detention and removal of undocumented criminal aliens. However, anti-immigrant activists wanted more enforcement, claiming that undocumented aliens caused moral depravity, a drain on the economy, and a rising crime rate. In 2006, the year in which this operation began, agents apprehended over one million aliens (U.S. Department of Homeland Security 2014a).

In 2005 the Bush administration initiated another program, Operation Streamline, memorably named since it effectively restructured the criminal justice system by limiting the availability of fundamental constitutional rights to those accused of entering the nation without authority (Hernandez 2015). To further "streamline" our system of justice as it relates to aliens, the federal government suspended the Constitution and federal criminal procedure law. For years, prosecutors presented criminal charges en masse, a practice criticized in 2013 by the Ninth Circuit.[21] Operation Streamline succeeded, if the objective was to increase the criminal aspects of undocumented entries. During the Clinton years, prosecutors obtained two thousand criminal convictions for illegal entry and reentry. In contrast, the Bush Justice Department obtained thirty thousand convictions in the three years after the "streamlining" began (Hernandez

2015). Questions about judicial procedures arose after a judge bragged about setting a record by sentencing seventy accused persons in under thirty minutes (Sakuma 2014).

DETENTIONS QUOTA POLICY: THE ROLES OF THE BUSH AND OBAMA ADMINISTRATIONS

On the campaign trail and in his first days in the White House, Barack Obama made several pledges to fix the broken immigration system. However, after the 2008 election, Congress avoided the politically charged comprehensive immigration control issue. Instead, it only took actions that projected an image of being "tough on crime."

In the preceding administration, the terrorist attacks of September 11, 2001, disrupted President George W. Bush's plan to submit an immigration proposal. During the seventeen years of inaction in Congress since the attacks, the entry of unauthorized immigrants slowed significantly, in part because of a decline in immigrants from Mexico, because of an increase in deportations by the Obama DHS, and because of fewer economic incentives to migrate after the 2008 recession. In addition, in what will come as a surprise to many, the evidence shows that President Obama was active in the enforcement of federal immigration removal statutes. It is worth noting that removals during the preceding Bush administration averaged about 251,000 annually, while removals during the Obama era averaged 403,000 (U.S. Department of Homeland Security 2014a). These statistics might explain why President Obama was cynically referred to as the "Deporter-in-Chief" by some civil rights leaders and immigration activists.

Another possible criticism against the Obama administration's policies centers on the detentions quota that appeared in 2009 as part of the DHS Appropriations Act of 2010. The Senate Appropriations Committee, chaired by Senator Robert Byrd (D-WV), first included language mandating that the DHS "maintain a level of not less than 33,400 detention beds" (National Immigrant Justice Center 2015). Regarding the quota policy, we witness another partisan split: Democrats want to remove the quota concept, while Republicans want to maintain the status quo.

The specific idea for a quota of 30,000-plus detainees derived from a DHS budget in 2009, President Obama's first year in office. However, the plan to raise the number of beds resulted from policies initiated under President Bush, Obama's immediate predecessor. First, the Intelligence Reform and Terrorism Prevention Act of 2004 (IRTPA), signed by Bush, increased the immigration detention capacity by at least 8,000 beds each year from fiscal year 2006 to 2010. Second, in 2006, during the signing of the DHS Appropriations Act for 2007, President Bush commented that the act "will allow us to add at least 6,700 new beds in detention centers," providing for a total of 27,500 beds. In September 2015, having seen the injustices that resulted from this strange policy, which primarily benefits private detention centers, Senator Bernie Sanders (I-VT), a 2016 candidate for the Democratic presidential nomination, introduced the "Justice Is Not for Sale Act of 2015," which seeks to eliminate the bed quota (National Immigrant Justice Center 2015).

U.S. Immigration and Customs Enforcement (ICE), DHS's interior enforcement agency, detains an average of 34,000 men, women, and children daily, or almost half a million people annually, in a network of 250 county jails, privately run contracted facilities, and federal facilities. The annual cost is more than two billion dollars. No other law enforcement agency in the nation operates with an actual or a perceived quota for its detainees (National Immigrant Justice Center 2015). What makes this cost even more foolish is that DHS has admitted that other alternatives, such as electronic monitors, could save Americans over one billion dollars annually (Hamilton and Alvarado 2014).

In August 2014, the DHS Office of the Inspector General (OIG) reported and conceded that the average daily population congressional mandate (i.e., the 34,000 quota) required ICE to decide whether to release a detainee "based on bed space availability, not whether detention is necessary for public safety or to effect removals." OIG urged that ICE be given the authority to determine when individuals should be detained, another matter in the hands of the Republican-controlled Congress (National Immigrant Justice Center 2015).

The quota, a policy for which both parties share responsibility, is a fiasco comparable to the 800-mile wall along the U.S.-Mexico border. As noted earlier, for years, the Democrats have urged an end to this quota injustice, while Republicans have taken a pit bull mentality in refusing to act. Financial reports by the Corrections Corporation of America (CCA) are troubling. For 2015, CCA reported $710,000 for its total lobbying expenses. A bar graph indicates that beginning with 2001 and through 2015, CCA has expended over 25 million dollars furthering its interests (Center for Responsive Politics 2015). One question that lingers is whether private prison detention companies like CCA and the GEO Group provide political contributions to the members of Congress. If so, considering the cost to the taxpayers and the misery the quota can cause, is this ethical? The question of whether "justice is for sale" is a fair one as it relates to immigration policies and the bed quota. Democrats have filed bills in the House to eliminate the quota. As expected, Republicans opposed them. The Republican-led Senate Appropriations Committee passed the 2016 DHS Appropriations Bill and recommended that funding provide the "resources necessary to maintain 34,000 detention beds" and urged "ICE to vigorously enforce all immigration laws under its purview" (National Immigrant Justice Center 2015).

In 2014, the *Los Angeles Times* urged Congress in an editorial to "Dump the Immigrant Detainee Quota." Calling it a peculiar provision in U.S. immigration law, the editorial board noted that the reasoning for the potential deportee quota is "murky" and "bizarre." The board also raised the policy implications of having the legal status of a detainee and his or her release on bond be based on budgetary and not judicial considerations, concluding with the assertion that "this is preposterous, unjust, and expensive, needlessly costing U.S. taxpayers hundreds of millions of dollars a year." Ironically, the quota continues even though unauthorized immigration has declined. The board further observed that DHS Secretary Jeh Johnson suggested that he would like to treat the 34,000-bed mandate as something other than a quota, but House Republicans disputed Johnson, stating that the secretary did not have the authority to interpret the budget law as he would like.

DUE PROCESS CONSIDERATIONS OF PROLONGED DETENTIONS OF ALIENS

In *Rodriguez v. Robbins* (2015) the Ninth Circuit Court of Appeals ruled that aliens detained by the government must be provided bond hearings when the detention exceeds six months.[22] The immigration judge is not mandated to release any single individual after this six-month period. Instead, the government must afford the detainee the minimal procedural safeguard and establish by clear and convincing evidence that the alien's release poses a danger to the community or risk of flight. Many of those held as unauthorized entrants have humanitarian bases to petition for asylum or refugee status or a reprieve based on some family emergency. These individuals would not have any interest in fleeing. The only issue then would be whether they pose a risk to the public.

The judicially imposed six-month standard has developed over the years.[23] In *Zadvydas v. Davis* (2001), the U.S. Supreme Court concluded that "freedom from imprisonment—from government custody, detention, or other forms of physical restraint—lies at the heart of the liberty that [the Due Process] Clause protects."[24] While the indefinite detention discussion in *Zadvydas* refers to a "once-admitted alien," those who enter seeking asylum and refugee status likewise should not be subjected to detentions that exceed the impermissible six-month period. The Supreme Court has also discussed other civil commitment circumstances where prolonged detention might be required. For example, the Court has upheld a nonpunitive statute that permits detention of sexually dangerous individuals after they have completed their criminal sentences. To justify this type of "indefinite involuntary commitment," the state must prove both "dangerousness" and an additional factor, such as a mental illness or mental abnormality.[25]

In *Rodriguez* the Ninth Circuit clarified that the government may not detain a legal permanent resident for "a prolonged period without providing him a neutral forum in which to contest the necessity of his continued detention."[26] The government bears the burden of proving "by clear and convincing evidence that an alien is a flight risk or a danger to the community to justify denial of bond."[27] According to the *Rodriguez* ruling, once the immigration judge hears a bond request for liberty pending a resolution of the alien's status, he or she must evaluate "the alien's criminal record, including the extensiveness of criminal activity, the recency of such activity, and the seriousness of the offenses."[28]

In *Casas-Castrillon v. Department of Homeland Security* (2008), a lawful permanent resident had been detained for nearly seven years while his petition for review of his removal order was pending. The Ninth Circuit stated that although the government has discretionary authority to detain the noncitizen, it distinguished between "detention being authorized and being necessary as to any particular person." The court ultimately concluded that Casas could not be held indefinitely or for a prolonged period of time "without providing him a neutral forum in which to contest the necessity of his continued detention."[29]

The same due process concerns apply to those detained persons who entered the United States without documentation, permission, or inspection. In a civil rights deprivation case involving aliens captured by the Border Patrol, the Ninth Circuit ruled that these victims of brutality by the agents were "persons" in the jurisdiction of the United States.[30] In that regard, these temporary visitors receive protection under the Constitution's Bill of Rights, including the Fourth Amendment right to be free from unreasonable seizures, the Fifth and Fourteenth Amendment rights to due process of law, and the Eighth Amendment right not to be subjected to cruel and unusual "punishment."

Even if the detention is for civil deportation, the holding itself becomes inhumane if certain conditions exist. For example, the detention can become prolonged based upon the incentives of the private detention center. Pursuant to the current DHS budget rules, these centers, primarily CCA and the GEO Group, as mentioned above, can profit from federal payments by having up to 34,000 beds filled annually (Ackerman and Furman 2014). Many detainees "work" either to have more freedom or, as in the case of some mothers, to have some funds to provide their minor children with candy and other goods not provided by the center (Hennessy-Fiske 2015). The "voluntary" work program, at one dollar per day, is itself questionable given the federal law prohibiting the hiring of undocumented persons and as a violation of the minimum wage statute. Further, in some cases, the detention centers set the thermostats at unbearably cold temperatures, which has led even employees of the centers to refer to the centers as a *hielera*, the Spanish word for icebox (Hamilton and Alvarado 2014; Zambrano

2015). Clearly, combining these adverse conditions with prolonged detention without access to liberty violates our nation's concept of basic human decency.

The *Los Angeles Times* (2014) expressed the view that the decision to detain a person should be decided "by judges and others charged with enforcing immigration laws, not by an arbitrary congressional budget mandate." The board acknowledged that the "current dysfunctional Congress is unlikely to enact immigration reform this year" (*Los Angeles Times* 2014). In fact, other than the Secure Fence Act, the detention quota, some minor matters, and partial funding ($1.6 billion) for Trump's border wall, Congress has not taken up any comprehensive immigration reform issues since the 2001 terrorist attacks.

SHOULD THE DREAMERS WHO CAN CONTRIBUTE TO OUR NATIONAL INTEREST BE DEPORTED?

In view of intensive enforcement efforts and the absence of legislative action, President Obama exercised his executive authority to protect "DREAMers," those who entered the country as minors with unauthorized immigrant parents. The term derives from the acronym of the proposed bill, the Development, Relief, and Education for Alien Minors (DREAM) Act, first presented in 2001 by Senator Richard Durbin of Illinois. President Obama signed an executive order to exempt DREAMers from immediate deportation (U.S. Department of Homeland Security 2012). Later, when he realized that many non-criminal aliens were being detained, President Obama, along with DHS Secretary Jeh Johnson, initiated the Priority Enforcement Program (PEP) in his Secure Communities memorandum, which enables DHS to work with state and local law enforcement to prioritize the custody of convicted criminals, those who participate in an organized criminal gang, and individuals who pose a danger to public safety or a national security threat (U.S. Department of Homeland Security 2014b). President Obama also issued executive actions in 2014 to grant about 5 million unauthorized immigrants protection from deportation and assisted DREAMers by expanding Deferred Action for Childhood Arrivals (DACA), the 2012 program that permits young people who arrived as children to apply for deportation deferrals and work permits. By 2014, about 1.2 million young immigrants were eligible (Parlapiano 2014).

President Obama said he preferred that Congress assume responsibility and overhaul the immigration system as the only way to provide permanent protection for immigrants and improve the nation's immigration laws. However, he felt compelled to issue executive orders after many members of the Republican-controlled House publicly disapproved of a plan that included a pathway to citizenship. Even though the DREAMers were children when they entered, the Republican members callously stated that their mere unauthorized presence justified deportation to a land they did not know. In other words, the DREAMers lacked protections from removal based on actions taken and decisions made when they were neither competent nor old enough to act.

In mid-2014, in response to an influx of Latino children at the Mexican border with Texas, Representative Darrell Issa (R-CA) urged an end to the DACA program and the deportation of the eleven million undocumented aliens. He specifically included those who qualify as DREAMers. Issa's declaration epitomizes shortsighted contradictions among many politicians who preach from the political pulpit to conservative elements, a group that includes not only Republicans and Tea Party activists but also Democrats from politically unsafe swing districts who desperately want to hold on to the financial security and perks of their congressional seats.

Our nation's public education systems have educated thousands of DREAMers. Many excelled scholastically and have been accepted into colleges, at great sacrifice paying their own way. Others, unfortunately, have performed quite well, but their status has prevented them from going to the better colleges where the financial costs are exorbitant and loan and scholarship assistance, for all practical purposes, is nonexistent. As one nation, we should be flexible and recognize that first, we have made an educational investment in these children, and second, that we have every right to seek a just return.

DREAMers can be, have been, and should be part of our nation's success. We owe it to them for having become productive members of U.S. society. An incredible story from Phoenix, Arizona, demonstrates my assertion. The incident involved an extraordinary group that included four undocumented Latino students from the poor side of town. This foursome competed in underwater robotics and defeated students from the Massachusetts Institute of Technology (MIT). When I heard this story during my first years as a law professor, I really believed it was an Internet hoax. It seemed incredible, considering the reputation that MIT has always had. It turned out, after all, to be a truly amazing and fantastic story.

A movie, *Spare Parts*, by Lionsgate and a documentary have been made about this 2004 team. The four students—Oscar Vazquez, Cristian Arcega, Luis Aranda, and Lorenzo Santillan—and their teachers, Faridodin Lajvardi and Allan Cameron, should receive accolades. To remove any suspicion that the victory against MIT was a fluke, the same high school with a team that included two of the four previous competitors defeated MIT again in 2005 and 2006 (Ruelas 2014). All four deserve detailed credits, but I will focus on Oscar Vazquez as probative of what our nation's support for DREAMers can produce.

All four entered the country as children with undocumented parents, and this status created obstacles to entering college or finding employment. The documentary producer

Mary Mazzio described them as "kids that can compete and that clearly are innovative, that love to build and to fuel the country forward," yet they faced barriers to full educational success. Cameron, one of the robotics program teachers, bluntly criticized America's shortsightedness with regard to the education of undocumented students and the resources our nation loses, angrily stating, "there will be people all over the world who will have you," but "the U.S. is too stupid to keep you" (Ruelas 2008).

Of the four, only Vazquez obtained a job in an engineering-related field. He attended Arizona State University and studied engineering. When the state enacted a law barring undocumented immigrants from receiving scholarships and in-state tuition, Vazquez took on extra jobs. He sought private scholarships. Upon graduation, Vazquez deported himself to Mexico, leaving his U.S.-citizen wife and daughter behind in Arizona. He hoped he could make a case to allow himself to reenter legally. Despite his having grown up "American," his stellar academic credentials, and his exemplary past, the U.S. government denied his request twice. Senator Dick Durbin of Illinois, the godfather of the DREAMers movement, eventually heard about Vazquez. Within ten days of Durbin's intervention, Vazquez had his visa. Vazquez then fulfilled a childhood dream and joined the U.S. Army. After basic training, he became a U.S. citizen. After becoming a paratrooper, Vazquez served our nation in Afghanistan, thereby fulfilling two of the alternative provisions for earning DREAMer status: serving the United States in the military and obtaining a college degree.

THE ROLE OF RACE IN IMMIGRATION ENFORCEMENT EFFORTS

In the debates over immigration enforcement, racist motives have surfaced. American history documents the reluctance of Anglo-Americans or whites to commingle with Mexicans. The superiority complex among whites arose from the nation's origins in which free white men administered governmental affairs. Exceptions occurred when wealthy Mexican businessmen and landowners in the Southwest permitted an Anglo to court and marry a daughter. By this time in U.S. history, the nation's racial foundations as established by the Founding Fathers provided that political representation would be determined by the total of all free persons plus "three fifths of all other Persons."[31] Thus slaves were treated as property and as less than any white person. In addition, all Americans know quite well the government's mistreatment of the original Native American inhabitants. Consequently, the application of these social and racial views to the swarthy Mexican mestizo who became a part of the population a few years later was not a surprise.

RACIAL PROFILING AND IMMIGRATION ENFORCEMENT

"Racial profiling" is the discriminatory police practice of suspecting individuals on the basis of race, ethnicity, religion, or national origin (American Civil Liberties Union 2017). Criminal profiling generally involves reliance on a stereotype or a group of characteristics that police associate with criminal activity. One of the earliest examples of anti-Latino profiling appeared in the 1855 statute known as the "Greaser Act" (Bender et al. 2008, 3). Whites commonly used the term "greaser" disparagingly to refer to persons of Mexican descent (Pitt 1966, 309). It grew to the point that regardless of the duration of a Latino's residence in California, whether twenty years or one week, Anglo society viewed all Latinos as "interlopers" and "greasers" (Pitt 1966, 53).

Anti-profiling policies traditionally prohibit focusing on a person as a suspect on the basis of his/her race, color, ethnicity, or national origin. An exemplary anti-profiling law today extends the protected status to political affiliation, language, sexual orientation, gender, gender identity, and disabilities. When a police stop is based on suspect classifications such as race and ethnicity, the constitutional protections of the Fifth Amendment's due process clause (federal agents)[32] and the Fourteenth Amendment's equal protection clause (state agents)[33] are triggered.

Lawyers for the Mexican American Legal Defense and Educational Fund (MALDEF) in a brief to a court argued: "It is not a crime to be of Mexican descent, nor is a person's Mexican appearance a proper basis for arousing an officer's suspicions. Those broad descriptions literally fit millions of law-abiding American citizens and lawfully resident aliens" (Johnson 2010, 1019). If Border Patrol agents can loosely decide who and what to search, experience confirms they will continue to focus on drivers and on passengers who meet these ethnic criteria as the most likely targets for routine or random vehicle searches.

America's racial and ethnic profiling dilemmas arise, in part, from the 1968 Supreme Court ruling in *Terry v. Ohio* where the court created the reasonable suspicion exception to the probable cause standard of the Fourth Amendment.[34] *Terry* basically holds that if an officer has knowledge of specific and articulable facts that lead to a reasonable suspicion of criminal behavior, the agent may conduct a temporary detention, even of a vehicle. In *Terry*, the court emphasized that suspicion cannot be based upon an "inchoate and unparticularized suspicion" or on a mere hunch.

A few years later, the court aggravated matters for Latinos when it extended the *Terry* rule in *United States v. Brignoni-Ponce* (1975), an immigration detention case. Federal immigration agents stopped a vehicle based strictly on the Mexican appearance of the driver and occupants, an action the court rejected.[35] In *Brignoni-Ponce*, the court specified that at locations away from the border and its functional equivalents, roving patrol officers may stop vehicles only "if they are aware of specific articulable facts, together with rational inferences from those facts, that reasonably warrant suspicion that the vehicles contain aliens who may be illegally in the country." However, in comments not essential for the court's primary holding, the court remarked that reasonable suspicion can be found where "Mexican appearance" is utilized along with another relevant factor to constitute the necessary specific and articulable facts.

In my opinion ethnicity is relevant for a stop only if the alleged suspect was described as being of a particular race or ethnicity. We must remember: "Not all Latinos are undocumented persons, and not all undocumented persons are Latinos" (Salinas and Colon-Navarro 2011, 5). Since Latinos make up the largest ethnic minority in the United States, this premise is especially important. *Brignoni-Ponce* extended *Terry* to immigration enforcement agents. With the advent of federal-state cooperative agreements under section 287(g) of the Illegal Immigration Reform and Immigrant Responsibility Act, the same standard became available to thousands of local police officers across the nation.[36]

The *Brignoni-Ponce* ruling also engaged in irresponsible conclusions by accepting certain comments by counsel for the government as reliable evidence. In its holding, the court highlighted the comment by a government lawyer that "trained officers can recognize the characteristic appearance of persons who live in Mexico, relying on such factors as the mode of dress and haircut." The court never explicitly approved this claim, but the mere mention of these words as an illustrative comment has been utilized to justify Border Patrol traffic stops. Consistent with the belief that Mexican immigrants can be spotted by their haircut, Maricopa County Sheriff Joe Arpaio, whose racial profiling practices have resulted in the payment of several million dollars in litigation costs and damages by the county, pledged to continue arresting persons whose "clothing, accents, and behavior betrayed them as likely illegal immigrants" (*New York Times* 2009).

The extremely unfair and overbroad *Brignoni-Ponce* ruling was reviewed by the Ninth Circuit in *United States v. Montero-Camargo* (2000).[37] The Ninth Circuit covers various states and court decisions that govern practices in large Latino-populated states like California and Arizona. In the *Montero-Camargo* decision, the court concluded that the *Brignoni-Ponce* principle had become obsolete in regard to California-based cases. *Montero-Camargo* applied the U.S. Latino population growth in 2000 and compared it to the *Brignoni-Ponce* 1970 census figures. The appellate court decided this population increase eliminated the probative value of Latino ethnic appearance and cautioned that "in an area in which a large number of people share a specific characteristic, that characteristic casts too wide a net to play any part in a particularized reasonable suspicion determination."

Rather than broadening the reach of law enforcement, using local police can cause immigrant crime victims to fear the police and also sidetrack police efforts to fight crime. Nationally, responsible sheriffs and police chiefs have looked at and rejected 287(g) programs. Programs like 287(g) rest on the dishonest premise that illegal immigrants are a vast criminal threat when only a small percentage are dangerous felons. According to the *New York Times* (2009), treating most undocumented immigrants as potential Americans and not as a criminal gang is the sound response to the problem.

THE LEGAL FOUNDATION FOR RACISM IN GOVERNMENT

For well over a century, America's immigration policy effectively promoted maintenance of a Caucasian race majority. Congressional leaders and the Supreme Court followed this ideology, barring the admission of Chinese and promoting efforts to curtail Mexican immigration (Gottheimer 2003; Salinas and Torres 1976). Congressional policy in the 1970s equalized the treatment toward the Eastern and Western Hemispheres by limiting each to 20,000 immigrants per country.[38] While on its face the policy appears equal, it disproportionately affected nonresident family members of U.S. Latinos and other Latinos who hoped to obtain documentation to migrate, leading to an increase in undocumented entries.

Beginning in the early years of the nineteenth century, American domestic and foreign policy contributed to the U.S. Latino presence. Moses Austin entered into a settlement agreement with Mexico, resulting in an Anglo migration from the American South to Mexican Texas. Racial and cultural conflicts between Mexicans and Anglos immediately developed and eventually led to a call for independence by the white immigrants and a few Mexican leaders (Lowrie 1932). Through rebellion, Texas became an independent republic, and in less than a decade the United States annexed the formerly Mexican state. However, this action was taken over the objection of Senator John C. Calhoun, who argued against the inclusion into the American nation of Mexicans, whom he viewed as racially inferior, pointing out that Spanish America failed when it treated "colored" people as equal to the white race (Salinas 2015; Weber 1973). The annexation further incited the "Manifest Destiny" desires to proceed westward (Voelker 2004). As documented in the PBS series *U.S.-Mexican War* and by various scholars (De León 1983, 2002, 2009; Griswold del Castillo 1998; Urbina, Vela, and Sánchez 2014), white Americans adhered to a belief that God ordained this expansion from coast to coast to expand democracy and freedom to those who were capable of self-government, excluding Native Americans and non-Europeans.

After the grossly unjust war with Mexico, the United States had no choice but to incorporate about seventy-five thousand Mexicans who remained in the conquered territory (De León 1983, 2009; McWilliams 1990). The U.S. Mexican population grew slowly, reaching larger numbers by 1930. The exclusion by Congress of Chinese immigrants from the 1880s to 1943 increased the demand for Mexican labor.[39] As a result, of the estimated fifty thousand railroad workers, persons of Mexican descent composed over 70 percent of the section crews and extra gangs (Taylor 1934).

Recall the 1920s effort in Congress by John Box of Texas to exclude the "degenerate" Mexican race. Half a century later similar sentiments surfaced. In the 1988 effort to make English the official language of Arizona, ophthalmologist John Tanton participated with Roger Conner, then executive director of the Federation for American Immigration Reform (FAIR), to win the English-only referendum. In a confidential memorandum that fell into the hands of a newspaper reporter, Tanton criticized, in callous and tactless terms, the high birth rate of Latinos. He described Latinos as "simply more fertile," bluntly adding "this is the first instance in which those with their pants up are going to get caught by those with their pants down!" Tanton later complained of being called a racist, and explained that all he wanted was for "all members of the American family" to "speak to each other" around the dinner table. Tanton apparently had little faith that Latino immigrants could learn English as other immigrants have historically done (Salinas 2007). But does his comment not express a prejudgment that Latinos have an intellectual difficulty in learning a language other than Spanish?

Other evidence of racist motives surfaced in immigration enforcement. The levels of hostility intensified when the federal government, pursuant to section 287(g) of the 1996 Immigration Acts, made arrangements with local police agencies for collaborative agreements (U.S. Department of Homeland Security 2009; U.S. Department of Justice 1996). This "great" idea overlooked the involvement of elected officials in communities with histories of bigotry. Terry Johnson, a North Carolina sheriff, singled out "Mexicans" as customarily approving of sex with twelve-year-old girls, as if whites and members of other ethnic groups never commit pedophilia. Another North Carolina sheriff, Steve Bizzell, complained that "Mexicans" rape, rob, and murder "American citizens" (Weissman 2009). Bizzell made this wild claim well before Donald Trump made his racist announcement for the Republican nomination for president in 2015, in which he stated that when Mexico sends its people, they are "sending people that have lots of problems. . . . They're bringing drugs. They're bringing crime. They're rapists. And some, I assume, are good people" (*Time* 2015).

HUMAN RIGHTS CONCERNS AND VIOLATIONS

After the death of President Franklin D. Roosevelt, his widow, Eleanor Roosevelt, assumed a significant role in bringing the Universal Declaration of Human Rights (UDHR) to fruition. In December 1945, President Harry Truman offered her a position among the first U.S. delegation to the United Nations. Although reluctant primarily because she lacked diplomatic experience, she quickly adapted. The most hotly debated issue at the meeting was the fate of the European refugees who had fled Eastern Europe or had been liberated from Nazi concentration camps. While the Soviet Union insisted that the refugees return to their countries of origin, the Western nations believed they should be allowed to settle elsewhere. Which ideological view would win out: the Western emphasis on the rights of the individual (i.e., the "person") or the belief in Communist countries that the "common interest is more important than the individual interest" (Sears 2008, 7).

As chair of the Commission on Human Rights subcommittee responsible for drafting the UDHR, Roosevelt insisted as her third year began that the subcommittee elect another chair to show the world that new leadership could effectively maintain continuity. One of her main accomplishments included persuading the Soviet Union and China to abstain from voting since their intense criticism indicated a vote against the UDHR. Ms. Roosevelt encountered difficulties with her own State Department, whose leadership contended that a declaration on human rights would not benefit American interests (Sears 2008). Recognizing the racial inequality in U.S. history, Ms. Roosevelt knew that some Americans, especially in the South, would oppose the UDHR. She thus believed in the importance of unequivocal anti-discrimination language that would also support the continuing American civil rights struggle in which she actively participated (Sears 2008).

ANTI-LATINO ABUSES BY OMISSIONS AND ACTS OF POLICE AND BORDER AGENTS

The comments herein will not be the first time that abuses perpetrated against U.S. Latino citizens, residents, and undocumented immigrants will be presented as human rights violations. Latinos in the United States have experienced discriminatory and oppressive abuses for centuries. In reaction to immigration enforcement abuses of the late 1920s and early 1930s, Latinos formed protective organizations (Balderrama and Rodriguez 1995). A few decades later, in 1959, Latino abuse victims filed a human rights violations complaint with the United Nations since they had not obtained protections from U.S. agencies. The petition alleged violations of the UDHR's Article 3, which guarantees the "right to life, liberty and security of person." The petition, "Our Badge of Infamy: A Petition to the United Nations on the Treatment of the Mexican Immigrant," alleged "indiscriminate mass round-ups" of Mexican Americans or anyone who "looks like a Mexican" (Cortes 1974, iii, viii–ix).

History unfortunately repeated itself in late 2008 when LatinoJustice PRLDEF filed a petition with the Inter-American Commission on Human Rights, an agency within the Organization of American States (OAS). LatinoJustice asserted that the United States failed to meet its "obligation to ensure the security" of Latinos, regardless of legal status, who reside in the United States. The petition before the OAS was based on the cases of eight Latinos, including three who died as a result of brutal attacks. Cesar Perales, former president of LatinoJustice, explained that he pursued this complaint approach owing to frustration with immigration policies and the ensuing hate crimes.

By ignoring the problem, Perales declared, the United States violated the very human rights it pledged to defend in 1948 as an essential aspect of democracy all over the world. He emphasized the absence of a legal remedy to control the climate of opinion that led to violent attacks against Latinos, resulting in a failure of the U.S. government to protect Latinos and others. Perales argued the UDHR provides protections for not only legal residents but also others who might be in an undocumented status, since all persons have the "right to be safe" (Ramos 2008; Salinas 2015).

Many human rights injustices arise from the private actions of racists. In some cases, the government is powerless and immune from responsibility. In other cases, however, official links to the violations exist, and government police agents do not always step forward to investigate, arrest, and prosecute the wrongdoers. Our nation's unfortunate civil rights history is a case study of how private discrimination became common enough to constitute a custom or routine. Private actions can become entwined with those of the government or its agents. Since the beginning of immigration enforcement, the tone of calls to remove certain immigrants has intensified. Today, the movement once led by die-hard white supremacists has been joined by mainstream anti-immigration activists, radio hosts, and politicians who implicitly encourage or even endorse violence by characterizing immigrants from Mexico and Central America as "illegals," invaders, and criminal aliens. Those who ultimately perpetrate violence range from racist skinheads to Border Patrol agents and otherwise common citizens who felt obligated to take action they thought would protect jobs and the nation from these presumed harmful intruders (Mock 2007).

I will describe only a few of the many kinds of hate crimes and acts of violence. In North Bergen, New Jersey, shortly after the 2006 pro-immigrant demonstrations attracted hundreds of thousands of immigrants and their supporters across the country, a neo-Nazi radio host berated immigrants and urged listeners to "Clean your guns. Have plenty of ammunition. Find out where the largest gathering of illegal aliens will be near you. Go to the area well in advance, scope out several places to position yourself and then do what has to be done." Similar comments by other talk show radicals have led to violence and death. Many Latinos, some aliens and some citizens, have been victims of hate crimes. In one case, a young man was kicked into unconsciousness by two teenagers and robbed. Once arrested, they told police they were "amigo shopping," a reference to looking for Latinos to victimize.

PHYSICAL ABUSES AT THE HANDS OF GOVERNMENT AGENTS

Government agents have committed crimes motivated by anti-Latino sentiment. For example, two Border Patrol agents in 2005 became heroes of the right-wing anti-immigrant community by shooting a suspected undocumented alien in the back as he fled toward Mexico. The shot struck the man in the buttocks, severed his urethra and lodged in his groin. Somehow, he managed to escape. The agents later found that the suspect's van contained a shipment of marijuana, but they were unaware of this when they fired their guns at him. They covered up their crime by picking up spent shell casings, by not reporting the shooting to their superiors, and by filing a false incident report by not admitting the shooting. The agents were later convicted of several federal crimes and sentenced to prison. Strangely, they became martyrs of the right wing and Republican conservatives, groups that vociferously claim support for law and order. Shooting a fleeing alien (this is all the agents reasonably believed at the time) who poses no deadly threat does not authorize shooting to kill.

Misguided support by supervisors has likely contributed to the use of unnecessary force by border agents. For almost a decade, these agents utilized deadly force to respond to rock throwers from Mexico. After many casualties, investigators reviewed U.S. Customs and Border Enforcement policies on the use of deadly force. One of the fatal shootings involved a teenager whom agents said was throwing rocks at them from across a fence in Mexico. Instead of retreating, the agents accepted the challenge. They obviously lost the right to assert credibly that they were in fear of the immediate loss of life. This would not be a "Stand Your Ground" situation. From 2010 to 2012 alone at least eighteen people were killed by Border Patrol agents. Eight of the deaths involved rock throwers (Associated Press 2012).

In one such rock-throwing incident, a Border Patrol agent shot and killed a fifteen-year-old near the El Paso–Ciudad Juárez port of entry. The family sued the United States and the agent. The Fifth Circuit Court of Appeals initially affirmed the dismissal against the government, but it allowed the action against the agent to proceed. Judge Edward Prado concluded that a "noncitizen injured outside the United States as a result of arbitrary official conduct by a law enforcement officer located in the United States may invoke the protections provided by the Fifth Amendment," which include the right not to be subjected to the "conscience-shocking use of excessive force across our nation's borders."[40] The Fifth Circuit en banc reversed the panel decision, holding that the victim's family failed to establish a Fourth Amendment claim and that the agent had qualified for immunity as to the Fifth Amendment arbitrary conduct claims.[41]

Another deadly force shooting in 2007 by Border Patrol agent Nicholas Corbett resulted in two mistrials. The government dismissed the charges and later settled with the victim's family (Jackman 2011). The physical evidence strongly discredited the agent's version of the events, but the national anti-immigration atmosphere made a conviction in Arizona difficult. Jury nullification essentially interfered with the jury's duty to return a verdict of guilty. The agent claimed self-defense, asserting that his victim, standing a few feet away near the front of his vehicle, picked up a rock and put him in fear for his life (Holstege 2008). Surveillance footage contradicts this claim, since Corbett confronted the alien at the rear of his vehicle. Witness accounts establish that the alien was fatally shot at close range while on his knees, a claim confirmed by the forensic proof that the bullet that killed the alien was fired from somewhere between three and thirty inches from the victim (Mock 2007) and left powder burns on his clothing. The evidence also indicates that the shot came from slightly behind and above the smaller man. Under those circumstances, the much larger agent was close enough to easily and physically control a man with a rock in his hand (Holstege 2008). Deadly force was neither objectively reasonable nor immediately necessary.

In 2014, a few years later after the Corbett injustice, the commissioner of Customs and Border Protection presented a report entitled *Use of Force Policy: Guidelines and Procedures Handbook*. This policy report provides agents with rules related to the appropriate use of force (U.S. Customs and Border Enforcement 2014). The agency recognized that agents face hazardous conditions, but it found that "in several cases where agents shot at rock throwers, the force appeared to be excessive" (Preston 2014; Salinas 2015).

U.S. CITIZEN APPREHENSIONS AND REMOVALS IN THE POST-REAGAN ERA

Even U.S. citizens of Puerto Rican descent, legislatively declared to be U.S. citizens even if born in Puerto Rico,[42] suffer detentions by immigration agents who operate on conjecture rather than facts. Eduardo Caraballo spent three days in a Chicago jail after his theft arrest when immigration questions led to the placement of a hold on him. He faced "deportation" on suspicion of unauthorized status since he could not answer questions to agents' satisfaction. Caraballo's mother had brought him to the U.S. mainland as an infant (Perez and Lutz 2011).

Another moving case involves Luis Alberto Delgado, an American by birth. Born in Houston and in possession of a Texas identification card, a Social Security card, and a birth certificate, Delgado was suspected by the deputy sheriff of using fake documents since he spoke only Spanish. These factors prompted the deputy to call a Border Patrol agent to assume custody. At this point, an unreasonable seizure (prolonged detention without probable cause) occurred. In Delgado's case, his mother had obtained a divorce and left Texas to live with family in southern Mexico. After endless hours of doubting his birth claims, the agent managed to coerce this U.S. citizen to "voluntarily" depart (Carroll 2010).

After Delgado had spent three long months in northern Mexico, immigration officials finally allowed his return (Lavender 2011). A question arises: If the agent really believed Delgado had false documents, why did he not pursue a felony charge of presenting forged documents, the alleged basis for his disbelief? Such a misrepresentation is an extremely serious felony, which amounts to an obstruction of justice (Salinas 2015). Nonprosecution on such a serious allegation is highly indicative that the agent did not seriously believe his assertion of criminal behavior by Delgado.

THE UNITED NATIONS AND THE UNIVERSAL DECLARATION OF HUMAN RIGHTS

As noted herein, the United Nations, formed in 1945, enacted the Universal Declaration of Human Rights (UDHR) in 1948. The UDHR preamble recognizes the inherent dignity and the equal and inalienable rights of all members of the human family as the foundation of freedom, justice, and peace in the world. The disregard of human rights has resulted in unconscionable barbarous acts that outrage humankind. To further the cause of human rights, people are entitled to freedom of speech and belief and freedom from fear and hunger as among the highest aspiration of the common people. To attain these standards, human rights should be protected by the rule of law. The U.N. member states consequently reaffirmed the "dignity and worth of the human person and . . . the equal rights of men and women" (United Nations 1948).

The language of the UDHR answers the question of whether the abusive treatment of undocumented aliens and other persons suspected of unauthorized entry during the enforcement, detention, and deportation by U.S. enforcement agents amounts to violations of human rights. Article 1 provides that all human beings are born free and equal in dignity and rights and endowed with reason and conscience. Article 2 states that everyone is entitled to all the rights and freedoms set forth in this Declaration "without distinction of any kind," as to race, color, sex, language, religion, political opinion, national origin, or other status. Furthermore, no distinction shall be made on the basis of the political, jurisdictional, or international status of the country or territory to which a person belongs.

Articles 3 through 9 are particularly relevant and applicable to the U.S. immigration detention system. Article 3 provides that "everyone has the right to life, liberty and security of person," while Article 4 partially states that "no one shall be held in slavery or servitude." Article 5 holds that no one should be subjected to "torture or to cruel, inhuman or degrading treatment or punishment," while Articles 6 and 7 provide everyone "recognition everywhere as a person before the law" as well as equality and a discrimination-free protection of the law. Quite critical is Article 8, which extends to all the right to an effective remedy by the competent national tribunals for acts violating the fundamental rights granted him or her by the constitution or by law. Finally, Article 9 provides that no one shall be subjected to "arbitrary arrest, detention or exile," as occurred with the U.S. citizens discussed earlier.

Other assorted articles address matters that concern today's immigrant population in the United States. Article 14 confirms that everyone, with some background limitations, has the right to seek and to enjoy asylum from persecution. Article 23 states that "everyone," again with some limitations, has the right to work, but more importantly the right to equal pay for equal work. Pertinent to the Central American refugee issues of 2014 and 2015, Article 25 pertinently emphasizes that "motherhood and childhood are entitled to special care and assistance. All children, whether born in or out of wedlock, shall enjoy the same social protection" (United Nations 1948).

Regrettably, in their real-world application, these enumerated rights are not as respected as Eleanor Roosevelt and others who fought for the UDHR would have wanted. For example, U.S. enforcement agents and local police violate the letter and spirit of the provisions of the UDHR more than one would expect. Recently, a federal district court judge approved a settlement critical of immigration enforcement officers who convinced aliens through deception to sign a "voluntary return" document, interfering with their right to see a judge and have their day in court.[43] The court order provides that noncitizens who signed these "voluntary" departure documents and were expelled to Mexico will be granted an opportunity to return to seek legal status. The ACLU commented that border protection cannot sacrifice rights guaranteed by the Constitution, particularly where the alien waives these rights as a result of "government practices that rely upon misinformation, deception, and coercion" (American

Civil Liberties Union 2015). In this case, the lead plaintiff experienced anguish created by government's actions that separated her and her autistic ten-year-old U.S.-citizen son from her two daughters. Federal agents encouraged her to sign a form for an immediate "voluntary" return, telling her she could then easily "fix" her papers from Mexico. Otherwise, her autistic child would be sent to a foster home while she was detained for months. During a three-year period, she was unable to obtain treatment for her child (American Civil Liberties Union 2015).

Arguably, the federal agents involved in this inhumane act against the mother and a U.S.-citizen child in need of medical assistance violated several provisions of the UDHR. These provisions hold that all human beings are entitled to be treated with dignity (Article 1), to respect for rights regardless of their race, national origin, or other status (Article 2), to the right to life, liberty, and security of person (Article 3), to avoidance of "cruel, inhuman or degrading treatment" (Article 5), to recognition as a person before the law (Article 6), to the right to access the competent national tribunals (Article 8), and to freedom from arbitrary and capricious exile (Article 9). A final provision pertinently emphasizes that "motherhood and childhood are entitled to special care and assistance" (Article 25).

Many Latinos suffer from racial profiling, a practice inconsistent with the status of being "free and equal in dignity and rights" (Article 1). UDHR Article 2, which guarantees everyone equal treatment "without distinction of any kind," such as race, color, language, or national origin, has been frequently violated by police agents, who detain individuals primarily on the basis of their "Mexican" or Latino appearance. Two federal court decisions in Arizona and New York[44] within the past few years illustrate the Latino community's concern that they will be judged and criminalized because of the color of their skin or their use of Spanish (Salinas 2015).

All abuses of this nature offend human dignity, but when abuses by federal, state, and local agents lead to the detention and deportation of U.S. citizens and permanent resident aliens, these practices violate UDHR Article 5, which admonishes against subjecting anyone to "cruel, inhuman or degrading treatment or punishment" (Romero and Serag 2005; Salinas 2015; Stevens 2011). Professor Jacqueline Stevens describes the horrific case of Mario Guerrero, who, though born in Mexico, derived U.S. citizenship at birth from his citizen father. After his conviction for robbery, the U.S. government placed Guerrero in removal proceedings. The "expert" government agent should have inquired about Guerrero's citizenship status. Instead, faced with a no-bail situation, Guerrero succumbed and signed papers that banished him to Mexico (Stevens 2011).

He returned a few times without "permission" and without establishing citizenship. Finally, a private attorney conducted the research the government official should have done, and, while he awaited trial, Guerrero's Certificate of Citizenship arrived, and the prosecution moved to dismiss the criminal charges. Unfortunately, Guerrero spent a substantial part of his life imprisoned for immigration crimes he could not have committed since he was a citizen (Stevens 2011).

Article 4 provides that "no one shall be held in slavery or servitude." Unfortunately, both legal and undocumented immigrant status exposes one to involuntary servitude. The Thirteenth Amendment provides that neither slavery nor involuntary servitude, *except as a punishment for crime*, shall exist.[45] The Fourteenth Amendment declares that no state shall "deprive any person of life, liberty, or property, without due process of law; nor deny to any person within its jurisdiction the equal protection of the laws."[46] The Fifth Amendment due process of law clause applies to federal prisons and, arguably, to those immigration detention centers with which the government contracts.

As stated earlier, there has been much criticism of using immigrant detainees to perform work in place of regular employees for the meager sum of one dollar per day. The cheap labor, 13 cents an hour for a regular workday, saves the government and private companies $40 million annually by circumventing the federal minimum wage (Urbina 2014; see also Urbina and Álvarez 2016). One of these involuntary servants was Pedro Guzman. While detained as a deportable immigrant, he worked as a cook and custodian as part of the detention center's "voluntary" work program. Guzman was held for almost twenty months while his immigration case was favorably resolved.

Immigrants like Guzman are assigned work duties by profit-making companies like the Corrections Corporation of America (CCA) at subminimum wage rates. CCA, the nation's largest detention facilities and prison operator, had pre-tax earnings of $96.4 million for 2012 (Kunichoff 2012). Over the last decade, CCA's revenues rose more than 60 percent and its stock price climbed to more than thirty dollars per share from less than three dollars. In 2013, CCA made $301 million in net income, while another detention center, the GEO Group, made $115 million (Urbina 2014; see also Urbina and Álvarez 2016). During that same year, the GEO Group had seven hundred asylum detainees without criminal records. The funds for these DHS "custody operations" were budgeted in fiscal 2014 at $1.84 billion. Taxpayers pay about $160 daily to detain each asylum seeker. DHS's own estimates, as cited earlier, indicate that if the agency used electronic ankle monitoring and alternatives other than detention, the government could save over $1 billion annually.

While President Obama called for an overhaul of immigration law, his administration deported about two million persons in the last five years, a rate higher than that of any of his predecessors. The administration explained that the number of detainees was partly the result of a requirement from Congress that ICE fill a daily quota of more than thirty thousand beds. Ironically, two private prison companies, CCA and the GEO Group, control most of the immigrant detention market. Detentions in these facilities after September 11, 2001, effectively revitalized the industry (Urbina 2014; Urbina and Álvarez 2016).

Professor Stevens describes the detainee work program as consistent with slave labor, since people work at non-negotiable rates below the minimum wage. In addition, she notes the contradictory practice of hiring persons unauthorized to work pursuant to the 1986 IRCA statute. She also points out that the Thirteenth Amendment, which permits forced prison labor, would not apply to civil immigration holds (Kunichoff 2012). The allegedly voluntary work program has been resisted by detainees, who are threatened with solitary confinement by the detention staff when they stage a work stoppage or hunger strike (Urbina 2014).

Congress enacted an anti-peonage statute to enforce the Thirteenth Amendment. The law forbids one from holding or returning any person to a condition of peonage, or from arresting any person with the intent of placing him in or returning him to a condition of peonage.[47] As an example of the persistence of peonage practices, in a 1980 case my U.S. Department of Justice (DOJ) colleague and I prosecuted an involuntary servitude case. A private business owner of a Bay Area seafood company paid a Houston resident $100 per undocumented worker from Mexico or Central America. Unaware that they had a built-in employment debt, the undocumented workers had their transportation fee deducted at the rate of $10 a day.[48] The jury convicted the owner of peonage, kidnapping, carrying away a person with the intent to hold that person as a slave, and of a separate charge for aiding and abetting the coyote (trafficker) in the transportation of unauthorized aliens (Salinas 2005).

Articles 3 and 5 of the UDHR relate specifically to the manner in which agents of the U.S. immigration detention system treat persons that come into their custody. Article 3 dictates that "everyone has the right to life, liberty and security of person," while Article 5 states that no one should be subjected to "torture or to cruel, inhuman or degrading treatment or punishment." Shockingly, a recent report by Americans for Immigrant Justice described conditions in a detention facility where the temperatures were so cold that Customs and Border Patrol officers referred to the facility as *la hielera* ("icebox"), where "fingers and toes turn blue" and blankets are not provided (Hamilton and Alvarado 2014).

Contrary to our commitment to these pledges since 1948, the DOJ issued a no-prosecution decision in a death case that startled many (Foley 2015). Five years after a Mexican national named Anastasio Hernández-Rojas died after being taken into custody by Border Patrol agents for unauthorized entry, DOJ reviewed the evidence and closed its investigation without pursuing any federal charges. Hernández-Rojas was detained by Border Patrol agents in May 2010 after another unauthorized entry in an attempt to rejoin his wife and five citizen children in San Diego. He allegedly resisted, a part not apparent on the video. Video footage shows the man being struck with a baton and shocked with a Taser while surrounded by agents and supervisors from the Border Patrol and Immigration and Customs Enforcement.[49]

A video undoubtedly in federal possession records the haunting sounds of Hernández-Rojas crying out in pain for two and a half minutes. When I heard it, the word "torture" immediately came to mind. In the video, Hernández-Rojas can be heard crying out in apparent pain for help. For twenty seconds he cries out in a prolonged and horrible-sounding "Noooh," at times desperately pleading loudly in Spanish to the other agents to help him. Some onlookers yelled for the agents to stop.

As a former federal prosecutor who has tried a few claims of excessive force, summary punishment, I wondered how the top-level officials in the nation's capital could conclude that not one count of deprivation of liberty without due process of law was seen as appropriate. Even if the experts in D.C. could disregard Hernández-Rojas's "acute methamphetamine intoxication, pre-existing heart disease, the level of physical exertion during the struggle, and the electro-shocks from the Taser and positional restraint," how in the world could they disregard the five broken ribs and the horrific wounds to his face and body (Reese and Dean 2015).

Two factors obviously call for reconsideration. Twelve agents, including four supervisors, should not have allowed the excessive force to occur. Second, the video clearly shows an agent telling the other agents to back up as he continued to tase a handcuffed man on the ground who could not possibly threaten any agent with bodily harm. The video reveals a sadistic application of excessive and unnecessary force, but the DOJ conclusion was that the agents involved had not willfully deprived Hernández-Rojas of a constitutional right. The department also found "there is no evidence that any of the federal agents deployed the Taser or restrained Hernández-Rojas with malice" (Foley 2015). A civilian could not have gotten away with this type of brutality. Yet the DOJ, contrary to our human rights commitment, looked the other way.

CONCLUSION

From the "decade of betrayal" during the Great Depression era through the Obama administration and into the first several months of the Trump administration, Latino immigrants have been "always running." For the past century the Latino community has not had any respite from La Migra. The constant vigilance affects permanent Latino residents and citizens as well as those who live on the run from federal agents. As a former immigration enforcement agent has stated, regardless of the level of enforcement, people from south of our border will continue to attempt to enter for what they see as a matter of survival (Acosta and Pulitzer 2012).

In raids that began in January 2016, authorities detained more than 120 persons, including children, as part of an operation to deport refugee families who had fled violence in Central America. In the process, the Fourth Amendment right to be free from unreasonable searches and seizures was violated with impunity. According to news reports, federal agents used deception in gaining entry into homes. Once inside, they began to interrogate individuals about their "papers" and their right to be in the United States. Through this deception, the agents circumvented the other aspect of the Fourth Amendment, the provision that entries into a home require that agents have a search warrant obtained from a neutral and detached magistrate and specifying the person who is the object of the search.[50]

Many swept up in this raid reportedly had asylum claims, but they were not afforded due process. An immigration appeals court halted their removals just hours before twelve persons were to be sent to El Salvador. The common thread in these cases appears to be denial of access to counsel. The pro bono attorneys were successful in their initial efforts to stay the removals, but they rightfully complained that the enforcement system treated the mothers and children as "lawbreakers" instead of the refugees they actually were (Goodman 2016).

Many Americans operate under the mistaken belief that undocumented aliens in the United States are not entitled to our nation's constitutional protections. The Fourth Amendment explicitly refers to the right of "people" to be free from "unreasonable searches and seizures." Another relevant constitutional provision is the Fourteenth Amendment's declaration that both "citizens" and "persons" are protected. The federal courts interpret this provision to mean that persons who are present in the country are subject to U.S. jurisdiction and entitled to constitutional protections, and this includes undocumented persons.[51] They obviously enjoy the constitutional right to due process and not to be detained indefinitely, for lengthy periods of time, or to undergo removal without an opportunity to resolve the petition for asylum or refugee status (Pistone 1999). According to a law school student interning at the Karnes County Family Detention Center,

> CBP systematically puts the wrong information on the I213. A lot of the women reported never being asked if they feared return. Others took the time to translate the transcripts and found things they never said or were never asked. For some time we saw a lot of I213 with exactly the same language saying that the reason to come here was "to work for three years," even on transcripts for little children. These inaccuracies bring great anxiety to the women. They have, in fact, been brought against the women in merits and bond hearings. One woman reported that when she told a CBP officer she was afraid of returning to her country due to gang violence (the gangs had threatened to kill her children resisting recruitment), the CBP officer said, "we have them here too, you'll never be safe." (Zambrano 2015)

Under American jurisprudence, due process of law includes an opportunity to resolve the petition for asylum or refugee status honestly and without false misrepresentation as to what the applicant stated or did not state to the detention officer or agent.[52]

Once the public and the courts agree that all persons have protected constitutional rights, regardless of their immigrant status, then we as a nation can begin the process of establishing a more just and equitable system built on the mutual respect among all the different racial and ethnic groups that truly makes us "one nation, with liberty and justice for all." One small step in the right direction is recognizing that unjust and harmful practices exist, without waiting for judicial declarations. Congress can accomplish this by not abdicating its duty.

Once the known inequities, such as the detention quota and the denial of due process hearings for refugees, are addressed and corrected, Americans can begin to develop an immigration policy that realistically addresses national economic and workforce needs based on the history that made us a nation of immigrants. Unless real change occurs in Washington, D.C., the current U.S. immigration laws and the resistance by Congress to address the politically delicate and apparently dreaded immigration issue will continue as usual. Operating under this mindset, the inaction by Congress will force immigrants of whatever status to constantly be on the alert for La Migra while they hope for a better life where employers will respect their right to fair pay and safe working conditions.

In closing, another factor to consider is that American demographers predict the need for continued immigration to the United States. Baby boomers did not produce the number of children necessary to maintain the future workforce. In 2002 demographers with the Office of Population Research at Princeton University reported that the United States needs about 464,000 immigrants annually for the next century just to maintain the population in the year 2100 at the same size as in 1980 and to provide for our ongoing labor needs as a nation (Wright 2001). Further, a study by the Immigration Policy Center found that while U.S. immigration cannot make up the developing deficits in Social Security and Medicare, younger immigrants can produce more children to overcome the low fertility rates among the native-born and can reduce the shortfall by contributing tax dollars to bolster Social Security (Ewing 2012).

Consequently, U.S. policy makers should plan decades ahead while recognizing the realities of the economics of immigration. First, immigrants and eventually their children fuel the U.S. economy. Second, despite the obvious economic importance of immigrants, the U.S. immigration system and policy makers remain "stubbornly oblivious to the forces of supply and demand that actually drive immigration" (Ewing 2012, 6). On the contrary, our leaders utilize "arbitrary numerical caps that bear little relationship to economic reality" (Ewing 2012, 6). The legislative leadership would be wise to legally admit those immigrants who can replace the retiring baby boomers, care for the growing elderly population, and strengthen the retirement and medical care systems with fresh tax dollars.

NOTES

1. The Antiterrorism and Effective Death Penalty Act (AEDPA) (1996), 18 U.S.C. § 2339B (a) (7) (2006); Illegal Immigration Reform and Immigrant Responsibility Act (IIRIRA) (1996), 8 U.S.C. § 1101 et seq. (2006); Padilla v. Kentucky, 559 U.S. 356, 369 (2010).

2. Secure Fence Act of 2006, 120 Stat. 2638, Pub. L. 109-367, Oct. 26, 2006.

3. See People v. Conroy, 958 N.Y.S.2d 224, 225 (2013) (Victim Marcelo Lucero).

4. Terry v. Ohio, 392 U.S. 1, 21 (1968); United States v. Brignoni-Ponce, 422 U.S. 873 (1975).

5. 347 U.S. 475 (1954).

6. See Dred Scott v. Sandford, 60 U.S. 393 (1857).

7. Agreement Between the United States of America and Mexico Respecting the Temporary Migration of Mexican Agricultural Workers, U.S.-Mex., Aug. 4, 1942, 56 Stat. 1759, amended by, 57 Stat. 1152 (1943) and Act of Dec. 13, 1963, Pub. L. No. 88-203, 77 Stat. 363 (expired Dec. 31, 1964) (popularly known as the Bracero Program).

8. Act of Oct. 3, 1965, Pub. Law No. 89-236, 79 Stat. 11, § 21 (e).

9. The Nicaraguan Adjustment and Central American Relief Act, 105 P.L. 139; 111 Stat. 2644 (1997).

10. 8 U.S.C. § 1255a (2006).

11. 8 U.S.C. § 1324a (2006).

12. The Antiterrorism and Effective Death Penalty Act (AEDPA), Pub. L. 104-142, § 401-443, 110 Stat. 1214, 1258-81 (1996), codified at 18 U.S.C. § 2339B (a) (7) (2006), combined with the Illegal Immigration Reform and Immigrant Responsibility Act (IIRIRA), Pub. L. 104-208, Div. C, 110 Stat. at 3009-546 through 3009-724 (1996), 8 U.S.C. § 1101 et seq. (2006), extensively amended the Immigration and Nationality Act of 1952 (INA), 66 Stat. 163 (1952), 8 U.S.C. § 1101 et seq. (2006).

13. 66 Stat. 163 (1952), 8 U.S.C. § 1101 et seq.

14. See 8 U.S.C. § 1227 (a) (2) (A)(iii) and § 1101 (a)(43) (A)-(U) (1999) (definition and descriptions of aggravated felonies).

15. Statement by President William Jefferson Clinton upon Signing S. 735 [The Antiterrorism and Effective Death Penalty Act of 1996], 142 Cong. Rec. 961-3, 110 Stat. 3009-749 (1996).

16. 8 U.S.C. § 1101, § 212 (c) (2006).

17. See 8 U.S.C. § 1229b (a) (cancellation of removal); § 1229b (b) (cancellation); § 1229c (voluntary departure); § 1231(b) (3) (restriction of removal); § 1225(a) (1) (withdrawal of application for admission); § 1158 (political asylum).

18. 110 Stat. 3009-597, § 304 (b), creating 8 U.S.C. § 1229b (a) (3) (1994 ed., Supp. V) (emphasis added); see 8 U.S.C. § 1101 (a) (43) (definition of aggravated felony).

19. For example, Marcello v. Bonds, 349 U.S. 302 (1955) (deported alien had been in the United States since the age of three).

20. 8 U.S.C. § 1101 (a) (43) (G); 8 U.S.C. 1101 (a) (43) (P), (R), and (S).

21. United States v. Arqueta-Ramos, 730 F.3d 1133, 1141-42 (9th Cir. 2013).

22. 804 F.3d 1060, 1089-90 (9th Cir. 2015).

23. Id. at 1066-67 (9th Cir. 2015).

24. 533 U.S. 678, 690 (2001).

25. Kansas v. Hendricks, 521 U.S. 346, 357, 358 (1997).

26. 804 F.3d 1060, 1069 (9th Cir. 2015), citing Casas-Castrillon v. Department of Homeland Security, 535 F.3d 942, 949 (9th Cir. 2008).

27. Singh v. Holder, 638 F.3d 1196, 1203, 1208 (9th Cir. 2011).

28. Rodriguez v. Robbins, 804 F.3d 1060, 1069 (9th Cir. 2015), citing Singh v. Holder, 638 F.3d 1196, 1206 (9th Cir. 2011) and In re Guerra, 24 I. and N. Dec. 37, 40 (BIA 2006).

29. Casas-Castrillon v. Department of Homeland Security, 535 F.3d 942, 948-49 (9th Cir. 2008).

30. United States v. Otherson, 637 F.2d 1276, 1281, 1283 (9th Cir. 1980).

31. See U.S. Const. art. I, § 2 cl. 3.

32. U.S. Const. amend. V.

33. U.S. Const. amend. XIV, § 1.

34. Terry, 392 U.S. at 1, 27.

35. United States v. Brignoni-Ponce, 422 U.S. 873, 876 (1975).

36. See 8 U.S.C. § 1357(g) (2006).

37. United States v. Montero-Camargo, 208 F.3d 1122, 1133 (9th Cir. 2000) (en banc).

38. Pub. L. No. 94-571 (Oct. 20, 1976) (effective January 1, 1977).

39. Chinese Exclusion Act, ch. 126, 22 Stat. 58 (1882), *repealed*, Act of Dec. 17, 1943, ch. 344, 57 Stat. 600.

40. Hernandez v. United States, 757 F.3d 249, 273 (5th Cir. 2014).

41. Hernandez v. United States, 785 F.3d 117 (5th Cir. 2015).

42. Congress declared that persons born in Puerto Rico between 1899 and 1941, and residing in Puerto Rico or other U.S territory, would be citizens of the United States, adding that all others born after January 13, 1941, would be citizens at birth. 8 U.S.C. § 1402 (2006).

43. Lopez-Venegas v. Johnson, First Amended Complaint, Cause No. 13-cv-03972 JAK (PLA) (C.D. Cal. Oct. 2, 2013).

44. Melendres v. Arpaio, 989 F. Supp. 2d 822 (D. Ariz. 2013), affirmed in part and vacated and remanded in part, 784 F.3d 1254 (9th Cir. 2015) (the appellate court affirmed in all respects with the exception that the remedial injunction broadly required the Monitor to consider and review disciplinary issues and violations of departmental policy that could subject sheriff employees to civil suits and criminal charges, even if they occur while the employee is not on duty); Floyd v. City of New York, 959 F. Supp. 2d 540 (S.D.N.Y. 2013), appeal dismissed, Nos. 13-3088-cv, 13-3123-cv, 14-2829-cv, 14-2848-cv, 14-2834-cv, at 5 (2d Cir. Oct. 31, 2014) (the appellate court granted the City's motion for voluntary dismissal of the appeals with prejudice).

45. U.S. Const. amend. XIII (emphasis added).

46. U.S. Const. amend. XIV. I add emphasis to show how the drafters of the Constitution distinguished "persons" and "citizens."

47. 18 U.S.C. § 1581 (2000).

48. United States v. Nelson, No. 81-2105 (S.D. Tex. 1980).

49. Estate of Hernandez-Rojas v. United States, 62 F. Supp. 3d 1169 (S.D. Cal. 2014).

50. Steagald v. United States, 451 U.S. 204 (1981).

51. For example, Plyler v. Doe, 457 U.S. 202 (1982) (the Fourteenth Amendment Equal Protection Clause provides protection from discrimination against undocumented alien children); United States v. Otherson, 637 F.2d 1276, 1281, 1283 (9th Cir. 1980).

52. Banks v. Dretke, 540 U.S. 668, 680, 683 n. 5 (2004), citing Brady v. Maryland, 373 U.S. 83, 87 (1963). ("Suppression by the prosecution of evidence favorable to an accused upon request violates due process where the evidence is material either to guilt or to punishment, irrespective of the good faith or bad faith of the prosecution.")

REFERENCES

Ackerman, A., and R. Furman. 2014. *The Criminalization of Immigration: Contexts and Consequences*. Durham, N.C.: Carolina Academic Press.

Acosta, H., and L. Pulitzer. 2012. *The Shadow Catcher*. New York: Atria Books.

Acuña, R. 1972. *Occupied America: The Chicano's Struggle Toward Liberation*. San Francisco: Canfield Press.

American Civil Liberties Union. 2015. "Families Separated by Coercive Immigration Practices Reunited in U.S." *ACLU*, February 26. https://www.aclu.org/news/families-separated -coercive-immigration-practices-may-be-reunited-us.

———. 2017. "Racial Profiling: Definition." *ACLU*. https://www.aclu.org/other/racial -profiling-definition.

Androff, D. K., and K. Y. Tavassoli. 2012. "Deaths in the Desert: The Human Rights Crisis on the U.S.-Mexico Border." *Social Work* 57: 165–73.

Associated Press. 2012. "Homeland Security Probing Border Patrol's Use of Force Policies Amid Claims of Brutality." *Washington Post*, October 18.

Balderrama, F. E., and R. Rodriguez. 1995. *Decade of Betrayal: Mexican Repatriation in the 1930s.* Albuquerque: University of New Mexico Press.

Bender, S. W., R. Aldana, G. P. Carrasco, and J. G. Ávila. 2008. *Everyday Law for Latino/as.* Boulder, Colo.: Paradigm.

Bernstein, N. 2009. "Target of Immigrant Raids Shifted." *New York Times*, February 3. http://www.nytimes.com/2009/02/04/us/04raids.html.

Biggers, J. 2012. *State Out of the Union: Arizona and the Final Showdown over the American Dream.* New York: Nation Books.

Box, J. 1928. "Immigration Restriction." *Digital History.* www.digitalhistory.uh.edu/disp_textbook.cfm?smtID=3&psid=594.

Carrigan, W., and C. Webb. 2003. "The Lynching of Persons of Mexican Origin or Descent in the US, 1848–1929." *Journal of Social History* 37: 411–38.

———. 2013. *Forgotten Dead: Mob Violence Against Mexicans in the United States, 1848–1928.* New York: Oxford University Press.

Carroll, S. 2010. "Man Born at Ben Taub Returns After He's Wrongly Deported." *Houston Chronicle*, September 14. http://www.chron.com/news/houston-texas/article/Man-born-at-Ben-Taub-returns-after-he-s-wrongly-1694617.php.

Center for Responsive Politics. 2015. "Annual Lobbying by Corrections Corp. of America." http://www.opensecrets.org/lobby/firmsum.php?id=D000021940&year=2017.

Chishti, M., D. Meissner, and C. Bergeron. 2011. "At Its 25th Anniversary, IRCA's Legacy Lives On." http://www.migrationpolicy.org/article/its-25th-anniversary-ircas-legacy-lives.

Chomsky, A. 2007. *"They Take Our Jobs!": And 20 Other Myths About Immigration.* Boston: Beacon Press.

Cook, M. 2003. "Banished for Minor Crimes: The Aggravated Felony Provision of the Immigration and Nationality Act as a Human Rights Violation." *Boston College Third World Law Journal* 23: 293–327.

Cortes, C. E., ed. 1974. *The Mexican American and the Law.* New York: Arno Press.

Davis, K. C. 2011. *Don't Know Much About History: Everything You Need to Know About American History but Never Learned.* New York: HarperCollins.

De León, A. 1983. *They Called Them Greasers: Anglo Attitudes Toward Mexicans in Texas, 1821–1900.* Austin: University of Texas Press.

———. 2002. *Racial Frontiers: Africans, Chinese, and Mexicans in Western America, 1848–1890.* Albuquerque: University of New Mexico Press.

———. 2009. *Mexican Americans in Texas: A Brief History.* 3rd ed. Wheeling, Ill.: Harland Davidson.

Delgado, R. 2009. "The Law of the Noose: A History of Latino Lynching." *Harvard Civil Rights–Civil Liberties Law Review* 44: 297–312.

DiNatale, S., and M. Sacchetti. 2015. "South Boston Brothers Allegedly Beat Homeless Man." *Boston Globe*, August 19. https://www.bostonglobe.com/metro/2015/08/19/homeless/iTagewS4bnvBKWxxPvFcAJ/story.html.

Ewing, W. A. 2012. "The Future of a Generation: How New Americans Will Help Support Retiring Baby Boomers." *American Immigration Council*. https://www.americanimmigrationcouncil.org/research/future-generation-how-new-americans-will-help-support-retiring-baby-boomers.

Fernandez, M. 2010. "L.I. Man Gets 25-Year Term in Killing of Immigrant." *New York Times*, May 27.

Flaccus, G. 2007. "L.A.-Area Immigration Sweep Nabs More Than 700." *Houston Chronicle*, January 24.

Foley, E. 2015. "DOJ: No Civil Rights Charges for Border Agents over Death of Anastasio Hernandez-Rojas." *Huffington Post*, November 6.

Frey, J. C. 2010. *The 800 Mile Wall*. Dir. John Carlos Frey. Gatekeeper Productions, 2010. DVD.

Fry, R. 2009. "Latino Children: A Majority Are U.S.-Born Offspring of Immigrants." *Pew Hispanic Center*, May 28. http://www.pewhispanic.org/reports/report.php?ReportID=110.

Galarza, E. 1964. *Merchants of Labor: The Mexican Bracero Story: An Account of the Managed Migration of Mexican Farm Workers in California, 1942–1960*. Charlotte, N.C.: McNally and Loftin.

Garcia, G. C. 1952. Testimony Given by American G.I. Forum Legal Counsel at Hearings on Migratory Labor Before the Subcommittee on Labor and Labor-Management Relations of the Senate Committee on Labor and Public Welfare. 82d Cong., 2d Sess., pt. 1.

Gibson, C., and K. Jung. 2002. "Historical Census Statistics on Population Totals by Race, 1790 to 1990, and by Hispanic Origin, 1970 to 1990, for the United States, Regions, Divisions, and States, Population Division." https://www.census.gov/content/dam/Census/library/working-papers/2002/demo/POP-twps0056.pdf.

Goodman, A. 2016. "Resistance and Outrage as Obama Administration Rounds Up Central American Refugees." *Democracy Now!*, January 8. http://www.truth-out.org/news/item/34343-resistance-and-outrage-as-obama-administration-rounds-up-central-american-refugees.

Gottheimer, J., ed. 2003. *Ripples of Hope: Great American Civil Rights Speeches*. New York: Basic Civitas Books.

Gottlieb, P. 1999. "A Decade Ago: A Terrorist Is Captured in Port Angeles." *Peninsula Daily News*, December 13. http://www.peninsuladailynews.com/article/20091213/news/312139990.

Griswold del Castillo, R. 1998. "The Mexican-American War and the Treaty of Guadalupe Hidalgo." *Southwestern Journal of Law and Trade in the Americas* 5: 31–43.

Hamilton, K., and F. Alvarado. 2014. "Seeking Asylum in U.S., Immigrants Become Long-Term Detainees Instead." *Broward-Palm Beach New Times*, April 10. http://www

.browardpalmbeach.com/news/seeking-asylum-in-us-immigrants-become-long-term
-detainees-instead-6353777.

Hennessy-Fiske, M. 2015. "Paid $1 to $3 a Day, Unauthorized Immigrants Keep Family Detention Centers Running." *Los Angeles Times*, August 3. http://www.latimes.com/nation/
immigration/la-na-detention-immigration-workers-20150803-story.html.

Hernandez, C. C. G. 2015. *Crimmigration Law*. Chicago, Ill.: ABA.

Hipsman, F., and D. Meissner. 2013. "Immigration in the United States: New Economic,
Social, Political Landscapes with Legislative Reform on the Horizon." *Migration Policy
Institute*, April 16. http://www.migrationpolicy.org/article/immigration-united-states-new
-economic-social-political-landscapes-legislative-reform.

Holstege, S. 2008. "Mistrial Ends Murder Case Against Ariz. Border Agent." *Arizona Republic*, November 5. http://archive.azcentral.com/arizonarepublic/news/articles/2008/11/05/
20081105corbett-verdict1105.html.

Jackman, J. R. 2011. "$850k Settlement for Family of Slain Illegal Immigrant." *Tucson Senti-
nel*, September 8. http://www.tucsonsentinel.com/local/report/090811_slain_immigrant
_settlement/850k-settlement-family-slain-illegal-immigrant/.

Johnson, K. R. 2005. "The Forgotten 'Repatriation' of Persons of Mexican Ancestry and Lessons
for the 'War on Terror.'" *Pace Law Review* 26: 1–26.

———. 2010. "How Racial Profiling in America Became the Law of the Land: *United States v.
Brignoni-Ponce* and *Whren v. United States* and the Need for Truly Rebellious Lawyering."
Georgetown Law Journal 98: 1005–77.

Johnson, K. R., and J. E. C. Ingram. 2013. "Anatomy of a Modern-Day Lynching: The Relationship Between Hate Crimes Against Latina/os and the Debate over Immigration Reform."
North Carolina Law Review 91: 1613–35.

Kunichoff, Y. 2012. "'Voluntary' Work Program Run in Private Detention Centers Pays
Detained Immigrants $1 a Day." *Truthout*, July 27. http://www.truth-out.org/news/
item/10548-voluntary-work-program-run-in-private-detention-centers-pays-detained
-immigrants-1-a-day.

Lavender, M. B. 2011. "Hispanic Profiling Happened Before Arizona's Stringent Immigration
Law." *ABC News*, February 3. http://abcnews.go.com/WhatWouldYouDo/hispanic-racial
-profiling-happened-arizonas-strict-immigration-law/story?id=12822819.

Lazarus, E. 1883. "The New Colossus." http://xroads.virginia.edu/~CAP/LIBERTY/lazarus
.html.

Liu, M. L., ed. 2012. *The World Almanac and Book of Facts 2012*. New York: World Almanac
Books.

Logan, J., and R. Turner. 2013. *Hispanics in the United States: Not Only Mexicans*. Report for
Russell Sage Foundation. http://www.s4.brown.edu/us2010/Data/Report/report03202013
.pdf.

Lopez, M. H., A. Gonzalez-Barrera, and D. Cuddington. 2013. *Diverse Origins: The Nation's 14 Largest Hispanic-Origin Groups*. Pew Hispanic Center. http://www.pewhispanic.org/files/2013/06/summary_report_final.pdf.

Los Angeles Times. 2014. "Dump the Immigrant Detainee Quota." May 8. http://www.latimes.com/opinion/editorials/la-ed-immigrant-detainee-quota-homeland-security-20140509-story.html.

Lowrie, S. H. 1932. *Culture Conflict in Texas: 1821–1835*. New York: Columbia University Press.

Martin, D. C., and J. E. Yankay. 2014. *Refugees and Asylees: 2013*. Washington, D.C.: U.S. Department of Homeland Security, Office of Immigration Statistics.

McWilliams, C. 1990. *North from Mexico: The Spanish-Speaking People of the United States*. New York: Praeger.

Miller, T. 2011. "Timeline: Guatemala's Brutal Civil War." *PBS NewsHour*. http://www.pbs.org/newshour/updates/latin_america/jan-june11/timeline_03-07.html.

Mock, B. 2007. "Immigration Backlash: Violence Engulfs Latinos." *Southern Poverty Law Center*, November 26. http://www.splcenter.org/get-informed/news/immigration-backlash-violence-engulfs-latinos.

National Immigrant Justice Center. 2015. "Immigration Detention Bed Quota Timeline." *National Immigrant Justice Center*. http://www.immigrantjustice.org/staff/blog/immigration-detention-bed-quota-timeline.

New York Times. 2009. "Wrong Paths to Immigration Reform." *New York Times*, October 12. http://www.nytimes.com/2009/10/12/opinion/12mon2.html.

Oboler, S., and D. J. González. 2005a. *The Oxford Encyclopedia of Latinos and Latinas in the United States*. Vol. 2. New York: Oxford University Press.

———. 2005b. *The Oxford Encyclopedia of Latinos and Latinas in the United States*. Vol. 4. New York: Oxford University Press.

Parlapiano, A. 2014. "What Is President Obama's Immigration Plan?" *New York Times*, November 20. https://www.nytimes.com/interactive/2014/11/20/us/2014-11-20-immigration.html?_r=0.

Passel, J., D. Cohn, and A. Gonzalez-Barrera. 2013. "Population Decline of Unauthorized Immigrants Stalls, May Have Reversed." *Pew Hispanic Center*, September 23. http://www.pewhispanic.org/2013/09/23/population-decline-of-unauthorized-immigrants-stalls-may-have-reversed/.

PBS. *U.S.-Mexican War*. Dir. Ginny Martin. KERA-Dallas/Fort Worth, 1998. https://www.pbs.org/kera/usmexicanwar/index_flash.html.

Perales, A. S. 1974. *Are We Good Neighbors?* New York: Arno Press.

Perez, A., and B. J. Lutz. 2010. "American Citizen Faced Deportation." *NBC Chicago*, June 30. http://www.nbcchicago.com/news/local/eduardo-caraballo-puerto-rico-deportion-94795779.html.

Pistone, M. R. 1999. "Justice Delayed Is Justice Denied: A Proposal for Ending the Unnecessary Detention of Asylum Seekers." *Harvard Human Rights Journal* 12: 197–265.

Pitt, L. 1966. *The Decline of the Californios: A Social History of the Spanish-Speaking Californians, 1846–1890*. Berkeley: University of California Press.

Preston, J. 2011. "Immigration Crackdown Also Snares Americans." *New York Times*, December 13.

———. 2014. "Book Guiding Border Agents on Force Is Released." *New York Times*, May 30. http://www.nytimes.com/2014/05/31/us/book-guiding-border-agents-on-force-is -released.html?src=rechp&_r=0.

Ramos, V. M. 2008. "Human Rights Complaint: U.S. Hispanics 'Are Being Targeted.'" *Orlando Sentinel*, December 18.

Reagan, Ronald. 1987. "Tear Down This Wall." *The History Place: Great Speeches Collection*. http://www.historyplace.com/speeches/reagan-tear-down.htm.

Reese, T., and J. Dean. 2015. "US Border Agents Cleared of Charges in Murder of Immigrant Anastasio Hernandez-Rojas." *World Socialist Web Site*, December 7. https://www.wsws.org/ en/articles/2015/12/07/bord-d07.html.

Reyes, R. 2008. "Hot Rhetoric Fuels Latino Hate Crimes." *USA Today*, December 5.

Romero, M., and M. Serag. 2005. "Violation of Latino Civil Rights Resulting from INS and Local Police's Use of Race, Culture and Class Profiling: The Case of the Chandler Roundup in Arizona." *Cleveland State Law Review* 52: 75–96.

Rosales, F. A. 2006. *Dictionary of Latino Civil Rights History*. Houston: Arte Público Press.

Ruelas, R. 2008. "For Carl Hayden Robotics Team, Beating Immigration Is Tougher Than Beating the Competition." *Arizona Republic*, July 31.

———. 2014. "10 Years Ago They Beat MIT. Today, It's Complicated." *Arizona Republic*, July 19.

Sakuma, A. 2014. "Operation Streamline: An Immigration Nightmare for Arizona Courts." *MSNBC*, June 22. http://www.msnbc.com/msnbc/operation-streamline-immigration -nightmare-arizona-courts.

Salinas, G., and I. D. Torres. 1976. "The Undocumented Mexican Alien: A Legal, Social, and Economic Analysis." *Houston Law Review* 13: 863–916.

Salinas, L. S. 2004. "Deportations, Removals, and the 1996 Immigration Acts: A Modern Look at the Ex Post Facto Clause." *Boston University International Law Journal* 22: 245–307.

———. 2005. "Latinos and Criminal Justice in Texas: Has the New Millennium Brought Progress?" *Thurgood Marshall Law Review* 30: 289–346.

———. 2007. "Immigration and Language Rights: The Evolution of Private Racist Attitudes into American Public Law and Policy." *Nevada Law Journal* 7: 895–932.

———. 2015. *U.S. Latinos and Criminal Injustice*. East Lansing: Michigan State University Press.

Salinas, L. S., and F. Colon-Navarro. 2011. "Racial Profiling as a Means of Thwarting the Alleged Latino Security Threat." *Thurgood Marshall Law Review* 37: 5–44.

Samora, J. 1971. *Los Mojados: The Wetback Story*. Notre Dame, Ind.: University of Notre Dame Press.

Sears, J. F. 2008. "Eleanor Roosevelt and the Universal Declaration of Human Rights." *FDR Presidential Library and Museum*. http://fdrlibrary.marist.edu/library/pdfs/sears.pdf.

Simanski, J. F. 2014. *Immigration Enforcement Actions: 2013*. Washington, D.C.: U.S. Department of Homeland Security, Office of Immigration Statistics.

Stevens, J. 2011. "U.S. Government Unlawfully Detaining and Deporting U.S. Citizens as Aliens." *Virginia Journal of Social Policy and the Law* 18: 606–720.

Taylor, P. S. 1934. *An American-Mexican Frontier: Nueces County, Texas*. Charlotte: University of North Carolina Press.

Time. 2015. "Here's Donald Trump's Presidential Announcement Speech." *Time*, June 16. http://time.com/3923128/donald-trump-announcement-speech/.

United Nations. 1948. *Universal Declaration of Human Rights*. http://www.un.org/en/documents/udhr/.

Urbina, I. 2014. "Using Jailed Migrants as a Pool of Cheap Labor." *New York Times*, May 24. http://www.nytimes.com/2014/05/25/us/using-jailed-migrants-as-a-pool-of-cheap-labor.html?_r=0.

Urbina, M. G., and S. E. Álvarez. 2016. "Neoliberalism, Criminal Justice, and Latinos: The Contours of Neoliberal Economic Thought and Policy on Criminalization." *Latino Studies* 14: 33–58.

Urbina, M. G., J. E. Vela, and J. O. Sánchez. 2014. *Ethnic Realities of Mexican Americans: From Colonialism to 21st Century Globalization*. Springfield, Ill.: Charles C Thomas.

U.S. Commission on Civil Rights. 1980. *The Tarnished Golden Door: Civil Rights Issues in Immigration*. Washington, D.C.: U.S. Government Printing Office.

U.S. Customs and Border Enforcement. 2014. *Use of Force Policy, Guidelines and Procedures Handbook*. Washington, D.C.: U.S. Government Printing Office. http://www.cbp.gov/sites/default/files/documents/UseofForcePolicyHandbook.pdf.

U.S. Department of Commerce. 1930. *Fifteenth Census of the United States: 1930, Justice Precinct 6, Victoria County, Texas, Enumeration Dist. No. 235-14*. U.S. Census Bureau.

U.S. Department of Homeland Security. 2009. "ICE Announces Standardized 287(g) Agreements with 67 State and Local Law Enforcement Partners." http://www.ice.gov/news/releases/0910/091016washingtondc.htm.

———. 2012. "Consideration of Deferred Action for Childhood Arrivals (DACA)." http://www.uscis.gov/humanitarian/consideration-deferred-action-childhood-arrivals-daca.

———. 2014a. *Yearbook of Immigration Statistics: 2013*. Washington, D.C.: U.S. Department of Homeland Security, Office of Immigration Statistics.

———. 2014b. "Priority Enforcement Program." http://www.ice.gov/pep.

U.S. Department of Justice. 1996. "Assistance by State and Local Police in Apprehending Illegal Aliens." http://www.justice.gov/olc/immstop01.htm.

U.S. Government Accountability Office. 2009. *Secure Border Initiative Fence Construction Costs.* Washington, D.C.: U.S. Government Printing Office. http://www.gao.gov/products/GAO -09-244R.

U.S. Immigration and Naturalization Service. 1964. *Annual Report of the Immigration and Naturalization Service.* Washington, D.C.: U.S. Government Printing Office.

———. 1974. *Annual Report of the Immigration and Naturalization Service.* Washington, D.C.: U.S. Government Printing Office.

Voelker, D. J. 2004. "John O'Sullivan Coins the Phrase 'Manifest Destiny.'" Excerpted from "Annexation," *United States Magazine and Democratic Review* 17 (July 1845): 5–10. http:// www.historytools.org/sources/manifest_destiny.pdf.

Warner, J. 2008. "U.S. Leads the World in Illegal Drug Use." *CBS News,* July 1. http://www .cbsnews.com/news/us-leads-the-world-in-illegal-drug-use/.

Weber, D. J., ed. 1973. *Foreigners in Their Native Land: Historical Roots of the Mexican Americans.* Albuquerque: University of New Mexico Press.

Weissman, D. M. 2009. "State and Local Enforcement of Immigration Laws." Statement Before the Committee on House Judiciary, Subcommittee on Constitution, Civil Rights, and Civil Liberties. *Congressional Quarterly,* April.

Wright, J. W., ed. 2001. *The New York Times Almanac 2002.* New York: Penguin.

Yardley, J. 2000. "Some Texans Say Border Patrol Singles Out Too Many Blameless Hispanics." *New York Times,* January 26. http://www.nytimes.com/2000/01/26/us/some-texans-say -border-patrol-singles-out-too-many-blameless-hispanics.html.

Zambrano, A. C. 2015. Personal communication with the author, September 13.

Zinn, H. 2005. *A People's History of the United States: 1492–Present.* New York: HarperCollins.

Chapter 7

CHALLENGES TO INTEGRATION

The Children of Immigrants and Direct and Indirect
Experiences with the Law

LEO R. CHÁVEZ

What we need to do is to have a sensible approach to
immigration. It needs to be open. It needs to be non-dogmatic
and non-bigoted. We need to be firm but reasonable in the way
we deal with the problem of illegal immigration. And we need
to try to get as many of our immigrants who want to do so to
become citizens as quickly as possible so that the American
people will all see that this is a part of the process of American
history, which is a good one for our country.

—BILL CLINTON

O N JUNE 16, 2015, Donald Trump officially began his campaign for president
by declaring, "When Mexico sends its people, they're not sending their best.
They're not sending you. They're not sending you. They're sending people that have
lots of problems, and they're bringing those problems with us. They're bringing drugs.
They're bringing crime. They're rapists. And some, I assume, are good people." Donald
Trump's incendiary and disparaging comments about Mexican immigrants when he
declared his candidacy renewed a long-simmering, often vitriolic, debate over the costs
and benefits of immigration (Chavez 2001, 2013a). It may be easy for scholars to dismiss Trump's hyperbolic statement. After all, scholars have long noted that immigrants
commit less crime than citizens (Dowling and India 2013; Kubrin, Zatz, and Martinez
2012; Rumbaut 2009a; Rumbaut and Ewing 2007; Sohoni and Sohoni 2013). However, crime and experiences with the judicial/legal system may have important consequences for the children of immigrants well beyond Trump's inflammatory rhetoric.

This chapter examines how direct and indirect experiences with the legal system,
especially immigration law, neighborhood crime, and experiences of arrest and incarceration, may influence two key indicators of how the children of immigrants are

integrating into U.S. society: years of schooling and personal income. In addition, integration is influenced by how one perceives being welcomed by the larger society, that is, by one's sense of belonging. So perceptions of prejudice and discrimination are also part of how the children of immigrants view their social environment. To examine these issues, this chapter relies on survey data collected on the adult children of Chinese, Filipino, Guatemalan, Korean, Mexican, Salvadoran, Taiwanese, and Vietnamese immigrants in the greater Los Angeles area.

Understanding what is meant here by "integration" and "belonging" is crucial. Integration, assimilation, acculturation, hybridization (blending), and joining the "mainstream" are terms used to capture the changes taking place among immigrants, their descendants, and other members of their communities and the nation (Alba and Nee 2003; Chávez 2006; Hirschman 2013). Specifically, integration implies that people of different racial or ethnic backgrounds are brought together into unrestricted and equal association ("to become integrated"). How well this process is working among the adult children of immigrants is examined in relation to education and income.

Several factors influence integration, not the least of which is immigration status (Gonzales and Chávez 2012; Massey and Pren 2012). Because undocumented children grow up steeped in U.S. culture, their illegality poses fundamental dilemmas. They must often make critical life decisions within the constraints created by their status. Catarina, who was twenty-one years old when interviewed (by author), was brought from Mexico to the United States at age eight. She explained the anxiety she felt trying to decide if going to college was a possibility for her.

> You become depressed, you become very depressed. You work so hard and now what? You start questioning yourself. Is it worth it? Was it worth it? And what now? You have two options. Either you take the college route because education is education, and I'm learning and I like what I'm learning, and I'm going to continue to learn. Or you take the other route, where you just say, that's it. I'm just going to start working. It wasn't worth it. My mom or my dad, or my neighbor, was right. Why am I still going to school if I am not going to be able to continue with my education? So two paths, you have to decide which one to take.

Catarina's comments reflect the depth of her anguish at her uncertain future as an undocumented child of immigrants. Ultimately, she decided to attend the University of California.

This discussion suggests that the integration of the children of immigrants must not be viewed as an either/or situation, integrated or not integrated. Rather, integration is a process that is affected by myriad factors, as we shall explore. U.S. immigration law plays a major role in the lives of immigrant families (Abrego 2011, 2014; Dreby

2012; Menjívar and Abrego 2012; Motomura 2014). An examination of ninety years of census data resulted in the conclusion that immigration law has been the most important factor shaping family structure, even more than race and ethnicity (Gratton, Gutmann, and Skop 2007). Immigration law constructs not only legal immigration but undocumented or unauthorized immigration status, the "illegal alien" (Ngai 2004). Immigration laws change over time and even the status of illegality is not fixed, as laws exist for regularizing an unauthorized status, though they have become much more restrictive over time. President Obama's Deferred Action for Childhood Arrivals (DACA) policy, which allows undocumented immigrants brought as children, the 1.5 generation, to request a grant of relief from the Department of Homeland Security, is an example of the flexible nature of immigration status (Chávez 2013b; Gonzales and Terriquez 2013). The U.S. Congress could pass immigration reform that would also provide further, broader avenues for regularization, as it did in 1986 with the Immigration Reform and Control Act (IRCA). The IRCA resulted in 70 percent of the nation's undocumented immigrants between 1986 and 1988 moving into a legal status, typically legal permanent residency (Yoshikawa and Kholoptseva 2013). The point here is that we must not consider illegality as the only factor affecting attachment to U.S. society, nor should it be the focus of policy on the social and cultural integration of immigrants and their children (Jones-Correa and Graauw 2013). At the same time, we must not minimize the effect that regularizing the status of undocumented 1.5-generation children of immigrants would have on their integration (Massey 2013). Finally, parents who enter the country as unauthorized migrants may also bequeath their children a legacy of obstacles to their social integration (Bean et al. 2013; Coutin 2013; Motomura 2006).

Clearly, integration involves sentiments of belonging, the emotional attachments immigrants and their children express about where they live and where they feel at home, which, in turn, are related to cultural identity (Massey and Sánchez R. 2010). For the children of immigrants, a sense of belonging and cultural identity are not something they are born with, nor something they acquire whole, fixed, and set for life (Vasquez 2011). As Stuart Hall (1990, 221) has observed about cultural identity: "It is not as transparent or unproblematic as we think. Perhaps instead of thinking of identity as an already accomplished fact . . . we should think, instead, of identity as a 'production,' which is never complete, always in process." This is similar for a sense of belonging, which is also always in a process of becoming a more or less positive sentiment.

Growing up in the United States pulls the children of immigrants toward a shared history with the larger society. This is an e pluribus unum sense of belonging, that one is part of a nation consisting of "one people" that transcends immigrant origins. However, other less harmonizing experiences influence sentiments of belonging. The

United States is a complex society, with many areas of difference: cultural beliefs and practices, economic disparities, educational attainment, and language are among the many differences that affect how the children of immigrants see themselves in relation to the larger society. Despite all the similarities that draw people in a society together, "there are also critical points of deep and significant *difference* which constitute 'what we really are'; or rather—since history has intervened—'what we have become'" (Hall 1990, 225).

Catarina's story exemplifies tensions in integrating and a sense of belonging that can sometimes arise among the children of immigrants.

> I think if you have obstacles to integrating, one, they don't want you to integrate. Obviously, they have the obstacles for you not to integrate, so you get to the point where you know what, I don't want to integrate, whether you will eventually want me to integrate for any reason, I am no longer willing to integrate. . . . After September 11, I felt American. And it's amazing because regardless of political inequalities, I think of my life and what would it have been if I had not been here. And here I am. There are obstacles, but it's better. It's better here even with the inequalities. I guess it's human nature. We just want something better.

Catarina's observations reflect her sense of belonging, which in turn can have implications for integration. As Nira Yuval-Davis (2006, 197) has observed, "Belonging is about emotional attachment, about feeling 'at home' and . . . about feeling 'safe.'" Home consists of both a sentiment and a set of social relationships, such as having family nearby, and a sense of safety and of the quality of life in one's neighborhood. For the children of undocumented immigrants, the neighborhood offers experiences outside the family, which may reduce or sharpen the effects of their parents', or even their own, immigration status. In this regard, Hirokazu Yoshikawa and Jenya Kholoptseva (2013, 8) have observed that "how children experience a parent's unauthorized status may differ—that is, any negative effects may be mitigated or exacerbated—depending on historical, policy, neighborhood, and network contexts."

Home is more than an idea or cognitive construct. One's home is also a material place, part of a neighborhood that can offer relative safety or can be beset with crime, gangs, and drugs. According to anthropologist E. N. Anderson (2005, 66), "Humans must feel safe and secure, above all." Broadening the idea of home to include the neighborhood raises the issue not just of safety but of relations with police and the legal system. In particular, the children of immigrants may experience arrests and incarcerations as part of their lived experiences (Armenta 2016; Light and Iceland 2016; Martinez 2016). As part of immigrant families, these young people have directly or indirectly experienced the increasing criminalization of immigrants and the growth of private immigrant detention centers, what Karen Manges Douglas and Rogelio Sáenz (2013) have characterized as the "immigration-industrial complex" (Rosas 2012; Urbina and Álvarez 2017). Further, it has become increasingly clear that arrest and incarceration experiences can have significant consequences for both individuals and society (Abrego and Menjívar 2012; Lerman 2013; Urbina 2018; Urbina and Álvarez 2017).

The experiences of adult children in relation to neighborhood crime, arrests and incarcerations, and perceptions of prejudice and discrimination will be further examined after presenting the study's methods of data collection, where logistic regression analyses will examine the relative influence of these factors on the dependent variables of education and income.

RESEARCH METHODS FOR THE CURRENT STUDY

PARTICIPANTS AND RESEARCH DESIGN

Data examined here come from the Immigration and Intergenerational Mobility in Metropolitan Los Angeles (IIMMLA) survey that was supported by a grant from the Russell Sage Foundation (Bean et al. 2006; Rumbaut, Massey, and Bean 2006).[1] Conducted in 2004, the study targeted the young-adult children of immigrants from large immigrant groups in the five-county metropolitan Los Angeles area (Los Angeles, Orange, Riverside, San Bernardino, and Ventura). Immigrants, or the foreign-born, accounted for 26.9 percent of California's population in 2013, surpassing New York (22.3 percent), Texas (16.5 percent), Florida (19.4 percent), and Illinois (14 percent) (Migration Policy Institute 2015a). The five counties in the study had about 5,510,900 immigrants in 2013, accounting for about 13.7 percent of the nation's immigrants (Migration Policy Institute 2015a). Latinos were 51.6 percent of California's immigrant population in 2013, and Asian Americans accounted for 32 percent (Migration Policy Institute 2015b).

Data was collected using a computer-assisted telephone interviewing system to gather information from 2,820 persons aged twenty to forty who had at least one immigrant parent from China (both mainland and Taiwan), El Salvador, Guatemala, Korea, Mexico, the Philippines, or Vietnam.[2] The study was designed to be a random probability sample of persons residing in households with telephones in the greater Los Angeles area.[3] Because of the centrality of the Mexican-origin group to the immigrant experience in Los Angeles, we oversampled the Mexican-origin population. The study's sample also included 1,860 individuals who are not considered here, including

U.S. whites, African Americans, other Latin Americans than those mentioned above, other Asians, and Middle Easterners. The surveys were administered between April 2004 and October 2004.[4] For the purposes of sample design, eligible adult immigrants were defined as "1.5 generation" if they came to the United States to live before the age of fifteen; as "2nd generation" if they were born in the United States and had at least one parent who was foreign-born; and as "3rd+ generation" if they and their parents were U.S.-born but had one or more foreign-born grandparents (3rd+ generation not included in this analysis).

TABLE 7.1. Characteristics of Adult Children of Latin American and Asian Immigrants in the Study

	MEXICAN	SALVADORAN-GUATEMALAN	ALL LATINOS	CHINESE/TAIWANESE	KOREAN	VIETNAMESE	FILIPINO	ALL ASIAN AMERICANS
	N = 843/%	N = 376/%	N = 1,219/%	N = 400/%	N = 399/%	N = 401/%	N = 401/%	N = 1,601/%
Gender (Male)	49.3	49.7	49.5	56.5	49.6	50.1	49.1	51.3
Age (30+)	39.0	30.9	36.5	39.0	37.6	33.9	35.4	36.5
Schooling 13+ Years	47.8	63.0	52.5***	94.3	91.5	90.5	88.3	91.1
Personal Income $30,000+	32.4	29.2	31.4***	53.3	49.1	35.9	42.0	45.0
Prefers English at Home Now	54.7	51.6	53.7***	53.0	63.2	52.1	86.8	64.3
GENERATION								
1.5 Generation	34.4	47.3	38.4	54.8	64.9	70.6	46.6	59.0
2nd Generation	65.6	52.7	61.6***	45.3	36.1	29.4	53.4	41.0
Married/Cohabitating	51.1	40.7	47.9***	29.3	33.1	27.7	39.7	32.4

TABLE 7.1. *continued*

	MEXICAN	SALVADORAN-GUATEMALAN	ALL LATINOS	CHINESE/TAIWANESE	KOREAN	VIETNAMESE	FILIPINO	ALL ASIAN AMERICANS
5+ Relatives Live Nearby	69.1	66.7	68.4***	49.4	49.2	59.5	68.2	56.6
Medical Insurance Through Work	54.9	58.1	55.9	58.2	50.4	51.5	59.8	55.0
Medical Insurance, Private or Government	70.5	72.1	71.0***	59.5	53.4	67.1	62.3	60.6
Belongs to 1 or More Community Organizations	15.2	13.3	14.6**	23.6	18.9	17.2	18.3	19.5
Ethnicity Important	60.9	63.0	61.6***	41.4	53.4	46.3	54.7	48.9

All Latinos compared to all Asian Americans: significance (X_2) for cross tabulations: *.05, **.01, ***.001.

Source: Rumbaut et al. 2004; N = 2,820.

Table 7.1 summarizes the characteristics of the adult children of immigrants who participated in the study. The respondents were about evenly distributed in terms of gender, and there was no difference among the groups in age breakdown. However, there were significant differences between the children of Latino and Asian immigrants. Asians were more likely to have one or more years of schooling beyond high school, and higher incomes. However, Filipinos preferred English. The children of Chinese/Taiwanese, Korean, and Vietnamese immigrants were similar to the children of Latino immigrants in their English preference. Asian Americans were also more likely than Latinos to belong to one or more community organizations. Latinos were more likely second generation; that is, U.S.-born Latinos and Asian American respondents were in the 1.5 generation, defined here as migrating when under fifteen years of age. Latinos were also more likely to be married or cohabiting than Asian American respondents, to have medical insurance, and to feel ethnicity was important.

A majority of both Latinos and Asian Americans preferred to speak English at home. However, the vast majority of the respondents grew up in a home where a non-English language was spoken, not surprising given that over three hundred languages are spoken in the United States, a testament to the adage that we are a "nation of immigrants" (Ryan 2013, 4). According to the U.S. Census, in 2011, in the Los Angeles, Long Beach, and Orange County area, 54 percent spoke a non-English language at home (Ryan 2013, 13). Despite this linguistic diversity, the same census study found that 75.1 percent of California's population spoke English very well (55.7 percent) or well (19.4 percent). Non-English language use among the children of immigrants in the greater Los Angeles area is on the wane, a pattern found nationally as well (Taylor and Cohn 2013). While individuals may be becoming more English-dominant, immigrants continue to come to the United States, replenishing linguistic diversity and ethnic endurance (Jimenez 2009).

FACTORS INFLUENCING INTEGRATION

IMMIGRATION LAW

Immigration law determines the conditions under which people migrate to the United States. Migrants who enter with an authorized status of some type typically do so with a permanent resident visa, tourist visa, student visa, temporary work permit of various sorts, or asylum status (or request for asylee status). Thus, for this study immigration status was assessed through a series of questions. Respondents were asked where they were born and if they were U.S. citizens. If foreign-born, they were asked if they were a permanent legal resident when they first came to the United States. If no, we then asked if any of the following applied to their immigration status at the time: refugee status, temporary work visa, or border-crossing card. The default category consisted of those without authorization to be in the United States. The respondents were asked similar questions about their mother's and father's migration history, and similar questions were asked about the respondents' and their parents' immigration status at the time of the interview.

Table 7.2 presents the immigration status at time of entry to the United States and at the time of the interview for the children of immigrants who themselves were immigrants, the 1.5-generation respondents, and all the respondents' parents. The 1.5-generation children of Latin American immigrants (45.5 percent) were more likely than the Asian

TABLE 7.2. Immigration Status at Time of Entry and at Time of Interview, Respondent and Parents

	MEXICAN		SALVADORAN-GUATEMALAN		CHINESE/TAIWANESE		KOREAN		VIETNAMESE		FILIPINO	
	1.5	2ND	1.5	2ND	1.5	2ND	1.5	2ND	1.5	2ND	1.5	2ND
	N = 290/%	N = 553/%	N = 178/%	N = 198/%	N = 219/%	N = 181/%	N = 255/%	N = 144/%	N = 283/%	N = 118/%	N = 187/%	N = 214/%
Respondent Unauthorized Entry to United States	51.4	NA	36.0	NA	13.7	NA	8.6	NA	3.5	NA	11.2	NA
Respondent Unauthorized at Interview	19.0	NA	8.4	NA	0.9	NA	1.6	NA	0	NA	1.1	NA
Mother Unauthorized Entry to United States	46.2	26.0	47.2	40.9	10.5	16.0	8.6	18.1	2.8	9.3	10.2	18.2
Father Unauthorized Entry to United States	41.4	29.7	31.5	41.4	6.8	17.7	5.9	13.9	3.9	11.0	6.4	17.3
Mother or Father Unauthorized at Entry to United States	59.3***	40.5	54.5	51.0	11.9**	22.1	10.2**	22.9	4.2**	12.7	12.8**	26.2
Mother or Father Unauthorized at Interview	12.1	3.4	7.3	3.5	1.4	2.2	1.6	0.0	0.0	0.0	2.1	1.9

Significance (X_2) for 1.5 vs. 2nd generation: * >.05, ** >.01, *** >.001.

American 1.5-generation respondents (8.8 percent) to have entered the United States without authorization (X_2 = <.001). However, 13.7 percent of Chinese/Taiwanese and 11.2 percent of Filipinos entered without authorization. Very few of the Asian American respondents (0.8 percent) were still unauthorized at the time of the interview, but 15 percent of the Latino respondents were unauthorized at the time of the interview (X_2 = <.001).

The mothers (36.3 percent) and fathers (34.5 percent) of Latinos were more likely to have entered the United States without authorization than the mothers (11.1 percent) and fathers (9.7 percent) of Asian American respondents (X_2 = <.001). However, as table 7.2 indicates, the second-generation Asian American respondents had significantly higher proportions of parents who entered the United States without authorization compared to their 1.5-generation counterparts. Having at least one parent who entered the country without authorization reached 26 percent among Filipino second-generation respondents, and above 20 percent for Chinese/Taiwanese and Korean respondents. Few of the Latino respondents' parents (6.1 percent) and even fewer of the Asian American parents (1.2 percent) were unauthorized at the time of the interview (X_2 = <.001). The important question here is, what legacy does unauthorized status at time of entry have for the integration of the children of immigrants into U.S. society?

LIFE AND CRIME IN THE NEIGHBORHOOD

The children of immigrants grow up in families that are mobile. While some may stay in one place after migrating, others make strategic decisions to move for opportunities and safety. As Catarina (introduced above) said, "I see that throughout the years, as my parents' economic situation got better, we moved into, not better neighborhoods at least into a better home. We started off like living in an apartment with my uncles, the typical big family thing where you really have no privacy. And then my father decided to try it on his own and start his own business, so we started moving. Now, he's paying the mortgage of the house we're living in. So my neighborhood at this point is, it's a nice neighborhood."

However, Catarina made clear that the neighborhood her family now lives in is "completely different" from the one she grew up in after coming to the United States, declaring: "I know there was like the drug problem. We moved into the apartments, you could see, like, people, alcohol abuse, everything. Kids were on the streets. So just the atmosphere was completely different. It's not that far [from where I live now], but yet, that area is still the same. Visibly noticeable kinds of problems."

Like Catarina, many of the children of immigrants grew up in neighborhoods where drugs, gang activity, and other criminal activity were problems. As table 7.3 indicates, drugs were somewhat of a problem or a big problem in the neighborhoods for almost half of the Mexican and Salvadoran-Guatemalan children of immigrants,

TABLE 7.3. Neighborhood Crime

	MEXICAN	SALVADORAN-GUATEMALAN	ALL LATINOS	CHINESE/TAIWANESE	KOREAN	VIETNAMESE	FILIPINO	ALL ASIAN AMERICANS
	N = 843/%	N = 376/%	N = 1,219/%	N = 400/%	N = 399/%	N = 401/%	N = 401/%	N = 1,601/%
DRUGS IN NEIGHBORHOOD GREW UP IN:								
No Problem	55.0	53.5	54.6***	86.3	82.2	74.8	74.6	79.5
Somewhat of a Problem	22.8	22.6	22.7	10.6	13.6	18.1	18.1	15.1
Big Problem	22.2	23.9	22.7	3.0	4.3	7.1	7.3	5.4
GANGS IN NEIGHBORHOOD GREW UP IN:								
No Problem	39.2	32.7	37.2***	70.8	71.4	54.1	59.4	63.9
Somewhat of a Problem	29.7	33.2	30.8	24.3	23.8	34.3	28.4	27.7
Big Problem	31.0	34.0	32.0	5.0	4.8	11.5	12.2	8.4
OTHER CRIME PROBLEMS IN NEIGHBORHOOD GREW UP IN:								
No Problem	46.3	40.1	44.4***	68.4	73.0	52.3	61.6	63.8
Somewhat of a Problem	31.1	37.9	33.2	27.6	21.9	39.6	32.2	30.3
Big Problem	22.6	22.0	22.4	4.0	5.0	8.1	6.3	5.8

Significance (X_2) for Latino by Asian American comparison: * >.05, ** >.01, *** >.001.

but for only about 20 percent of the children of Asian immigrants, a significant difference. However, about one in four of the Vietnamese and Salvadorans grew up in neighborhoods where drugs posed somewhat of or a big problem. Among the children of Mexican immigrants there was a significant difference between the 1.5 generation (more likely) and second generation on this issue of drugs being a big or somewhat of a problem in their neighborhoods when growing up (X_2 = <.01). The second-generation Vietnamese were significantly more likely than the 1.5 generation to have grown up in neighborhoods where drugs were somewhat of or a big problem (X_2 = <.01).

Gang activity was somewhat of or a big problem for both Latinos (62.8 percent) and Asian Americans (36.1 percent), although the difference was significant. About similar proportions of all groups, however, said gangs were somewhat of a problem. Once again, the children of Vietnamese (45.9 percent) and Filipino (40.1 percent) immigrants were more likely than children of Chinese/Taiwanese (29.2 percent) and Korean (28.6 percent) immigrants to indicate that gangs were somewhat of a big problem in the neighborhood where they grew up. Only the 1.5-generation children of Mexican immigrants (more likely) were significantly different from their second-generation counterparts (X_2 = <.01).

Neighborhoods could also have a problem with other types of criminal activity. A majority (55.6 percent) of the Latino groups indicated that other criminal activity was a big or somewhat of a problem, compared to 36.2 percent of the children of Asian immigrants, although higher among Vietnamese (47.7 percent). Only among the Filipinos was there a significant difference between the 1.5 generation (less likely) and second generation in terms of other criminal activity being somewhat of or a big problem (X_2 = <.01).

TABLE 7.4. Number of Neighborhood Crime Problems

	MEXICAN	SALVADORAN-GUATEMALAN	ALL LATINOS	CHINESE/TAIWANESE	KOREAN	VIETNAMESE	FILIPINO	ALL ASIAN AMERICANS
	N = 843/%	N = 376/%	N = 1,219/%	N = 400/%	N = 399/%	N = 401/%	N = 401/%	N = 1,601/%
NEIGHBOR-HOOD GREW UP IN HAD:								
No Crime Problems	31.0	25.3	29.2***	57.3	58.9	39.7	45.1	50.2
One Problem (Drugs, Gangs, Other Crime)	15.7	15.7	15.7	20.5	19.5	22.4	23.2	21.4
Two Problems (Drugs, Gangs, Other Crime)	17.2	20.2	18.1	13.0	11.0	18.5	14.2	14.2

TABLE 7.4. *continued*

	MEXICAN	SALVADORAN-GUATEMALAN	ALL LATINOS	CHINESE/TAIWANESE	KOREAN	VIETNAMESE	FILIPINO	ALL ASIAN AMERICANS
Three Problems (Drugs, Gangs, Other Crime)	36.2	38.8	37.0	9.3	10.5	19.5	17.5	14.2
One or More Crime-Related Problems	69.0	74.7	70.6***	47.2	41.1	60.3	54.9	49.6

Significance (X2) for Latino by Asian American comparison: * >.05, ** >.01, *** >.001.

While many of the children of immigrants grew up with one or more of these problems (gangs, drugs, or other criminal activities), Latinos (70.6 percent) were significantly more likely to have done so compared to Asian Americans (49.6 percent), as illustrated in table 7.4. However, almost half of Chinese/Taiwanese (47.2 percent) and a majority of Filipinos (54.9 percent) and Vietnamese (60.3 percent) grew up in neighborhoods with crime problems. The question here is, to what extent do these experiences growing up in neighborhoods with crime predict social integration?

ARRESTS AND INCARCERATIONS

Neighborhood conditions and perceptions of discrimination have material consequences for the lives of the children of immigrants. This is especially true when considering relations with the police and legal system. The issue of crime is especially complicated for the 1.5-generation unauthorized children of immigrants, for whom just being in the United States may be seen as a "criminal" activity. When undocumented 1.5ers try to work or even just engage in everyday activities that most citizens and legal residents take for granted, their illegality becomes an issue. As Lupita explains:

> I didn't want to break the law, but everything you do is illegal because you are illegal. Everything you do will be illegal. Otherwise you can't live. But I am still afraid. I don't want to jeopardize anything. I mean, I guess I am just ashamed. I looked [for work] in most restaurants and they would be like, "Why do you want to work for us if you have a

B.A.? So, I am going to have to lie and I am going to have to tell them that I just dropped out of high school. But eventually they are going, it is going to come out, I know it. The people [working] at those places, like the cooks and the cashiers, they are either really young people, and I feel really old, like what am I doing there if they are all like 16, 17 years old. The others are like señoras who are 35 and have little kids; they dropped out of school, but because they have little kids they are still working at the restaurant. Thinking about that, it makes me feel so fucking stupid. And like the factories, too, because they ask me, "Que estas haciendo aqui? ["What are you doing here?] You can speak English. You graduated from high school. You can work anywhere." They don't stop bugging me. (Qtd. in Gonzales and Chavez 2012, 264)

While Lupita's status may raise questions about what she is legally able to do (work, for example), arrest and incarceration experiences are more clear-cut. As table 7.5 indicates, many of the interviewees or their family members had been arrested and/or incarcerated (reform school, detention center, jail, or prison). While the proportions

TABLE 7.5. Arrest/Incarceration

	MEXICAN	SALVADORAN-GUATEMALAN	ALL LATINOS	CHINESE/TAIWANESE	KOREAN	VIETNAMESE	FILIPINO	ALL ASIAN AMERICANS
	N = 843/%	N = 376/%	N = 1,219/%	N = 400/%	N = 399/%	N = 401/%	N = 401/%	N = 1,601/%
Self-Arrested	16.0	17.3	16.4***	4.8	9.0	5.0	7.5	6.6
Self or Family Ever Arrested	34.0	31.4	33.2***	8.8	16.5	13.7	16.7	13.9
Self Ever Incarcerated: in Reform School, Detention Center, Jail, Prison	9.8	8.5	9.4***	1.8	2.8	3.2	4.2	3.0
Self or Family Member Ever Incarcerated: in Reform School, Detention Center, Jail, Prison	25.0	21.8	24.0***	5.0	10.5	11.0	12.0	9.6
Self-Arrested or Incarcerated	16.8	17.8	17.1***	4.8	9.5	5.2	8.2	6.9
Self or Family Arrested or Incarcerated	36.3	34.0	35.6***	9.8	18.3	16.0	17.7	15.4

Significance (X2) for 1.5 vs. 2nd generation: * >.05, ** >.01, *** >.001.

vary among the groups, Latinos were significantly more likely than Asian Americans to either personally have been arrested or incarcerated or to have had family members arrested or incarcerated. However, arrest and incarceration rates among Filipino, Korean, Vietnamese, and those in the *Other* category indicate that problems with the criminal justice system are an important area of concern for them as well. When arrest and incarceration rates for the interviewee and/or other family members are combined, Filipinos, Koreans, and Vietnamese often have direct or indirect experiences with the criminal justice system. Lastly, second-generation interviewees were significantly more likely than the 1.5 generation to have been arrested only among the children of Mexican ($X_2 < .01$) and Salvadoran-Guatemalan ($X_2 < .05$) immigrants. To what extent the experiences of arrest and incarceration predict social integration will also be examined in logistic regression analysis.

PERCEPTIONS OF PREJUDICE AND DISCRIMINATION

There was no statistical difference between Latinos and Asian Americans in response to the question about having experienced prejudice or discrimination because of their ethnicity or race in the year previous to the interview. About a third of all interviewees in each of the groups indicated they had experienced prejudice or discrimination because of their race or ethnicity in the past year, with no significant difference between Latinos and Asian Americans, as illustrated in table 7.6. Koreans were most likely (39.1 percent) of all the groups to believe they had been the victim of prejudice or discrimination. Although the second generation was generally more likely to feel themselves to be the recipient of prejudiced or discriminatory behavior, there was only a significant generational difference among the Filipino ($X_2 < .05$) and Vietnamese children of immigrants ($X_2 < .01$).

Latinos (25 percent) were more likely than Asian American children of immigrants (11.3 percent) to feel they had experienced prejudice or discriminatory treatment from the police ($X_2 < .001$). However, many Vietnamese also indicated negative treatment by police (17.2 percent). Mexicans (43.8 percent) and Salvadoran-Guatemalans (45.2 percent), in particular, cited the workplace or looking for work as sites where they encountered prejudice. Although Latinos differed significantly from Asian American children of immigrants ($X_2 < .001$), many of the Vietnamese (37.1 percent) and Filipinos (35.6 percent) also indicated problems of prejudice related to work.

Housing discrimination was also cited more by Latinos than Asian American children of immigrants ($X_2 < .001$). Asian Americans were significantly more likely than Latinos to indicate that they had experienced prejudice or discrimination in "other" situations. However, a majority of all groups felt they had been victims of

TABLE 7.6. Prejudice/Discrimination

	MEXICAN	SALVADORAN-GUATEMALAN	ALL LATINOS	CHINESE/TAIWANESE	KOREAN	VIETNAMESE	FILIPINO	ALL ASIAN AMERICANS
	N = 843/%	N = 376/%	N = 1,219/%	N = 400/%	N = 399/%	N = 401/%	N = 401/%	N = 1,601/%
Felt Prejudice or Discrimination Because of Ethnicity or Race in Past Year	32.5	33.5	32.8	29.3	39.1	37.7	32.9	34.7
EXPERIENCED PREJUDICE OR DISCRIMINATION (MULTIPLE RESPONSES RECORDED):	N = 274/%	N = 126/%	N = 400/%	N = 117/%	N = 156/%	N = 151/%	N = 132/%	N = 556/%
From Police	26.3	22.2	25.0***	3.4	10.3	17.2	12.9	11.4
At Work or Looking for Work	43.8	45.2	44.4***	22.2	19.9	37.1	35.6	28.8
Looking for House/Apartment	15.0	11.9	14.0***	4.3	5.1	5.3	5.3	5.0
Other Setting	63.5	73.8	66.8***	82.9	84.6	73.5	72.7	78.4
DISCRIMINATED BY:								
White	74.8	73.0	74.3	70.8	76.8	65.2	71.2	70.9
African American	12.4	15.9	13.5*	6.8	11.5	7.3	9.8	9.0
Asian American	7.3	4.0	6.3	3.4	3.2	4.6	13.6	6.1
Latino	8.8	8.7	8.8**	17.1	9.0	22.5	18.9	16.7

Significance (X2): * >.05, ** >.01, *** >.001.

prejudice or discrimination in some other setting. Sometimes it could be a feeling of being unwelcomed or viewed as out-of-place. Catarina provides an example of being made to feel she was intruding into an event she attended—not by staff at the Orange County Performing Arts Center, but by some other attendees: "They looked at me like I didn't belong. Even if you are dressed up you are still Mexican. You still don't belong. They look at you from top to bottom and they don't stop looking at you. This is an experience I had in high school, because we had to go see a play. There was this couple with a little girl, they were white, and they just kept looking at us, like saying what you are doing here."

Catarina also related an experience she recently had at Starbucks:

And I just had an experience at Starbucks this week. I went in and I ordered a coffee and something went wrong with the name the girl wrote down, and I said, "I'm sorry this is not what I asked for." She turns her head and she doesn't even answer, and I said, "Excuse me." And she goes, "I'm not even talking to you." And I said, "Oh, I'm sorry." And I looked at her, and she went on talking with her co-worker discussing whatever had happened with the coffee. And she goes, "Are you gonna want this or not?" And I'm like, "Excuse me," and she goes, "Do you want me to switch the cup?" And I just said it's okay. And she then starts screaming at me, and I thought, if I had been white would she have done this to me? And it's interesting because they serve Mexicans, you know.

We asked respondents from whom they received discriminatory treatment. A majority in all groups who had experienced prejudice or discrimination attributed it to whites (non-Latinos), as reported in table 7.6. However, prejudice or discriminatory behavior was also attributed, but much less frequently, to other ethnic/racial groups. Although Latinos were significantly more likely than Asian American children of immigrants to cite African Americans as the source of discriminatory behavior ($X_2 < .05$), Koreans (11.5 percent) and Filipino (9.8 percent) were close to the proportion of Mexicans (12.4 percent) citing African Americans. Asian Americans generally were not cited as often as the source of prejudice or discriminatory behavior. Interestingly, however, Filipinos (13.6 percent) were the most likely to cite other Asians as discriminators. The children of Mexican immigrants (7.3 percent) cited Asian Americans more frequently than Salvadoran-Guatemalans and the other Asian American groups besides Filipinos.

Latinos were also cited as the source of prejudice and discriminatory behavior. Reportedly, there was a significant difference between Latinos, 8.8 percent, and Asian American children of immigrants, 16.7 percent ($X_2 = < .01$). More than one-fifth (22.5 percent) of the Vietnamese, and many of the Filipinos (18.9 percent) and Chinese-Taiwanese (17.1 percent), also cited Latinos. However, it should be noted that Mexicans (8.8 percent) and Salvadorans (8.7 percent) also cited Latinos more often than either group cited Asian Americans for prejudiced behavior. Once again, Catarina provides an incident where she felt she was treated unfairly by a Latino: "It's interesting because [discrimination] happens with like my own people. I walked into the shoe store [at a major mall], and there is this sales representative, and he doesn't approach me. Nothing. And I'm looking there and this lady, white lady, comes in, and he's already right there helping her. I was like okay."

Isela, who was twenty-two at the time the author interviewed here, was brought to the United States without authorization at age nine. She felt classmates, teachers, and random people had treated her unfairly at various times in her life. She related two experiences, one as a child in Las Vegas and the other after 9/11:

> One time we were in Vegas with my family and we were walking, and our first time in Vegas, we were little kids. I was probably eleven, so we were, you know, walking around, in front of my parents, kinda laughing. And there was a man walking a dog, and we were like, oh look at the cute dog, and the man said, "Go back to your country!" And you know, we were like, oh my God. We had never experienced that before. People, the way people look at me certain times, especially after 9/11. People thought I was Middle Eastern, so at the mall I get a lot of stares, and it frustrates me.

Situating prejudice and discrimination within a broader context, we analyzed additional factors (below), while trying to better understand a focal question: To what extent do perceptions of prejudice and discrimination predict social integration?

LANGUAGE USE

Other factors that influence social integration are language use and a sense of belonging. Language use is an important indicator of cultural integration, ethnic resilience, economic mobility, and educational attainment (Portes and Schauffler 1996; Rumbaut 2009b; Urbina and Wright 2016). Use of English also indicates acculturation, a process that the children of immigrants can find stressful and anxiety provoking as they attempt to "fit in" to American culture (Guendelman, Cheryan, and Monin 2011). Language use, then, is about more than the facility to communicate. It carries with it much larger political significance for issues of cultural identity and ethnic persistence, as well as integration into the life of the nation. The politics over language, then, is a politics over belonging. According to Nira Yuval-Davis (2006, 207): "Much of the contemporary debates on the politics of belonging surround that question of who 'belongs' and who does not, and what are the minimum common grounds—in terms of origin, culture and normative behavior—that are required to signify belonging." Catarina pointed out that bilingualism has definite benefits and she would try to ensure her children could speak Spanish, declaring, "One is the culture thing. If you know Spanish and if you're Mexican, or that's your cultural background, you have to teach [children] some culture. It's essential for their identity, self-identity, self-esteem, and two languages, especially here, let's say in the United States, and in California, Spanish and English, that's plus." Despite the benefits, the generation after Catarina's will probably prefer to speak English in even higher proportions.

A SENSE OF BELONGING

Almost all (94.6 percent) of the children of immigrants in our study indicated that the United States feels most like home, even when compared to their parents' home country.[5] For those in the 1.5 generation, who spent a few years in their country of origin, there is more ambivalence, a sense of home in both places. For example, Catarina, who was twenty-one when interviewed and was brought from Mexico to the United States when she was eight, explained her sense of home and how she felt about her local community:

> Like home, I would have to say probably the U.S. at this point. Although there's this holding on of your native country, and I think just by the fact that I went to school there for a while, and my grandparents were there, and some of my childhood was there, it's still my home as well. But I guess at this point most of my life I've been here. . . . If I define [it as,] Do I feel part of my community, like my neighborhood and everything, yes because, although I don't participate in events that they do hold, my entire neighborhood is kind of close together. I think they all help each other when there's need and everything. Like for example, when someone dies and they need to raise funds, in different events.

Catarina's comments suggest the importance of community engagement for a sense of belonging, a factor that we will explore below.

Clearly, immigration law can influence a sense of belonging. For example, Lupita, twenty-seven at the time of the interview, excelled academically in high school and was heavily involved in extracurricular activities. She completed a BA at a University of California campus and would someday like to get a PhD or law degree. At the time of the interview, however, she was working and trying to survive as an undocumented immigrant. Lupita spoke of how her life is constrained because of her unauthorized status:

> I know I can do so much more, but I can't because I can't live wherever. I can't choose where I live. I can't choose where I work. And the worst thing is that I can't choose my friends. In high school I was able to do that. I can't anymore. I can't hang out with my friends anymore. I can't even hang out with my high school friends anymore and that hurts a lot. Yeah, they want to do grown-up stuff. I can't do anything that is eighteen and over. I can't do anything. I can only hang out where little kids hang out. I can't hang out with them. I can't travel with them. I can't go out to dinner with them. I can't go to Vegas with them. If I want to go to a bar, I don't even have a drink. If they want to go to San Diego, if they want to go visit museums down there, if they want to go to Sea World,

I can't go with them. I can't go to Los Angeles. I can't go to any clubs in L.A. (Qtd. in Gonzalez and Chavez 2012, 264)

As these comments indicate (her cry to be understood, be heard, and a call for help), a sense of belonging is influenced by social relationships with family, friends, and the community. A belief that one's ethnic identity is important may also contribute to a sense of belonging, which may influence, positively or negatively, social integration (Barth 1982; Stepick and Stepick 2010).

LOGISTIC REGRESSION ANALYSES

To further delinate and statistically quantify the influence of these various factors on social integration, we now utilize a more advanced statistical technique (logistic regression analyses), using education and income as dependent variables. Before presenting our findings, though, we define our dependent variables: individual characteristics; experiences with crime, law, and discrimination; belonging and community; and analysis.

DEPENDENT VARIABLES AND INDIVIDUAL CHARACTERISTICS

Years of schooling was dichotomized: o = 12 years or less; 1 = 13 years or more. Personal yearly income was dichotomized using the sample median: o = <$30,000; 1 = $30,000 or more. Individual characteristics include gender with the values o = female; 1 = male, and age: o = 30 or younger; 1 = 31 or older. Language preference was dichotomized as prefers to speak English at home: o = No; 1 = Yes. Those indicating they preferred both English and another language were categorized as o. Generation in the United States included the 1.5 generation (defined as coming to United States under fifteen years of age) and the second generation, those born in the United States with an immigrant parent. The generation variable was dichotomized: o = 1.5 generation; 1 = 2nd generation. Marital status was dichotomized: o = single, divorced, or widowed; 1 = married or living together. Medical insurance through work is an indicator of integration labor force integration, with "better" jobs providing medical insurance (Liebig 2008); and the variable was dichotomized as o = No medical insurance through work; 1 = Yes, medical insurance through work.

EXPERIENCES WITH CRIME, LAW, AND DISCRIMINATION

Having experienced prejudice or discrimination in the past year was dichotomized: o = No; 1 = Yes. Having grown up in a neighborhood characterized with problems related to drug use, gang activity, or other types of crime problems was dichotomized: 0 = Yes; 1= No; and if the respondent or immediate family member had been arrested and/or incarcerated was dichotomized: 0 = Yes; 1 = No. Immigration status was assessed through a series of questions. We asked where the respondents were born and if the respondent was a U.S. citizen. If foreign-born, they were asked if they were a permanent legal resident when they first came to the United States. If no, we then asked if any of the following applied to their immigration status at the time: refugee status, temporary work visa, or border-crossing card. The default category consisted of those without authorization to be in the United States. The respondents were asked similar questions about their mother's and father's migration history. The immigration-related variables in the analysis are: respondent entered the United States without authorization (0 = No; 1 = Yes), and mother and/or father entered the United States unauthorized (0 = No; 1 = Yes). The first variable compares those with an unauthorized immigration status when migrating to the United States to respondents who were authorized when coming to the United States or who were U.S.-born citizens since birth. When included in the logistic regression, it indicates if that status at entry predicts self-rated health—similar to the comparison of respondents who had at least one unauthorized immigrant parent versus those whose parents were authorized immigrants or citizens.

BELONGING AND COMMUNITY

A sense of belonging was assessed through a belief that ethnicity is important: 0 = No; 1 = Yes; and having relatives living nearby, dichotomized as 0 = 0 to 4 relatives living nearby; 1 = 5 or more relatives living nearby. Children of immigrants were assigned values of 0 = Latin American parents; 1 = Asian immigrant parents. Respondents' community engagement was assessed broadly. Respondents were asked: Do you belong to any community organizations, work-related organizations, sports teams, or other nonreligious organizations? Community organizations could include ethnic or nonethnic defined groups. Community engagement was dichotomized: 0 = zero participation; 1 = participating in one or more community organization.

ANALYSIS

Data were analyzed using the Statistical Package for the Social Sciences (PASW 21). Variables were analyzed using frequencies (means, medians), cross-tabulations (chi-square tests), and logistical regression (odds ratios and confidence intervals). Logistic regression analysis provides the odds ratio, which indicates the odds of the 1 value, of a dichotomous variable with 0 and 1 values, predicting the dependent variable, holding other variables in the model constant. Cases with missing values were excluded from the analyses.[6] Three logistic regression models were used to estimate the odds ratios (OR) for each of the two dependent variables (years of schooling and personal income). Model 1 included only the Latino respondents, Model 2 included only the Asian American respondents, and Model 3 included both Latino and Asian American respondents.

TABLE 7.7. Logistic Regression Analysis of Years of Schooling (1 = 13 or More Years; 0 = 12 Years or Less), Latino and Asian American 1.5- and 2nd-Generation Children of Immigrants in the Greater Los Angeles Metropolitan Area

PREDICTORS	MODEL 1: LATINOS		MODEL 2: ASIAN AMERICANS		MODEL 3: ALL	
	ODDS RATIO	95% CI	ODDS RATIO	95% CI	ODDS RATIO	95% CI
INDIVIDUAL CHARACTERISTICS						
Gender: 1 = Male; 0 = Female	0.61***	0.46–0.80	0.71	0.47–1.07	0.66***	0.53–0.84
Age: 1 = 30+; 0 = Under 30	1.08	0.79–1.47	0.89	0.53–1.52	1.04	0.79–1.35
Yearly Income: 1 = $30,000+; 0 = <$30,000	2.43***	1.74–3.38	4.09***	2.38–7.02	2.92***	2.20–3.86
Prefers to Speak English at Home: 1 = Yes; 0 = No	1.40*	1.06–1.85	1.36	0.88–2.11	1.33*	1.05–1.67
Marital Status: 1 = Married/Cohabit; 0 = Single	0.51***	0.38–0.68	0.56*	0.34–0.94	0.53***	0.41–0.68
Medical Insurance Through Work: 1 = Yes; 0 = No	1.52**	1.14–2.03	0.72	0.46–1.11	1.20	0.95–1.53
Generation: 1 = 2nd Generation; 0 = 1.5 Generation	1.73	0.87–3.45	1.74	0.29–1.88	1.29	0.75–2.22
CRIME, LAW, DISCRIMINATION						
Problem Neighborhood: 1 = No; 0 = Yes	0.97	0.72–1.31	1.81**	1.18–2.78	1.20	0.94–1.53

TABLE 7.7. *continued*

PREDICTORS	MODEL 1: LATINOS		MODEL 2: ASIAN AMERICANS		MODEL 3: ALL	
Self or Family Member Arrested and/or Jail: 1 = No; 0 = Yes	1.53^{**}	$1.15-$ 2.04	2.39^{***}	$1.52-$ 3.77	1.72^{***}	$1.35-$ 2.20
Respondent Unauthorized when Entered the United States: 1 = Yes; 0 = No	0.80	$0.51-$ 1.26	0.66	$0.27-$ 1.62	0.74	$0.50-$ 1.08
Mother and/or Father Unauthorized when Entered the United States: 1 = Yes; 0 = No	1.31	$0.99-$ 1.74	0.98	$0.53-$ 1.83	1.24	$0.96-$ 1.60
Prejudice or Discrimination: 1 = Yes; 0 = No	1.62^{**}	$1.21-$ 2.18	0.94	$0.62-1.4$	1.37^{*}	$1.07-$ 1.74
BELONGING AND COMMUNITY						
Ethnicity Important: 1 = Yes; 0 = No	1.04	$0.79-$ 1.38	1.08	$0.72-$ 1.61	1.08	$0.86-$ 1.35
Five or More Relatives Live Nearby: 1 = Yes; 0 = No	1.19	$0.89-$ 1.60	1.09	$0.72-$ 1.64	1.16	$0.92-$ 1.47
Belongs to One or More Community Organizations: 1 = Yes; 0 = No	1.90^{**}	$1.28-$ 2.83	1.54	$0.87-$ 2.71	1.77^{**}	$1.27-$ 2.45
Ethnicity: 1 = Asian American; 0 = Latino					7.07^{***}	$5.38-$ 9.31
X2	133.31^{***}		71.67^{***}		692.61^{***}	
DF	15		15		16	

Significance: * p <.05; ** p < .01; *** p < .001.

Source: Rumbaut et al. 2004.

Model 1: N in analysis = 1,028; missing cases 191.

Model 2: N in analysis = 1,348; missing cases 253.

Model 3: N in analysis = 2,376; missing cases 444.

FINDINGS FOR THE CURRENT STUDY

Table 7.7 displays the findings from three models for the dependent variable years of schooling. The children of Asian immigrants were seven times more likely than the children of Latin American immigrants to have had thirteen or more years of education. However, both groups had similar predictors of fewer and more years of schooling, especially relations with the law. Male children of Latin American immigrants were significantly less likely than Latinas to have had thirteen or more years of schooling, a pattern that follows national trends (U.S. Census Bureau 2011). Gender was not significant for the children of Asian immigrants, although gender was significant in Model 3, with all respondents in the analysis. In all three models, married respondents or those living with a partner were significantly less likely to have had thirteen or more years of education, perhaps due to the additional responsibilities that accompany family formation.

Among Latino respondents, preferring to speak English at home significantly predicted being in the higher education category, but not so for Asian Americans. However, English preference was significant in Model 3. Also among Latinos, having medical insurance through work, an indicator of better jobs, was also significantly correlated with more years of education. More years of schooling is significantly correlated with higher personal incomes among Latinos, Asian Americans, and all respondents. Among Latinos, those with more education were almost two-and-a-half times more likely to earn more than $30,000 a year. Among Asian Americans, those with more schooling were four times as likely as those with less schooling to be in the higher personal income category.

Experiences with the law also predicted years of schooling. Latinos who had never personally been arrested nor had a family member who had been arrested and/or incarcerated were 53 percent more likely to have had thirteen or more years of schooling compared to respondents who did have negative experiences with the criminal justice system. Among Asian Americans, those without arrest and/or incarceration experiences were 2.39 times as likely to be in the higher years of schooling category than those with negative experiences with the criminal justice system. The predictability of arrests and incarcerations for schooling is significant when all respondents are included in the analysis (Model 3). Asian Americans growing up in a neighborhood without crime problems were 81 percent more likely to have thirteen or more years of education than those who did experience neighborhoods with crime when growing up. Among Latinos, perceived experiences of prejudice and discrimination were positively associated with more years of education. The variable perceptions of prejudice and/or discrimination were significant in Model 3 as well. Respondents' and parents' immigration statuses when coming to the United States were not significant predictors of years of schooling. Also, the respondents' beliefs about the importance of ethnic identity and having five or more relatives living nearby were not significant factors in this study. However, Latinos who participated in at least one community organization were 90 percent more likely to have thirteen or more years of education than Latinos who were not community engaged.

TABLE 7.8. Logistic Regression Analysis of Personal Income (0 = <$30k; 1 = $30k or More), Latino and Asian American 1.5- and 2nd-Generation Children of Immigrants in the Greater Los Angeles Metropolitan Area

PREDICTORS	MODEL 1: LATINOS		MODEL 2: ASIAN AMERICANS		MODEL 3: ALL	
	ODDS RATIO	95% CI	ODDS RATIO	95% CI	ODDS RATIO	95% CI
INDIVIDUAL CHARACTERISTICS						
Gender: 1 = Male; 0 = Female	1.69**	1.22–2.36	1.16	0.88–1.53	1.40**	1.13–1.76
Age: 1 = 30+; 0 = Under 30	3.19***	2.29–4.45	3.81***	2.78–5.23	3.50***	2.79–4.38
Years of Schooling: 1 = 13 or More Years; 0 = 0–12 Years	2.37***	1.70–3.30	3.86***	2.26–6.59	2.83***	2.14–3.73
Prefers to Speak English at Home: 1 = Yes; 0 = No	1.54*	1.10–2.14	1.36*	1.01–1.84	1.41**	1.14–1.76
Marital Status: 1 = Married/Cohabit; 0 = Single	1.97***	1.43–2.73	2.41***	1.75–3.32	2.26***	1.80–2.83
Medical Insurance Through Work: 1 = Yes; 0 = No	5.09***	3.59–7.21	5.50***	4.18–7.24	5.29***	428–6.55
Generation: 1 = 2nd Generation; 0 = 1.5 Generation	0.91	0.41–2.03	0.90	0.49–1.66	0.90	0.56–1.44
CRIME, LAW, DISCRIMINATION						
Problem Neighborhood: 1 = No; 0 = Yes	1.02	0.72–1.46	1.44**	1.10–1.89	1.29*	1.043–1.60
Self or Family Member Arrested and/or Jail: 1 = No; 0 = Yes	1.05	0.75–1.47	1.44	0.99–2.10	1.18	0.92–1.51

TABLE 7.8. *continued*

PREDICTORS	MODEL 1: LATINOS		MODEL 2: ASIAN AMERICANS		MODEL 3: ALL	
Respondent Unauthorized when Entered the United States: 1 = Yes; 0 = No	0.56*	0.32–0.97	0.99	0.52–1.89	0.69	0.46–1.03
Mother and/or Father Unauthorized when Entered the United States: 1 = Yes; 0 = No	1.13	0.82–1.57	0.86	0.53–1.83	1.00	0.76–1.29
Prejudice or Discrimination: 1 = Yes; 0 = No	0.96	0.68–1.35	0.94	0.57–1.31	0.99	0.80–1.23
BELONGING AND COMMUNITY						
Ethnicity Important: 1 = Yes; 0 = No	0.95	0.69–1.31	1.11	0.85–1.46	1.05	0.86–1.29
Five or More Relatives Live Nearby: 1 = Yes; 0 = No	1.27	0.90–1.81	0.95	0.72–1.25	1.06	0.85–1.31
Belongs to One or More Community Organizations: 1 = Yes; 0 = No	1.67*	1.10–2.53	1.05	0.75–1.48	1.26	0.97–1.64
Ethnicity: 1 = Asian American; 0 = Latino					1.63***	1.27–2.11
X2	313.69***		547.11***		890.64***	
DF	15		15		16	

Significance: * p <.05; ** p < .01; *** p < .001.

Source: Rumbaut et al. 2004.

Model 1: N in analysis = 1,028; missing cases 191.

Model 2: N in analysis = 1,348; missing cases 253.

Model 3: N in analysis = 2,376; missing cases 444.

Table 7.8 presents the logistic regression analysis on personal income (0 = <$30,000; 1 = $30,000 or more) as the dependent variable. The children of Asian immigrants were 63 percent more likely than the children of Latin American immigrants to be in the higher-income category, which, given the imbalance in years of education, is an "interesting" finding. Almost all the respondents' individual characteristics are significant predictors of personal income. Males earn more than females among Latinos;

older respondents earn more than younger ones among all respondents. More years of schooling, being married or living together, and preferring to speak English at home all significantly predicted higher personal income for all respondents. Medical insurance through work, an indicator before the Affordable Care Act of a "better" job, was also significantly associated with higher personal income for all respondents. Asian Americans who did not grow up in neighborhoods with crime were 44 percent more likely to be in the higher personal income category, which was also significant in Model 3, with all respondents. Among Latinos, those who entered the United States without authorization were significantly less likely to be in the higher-income category than those who entered with authorization or were born in the United States. Lastly, among the belonging and community variables, Latinos who belonged to one or more community organizations were 67 percent more likely to be in the upper-income category than their less community-engaged counterparts.

DISCUSSION

As delineated herein, schooling and personal income are two key indicators of social integration. These indicators are not independent factors in that the amount of schooling one receives influences later earnings potential. The findings indicate the negative effect on schooling the children of immigrants experience as a result of arrest or incarceration, affecting either themselves or family members. Early life experiences in neighborhoods with crime can also affect schooling, especially among the children of Asian immigrants. Interestingly, Latinos who perceived themselves as the victims of prejudice or discrimination actually did better in terms of schooling. Either their education made them more aware or sensitive to possible instances of prejudice and discrimination, or they excelled to overcome a sense of social exclusion instilled by such experiences, or, as reported by Martin Guevara Urbina and Claudia Rodriguez Wright in *Latino Access to Higher Education: Ethnic Realities and New Directions for the Twenty-First Century* (2016), they possessed *ganas* (desire/will) to overcome all obstacles to stay in school and graduate, and subsequently obtain a better life.

Importantly, immigration status at time of entry was not a significant predictor of schooling among the participating respondents. The study was conducted after AB 540 was signed into law in California in 2001, allowing undocumented students to pay resident tuition to attend public colleges and universities. Previous to AB 540, unauthorized students had to pay nonresident tuition, much higher than the amount paid by residents, often limiting the years of schooling or forcing attendance at a less costly public university or community college. The finding that parents' immigration status when coming to the United States was not a significant predictor of years of schooling may reflect the inclusion of a broad range of community and policing variables, in contrast to other studies that do find a continued effect of immigration status over generations (Bean, Brown, and Bachmeier 2015). Personal income was predicted by many of the respondents' individual characteristics. However, schooling was highly significant, and as these findings suggest, schooling is affected by negative experiences with the criminal justice system. Although being arrested and/or incarcerated was not a significant predictor of personal income, such experiences had an indirect effect through negatively affecting years of schooling. Growing up in crime-ridden neighborhoods had a direct effect on personal earnings among Asian Americans and respondents generally.

Immigration law was a significant factor in earnings for the children of Latin American immigrants. Latinos who entered the country without authorization were significantly less likely to be in the higher-income category. The study was conducted before the Deferred Action for Childhood Arrivals program in 2012. Although undocumented young people could go to college or university at the time of study, they could not work legally, and doing so would jeopardize their chances of obtaining legal resident status. As these findings indicate, this appears to have negatively influenced personal income among these respondents.

CONCLUSION

Evidently, experiences with law and crime play an important role in the social integration of the children of immigrants, though not in the ways indicated in the statement by Donald Trump quoted at the beginning of this chapter. The children of immigrants who had negative experiences with the criminal justice system and who grew up in neighborhoods with drugs, gangs, and other crimes faced significant obstacles to their social integration. They were less likely to continue with their schooling and less likely to experience mobility in their personal earnings. Among the children of Mexican, Salvadoran, and Guatemalan immigrants, if they came to the United States without authorization they experienced additional obstacles to their earnings potential. Working at formal jobs increased the risk of deportation and reduced or even eliminated the possibility of acquiring legal resident status. They would, therefore, face limitations to working in better-paying jobs, such as those that provided medical insurance, which was also a significant predictor of higher personal income.

Broadly, these findings support legislative efforts to regularize the status of the undocumented children of immigrants as a way to improve social integration. Further, these findings underscore the need for interventions to ameliorate community and police relations and to reduce negative experiences with the criminal justice system among the children of both Asian and Latin American immigrants (see Urbina 2018; Urbina and Álvarez 2015, 2017). Attention to such efforts would improve educational attainment and thus social integration. Finally, immigrants and their children should not be penalized because of the neighborhoods they can afford to live in. All people deserve safe neighborhoods, but the findings here underscore the obstacles that neighborhoods with drugs, gangs, and crime add for the social integration of children of immigrants. While the situation for these children reveals a continued struggle, thousands of immigrant children (undocumented and documented) across the United States are experiencing not only the historical realities detailed herein, but also the current implications and consequences of Trump's anti-immigrant, anti-Mexican, anti-Latino, and anti-minorities movement. The findings presented illustrate the pressing call for action as we strive for understanding, tolerance, social integration, transformation, and unity in a highly multiethnic, multiracial, and multicultural American society.

NOTES

1. Co-principal investigators of the IIMMLA study were Rubén G. Rumbaut, Frank D. Bean, Susan K. Brown, Leo R. Chávez, Louis DeSipio, Jennifer Lee, and Min Zhou.

2. The Field Research Corporation conducted the telephone interviews.

3. Before the start of the interviewing, targeted quotas for the ethnic strata were established for eligible respondents aged twenty to forty years in the five-county area, placing special emphasis on the largest and most significant group—the Mexican-origin population. The IIMMLA also sampled a strategic handful of other large immigrant refugee origin-groups that were expected to be different in their modes of incorporation into U.S. society, including Chinese, Filipinos, Koreans, and Vietnamese, along with Salvadorans and Guatemalans taken together. All groups were assigned a separate sampling stratum for 1.5- and 2nd-generation respondents. The final design called for completing approximately 2,800 closed-ended telephone interviews with random samples of eligible 1.5- and 2nd-generation Latino and Asian American respondents. Multiframe sampling procedures were used to improve the chances of finding and interviewing members of targeted populations. The first stage used random digit dialing (RDD) to sample and screen households in the five-county area, and using this approach the IIMMLA was able to complete sample quotas for Mexicans. For the other groups, samples were compiled using RDD until the incidence rates of eligible respondents became prohibitively low. At this point, more specific geographic and race-ethnic sampling frames were used, targeting RDD to households in high-density Asian residential areas and those on lists of Chinese, Filipino, Korean, and Vietnamese surnames. Sixty-one percent of

the completed interviews were derived using solely first-stage RDD sampling, while 39 percent resulted from interviews using the augmented samples. The surveys were administered in English or Spanish using a computer-assisted telephone interviewing system. The number of questions asked varied by generation status, yielding an average interview length of thirty-two minutes for those in the 2nd generation and thirty-four minutes for those in the 1.5 generation. Respondents received $20 for participating in the survey. The response rate for the survey's main questionnaire was 55.6 percent.

4. An important consideration discussed by the study team prior to the launching of the study was the extent to which non-English languages would be required for the telephone survey. Data from the U.S. Census Bureau pertaining to 1.5/2nd- and 3rd+- generation immigrants residing in the Los Angeles metropolitan area, as well as the results of a preliminary pilot test conducted in 2003 for UCI by the Field Research Corporation, indicated that relatively small proportions of the 1.5-, 2nd-, and 3rd+- generation respondents were not fluent in English. Nevertheless, due to the presence of the large Spanish-speaking population, a courtesy Spanish-language version of the questionnaire was prepared and made available to those who requested it. Results from the survey indicated that greater than 90 percent of all eligible Latino adults chose to be interviewed in English.

5. Researchers at the Pew Research Center (Taylor and Cohn 2013, 48) found that 61 percent of U.S.-born children of Hispanics and Asian Americans consider themselves to be "typical Americans," which was double that of the 1.5-generation Hispanics (33 percent) and Asian Americans (30 percent).

6. A correlation matrix with all variables included found that none of the variables were highly enough correlated to be included in the analysis.

REFERENCES

Abrego, L. 2011. "Legal Consciousness of Undocumented Latinos: Fear and Stigma as Barriers to Claims-Making for First- and 1.5-Generation Immigrants." *Law and Society Review* 45: 337–70.

———. 2014. *Sacrificing Families: Navigating Laws, Labor, and Love Across Borders*. Stanford, Calif.: Stanford University Press.

Abrego, L., and C. Menjivar. 2012. "Legal Violence: Immigration Law and the Lives of Central American Immigrants." *American Journal of Sociology* 117: 1380–1421.

Alba, R., and V. Nee. 2003. *Remaking the American Mainstream: Assimilation and Contemporary Immigration*. Cambridge, Mass.: Harvard University Press.

Anderson, E. N. 2005. *Everyone Eats: Understanding Food and Culture*. New York: New York University Press.

Armenta, A. 2016. "Racializing Crimmigration: Structural Racism, Colorblindness, and the Institutional Production of Immigrant Criminality." *Sociology of Race and Ethnicity* 3: 82–95.

Barth, F., ed. 1982. *Ethnic Groups and Boundaries: The Social Organization of Cultural Difference*. Oslo: Universitetsforlaget.

Bean, F. D., S. K. Brown, and J. D. Bachmeier. 2015. *Parents Without Papers: The Progress and Pitfalls of Mexican American Integration*. New York: Russell Sage Foundation.

Bean, F. D., S. K. Brown, M. Leach, J. Bachmeier, L. R. Chávez, L. DeSipio, R. G. Rumbaut, J. Lee, and M. Zhou. 2006. "How Pathways to Legal Status and Citizenship Relate to Economic Attainment Among the Children of Mexican Immigrants." Washington, D.C.: Pew Hispanic Center.

Bean, F. D., S. K. Brown, M. A. Leach, J. D. Bachmeier, and J. V. Hook. 2014. "Unauthorized Mexican Migration and the Socioeconomic Integration of Mexican Americans." In *Diversity and Disparities: America Enters a New Century*, edited by J. R. Logan, 341–74. New York: Russell Sage Foundation.

Chávez, L. R. 2001. *Covering Immigration: Popular Images and the Politics of the Nation*. Berkeley: University of California Press.

———. 2006. "Culture Change and Cultural Reproduction: Lessons from Research on Transnational Migration." In *Globalization and Change in Fifteen Cultures: Born in One World and Living in Another*, edited by J. Stockard and G. Spindler, 283–303. Belmont, Calif.: Thomson-Wadsworth.

———. 2013a. *The Latino Threat: Constructing Immigrants, Citizens, and the Nation*. Stanford, Calif.: Stanford University Press.

———. 2013b. "Illegality Across Generations: Public Discourse and the Children of Undocumented Immigrants." In *Constructing "Illegality": Critiques, Immigrants' Experiences, and Responses*, edited by C. Menjivar and D. Kanstroom, 84–110. Cambridge: Cambridge University Press.

Coutin, S. 2013. "Place and Presence Within Salvadoran Deportees' Narratives of Removal." *Childhood* 20: 323–36.

Douglas, K. M., and R. Sáenz. 2013. "The Criminalization of Immigrants and the Immigration-Industrial Complex." *Daedalus* 142: 199–227.

Dowling, J. A., and J. X. India, eds. 2013. *Governing Immigration Through Crime: A Reader*. Stanford, Calif.: Stanford University Press.

Dreby, J. 2012. "The Burden of Deportation on Children in Mexican Immigrant Families." *Journal of Marriage and Family* 74: 829–45.

Gonzales, R. G., and L. R. Chávez. 2012. "'Awakening to a Nightmare': Objectivity and Illegality in the Lives of Undocumented 1.5 Generation Latino Immigrants in the United States." *Current Anthropology* 53: 255–81.

Gonzales, R. G., and V. Terriquez. 2013. "How DACA Is Impacting the Lives of Those Who Are Now DACAmented: Preliminary Findings from the National UnDACAmented Research

Project." Immigration Policy Center, Center for the Study of Immigrant Integrant, University of Southern California. http://www.immigrationpolicy.org/just-facts/how-daca-impacting-lives-those-who-are-now-dacamented.

Gratton, B., M. P. Gutmann, and E. Skop. 2007. "Immigrants, Their Children, and Theories of Assimilation: Family Structure in the United States, 1880–1970." *History of the Family* 12: 203–22.

Guendelman, M. D., S. Cheryan, and B. Monin. 2011. "Fitting In but Getting Fat: Identity Threat and Dietary Choices Among U.S. Immigrant Groups." *Psychological Science* 22: 959–67.

Hall, S. 1990. "Cultural Identity and Diaspora." In *Identity: Community, Culture, Difference*, edited by J. Rutherford, 222–37. London: Lawrence and Wishart.

Hirschman, C. 2013. "The Contributions of Immigrants to American Culture." *Daedalus* 142: 26–47.

Jimenez, T. 2009. *Replenished Ethnicity: Mexican Americans, Immigration, and Identity*. Berkeley: University of California Press.

Jones-Correa, M., and E. de Graauw. 2013. "The Illegality Trap: The Politics of Immigration and the Lens of Illegality." *Daedalus* 142: 185–98.

Kubrin, C. E., M. S. Zatz, and R. Martinez, eds. 2012. *Punishing Immigrants: Policy, Politics, and Injustice*. New York: New York University Press.

Lerman, A. E. 2013. *The Modern Prison Paradox: Politics, Punishment, and Social Community*. Cambridge: Cambridge University Press.

Liebig, T. 2008. "Labor Market Integration of the Children of Immigrants." The Integration of the European Second Generation Academic Conference. Amsterdam, Netherlands.

Light, M., and J. Iceland. 2016. "The Social Context of Racial Boundary Negotiations: Segregation, Hate Crime, and Hispanic Racial Identification in Metropolitan America." *Sociological Science* 3: 61–84.

Martinez, R. 2016. "Latina/o Immigrants, Crime, and Justice." In *Latinos and Criminal Justice: An Encyclopedia*, edited by J. L. Morin. Santa Barbara, Calif.: Greenwood.

Massey, D. 2013. "America's Immigration Policy Fiasco: Learning from Past Mistakes." *Daedalus* 142: 5–15.

Massey, D., and K. Pren. 2012. "Unintended Consequences of US Immigration Policy: Explaining the Post-1965 Surge from Latin America." *Population and Development Review* 38: 1–29.

Massey, D., and M. Sánchez R. 2010. *Brokered Boundaries: Creating Immigrant Identity in Antiimmigrant Times*. New York: Russell Sage Foundation.

Menjivar, C., and L. Abrego. 2012. "Legal Violence: Immigration Law and the Lives of Central American Immigrants." *American Journal of Sociology* 117: 1380–1421.

Migration Policy Institute. 2015a. "U.S: Immigrant Population by State and County." Washington, D.C.: Migration Policy Institute. http://www.migrationpolicy.org/programs/data-hub/charts/us-immigrant-population-state-and-county.

———. 2015b. "State Immigration Data Profiles." Washington, D.C.: Migration Policy Institute. http://www.migrationpolicy.org/programs/data-hub/state-immigration-data-profiles.

Motomura, H. 2014. *Immigration Outside the Law*. New York: Oxford University Press.

Motomura, H. 2006. *Americans in Waiting: The Lost Story of Immigration and Citizenship in the United States*. New York: Oxford University Press.

Ngai, M. 2004. *Impossible Subjects: Illegal Aliens and the Making of Modern America*. Princeton, N.J.: Princeton University Press.

Portes, A., and R. Schauffler. 1996. "Language Acquisition and Loss Among Children of Immigrants." In *Origins and Destinies: Immigration, Race, and Ethnicity in America*, edited by S. Pedraza and R. Rumbaut, 432–43. Belmont, Calif.: Wadsworth.

Rosas, G. 2012. *Barrio Libre: Criminalizing States and Delinquent Refusals of the New Frontier*. Durham, N.C.: Duke University Press.

Rumbaut, R. G. 2009a. "Undocumented Immigration and Rates of Crime and Imprisonment: Popular Myths and Empirical Realities." In *The Role of Local Police: Striking a Balance Between Immigration Enforcement and Civil Liberties*, edited by M. Malina, 119–39. Washington, D.C.: Police Foundation.

———. 2009b. "A Language Graveyard? The Evolution of Language Competencies, Preferences, and Use Among Young Adult Children of Immigrants." In *The Education of Language Minority Immigrants in the United States*, edited by T. G. Wiley, J. S. Lee, and R. Rumberger, 35–71. Clevedon, UK: Multilingual Matters.

Rumbaut, R. G., and W. Ewing. 2007. *The Myth of Immigrant Criminality and the Paradox of Assimilation: Incarceration Rates Among Native and Foreign-Born Men*. Washington, D.C.: Immigration Policy Center.

Rumbaut, R. G., D. S. Massey, and F. D. Bean. 2006. "Linguistic Life Expectancies: Immigrant Language Retention in Southern California." *Population and Development Review* 32: 447–60.

Rumbaut, R. G., F. D. Bean, L. R. Chávez, J. Lee, S. K. Brown, L. DeSipio, and M. Zhou. 2004. *Immigration and Intergenerational Mobility in Metropolitan Los Angeles (IIMMLA)*. ICPSR22627-VI. Ann Arbor, Mich.: Inter-university Consortium for Political and Social Research [distributor], 2008-07-01. https://doi.org/10.3886/ICPSR22627.VI.

Ryan, C. 2013. *Language Use in the United States: 2011*. Washington, D.C.: U.S. Census Bureau, U.S. Department of Commerce, Economics and Statistics Administration.

Sohoni, D., and T. W. P. Sohoni. 2013. "Perceptions of Immigrant Criminality: Crime and Social Boundaries." *Sociological Quarterly* 55: 49–71.

Stepick, A., and C. D. Stepick. 2010. "The Complexities and Confusions of Segmented Assimilation." *Ethnic and Racial Studies* 33: 1149–67.

Taylor, P., and D. Cohn. 2013. *Second-Generation Americans: A Portrait of the Adult Children of Immigrants*. Washington, D.C.: Pew Research Center.

Urbina, M. G., ed. 2018. *Hispanics in the U.S. Criminal Justice System: Ethnicity, Ideology, and Social Control.* 2nd ed. Springfield, Ill.: Charles C Thomas.

Urbina, M. G., and S. E. Álvarez, eds. 2015. *Latino Police Officers in the United States: An Examination of Emerging Trends and Issues.* Springfield, Ill.: Charles C Thomas.

——. 2017. *Ethnicity and Criminal Justice in the Era of Mass Incarceration: A Critical Reader on the Latino Experience.* Springfield, Ill.: Charles C Thomas.

Urbina, M. G., and C. R. Wright. 2016. *Latino Access to Higher Education: Ethnic Realities and New Directions for the Twenty-First Century.* Springfield, Ill.: Charles C Thomas.

U.S. Census Bureau. 2011. *More Working Women Than Men Have College Degrees.* http://www .census.gov/newsroom/releases/archives/education/cb11-72.html.

Vasquez, J. M. 2011. *Mexican Americans Across Generations: Immigrant Families, Racial Realities.* New York: New York University Press.

Yoshikawa, H., and J. Kholoptseva, J. 2013. "Unauthorized Immigrant Parents and Their Children's Development: A Summary of the Evidence." Migration Policy Institute. http://www .migrationpolicy.org/pubs/COI-Yoshikawa.pdf.

Yuval-Davis, N. 2006. "Belonging and the Politics of Belonging." *Patterns of Prejudice* 40: 197–214.

Chapter 8

BORDERS AND DREAMS

Immigration, Diversity, and Multiculturalism in the New Millennium

BRENDA I. GILL AND MARY C. SENGSTOCK

> Our nation was born in genocide when it embraced the doctrine
> that the original American, the Indian, was an inferior race.
> Even before there were large numbers of Negroes on our shore,
> the scar of racial hatred had already disfigured colonial society.
> From the sixteenth century forward, blood flowed in battles over
> racial supremacy. We are perhaps the only nation which tried as a
> matter of national policy to wipe out its indigenous population.
> Moreover, we elevated that tragic experience into a noble
> crusade. Indeed, even today we have not permitted ourselves to
> reject or feel remorse for this shameful episode. Our literature,
> our films, our drama, our folklore all exalt it. Our children are
> still taught to respect the violence which reduced a red-skinned
> people of an earlier culture into a few fragmented groups herded
> into impoverished reservations.
>
> —JOHN F. KENNEDY

A S NOTED THROUGHOUT this book, the immigration discourse has historically revolved around various intertwining and influential factors, principally
diversity and most recently multiculturalism. However, after centuries of social transformation, and in the midst of the hotly debated immigration discourse, what is "multiculturalism" in twenty-first-century America? The term arouses emotional reactions
in nearly everyone who hears it. Some find it pleasant or exciting. Usually they have
had previous contacts with persons different from themselves and have found the

This chapter is a revised version of the chapter "Multiculturalism in Twenty-First Century America," in
Twenty-First Century Dynamics of Multiculturalism, edited by Martin Guevara Urbina (Springfield, Ill.:
Charles C Thomas Publisher, Ltd.). Used with permission.

experience to be pleasant or interesting. Many people, however, find it *threatening*. They seek a "unified society," with one people, one race, one culture, one religion, one language, and one color. For these individuals, the presence of people different from themselves is viewed as a threat to their sense of identity and their ability to relate to others. For instance, hearing others who speak a different language, have an unfamiliar accent, have a different color of skin, or wear clothing that looks strange all threaten their sense of comfort. This is the situation the United States faces in the early twenty-first century. Americans who are uncomfortable with the modern dynamics of diversity and multiculturalism—highly influenced by immigration—often express a longing for what are perceived to be the "good old days," in which America was allegedly "one language, one culture, one people," where Americans did not worry about encountering or interacting with persons different from themselves.

However, the reality is that throughout its history the United States has been a diverse nation; that is, a nation not composed of a single racial or cultural group but made up of a number of different subgroups of people, originating from different racial, ethnic, or cultural backgrounds. As various scholars have pointed out, images of our country as a unified, "one-people" nation are greatly manipulated, skewed, or exaggerated—if not downright false (Coontz 2000; Loewen 2007). In reality, America has been a diverse nation since its earliest colonial days, and management of the varying races, ethnicities, and cultures that made up the nation has been problematic—normally seen by the dominant majority as threatening.

COLONIAL AMERICAN DIVERSITY

When white Americans think about "diversity" or "multiculturalism," they generally are referring to someone other than themselves. In their view, they are certainly not part of the "multicultural mix." Rather, they are the "normal" ones, the "real Americans." The right of some groups to claim the title of "American" might be questioned, but surely theirs wouldn't be. For example, in the twenty-first century, there was the charge that President Barack Obama was not born in the United States; and Latinos, including children, could not walk or drive down a street without the legitimacy of their residency being questioned. This questioning, of course, would not be an issue with "white" Americans.

In truth, white Americans are as much a part of the "American mix" as any other racial or ethnic group. This can be seen from an examination of the earliest colonial period. In fact, America's social diversity predates the arrival of European colonists. Studies reveal that prior to European colonization, North America was home to approximately one million Native Americans—with some scholars estimating as many as eighteen million. The colonists referred to the natives as "Indians" due, in part, to the erroneous conclusion that the explorers had reached the Far East. They also assumed the Native Americans were a single group, when in fact they consisted of approximately three hundred different groups, each with its own language, culture, and societal structure (John 1998; Sutton and Broken Nose 2005; Tafoya and Vecchio 2005). Even prior to the arrival of the Europeans, America was home to a culturally diverse population.

Native Americans were in no way perceived to be equals by the colonists, who viewed their own entry onto the scene as that of a *conquering power* even though in many instances the skills of the natives were needed to help the colonists adapt to a different environment. Over the years, English colonists and politicians who represented them were eager to take over large tracts of land used by Native Americans for hunting and grazing, so they were "removed" from the lands they had held for generations; children were separated from their families, culture, and religion and forcefully indoctrinated by Christian missionaries who saw themselves as superior. Native Americans were forbidden to speak their languages or follow their traditional cultural activities. Worse, the Native American population was decimated by European diseases. In fact, to this day, Native American health is worse than that of any other ethnic group in America, an issue compounded by astronomical rates of alcoholism and suicide (Hooyman and Kiyak 2005; John 1998; Sutton and Broken Nose 2005; Tafoya and Vecchio 2005).

RELIGIOUS AND ETHNIC (NATIONAL) DIVERSITY

Also contrary to popular belief, the colonial arrivals were quite diverse. For instance, while the earliest colonists were from England, spoke the English language, and practiced the Protestant religion, they were not from a single denomination. Some were Anglicans, others Congregationalists, with different views of the proper religious beliefs and structures, and they settled in different areas, mainly Massachusetts or Virginia (Anderson 1970). Yet people today view the "founders" of the American nation as a single unified group, a portrait that fails to recognize that the formation of separate colonies was partly due to their inability to get along with one another.

These differences only increased with subsequent waves of immigrants in the 1600s, when Baptists and Reformed Protestant groups began to arrive. Their different views on religion was in fact part of the reason for leaving England. Anglicans, for example, conformed to the hierarchical structure of the English church, with most other groups considering such structure to be too similar to the "Popish" Catholic Church

(Anderson 1970). In effect, differences that modern Protestants may view as relatively unimportant were of great concern to the early arrivals, so much that many left their homeland to avoid one another. Indeed, since the continent was sparsely populated, they were able to remain quite separate once they arrived in America.

The 1700s brought even more—not less—diversity to the colonial population, both in religion and national origin. Lutherans, Presbyterians, and Methodists, as well as some smaller sects, arrived, with Methodists becoming the largest Protestant group (Lipset 1963). Their religious views were quite different from those of the founding English Protestants. Denomination was only the beginning of their differences, since the new arrivals were of different national origins, primarily from Germany and other Germanic-speaking areas, including Austria, Switzerland, and Holland. While today's Protestant Americans tend to downplay these differences, they were viewed as quite problematic by the earlier English colonists. Benjamin Franklin, one of the founding fathers, is said to have had serious concerns about their increasing numbers and some of their behaviors (Cross 1973). The introduction of the German language, for example, raised anxieties among the English. Differences between German- and English-speaking Protestants persisted for some time. Many Germans chose not to become part of the "White Protestant majority," and thus the German language persisted in Pennsylvania as late as the twentieth century (Anderson 1970, 82). In fact, several of these German-speaking groups have been among the groups most resistant to merging into mainline Protestantism, including the Missouri Synod Lutheran denomination, the Amish, and the Mennonites (Huntington 1998).

Of course, it is not simply the resistance of incoming groups to accepting the culture of earlier arrivals that affects assimilation into a single group and culture. The degree of acceptance that newcomers encounter from their predecessors also plays a role. Protestants from other parts of the British Empire were often received no more hospitably than those from German-speaking groups. For example, arrivals from the Scottish Highlands were Protestants, but they were Presbyterian, a strange faith to the proper English settlers who preceded them. They also spoke their unfamiliar Celtic language, often wore their clan garb, and were prone to drink and use language the English considered blasphemous (Anderson 1970; Graham 1956). Although today the Scots and Scots-Irish would be considered "white Protestants," colonial treatment of them was often as discriminatory as that received by newcomers from non-Christian religions in later eras. For instance, they were shunned by the English Bostonians, banned from the Carolinas (Anderson 1970), and barred from holding public office in colonial times. Some Scots-Irish Presbyterian churches were targeted by vandals (Jones 1960). Their reception was influenced not only by their religious beliefs but by the view that they were short-tempered and not very industrious (Anderson 1970; Leyburn 1962).

Another segment of the so-called white Protestant population that was initially viewed as radically different and unacceptable was the Scandinavian group from Norway, Finland, and Sweden. While some came during the colonial period, the majority came during the major immigration period of the late nineteenth and early twentieth centuries. They were descended from the Vikings, not the Anglo-Saxons as were the English (Anderson 1970). Their version of the Protestant faith was a particularly strict Lutheranism, rigidly enforced by Scandinavian pastors (Anderson 1970). Their different languages and isolation in the largely rural Midwest meant that Scandinavians maintained their separation from the larger society for an extended time. Finnish Lutherans in particular remained separate well into the twentieth century (Anderson 1970). Assimilation with other Scandinavians occurred before most moved into the broader Protestant group.

In summary, early immigrants into the United States were primarily Protestant, but they also came from a broad array of nationalities, languages, and versions of the Protestant faith. These traits led to considerable division among the groups, sometimes resulting in actions that would today be characterized as "prejudice" or "discrimination." Over time, they came to view themselves as the quintessential "white Americans." Only with the increasing diversity of the American population, together with its focus on ethnic identity, which occurred in the mid-twentieth century, did many become more conscious of their common ties to the broader Protestant religion (Anderson 1970). In fact, many of the Protestant groups continue to maintain some of the cultural characteristics of their national and religious denominational origins. For example, the family patterns of numerous European Protestant groups are sufficiently different to justify being considered different family types in manuals used for training family counselors (McGoldrick, Giordano, and García-Pareto 2005).

Seeking to understand diversity and multiculturalism, among other issues, in twenty-first-century America, we can learn much from the experiences of these early arrivals—immigrants—to American shores. Although today they are viewed as relatively similar—all Protestants, all of European stock, all from the so-called white race—they were by no means seen as such on their arrival in present-day United States. Their different ethnic origins (Anglo-Saxon vs. Germanic vs. Viking), their different languages (English, German, and the various Scandinavian languages), and the different denominational approaches to the Protestant religion all contributed to their being viewed as "different" groups from the early colonial period until the late nineteenth or even twentieth centuries.

Together, there are three important lessons to take from the white Protestant experience. First, it illustrates how the differences that groups perceive in each other are not necessarily obvious to an objective outside observer. The seventeenth-century English and Scots-Irish Protestants may look the same to us, but they did not look that way to each other. Second, intergroup relations always tend to go in two directions. Not only must the original group be willing to accept the incoming group, but newcomers must also desire to become part of the original group. Reluctance by either group can jeopardize the exchange. Third, the basic cultural difference that groups bring with them can be persistent; trends may continue for several generations, often long after members of the group are even aware of their existence. Therefore, an apparently "white Protestant American" couple who plans to marry may be totally unaware of the existence of longstanding family traditions, which each retains and may be radically different from those of the other.

Descendants of these early groups also tend to view themselves as the "dominant" group, with a superior culture and not part of the mix, not part of a pluralistic culture. In retrospect, they think of the "white Protestant culture" as *the* American culture, with the practices of other incoming groups deviating from that pattern. In truth, the earliest Protestant settlers had several distinct cultures, and multiple components of the numerous cultures remain in various forms in the twenty-first century. In effect, the United States is currently composed of a mixture of cultures, many of them being remnants of the several European nationalistic, religious, and linguistic variations that existed in the "Old World" during the time of conquest and colonization.

These variations remain today, though most Americans, including descendants of the original groups, are unaware of the historical variations. In fact, in the early years, some people were even considered to be from a different "race," even though they did not look physically different. Immigrants who were perceived to be radically "different" and not easily assimilated were viewed as unacceptable and thus were targets of prejudice and discrimination by their predecessors. These views formed part of the basis for the immigration restrictions and quota system of the 1920s, with strong support for such limitations on immigration during the first two decades of the twentieth century. Further revealing of historical shifts, some groups now considered to be "white" were, at that time, considered to be of a different "race," as evidenced by the fact that early English and Dutch settlers considered marriage between different cultural groups to be as unacceptable as marriage between physically different races (Fernández 1996). As such, groups who were not considered white were not favored in the immigration quota system (Barrett and Roediger 1997; Jacobson 1998; Ngai 1999). In fact, even legendary President Theodore Roosevelt, following his departure from the White House, was a prominent supporter of these views, insisting that immigrants must renounce their nations of origin and that only English was to be taught in schools (Hart and Ferleger 1989; Roosevelt 1919). Thus, before it was situated and promoted as having a biological basis, *"race" was used by people in power to manage and control those they disliked*—although the logic of the categories has rarely been examined (Spickard 1992).

The most important conclusion to draw from the experiences of early immigrants is that they were not received graciously by the groups who preceded them—even though they were not remarkably different from the original English Protestant settlers. Such differential treatment set the stage for the handling of later newcomers, especially since immigrants who followed tended to vary more and more dramatically from the dominant white America.

INTRODUCING ANOTHER NEW CULTURE INTO THE "NEW" NATION

Within a few decades after the establishment of the American nation, its citizens began searching for new areas to establish homesteads, and they had already made clear that they intended to remove and displace Native Americans—taking total control of the conquered lands while seeking further expansion. However, another group stood in the way of the expansion of the "new" American nation, for the present-day western states had already been claimed by Spain and later Mexico—and this area was already home to many Mexican citizens. Still, in the early decades of the nineteenth century, white settlers from the eastern states began moving into what are now the states of Arizona, California, Colorado, New Mexico, and Texas—invading territory already populated by people of Mexican descent. Under the expansionist ideology of Manifest Destiny, the incoming white Americans sought not only to take possession of these areas but also to quickly transform them into territories under Anglo-American rule. These lands were taken over by the U.S. government using various strategies (Acuña 2014; Almaguer 2008; De León 1983, 1997, 2002, 2009; McWilliams 1990; Urbina, Vela, and Sánchez 2014), though primarily through the Texas rebellion (1836), the Battle of San Jacinto (1836), and the Gadsden Purchase in 1853 (Alba and Nee 2003; Moore 1970). Subsequently, a new group of Americans of Mexican descent, who, like Native Americans, were not immigrants but natives of the Southwest, automatically became American "citizens" (on paper) when their homelands became part of the United States. As documented by David López and Ricardo Stanton-Salazar (2001), by the mid-nineteenth century, the Anglo presence in the Southwest had largely overwhelmed the Mexican presence.

Other than the original Mexican Americans, who were not immigrants but a conquered people like Native Americans, all subsequent people of Mexican heritage have been part of a free rather than a forced migration. In that respect, Mexican migration is similar to that of other immigrant groups. As for the original Mexican inhabitants, while the government treaties were to have guaranteed the original Mexicans' rights to their property and cultural freedom, the formal treaties and promises were rarely respected (Acuña 2014; Alba and Nee 2003; Almaguer 2008; Bender 2003; De León and Del Castillo 2012; Mirandé 1987; Urbina, Vela, and Sánchez 2014). In part, such oppressive treatment was due to the fact that, like other culturally different groups, Mexicans were defined as a "different race." Although, as Joan Moore (1970) reports, it is difficult to comprehend how the mixture of Spanish and Native American, which describes many Mexicans, would constitute a different race. Yet the problems of Mexican Americans were to be exacerbated by later movements of Spanish-speaking migrants into the United States—eventually resulting in a legacy of hate against immigrants, especially Mexican immigrants.

SPECIAL TREATMENT OF PEOPLE OF COLOR BY THE FOUNDERS OF THE AMERICAN NATION

While we have been stressing the fact that all groups viewed as "different" were treated, in large part, as undesirable interlopers by the original colonists, there is also no doubt that some groups were clearly more unequal than others, as evidenced by the brutal and discriminatory treatment of Native Americans and Mexican Americans. The unenviable position, however, was undoubtedly reserved for people who had the most obvious physical differences, mainly different *skin color*: blacks, Mexicans, and Asians, in addition to Native Americans. The discrimination against ethnic and racial groups was clearly much more severe than the treatment of whites from different cultural backgrounds.

Some critics, for instance, document that African Americans have historically been the target of a far greater degree of prejudice and discrimination than any other group (Baldwin 1963). African Americans were the only group for whom migration to the Americas was exclusively forced migration, followed by a social system that forced them to live in slavery for two hundred years (Pinkney 1993). While many immigrant groups have included migrants who did not freely choose to come to America, only for blacks was migration a forced choice for all. From the outset, blacks were also banned from full participation in society, the result of an act of Congress in the years immediately preceding the establishment of the nation. In 1790 citizenship was limited to "free White persons" (Alba and Nee 2003, 168).

Free migrants rarely come alone. That is, they tend to migrate as part of a family or village community, and they often know persons in the new environment who will assist them on arrival—easing their adjustment to their new homes. In turn, they maintain contact with their places of origin and often assist those who wish to follow them to the United States, a process that helps in their adjustment to a strange new place (Sengstock 1976). Forced migration, like that created by slavery, represents a radical change of both environment and culture for the newcomer. Forced immigrants, for instance, have no control over the place to which they will be sent. Further, forced immigrants are deliberately separated from all contact with anyone who shares their social patterns, culture, or language. Often they were completely alone, making them totally dependent on the slaveholders. If slaves did develop familial or other social contacts, they were often sold to widely separated owners to forestall possible slave uprisings (Pinkney 1993). Labor was forced, living conditions were appalling, and punishment was brutal, even for minor infractions of the established slave system. In fact, Africans were not defined as "human" by most European religions; subsequently, they were not entitled to basic human rights (Black and Jackson 2005; Pinkney 1993).

According to some critics, *even the most hated white immigrants were not subjected to such restrictions*, so long as they agreed to relinquish their former cultures (Hart and Ferleger 1989; Roosevelt 1919). Technically, the Civil War (1861–65) and the Emancipation Proclamation of the mid-1800s freed the slaves. However, in the succeeding Reconstruction period (1865–77) a differential system *designed* specifically for blacks was rapidly reestablished—miscegenation laws were passed preventing intermarriage between blacks and whites, and Jim Crow laws were implemented preventing the races from interacting in all types of settings for decades. The supposed "separate but equal" treatment, which was hardly equal, persisted until the civil rights movement of the mid-twentieth century (Nakashima 1992; Pinkney 1993).

Asian immigrants, who were, like blacks, physically identifiable as "different" from whites, also experienced significant prejudice and discriminatory treatment. Chinese immigrants were the first Asians to come to the United States in significant numbers, the earliest immigrants coming in the mid-nineteenth century. Most Asian immigrants settled in the western states, not surprising in view of its greater proximity to the Asian continent (Lee and Mock 2005). Like blacks, Asians were subject to the 1790 law banning nonwhites from U.S. citizenship (Alba and Nee 2003). Congress also found other ways of limiting Chinese migration, such as the Chinese Exclusion Act of 1882, which prohibited Chinese from bringing family members to the United States. As such, Chinese immigration primarily involved a migration of male workers, not of families (Alba and Nee 2003; Lee and Mock 2005; Shibusawa 2005).

Once Chinese migration was halted, Japanese men largely took their place, and therefore these two groups largely represented Asian migration to the United States prior to the twentieth century. While the Japanese immigrants fared a little better than the Asians who preceded them, they too were banned from citizenship and prohibited from owning land. To some critics, Japanese experienced the most dramatic discrimination against immigrants on American soil: the internment of thousands of Japanese Americans, immigrants and U.S.-born citizens alike, in concentration camps following the bombing of Pearl Harbor in 1941 (Bosworth 1967; Kitano 1969). In the later twentieth century, reparation efforts were made for the damages the Japanese experienced, but many Americans, remembering World War II, resisted these efforts, illustrating again that considerable prejudice against Asians remained (Shibusawa 2005).

MID-TO LATE NINETEENTH CENTURY: THE "REALLY DIFFERENT" WHITE IMMIGRANTS ARRIVE

The mid-1800s began an era of dramatic change for the American nation. Prior to that time, free migration into the country had been relatively slow, and those entering had been primarily from northern Europe and followed some variant of the Protestant faith. With the failure of the potato crop in Ireland, immigration trends quickly changed. The resulting famine forced impoverished Irish peasants, the vast majority being Roman Catholic, to seek refuge in the United States, producing a dramatic change in the American population. For example, the first U.S. Census in 1790 showed a total population of approximately four million, including 200,000 Irish, nearly all of them Protestant (Fallows 1979). Yet by the 1830s, a totally different group of Irish began to arrive in the United States. During that decade, the number of Irish in the United States more than doubled, with 300,000 new Irish arriving in America, the majority of them Catholic (Fallows 1979). The new Irish immigrants were not only impoverished but were perceived to be lazy, frivolous, immoral, and addicted to alcohol, traits detested by the staid English Protestants (Alba and Nee 2003; Anderson 1970; Fallows 1979). To make matters worse, the new Irish instituted the "pub," the typical Irish meeting place and bar (Fallows 1979), not the best signal to the long-time residents of their new community. The Irish also quickly began developing the religious institution they had cherished in their homeland, establishing churches for worship and schools to ensure that their children would not be educated into the Protestant tradition of the early American settlers (Fallows 1979). As such, the Irish were rapidly labeled "Papists" to symbolize their affiliation with the Catholic religion (Anderson 1970). Numerous authors have shown that the animosity toward Catholics in nineteenth-century American life cannot be overstated, as it was a major unifying force for Protestants at that time (Anderson 1970; Fallows 1979; McGrath 2007).

With new riches to be discovered in the newly conquered land, the Irish were rapidly followed by other immigrants, most of whom bore characteristics that made them equally unwelcome. For instance, Italian and Polish people were also Catholic and thus, like the Irish, suspect. However, like the Scots-Irish, who came in the earliest days of American colonization, their religious patterns were significantly different from those of the Irish Catholics who preceded them. In effect, Irish Catholicism was heavily rule-driven, the Church being viewed as a mechanism for avoiding hell, while both Italian and Polish people valued the church for its pageantry and rituals. Consequently, these new ethnic groups began establishing a new set of Catholic churches and schools, separate from those of the Irish, to serve their own respective religious preferences (Gambino 1974; Giordano, McGoldrick, and Klages 2005; Lopata 1976; Nelli 1980).

Contrary to the popular imagination, these groups, like the various nationality groups that preceded them, were not particularly interested in acculturating and assimilating into the American society and culture—or even into the cultures of other groups similar to themselves. Conversely, there were reasons each group was not considered appropriate for acceptance by other so-called Americans at the time. While the Irish were considered irresponsible alcoholics, Italians had the additional characteristic of having the darker skin color of southern Europeans and often were associated with organized crime and the Mafia (Giordano, McGoldrick, and Klages 2005). The Italians, like the Polish, were generally poor, uneducated, and employed in unskilled occupations (Lopata 1976), and both groups were singled out by former President Woodrow Wilson as undesirable citizens for the United States (Gerson 1972).

While new immigrants confronted various barriers, religious difference was clearly a key factor in their conflictive relationships, as none were inclined to abandon their Catholic beliefs and instead began building an extensive set of institutions to establish a strong Catholic presence in the United States—resulting in three different sets of institutions, each serving a different ethnic population. At the same time, the U.S. population remained highly resistant to including followers of the Roman Catholic faith in the already existing institutions. The earlier bans against Catholics holding office had been eliminated after the American Revolution (1775–83), but there were regular movements to revise restrictions once major Catholic groups began arriving in America. Some of the groups espousing these views were the American Protestant Union, Protestant Reformation Society, Know-Nothing Party, American Protective Association, and Ku Klux Klan, one of whose first targets were Catholics (Alba and Nee 2003; Anderson 1970). In the twenty-first century, all three of these Catholic groups are considered part of the "white" or "European" population.

AMERICA'S JEWISH POPULATION: THE FIRST NON-CHRISTIANS ON THE AMERICAN SCENE

Most Americans have been unaware that Jews were present in the American population in small numbers long before the American Revolution. Jewish refugees from Brazil, for instance, were present in the colonies as early as the mid-1600s (Schuck 2003). Sephardic Jews from Spanish and Portuguese backgrounds came to New

Amsterdam in the mid-1700s; after experiencing a less-than-positive reception, they moved on to Newport, Rhode Island, where they established the first synagogue in America (Tauro Synagogue 2007). A second wave of Jews, following the Reform tradition, came from Germany in the mid-1800s, with many of them being merchants who became successful in business and finance (Farber, Lazerwitz, and Mindel 1998). However, until the last few decades of the nineteenth century, Jews remained a small proportion (about 200,000, or less than 0.5 percent) of the U.S. population (Goldstein and Goldschneider 1968).

The majority of Jewish immigrants were part of the major migration occurring at the end of the nineteenth century and in the early twentieth. This group of immigrants, however, was quite different from its predecessors, as most were from Eastern Europe and practiced the ritually Orthodox version of Judaism (Farber, Lazerwitz, and Mindel 1998). The earliest arrivals tended to be lower class, unskilled workers, but after the turn of the twentieth century, they were succeeded by members of the skilled trade class, who arrived with aspirations to move into business, white-collar, and professional occupations (Goldstein and Goldschneider 1968; Rosen and Weltman 2005; Sherman 1965). Eventually, they were perceived as the "model" ethnic group, attaining success through their industry (Glazer and Moynihan 1963).

It is not surprising that Jews tended to remain united as a community once they arrived in the United States. While they immigrated from a wide diversity of nations, most did not identify with their countries of origin. Once they were in the United States, they simply identified themselves as Jews (Goldstein and Goldschneider 1968). Further, despite the original tension between the more economically successful Sephardic and German Jews of the earlier migration and the eastern European Jews who arrived later, the community became unified and developed an extensive set of religious, educational, and social welfare institutions to assist new Jewish immigrants as they arrived and to maintain a strong sense of identity within the community, even as they moved into the second and subsequent generations. As reported in various studies, members of the Jewish community have a high rate of marriage within the community, with stable marriages. Intermarriages tend to result in the non-Jewish partner becoming Jewish rather than deviating from the community (Goldstein and Goldschneider 1968; Rosen and Weltman 2005).

Maintenance of *ethnic identity* is essential for newcomers to remain a separate community, which is influenced by the degree of acceptance they encounter from mainstream society. Invariably, given the manner in which Jews were viewed and treated in Europe throughout the centuries, it is not surprising that the European colonists who had settled in the United States were not pleased with the arrival of large numbers of Jewish immigrants. Like Catholics, who were disliked by American Protestants, Jews became a major target for various groups, including the Ku Klux Klan (Alba and Nee

2003; Urbina, Vela, and Sánchez 2014). In fact, from the outset, they experienced prejudice and discrimination in community settings and institutions, including housing, employment, and education (Alba and Nee 2003). In the early twentieth century, for example, some Ivy League universities established quotas for the number of Jews who could be admitted to ensure that such revered white Protestant institutions would remain Protestant white men's universities (Klein 2005; see also Acuña 1998, 2011; Mirandé 2005; Moore 2007; Urbina 2003; Urbina and Wright 2016; Zuberi and Bonilla-Silva 2008). Clearly, Jews were not defined as members of the "white" race by white America (Alba and Nee 2003). Even at the beginning of the twenty-first century, anti-Semitism remains strong in some Christian groups (Allen and Beitin 2007; Americans United for Separation of Church and State 2007). Getting accepted as a member of the "white" race still remains an elusive *privilege* in twenty-first-century America (Bonilla-Silva 2006; Feagin 2013; Feagin and Cobas 2008, 2014; López 2003, 2006; Urbina 2014; Urbina and Álvarez 2017; Urbina and Wright 2016), as recently illustrated by Wendy Leo Moore in *Reproducing Racism: White Space, Elite Law Schools, and Racial Inequality* (2007) and Joe Feagin in *White Party, White Government: Race, Class, and U.S. Politics* (2012).

POLITICAL REACTIONS TO THE IMMIGRATION SURGE AT THE TURN OF THE TWENTIETH CENTURY

The closing decade of the nineteenth century and the early decades of the twentieth century saw the influx of a huge number of immigrants—more than eighteen million new arrivals from 1890 to 1920 (Schuck 2003). British, Irish, Jews, Scandinavians, and southern and eastern Europeans continued to come, but they were joined by Canadians, Japanese, Mexicans, and residents of the Caribbean and Pacific Islands. Among the eastern and southern Europeans who arrived were Greeks, Slavs, and people from other nations who were migrating for the first time. With a broad and diverse spectrum of newcomers, anti-immigration movements quickly arose, including a series of congressional hearings, led by Senator William Dillingham of Vermont (House-Senate Commission on Immigration 1911). These hearings resulted in restrictive laws against immigration in the 1920s, known as the "quota system." To ensure that the majority of new arrivals would resemble the earlier arrivals, lawmakers went back to the 1890 census rather than later censuses to determine the "appropriate" numbers of new admissions.

After the hearings, the commission concluded that the "new" immigrants were radically different from those who had come earlier, incapable of being acculturated into the mainstream America. Consequently, government officials argued that the nation needed to impose severe restrictions on the number of new arrivals from certain countries in the future, leading to the enactment of subjective quota restrictions and enforcement. Scholars have reported that the commission based its conclusions on seriously erroneous information, a situation that became known as the "Dillingham Flaw," after the chair of the commission (Parillo 1994, 2000). The underlying error was the failure to recognize that all immigrants, earlier ones as well as those arriving in the 1890–1920 period, required a relatively long period of adjustment, and later immigrants also had a technologically more advanced and urbanized society to which they had to adapt. This failure to understand the assimilation and acculturation process, with its corresponding elements, continues in the twenty-first century. In fact, social scientists and other professionals have recognized that cultural difference may persist for several generations, not only among Asians, blacks, or Jews, but also among people of white Anglo-Saxon Protestant (WASP) backgrounds (McGoldrick, Giordano, and Garcia-Parto 2005).

CHANGES IN IMMIGRATION PATTERNS IN MID- AND LATE TWENTIETH-CENTURY AMERICA

The mid-twentieth century brought more changes to the existing immigration policies. As noted, the immigration restrictions of the 1920s had purposely limited the number of people who could enter the United States, with particularly severe restrictions on immigrants from Third World countries and people of color. The purpose was clearly to ensure that the majority of new immigrants would more closely resemble the white Protestant "founders" of the United States. However, after centuries of ethnic and racial oppression, the civil rights movement of the 1960s raised serious questions about racial prejudice and discrimination, altering the perspective of many Americans about the basic fairness of legal limitations on racial equality (Alba and Nee 2003). Eventually, these sentiments led to the adoption of the Immigration and Nationality Act of 1965, which restructured the old quota system and allowed greater numbers of non-European immigrants to enter the United States (Schuck 2003).

These changes in immigration policy quickly resulted in major demographic shifts, along with shifts in diversity. For example, in just five years following the enactment of the new law, Asian immigrants increased over fourfold, from 21,000 in 1965 to 93,000 in 1970 (Schuck 2003). There were also substantial increases in the number of Africans and especially Afro-Caribbean residents from the West Indies. Of course, since the 1965 act had basically rearranged the national quota by taking the quotas destined for European and North American nations and awarding them to other countries, the act also imposed a quota, for the first time, on Western Hemisphere nations. The new immigration policy *strategically* placed limitations on immigration from Mexico, which produced the "undocumented" immigrant dilemma that has strained the U.S.-Mexico border ever since (Alba and Nee 2003).

In 2000, the U.S. Census found that approximately 20 percent of Americans (one in five) were either foreign-born or children of foreign-born parents, with most immigrants being concentrated near points of entry, such as New York, and border states, like Arizona, California, Florida, and Texas (Alba and Nee 2003). California, in particular, has experienced a major shift in its population composition. For example, in the last two decades of the twentieth century, the Latino portion of California's population increased by one-third, with the Asian population increasing by 40 percent. In contrast, the proportion of non-Latino whites dropped to less than half, compared with over 60 percent in previous decades (Alba and Nee 2003). Since most newcomers settled in the Los Angeles area, Los Angeles was significantly transformed in terms of diversity and multiculturalism.

Analyzing recent demographic shifts, Alba and Nee (2003, 10–14) characterize the remapping process as "remaking the American mainstream." As seen in cities across the United States, not only do immigration trends result in racial and ethnic differences, they also produce extreme cultural differences. Asians, for example, bring with them over thirty different languages as well as regional dialects. With multiple foreign languages and great cultural variation, some institutions are "forced" to alter their operating mechanisms. Schools, for example, must teach children whose first language is not English, and government programs have found it necessary to provide translation in public buildings (Bloomberg 2006; Urbina and Wright 2016). Similarly, some newcomers bring with them radically different religious beliefs. Many Americans believe that language differences threaten the character of America as an English-speaking country (Alba and Nee 2003; Doucet and Hamon 2007), and if the Protestant settlers felt threatened by European Catholics and Jews, how much more must they feel threatened by the entry of Muslims, Hindus, Taoists, or followers of Confucius or Buddha (Lee and Mock 2005). For many white Americans, these dramatic differences represent a serious threat to their historically cherished cultural patterns of absolute power, control, and dominance, resulting in major reactions by people like Donald Trump, Bill O'Reilly, Sean Hannity, Rush Limbaugh, Ann Coulter, and Ted Cruz.

WHITE MAINSTREAM RESPONDS: REASSERTING THE SUPERIORITY OF "WHITENESS"

For a brief period in the 1990s, studies have shown, Americans were more receptive to cultural differences than in the past. However, at the same time, Americans continue to believe that certain elements of the dominant "white" culture must be maintained, and that new arrivals should accept established patterns as quickly as possible (Alba and Nee 2003) or suffer the consequences, like prejudice and discrimination. In fact, contrary to the notion that America is becoming more tolerant of ethnic, racial, and cultural diversity, some critics observe that the U.S. population is in fact becoming more conservative (Acuña 1998, 2013, 2014; Pinkney 1993). Some critics also suggest that Americans are not less prejudiced but simply less overt about their prejudices (Quillian 2006; see also Bonilla-Silva 2006; Cobas, Duany, and Feagin 2009; Feagin 2013; Feagin and Cobas 2014), expressing liberal attitudes in general but not supporting specific programs to assist racial and ethnic minorities (Acuña 2011; Krysan 2000; Urbina and Wright 2016). Numerous reactions across the United States clearly illustrate that white Americans are increasingly reasserting the superiority of "whiteness" and white people's right to dominate the American society (Acuña 2011, 2013; Feagin 2012; McDermott and Samson 2005; Urbina and Álvarez 2015, 2016, 2017). For instance, some of the errors in the Dillingham Commission report one hundred years ago can once again be seen in congressional immigration discussions in the first fifteen years of the twenty-first century (Gutiérrez 1997; Parillo 1994, 2000; Posadas and Medina 2012; Romero and Sánchez 2012; Salinas 2015).

Ironically, some of the most strident supporters of today's white supremacy movement are descendants of the "second-wave" immigrants, both Protestant and Catholic, who were targets of severe discrimination on their arrival in the United States a century ago. This twenty-first-century mentality is consistent with the fact that members of these groups, in their early days in the country, often found that they could move ahead by distinguishing themselves from blacks (Alba and Nee 2003). They have learned that focusing on their "whiteness" and a commitment to traditional American values are keys to advancement in America—*white privilege*. In the twenty-first century, four major dimensions continue to characterize this movement: resistance to immigration, defense of the English language, opposition to affirmative action, and reassertion of Christian fundamentalism.

RESISTANCE TO IMMIGRATION

Resistance to immigration has taken several forms in recent years. For instance, the 1994 General Social Survey showed that nearly three-fourths of respondents were uncomfortable with increased immigration and believed immigrants threatened American unity (Alba and Nee 2003). The degree to which Asians and other non-whites took advantage of new opportunities was probably not anticipated by the dominant white majority. Further, the limitations placed on Western Hemisphere immigration also failed to recognize the various dimensions of immigration from Mexico, particularly economic and political issues (Alba and Nee 2003), resulting in the current focus on "undocumented" migration and numerous efforts to "secure" the Mexican border (Kiely 2006; Krauthammer 2006).

In fact, in the twenty-first century, undocumented immigration has become a focal issue, exacerbated after 9/11 and blown out of proportion during the 2016 presidential election by Donald Trump and the other sixteen Republican presidential candidates, as well as by other immigration hawks, political pundits, conservative bigots, and some intellectual racists. Consequently, as state and local governments become increasingly dissatisfied with federal programs to "control the border," more and more state and local governments are adopting their own anti-immigration initiatives (Brezosky 2007; Democracy Now 2005; Gazelem 2007; Invasion USA 2005; Lucas 2005; Robbins 2007). The anti-immigrants movement has also strongly opposed a broad variety of services to undocumented immigrants, including health care, education, and social assistance in various states, including California with Proposition 187 in 1994 (Lucas 2005; Mailman 1995). However, the distinction between a "legal" and an "illegal" immigrant is not always an easy one, resulting in some documented immigrants, even U.S. citizens, being targeted as well—an approach that many Americans find acceptable, resulting in further prejudice and discrimination. Studies show that two-thirds of legal immigrants believe these restrictions are causing difficulties for them and their families (Bendixen and Associates 2006).

DEFENSE OF THE ENGLISH LANGUAGE

Americans have always been assertive about the significance of the English language for maintaining a unified white culture. According to public opinion polls, respondents consider it essential that immigrants and their children be required to learn English as quickly as possible and think that native languages should be allowed for only a few years. In fact, some people have rejected the use of any other language in schools at any time (Alba and Nee 2003; Boulet 2001; Urbina and Wright 2016), presenting a serious problem since schools are the major mechanism for promoting new language skills. Still, several states have introduced "English only" requirements for schools, banned the use of other languages in public places, and even attempted to force immigrants to eliminate "accents" that would distinguish their speech from other Americans (English First 2007; Luongo 2007; Swift 2007; Urbina and Wright 2016; U.S. English 2005). Although not designed to help establish English-language primacy, the federal government's No Child Left Behind Act of 2001 also had the effect of discouraging foreign language use in schools; it set penalties for schools that did not meet the established criteria for improvement, meaning that certain programs, such as remedial English for foreign students, have been nearly impossible to sustain (Crawford 2004a, 2004b, 2006, 2007).

OPPOSITION TO AFFIRMATIVE ACTION

Affirmative action programs were established in the wake of the civil rights movement (1955–68) to ensure that minorities, particularly African Americans, would be accorded certain rights, such as equal opportunity for jobs and admission to educational programs. These programs are based on the notion that minorities have historically been discriminated, marginalized, and oppressed, and therefore minorities should be provided opportunities to make up for past disadvantages. In the 1960s and 1970s, courts generally supported the mission and legality of such reform efforts (Alba and Nee 2003; DiPrete and Eirich 2006). However, there has been resistance to leveling programs by many whites. As noted herein, while whites have become more accepting of diversity and multiculturalism (at least in principle), they have become less accepting of specific programs promoting certain rights, which they perceive as an intrusion into their own personal rights. In fact, surveys show that opposition has increased in recent years, and court decisions are more likely to favor the elimination of such leveling programs (Alba and Nee 2003), as illustrated by the *Bakke* (1978) case in California, and cases against the University of Michigan (Katznelson 2005; Pinkney 1993). In essence, the rights of minorities, particularly blacks and Latinos, and immigrants are being pitted against the individual rights of the white majority, and the dominant whites are determined to maintain their historically privileged positions of power, control, and dominance (Acuña 2011, 2013, 2014; Bonilla-Silva 2006; Chávez 2013; Cobas, Duany, and Feagin 2009; Feagin 2012; Gonzales 2014; Katznelson 2005; Urbina and Álvarez 2015, 2016; Urbina and Wright 2016).

CHRISTIAN FUNDAMENTALIST MOVEMENT

Christian fundamentalism is another dimension of the national movement to suppress immigration, which is seen not only as a threat to the racial makeup of society but also to what is viewed as the "Christian" character of the American society. In fact, white Americans, Catholic and Protestant, have historically viewed the influx of diverse new religious beliefs as a threat to Christian values, which are perceived to be the building blocks of American society. In what are often seen to be the "good old days," most people spent their lives with family and close associates who shared similar values and traditions (Emerson and Hartman 2006). In today's world, however, people are constantly confronted with persons who differ from themselves, who question and challenge their cherished norms, values, and ideologies. In the twenty-first century, many continue to long for a time in which everyone, arguably, held the same beliefs about faith and family traditions. Therefore, while the dominant white majority has always found incoming immigrants to be a threat to what they consider the original base of the American society, because of major demographic shifts during the first fifteen years of the twenty-first century, some people are now seeing these changes as a major threat to the stability of their own values and the existing social structure—not to mention shifts in the economic, educational, and political systems.

In response to these fears, some people are relying on the "fundamentals" of the Protestant faith to, supposedly, reestablish social order—or, more precisely, control and domination. In its initial form in the early twentieth century, it was a movement of conservative Protestant leaders aimed not at members of other religions but at other Protestants who were seen as diverging from the true Christian message (Emerson and Hartman 2006). Key issues represented in Christian fundamentalism include the view that pure evil exists in the world, a need for religion to be the guiding force in society, a need for a clearly defined and charismatic religious leader, belief in the coming of a divinely ordained end, specific behavioral requirements such as an emphasis on the patriarchal family, clear roles for men and women, opposition to homosexuality and abortion, and the primacy of religion over science (Emerson and Hartman 2006). Today, however, this movement has been adopted by other groups, notably conservative Catholics, whose views would have been anathema to the original founders of Christian fundamentalism. In the twists and turns of social life, these groups have allied in a political effort to restore their version of religion to what they perceive to be its proper place in guiding social life in America.

In the twenty-first century, however, the major problem with the Christian fundamentalist position is the obvious absence of a unitary religion in what is now, unquestionably, a multiethnic, multiracial, and multicultural American society. Not only are there increasing numbers of non-Christians, such as Jews, Muslims, Hindus, other Asian religions, and atheists, but for many Christians, the title "Christian" may be the only thing they have in common. For instance, there can be dramatic disagreement about the so-called fundamentals of Christian belief (Myers and Scanzoni 2005). In fact, in many of their publications, the fundamentalists deny the right to be called "Christian" to those who reject their perspective on the fundamentals. Clearly, the "Christian religion" hardly qualifies as a common value system on which to base the social structure of a complex, diverse, and multicultural society.

In summary, while a large proportion of Americans may wish to live in the "good old days," twenty-first-century America is now a multicultural society, with corresponding dimensions. As for race and ethnicity, in the last decades of the twentieth century, over 80 percent of immigrants were non-Europeans (Farley 1996), with most new arrivals being nonwhite and practicing non-Christian religions. The arguments of religious leaders for developing laws based on Christian fundamentalism or of politicians for restricting affirmative action or the use of languages other than English are becoming moot. New arrivals, some non-Christians and foreign-language speakers, are already here! Will they assimilate? If past experience is any indication, the answer is a resounding "Yes!" We do not need "English only" laws to force immigrants to learn English, as most speak English fluently within a generation or two (Alba and Nee 2003). Religious differences are more persistent, but over time, even drastically different religions adopt social patterns similar to those of the denominations that preceded them (Sengstock 2011). In effect, the diversity of today, extensive as it may be, is not fundamentally different from the diversity of past generations. Religions may seem more different, and the languages may sound stranger or use an unfamiliar alphabet, but past experience indicates that new immigrants will adopt the language and most of the cultural patterns of mainstream America within a relatively short time—simply remaking the American mainstream, as has occurred for centuries (Alba and Nee 2003).

TRANSNATIONALISM: IMMIGRATION CHARACTERISTICS IN THE TWENTY-FIRST CENTURY

Various unprecedented characteristics have developed with the immigration of the late twentieth and early twenty-first centuries. As once noted by Professor Arifa Javed during a conversation, previous generations of immigrants could be characterized as "one-way ticket immigrants," in that until the last quarter of the twentieth century, most immigrants left their homelands for the desired new homeland with little expectation that they would return, at least not in the foreseeable future. Some immigrants did return, but most did so after many years and after becoming fairly well adjusted to their new homelands. Indeed, on return to their countries of origin, most discovered that they had little in common with those of their former country, due not only to their adjustment to American culture, but also to extensive changes in their homelands during the time they were living in the United States.

Advances in transportation and communication have given today's immigrants a different connection to their countries of origin. Travel is much easier, for those who wish only to visit and those who opt to return home, and thus home visits tend to be more frequent, while friends and relatives from "back home" also visit the United States. Transnational communication also enables immigrants to quickly communicate with their country of origin. Cell phones, for example, provide near instantaneous contact with their friends/relatives at any given time. So while the immigrants of a century ago might not learn of homeland events for weeks or even months, today's immigrants can learn of births, deaths, and other life events as they happen. Modern immigrants are able to maintain continual contact with the culture and social structure in their original homeland, so that home culture and its influence are maintained for a much longer period, perhaps indefinitely. In past generations, frequent contacts existed only for groups, such as Mexicans, who shared a border with the United States. Today, with globalization, including the globalization of technology and knowledge, such contacts exist for nearly all immigrants residing in the country.

LATINO MIGRATION: GLOBALIZING AMERICAN MULTICULTURALISM

As noted throughout this book, the Spanish-speaking population is somewhat different from other American ethnic and racial groups in several aspects, including accessibility, internal diversity, continued in-migration, and the issue of "color." Perhaps more than any other ethnic or racial group in history, Latinos have influenced, shaped, and reshaped the dynamics of American multiculturalism over the centuries, and they have also been influenced by the historical forces of diversity and culture. Thus the everyday life of the Latino community, and of the various ethnic groups within the Latino population, has been redefined, as evidenced by Mexicans, Cubans, and Puerto Ricans—historically the three largest ethnic (Latino) groups in the United States.

ACCESSIBILITY

For most Latinos, moving to the United States has been, on some levels, a simpler process than for other ethnic groups simply because of the geographic proximity, which facilitates both migration and contact with their homeland. Unlike for other groups, this pattern has existed throughout most of the history of U.S. immigration, with the first group of Mexicans becoming "citizens" when the United States absorbed the southwestern territory in 1848. Because of proximity and economic and political reasons, Mexicans have been handled differently within the U.S. quota system, which once applied only to countries outside the Western Hemisphere, giving Mexicans, arguably, the greatest advantage. With a high demand for cheap laborers to work the newly conquered lands, over several decades laws were continually altered to allow Mexicans to enter the United States, sometimes permanently, at other times as contract laborers or commuters (Moore 1970). Therefore, in part, the U.S.-Mexico border as a crossing point remained generally "easier" for Mexicans and people from other

Latin American countries than other entry points did for would-be immigrants from other countries. Of course, the advantage can be conceptualized in different ways: as truly benefiting Mexicans, or as facilitating exploitation and oppression to the benefit of corporate white America.

For Puerto Ricans, as citizens under commonwealth status, travel is open for both migration and visits. More important, on their arrival, Puerto Ricans are not "immigrants" but U.S. citizens. The ability to fly from San Juan to New York has not only eased the original migration but also visits, in both directions, for weddings, graduations, and other social events (Fitzpatrick 1987). For Cubans, immigration policy has been strict yet highly accommodating for Cuban "immigrants" who manage to land on U.S. territory (Urbina 2007, 2011). Clearly, historical forces have shaped and reshaped the contours of immigration policy, varying not only from racial group to racial group, but also from ethnic group to ethnic group—and so redefining the dynamics of diversity, culture, and multiculturalism, as recently documented by Urbina in *Twenty-First Century Dynamics of Multiculturalism: Beyond Post-Racial America* (2014).

INTERNAL DIVERSITY

Another characteristic of the Latino population in the United States is internal diversity, with multiple elements, like tradition, culture, and ideology. In fact, more than at any other time in history, the Latino population is now composed of multiple ethnic groups, representing a wide range of national origins and different periods of arrival in the United States. For instance, while Mexicans have a long history in the United States (Acuña 2014; Almaguer 2008; Bender 2003; De León 1983, 1997, 2002, 2009; De León and Del Castillo 2012; McWilliams 1990; Mirandé 1987; Urbina, Vela, and Sánchez 2014), Puerto Ricans did not begin coming to the mainland, primarily to New York, until the mid-twentieth century (Fitzpatrick 1987), and Cubans have historically settled in Florida (Pérez 2001). For years, Anglos, the U.S. government, and the American media have searched for a common term to apply to this community (typically "Hispanic"), in the process promoting the Latinos as a monolithic population. In truth, each individual group comes with distinctive cultural patterns and a sense of national identity, at different points in time, and with a different migration experience.

The diversity within ethnic groups has historical roots, which have been redefined with the interaction of political, economic, structural, and ideological forces. As noted earlier, "Irish-Americans" have included both Protestants and Catholics, groups that did not get along in their homeland. Similarly, "Polish" origin often belies a major difference between the Catholic majority of people of Polish origin and the substantial population of Polish Jews who also immigrated. Similarly, wide differences exist within the Latino population, the largest minority group in the United States. Therefore, members of the Latino population sometimes express resentment when generic terms are utilized. Mexican Americans, for example, have referred to themselves as La Raza, but this term is "appropriate" only for Mexicans, not other Latinos (García-Pareto 2005). Conversely, Mexicans have rejected the term "Hispanic" (Ramírez 1996), which is widely used by Cuban Americans (Urbina, 2007, 2011). In the twenty-first century, members of the Latino population, like many of their predecessors, do not share a unified identity, nationality, or culture; in fact, the different Latino subgroups are proud of their own unique heritage and thus are sometimes resentful of attempts to force them into a single mold.

Marginalizing and neglecting the essence of immigration and thus diversity and multiculturalism, the American public, government officials, and the media tend to ignore internal differences within highly diverse ethnic populations. Just as Japanese Americans were all herded into concentration camps during World War II (1939–45), without recognition of their immigration status, members of ethnic groups are merged based on some perceived common characteristic, such as language or national origin, regardless of whether they are indeed part of a single group (Bosworth 1967; Kitano 1969; Shorris 1992). In fifty years of studying immigrants from the Middle East, the coauthor of this chapter, Mary C. Sengstock, has persistently had difficulty convincing members of the general public that not all Middle Easterners, regardless of language, nationality, or religion, are "Arabs" or "Muslims." Many simply shrug their shoulders and remark, "Oh, they're Arabs." In the new millennium, after centuries of living in the United States, Latinos who prefer to be recognized as originating from their specific nation of origin continue to be labeled "Hispanic," "Mexican," or whatever the observer considers the appropriate term of reference for the given situation, often consciously governed by economic, political, or ideological motives.

CONTINUED IN-MIGRATION

While the recent anti-immigrants movement has aggressively targeted Latinos, both Mexicans and Puerto Ricans have immigrated to the United States in substantial numbers during the last decades. In fact, even with the immigration challenges of the twenty-first century, barring major legal changes, travel and communication between the United States and immigrants' homelands will continue, possibly for generations. Even if the U.S.-Mexico border is completely sealed off to foreigners, as proposed by Donald Trump, Latinos will continue to maintain contact with their homelands and so continue to influence the ethnic community, its diversity and multiculturalism.

With the arrival of new immigrants and assisted by advanced technology, constant communication with home countries will continue to influence not only the Mexican, Puerto Rican, and Cuban experience in the United States, but the entire Latino community—ultimately redefining and reshaping the diversity and multiculturalism of American society.

However, given the current anti-immigrants sentiment, continued migration and immigrants' ongoing contact with their homeland tend to aggravate the public perception of the ethnic community as a "problem group" or, as historically propagated, the "Mexican problem." In the racial/ethnic communities of a century ago, immigration generally occurred for a few decades and then tapered off, allowing the community to become more acculturated and assimilated, and thus more acceptable to the dominant white majority. In the twenty-first century, however, with continued migration and constant homeland contact, ethnic groups are likely to be viewed by mainstream America as "new immigrant communities" for a much longer time, influencing the ethnic experience in most, if not all, areas of social life, including education, employment, health care, and community governance (Urbina 2014; Urbina, Vela, and Sánchez 2014; Urbina and Wright 2016).

THE COLOR "LINE"

Similar to African Americans, Latinos exhibit a wide range of skin colors. Consequently, Latinos have historically been subjected to the same or similar prejudice and discrimination on the basis of skin color (Alba and Nee 2003; Urbina, Vela, and Sánchez 2014). The color line presents a critical problem for Latinos, who tend to be divided between those who identify themselves as "white" and those who do not, with most Latinos who do not identify themselves as "white" preferring to be characterized as "other" (Alba and Nee 2003; see also Fitzpatrick 1987; Shorris 1992). Worse, for Latinos, skin color combined with immigration status, especially if undocumented, tends to exacerbate fear, prejudice, and discrimination, sometimes resulting in conflict and violence (Acuña 2014; Almaguer 2008; De León and Del Castillo 2012; Urbina et al. 2014). Although the degree of maltreatment varies by geography, Latinos, particularly Mexicans, have been a prime target of anti-Latino movements throughout the country, with various states introducing limits on education, medical care, and other services, and English-only laws have restricted Spanish-language programs in public areas, including schools (Acuña 2011, 2013; Fitzpatrick 1987; García-Pareto 2005), as recently documented by Urbina and Wright in *Latino Access to Higher Education: Ethnic Realities and New Directions for the Twenty-First Century* (2016). Having long histories in the United States, Latinos and African Americans have been targets of extreme prejudice and discrimination by those who wish to maintain the historical legacy of oppression, dominance, and control (Acuña 2014; Almaguer 2008; De León 2002; Gómez 2007; McWilliams 1990; Mirandé 1987; Morín 2009; Salinas 2015; Urbina and Álvarez 2015, 2016, 2017; Urbina, Vela, and Sánchez 2014). As such, these groups have made efforts to work together to achieve equality, representation, and justice. While past efforts have been marred by feelings of competition (Fitzpatrick 1987), there is great potential for these two groups to unify efforts in their mission for a better life in the twenty-first century.

CONCLUSION

Latinos are one of the oldest and one of the newest cultural groups in America. Spanish-speaking people settled in the areas that now constitute the American Southwest long before the United States existed as a nation. At the same time, continued migration from Cuba, Mexico, Puerto Rico, and more distant countries in Central and South America continue to influence the everyday life of Latinos and the overall American experience. For instance, while many Latinos are lifelong U.S. residents or citizens, with many being descendants of several generations of American citizens, most longtime Latino Americans continue to be asked by non-Latinos when they came to the United States. For example, upon being asked when he had "arrived" in America, former U.S. representative Eligio de la Garza, popularly known as "Kika," said his family had lived in Spain, then in Mexico, then in the Independent Republic of Texas, and finally in the United States—all without leaving their home in Hidalgo County, Texas. As recently documented by Urbina, Vela, and Sánchez in *Ethnic Realities of Mexican Americans: From Colonialism to 21st Century Globalization* (2014), in contrast to both Native Americans and Mexicans, the English colonists were relative newcomers.

As detailed herein, English settlers who formed the core of the "founders" of the United States should be viewed as only one part of the multiracial, multiethnic, and multicultural populations that now make up the American population. And with the globalization movement in full swing and significant demographic shifts, diversity and multiculturalism are likely to increase as we advance into the twenty-first century. Already in the first fifteen years of the new millennium, so-called white Americans are rapidly becoming a minority in some parts of the country, particularly in states with a high concentration of Latinos. Further, while seldom mentioned in public discussions, the ethnic and racial landscape is also being transformed by the large migrations from countries in Asia, the Middle East, Africa, and the Caribbean as a result of the elimination of the quota system in the 1960s. Of course, increases in the ethnic and racial minority population are a result not only of actual migration but also of an increase in ethnic/racial minority births. Ultimately, the current demographic trends will (re)produce an American population in which so-called minorities will begin to constitute the American majority, with Latinos constituting the largest majority of the new majority. In fact, the proportion of "non-Latino" whites is projected to decrease from 70 percent in 2000 to barely half (50.1 percent) in 2050 (Parillo 2009), in which case Alba and Nee's (2003) prediction that the "American mainstream" will be remade will become a "multicultural" reality by midcentury.

REFERENCES

Acuña, R. 1998. *Sometimes There Is No Other Side: Chicanos and the Myth of Equality*. Notre Dame, Ind.: University of Notre Dame Press.

———. 2011. *The Making of Chicana/o Studies: In the Trenches of Academe*. Piscataway, N.J.: Rutgers University Press.

———. 2013. "Los Muertos de Hambre: The War on Chicana/o Studies—Unmasking the Illusion of Inclusion." http://mexmigration.blogspot.com/2013/11/acuna-on-war-against -chicanao-studies.html.

———. 2014. *Occupied America: A History of Chicanos*. 8th ed. Boston: Pearson.

Alba, R., and V. Nee. 2003. *Remaking the American Mainstream: Assimilation and Contemporary Immigration*. Cambridge, Mass.: Harvard University Press.

Allen, K. R., and B. K. Beitin. 2007. "Gender and Class in Culturally Diverse Families." In *Cultural Diversity and Families: Expanding Perspectives*, edited by B. S. Trask and R. R. Hamon, 63–79. Thousand Oaks, Calif.: Sage.

Almaguer, T. 2008. *Racial Fault Lines: The Historical Origins of White Supremacy in California*. Berkeley: University of California Press.

Americans United for Separation of Church and State. 2007. "Lest We Forget: The Jerry Falwell Saga." *Church and State*, August, 7–9.

Anderson, C. H. 1970. *White Protestant Americans: From National Origins to Religious Group*. Englewood Cliffs, N.J.: Prentice Hall.

Baldwin, J. 1963. *The Fire Next Time*. Merchantville, N.J.: Dial Press.

Barrett, J. R., and D. Roediger. 1997. "In Between Peoples: Race, Nationality and the 'New Immigrant' Working Class." *Journal of American Ethnic History* 16: 3–44.

Bender, S. W. 2003. *Greasers and Gringos: Latinos, Law, and the American Imagination*. New York: New York University Press.

Bendixen and Associates. 2006. "Multilingual Poll of Legal Immigrants on U.S. Immigration Policy." http://www.americanprogress.org/kf/imm_policy_poll.pdf.

Black, L., and V. Jackson. 2005. "Families of African Origin: An Overview." In McGoldrick, Giordano, and García-Parto, *Ethnicity and Family Therapy*, 77–86.

Bloomberg, M. 2006. "Mayor Michael Bloomberg Delivers Slate 60 Dinner Keynote Address at William J. Clinton Presidential Library." November 12. http://www.mikebloomberg.com/ en/issues/education/mayor_michael_bloomberg_delivers_slate_60_dinner_keynote _address_at_william_j_clinton_presidential_library.htm.

Bonilla-Silva, E. 2006. *Racism Without Racists: Color-Blind Racism and the Persistence of Racial Inequality in the United States*. Lanham, Md.: Rowman and Littlefield.

Bosworth, A. R. 1967. *America's Concentration Camps*. New York: W. W. Norton.

Boulet, J. 2001. "Assimilation, Not Amnesty." http://www.nationalreview.com/comment/ comment-boulet082101.shtml.

Brezosky, L. 2007. "Texas Governor Signs Compromise Border Security Bill." http://www .mysanantonio.com/sharedcontent/APStories/stories/D8PJJA0O0.html.

Chávez, L. R. 2013. *The Latino Threat: Constructing Immigrants, Citizens, and the Nation*. Stanford, Calif.: Stanford University Press.

Cobas, J., J. Duany, and J. Feagin. 2009. *How the United States Racializes Latinos: White Hegemony and Its Consequences*. Boulder, Colo.: Paradigm.

Coontz, S. 2000. *The Way We Never Were*. New York: Basic Books.

Crawford, J. 2004a. *Educating English Learners: Language Diversity in the Classroom*. 5th ed. Los Angeles: Bilingual Education Service.

———. 2004b. "No Child Left Behind: Misguided Approach to School Accountability for English Language Learners." Presentation to the Forum on Ideas to Improve the NCLB Accountability Provisions for Students with Disabilities and English Language Learners. http://users.rcn.com/crawj/langpol/misguided.pdf.

———. 2006. "The Decline of Bilingual Education: How to Reverse a Troubling Trend?" http://users.rcn.com/crawj/langpol/Crawford_Decline_of_BE.pdf.

———. 2007. "A Diminished Vision of Civil Rights. *Education Week*, June 6. http://www .elladvocates.org/media/NCLB/EdWeek6jun07.html.

Cross, R. D. 1973. "How Historians Have Looked at Immigrants to the United States." *International Migration Review* 7: 4–22.

De León, A. 1983. *They Called Them Greasers: Anglo Attitudes Toward Mexicans in Texas, 1821–1900*. Austin: University of Texas Press.

———. 1997. *The Tejano Community, 1836–1900*. Dallas: Southern Methodist University Press.

———. 2002. *Racial Frontiers: Africans, Chinese, and Mexicans in Western America, 1848–1890*. Albuquerque: University of New Mexico Press.

———. 2009. *Mexican Americans in Texas: A Brief History*. 3rd ed. Wheeling, Ill.: Harland Davidson.

De León, A., and R. Del Castillo. 2012. *North to Aztlán: A History of Mexican Americans in the United States*. 2nd ed. Hoboken, N.J.: Wiley-Blackwell.

Democracy Now. 2005. "Governor Richardson Calls for Tighter Border Security." http://www .democracynow.org/article.pl?sid=05/09/22/1846255.

DiPrete, T. A., and G. M. Eirich. 2006. "Cumulative Advantage as a Mechanism for Inequality: A Review of Theoretical and Empirical Developments. *Annual Review of Sociology* 32: 271–97.

Doucet, F., and R. R. Hamon. 2007. "A Nation of Diversity: Demographics of the United States and Their Implications for Families." In *Cultural Diversity and Families: Expanding Perspectives*, edited by B. S. Trask and R. R. Hamon, 20–43. Thousand Oaks, Calif.: Sage.

Emerson, M. O., and D. Hartman. 2006. "The Rise of Religious Fundamentalism." *Annual Review of Sociology* 32: 127–44.

English First. 2007. *English First.* http://www.englishfirst.org/.

Fallows, M. R. 1979. *Irish Americans: Identity and Assimilation.* Englewood Cliffs, N.J.: Prentice Hall.

Farber, B., B. Lazerwitz, and C. H. Mindel. 1998. "The Jewish-American Family." In Mindel, Habenstein, and Wright, *Ethnic Families in America*, 422–49.

Farley, R. 1996. *The New American Reality: Who We Are, How We Got Here, Where We Are Going.* New York: Russell Sage Foundation.

Feagin, J. R. 2012. *White Party, White Government: Race, Class, and U.S. Politics.* New York: Routledge.

———. 2013. *The White Racial Frame: Centuries of Racial Framing and Counter-Framing.* 2nd ed. New York: Routledge.

Feagin, J. R., and J. A. Cobas. 2008. "Latino/as and the White Racial Frame: Procrustean Bed of Assimilation." *Sociological Inquiry* 78: 39–53.

———. 2014. *Latinos Facing Racism: Discrimination, Resistance, and Endurance.* Boulder, Colo.: Paradigm.

Fernández, C. 1996. "Government Classification of Multiracial/Multiethnic People." In *The Multiracial Experience: Racial Borders as the New Frontier*, edited by M. M. P. Root, 15–36. Thousand Oaks, Calif.: Sage.

Fitzpatrick, J. P. 1987. *Puerto Rican Americans: The Meaning of Migration to the Mainland.* Englewood Cliffs, N.J.: Prentice Hall.

Gambino, R. 1974. *Blood of My Blood: The Dilemma of Italian-Americans.* New York: Doubleday.

García-Pareto, N. 2005. "Latino Families: An Overview." In McGoldrick, Giordano, and García-Parto, *Ethnicity and Family Therapy*, 153–65.

Gazelem. 2007. "Key Utah Legislators Oppose the Border Security and Immigration Reform Act of 2007." http://gazelem.blog-city.com/utah_legislatures_oppose_immigration_act.htm.

Gerson, L. 1972. *Woodrow Wilson and the Rebirth of Poland, 1914–1920.* Hamden, Conn.: Archon Books.

Giordano, J., M. McGoldrick, and J. G. Klages. 2005. "Italian Families." In McGoldrick, Giordano, and García-Parto, *Ethnicity and Family Therapy*, 616–28.

Glazer, N., and D. P. Moynihan. 1963. *Beyond the Melting Pot.* Cambridge, Mass.: MIT Press.

Goldstein, S., and C. Goldscheider. 1968. *Jewish Americans: Three Generations of a Jewish Community.* Englewood Cliffs, NJ: Prentice Hall.

Gómez, L. E. 2007. *Manifest Destinies: The Making of the Mexican American Race*. New York: New York University Press.

Gonzales, A. 2014. *Reform Without Justice: Latino Migrant Politics and the Homeland Security State*. New York: Oxford University Press.

Graham, I. C. 1956. *Colonists from Scotland: Emigration to North America 1707–1783*. Ithaca, N.Y.: Cornell University Press.

Gutiérrez, D., ed. 1997. *Between Two Worlds: Mexican Immigrants in the United States*. Wilmington, Del.: Jaguar Books.

Hart, A. B., and H. R. Ferleger, eds. 1989. *Theodore Roosevelt Cyclopedia*. 2nd ed. New York: Theodore Roosevelt Association.

Hooyman, N. R., and H. A. Kiyak. 2005. *Social Gerontology: A Multidisciplinary Perspective*. 7th ed. Boston: Pearson Education/Allyn and Bacon.

House-Senate Commission on Immigration. 1911. *The Dillingham Commission Reports*. Washington, D.C.: U.S. Government, 61st Cong. http://library.stanford.edu/depts/dlp/ebrary/dillingham/body.shtml.

Huntington, G. E. 1998. "The Amish Family." In Mindel, Habenstein, and Wright, *Ethnic Families in America*, 450–79.

Invasion USA. 2005. "Texas Governor Hot over Border Security." *World Net Daily*, October 13. http://www.worldnetdaily.com/news/article.asp?ARTICLE_ID=46814.

Jacobson M. F. 1998. *Whiteness of a Different Color: European Immigrants and the Alchemy of Race*. Cambridge, Mass.: Harvard University Press.

John, R. 1998. "Native American Families." In Mindel, Habenstein, and Wright, *Ethnic Families in America*, 382–421.

Jones, M. A. 1960. *American Immigration*. Chicago: University of Chicago Press.

Katznelson, I. 2005. *When Affirmative Action Was White: An Untold History of Racial Inequality in Twentieth Century America*. New York: W. W. Norton.

Kiely, K. 2006. "GOP Leaders Oppose Immigration Felony." *USA Today*, April 12. http://www.usatoday.com/news/washington/2006-04-12-immigration-congress_x.htm.

Kitano, H. H. L. 1969. *Japanese Americans: The Evolution of a Subculture*. Englewood Cliffs, N.J.: Prentice Hall.

Klein, J. M. 2005. "Merit's Demerits." *Chronicle of Higher Education*, November 4, B12–B13.

Krauthammer, C. 2006. "Why Is Border Security Conservative?" *Washington Post*, May 18, A21.

Krysan, M. 2000. "Prejudice, Politics, and Public Opinion: Understanding the Sources of Racial Policy Attitudes." *Annual Review of Sociology* 26: 135–58.

Lee, E., and M. R. Mock. 2005. "Chinese Families." In McGoldrick, Giordano, and García-Parto, *Ethnicity and Family Therapy*, 302–18.

Leyburn, J. G. 1962. *The Scotch-Irish: A Social History*. Chapel Hill, N.C.: University of North Carolina Press.

Lipset, S. M. 1963. *The First New Nation*. New York: Basic Books.

Loewen, J. W. 2007. *Lies My Teacher Told Me: Everything Your American History Textbook Got Wrong*. New York: New Press.

Lopata, H. Z. 1976. *Polish-Americans*. Englewood Cliffs, N.J.: Prentice Hall.

López, D. E., and R. D. Stanton-Salazar. 2001. "Mexican-Americans: A Second Generation at Risk." In *Ethnicities*, edited by R. G. Rumbaut and A. Portes, 57–90. Berkeley: University of California Press.

López, I. F. H. 2003. *Racism on Trial: The Chicano Fight for Justice*. Cambridge, Mass.: Belknap Press of Harvard University Press.

———. 2006. *White by Law: The Legal Construction of Race*. New York: New York University Press.

Lucas, G. 2005. "Sacramento: Border Security Debate Revived: Governor's Praise of Minutemen Leads to Talk of Costs, Benefits." *San Francisco Chronicle*, May 16. http://sfgate.com/cgi-bin/article.cgi?file=/c/a/2005/05/16/IMMIG.TMP.

Luongo, M. T. 2007. "In U.S., Expatriate Professionals See 'Accent Reduction' as a Sound Investment." *International Herald Tribune*, June 5. http://www.iht.com/articles/2007/06/05/business/accents.php.

Mailman, S. 1995. "California's Proposition 187 and Its Lessons." *New York Law Journal* 3: 3. http://ssbb.com/article1.html.

McDermott, M., and F. L. Samson. 2005. "White Racial and Ethnic Identity in the United States." *Annual Review of Sociology* 31: 245–61.

McGoldrick, M., J. Giordano, and N. García-Parto, eds. 2005. *Ethnicity and Family Therapy*. 3rd ed. New York: Guilford.

McGrath, A. 2007. *Christianity's Dangerous Idea: The Protestant Revolution—A History from the Sixteenth Century to the Twenty-First*. New York: HarperOne.

McWilliams, C. 1990. *North from Mexico: The Spanish-Speaking People of the United States*. New York: Praeger.

Mindel, C. H., R. W. Habenstein, and R. Wright, eds. *Ethnic Families in America: Patterns and Variations*. 4th ed. Upper Saddle River, N.J.: Prentice Hall.

Mirandé, A. 1987. *Gringo Justice*. Notre Dame, Ind.: University of Notre Dame.

———. 2005. *The Stanford Law Chronicles: Doin' Time on the Farm*. Notre Dame, Ind.: University of Notre Dame Press.

Moore, J. 1970. *Mexican Americans*. Englewood Cliffs, N.J.: Prentice Hall.

Moore, W. L. 2007. *Reproducing Racism: White Space, Elite Law Schools, and Racial Inequality*. Lanham, Md.: Rowman and Littlefield.

Morín, J. L. 2009. *Latino/a Rights and Justice in the United States: Perspectives and Approaches*. 2nd ed. Durham, N.C.: Carolina Academic Press.

Myers, D. G., and L. D. Scanzoni. 2005. *What God Has Joined Together? A Christian Case for Gay Marriage*. San Francisco: Harper San Francisco.

Nakashima, C. L. 1992. "An Invisible Monster: The Creation and Denial of Mixed-Race People in America." In *Racially Mixed People in America*, edited by M. P. P. Root, 162–80. Thousand Oaks, Calif.: Sage.

Nelli, H. S. 1980. "Italians." In *Harvard Encyclopedia of American Ethnic Groups*, edited by S. Thernstrom, A. Orlov, and O. Hanlin, 545–60. Cambridge, Mass.: Harvard University Press.

Ngai, M. 1999. "The Architecture of Race in American Immigration Law: A Reexamination of the Immigration Act of 1924." *Journal of American History* 86: 67–92.

Parillo, V. N. 1994. "Diversity in America: A Sociohistorical Analysis." *Sociological Focus* 9: 523–45.

———. 2000. *Strangers to These Shores: Race and Ethnic Relations in the United States*. 6th ed. Needham Heights, Mass.: Allyn and Bacon.

———. 2009. *Diversity in America*. 3rd ed. Los Angeles: Pine Forge Press.

Pérez, L. 2001. "Growing Up in Cuban Miami." In *Ethnicities*, edited by R. G. Rumbaut and A. Portes, 91–126. Berkeley: University of California Press.

Pinkney, A. 1993. *Black Americans*. 4th ed. Englewood Cliffs, N.J.: Prentice Hall.

Posadas, C., and C. Medina. 2012. "Immigration Lockdown: The Exclusion of Mexican Immigrants Through Legislation." In *Hispanics in the U.S. Criminal Justice System: The New American Demography*, edited by M. G. Urbina, 80–93. Springfield, Ill.: Charles C Thomas.

Quillian, L. 2006. "New Approaches to Understanding Racial Prejudice and Discrimination." *Annual Review of Sociology* 32: 299–328.

Ramírez, D. A. 1996. "Multiracial Identity in a Color-Conscious World." In *The Multiracial Experience: Racial Borders as the New Frontier*, edited by M. P. P. Root, 49–62. Thousand Oaks, Calif.: Sage.

Robbins, T. 2007. "States Fret at Easing of Border Security Plan." *NPR*, May 23. http://www.npr.org/templates/story/story.php?storyId=10357984.

Romero, M., and G. Sánchez. 2012. "Critical Issues Facing Hispanic Defendants: From Detection to Arrest." In *Hispanics in the U.S. Criminal Justice System: The New American Demography*, edited by M. G. Urbina, 63–79. Springfield, Ill.: Charles C Thomas.

Roosevelt, T. 1919. Letter to the American Defense Society. January 3. http://urbanlegends.about.com/library/bl_roosevelt_on_immigrants.htm.

Rosen, E. J., and S. F. Weltman. 2005. "Jewish Families: An Overview." In McGoldrick, Giordano, and García-Parto, *Ethnicity and Family Therapy*, 667–79.

Salinas, L. S. 2015. *U.S. Latinos and Criminal Injustice*. East Lansing: Michigan State University Press.

Schuck, P. H. 2003. *Diversity in America: Keeping Government at a Safe Distance*. Cambridge, Mass.: Belknap Press of Harvard University Press.

Sengstock, M. C. 1976. "Importing an Ethnic Community." In *Culture, Community, and Identity*, edited by J. Gardner and R. McMann, 235–49. Detroit, Mich.: Wayne State University.

———. 2011. "Iraqi Immigrants." In *Multicultural America: An Encyclopedia of the Newest Americans*, edited by R. Bayor, 1111–48. San Francisco: Greenwood Press.

Sherman, C. B. 1965. *The Jew Within American Society*. Detroit, Mich.: Wayne State University Press.

Shibusawa, T. 2005. "Japanese Families." In McGoldrick, Giordano, and García-Parto, *Ethnicity and Family Therapy*, 339–48.

Shorris, E. 1992. *Latinos: A Biography of the People*. New York: W. W. Norton.

Spickard, P. R. 1992. "The Illogic of American Racial Categories." In *Racially Mixed People in America*, edited by M. P. P. Root, 12–23. Thousand Oaks, Calif.: Sage.

Sutton, C. T., and M. A. Broken Nose. 2005. "American Indian Families: An Overview." In McGoldrick, Giordano, and García-Parto, *Ethnicity and Family Therapy*, 43–54.

Swift, M. 2007. "Those Who Sound Too Different Face Social or Career Barriers." *Mercury News*, December 7. http://www.mercurynews.com/valley/ci_7667096?nclick_check =1.

Tafoya, N., and A. Vecchio. 2005. "Back to the Future: An Examination of the Native American Holocaust Experience." In McGoldrick, Giordano, and García-Parto, *Ethnicity and Family Therapy*, 55–63.

Tauro Synagogue. 2007. http://www.tourosynagogue.org/timeline/timeline.html.

U.S. English. 2005. "Making English the Official Language." http://www.us-english.org/inc/.

Urbina, M. G. 2003. "The Quest and Application of Historical Knowledge in Modern Times: A Critical View." *Criminal Justice Studies: A Critical Journal of Crime, Law and Society* 16: 113–29.

———. 2007. Latinas/os in the Criminal and Juvenile Justice Systems. *Critical Criminology: An International Journal* 15: 41–99.

———. 2011. *Capital Punishment and Latino Offenders: Racial and Ethnic Differences in Death Sentences*. El Paso, Tex.: LFB Scholarly Publishing.

———, ed. 2014. *Twenty-First Century Dynamics of Multiculturalism: Beyond Post-racial America*. Springfield, Ill.: Charles C Thomas.

Urbina, M. G., and S. E. Álvarez, eds. 2015. *Latino Police Officers in the United States: An Examination of Emerging Trends and Issues*. Springfield, Ill.: Charles C Thomas.

———. 2016. "Neoliberalism, Criminal Justice, and Latinos: The Contours of Neoliberal Economic Thought and Policy on Criminalization." *Latino Studies* 14: 33–58.

———. 2017. *Ethnicity and Criminal Justice in the Era of Mass Incarceration: A Critical Reader on the Latino Experience*. Springfield, Ill.: Charles C Thomas.

Urbina, M. G., J. E. Vela, and J. O. Sánchez. 2014. *Ethnic Realities of Mexican Americans: From Colonialism to 21st Century Globalization*. Springfield, Ill.: Charles C Thomas.

Urbina, M. G., and C. R. Wright. 2016. *Latino Access to Higher Education: Ethnic Realities and New Directions for the Twenty-First Century*. Springfield, Ill.: Charles C Thomas.

Zuberi, T., and E. Bonilla-Silva, eds. 2008. *White Logic, White Methods: Racism and Methodology*. Lanham, Md.: Rowman and Littlefield.

Chapter 9

FIVE MYTHS ABOUT IMMIGRATION

Immigrant Discourse, Locating White Supremacy, and the Racialization of Latino Immigrants in the United States

DANIEL JUSTINO DELGADO

> I have almost reached the regrettable conclusion that the Negro's
> great stumbling block in the stride toward freedom is not the
> White Citizen's Council or the Ku Klux Klanner, but the white
> moderate who is more devoted to "order" than to justice; who
> prefers a negative peace which is the absence of tension to a
> positive peace which is the presence of justice; who constantly
> says "I agree with you in the goal you seek, but I can't agree with
> your methods of direct action"; who paternalistically feels he can
> set the timetable for another man's freedom; who lives by the
> myth of time and who constantly advises the Negro to wait until
> a "more convenient season."

—REV. MARTIN LUTHER KING

IN OCTOBER 2010, sixteen-year-old Jose Antonio Elena Rodriguez was killed by the U.S. Border Patrol. It was reported in national media by *USA Today* and a few other large news agencies, but was on the whole a small blip on the media radar. It was a controversial death because Jose was killed not on the U.S. side of the border, but rather on the Mexican side. The Border Patrol claimed that because Jose was throwing rocks, they were justified in using deadly force. The news coverage of the event reports that numerous people were throwing rocks, but Jose was the only one who was killed (Skoloff 2013). There was little evidence that any rocks were thrown, nor was there any evidence that the agents provided adequate warnings to the individuals to cease their actions (Skoloff 2013). While Jose's death was largely ignored by much of the national news media, the prevailing discourse at the time focused on "illegal" immigration, criminal immigrants, violence on the border, human trafficking, and drug smuggling.

No state exemplified this immigrant hysteria better than Arizona, the state in which Jose's killers were patrolling the border. At the time of Jose's death, Arizona was gearing up to have its anti-immigrant bill, S.B. 1070, institutionalized. With several other states following Arizona's lead, the fevered pitch of anti-Latino immigration discourse was reaching a pinnacle. The Latino immigrant threat had a face, and it looked very much like Jose's. His death was not a problem, but instead came to be understood as the solution to alleviating white people's panic regarding immigration. Immigrant deaths and murders fly under the moral and ethical radars of many white Americans, and the discursive logics of racist anti-immigration policy enable these blind spots in American conceptualizations of immigration and compassion.

Jose Antonio Elena Rodriguez is not alone. Between 2005 and 2013, an estimated 42 immigrants were killed by Border Patrol agents (U.S. Border Patrol 2014). According to Border Patrol statistics, between 1998 and 2014, 6,330 immigrants died on the Southwest border (U.S. Border Patrol 2014). This means that every year an average of 372 people die there because of the perils associated with crossing, living, and merely existing in the border space. It should also be noted that these deaths are only those recorded by the Border Patrol and exclude the many other immigrants who die from other border-related activities such as human trafficking, drug smuggling, and simply dying in the desert from dehydration and exhaustion. These deaths are rarely reported in national news, nor are they the centerpiece of a national discourse on immigration. Instead, a simple Internet search on immigration uncovers scores of articles, blogs, and other Internet detritus locating immigration as the source of the social woes of the twenty-first-century United States.

This chapter argues that all these deaths and the discourse about Latino immigrants in the borderland can be understood as directly tied to the racialized narratives on immigration in this country. Anti-Latino immigrant discourse has been present in the United States since its inception (Acuña 2014; Navarro 2005), and its effects have shaped the experiences of Latinos, both immigrants and citizens. This chapter looks at several broad themes that organize these discourses while recognizing that undergirding these narratives is a historical, systemic, and everyday process of racialization. While discourse on immigration has been shown to consistently and repeatedly interpret immigrants as noncitizens and nonhuman (Saenz, Menjivar, and García 2013), it ultimately accomplishes this through various racially coded processes. However, much of the academic scholarship has focused on immigration in terms of human rights violations, and from these human rights violations arise subsequent violations associated with policing, surveilling, and patrolling the border space (Saenz, Menjivar, and García 2013). However, much of this ignores the realities of racial histories that pervade South, Central, and North America—histories that organize racial hierarchies and institutional narratives in all the nations of this hemisphere. This chapter argues that human rights violations are fundamental to the functioning of social systems in these nations, the United States in particular, and are ultimately the result of a history of white European settler colonialism and white supremacy. These racial histories have led to the normalization of everyday white supremacy, beliefs in white virtuousness (Feagin 2013), and a focus on immigrants as the racial Other. I argue that because of these racial histories the biggest myth surrounding immigration is that immigration is not about race. Instead, I argue that race *is* the central organizing principle of these various discourses, myths, and narratives on immigration.

The scholarship on Latino immigration to the United States is vast, with numerous articles, books, and edited volumes covering the complex issues faced by Latino immigrants coming to the Americas for what they believe is a better life. However, the context of reception (Alba and Nee 2003) is less than hospitable for Latino immigrants. Their rights are stripped, they are attacked, they are exploited, they are demonized, they are described as diseases and diseased, and they are generally assumed to be less worthy of equal treatment than the rest of U.S. citizenry. Two factors largely shape the context of reception for Latino immigrants in this nation: race and citizenship. These two factors organize how immigrants are treated once they enter the United States, and they organize how immigrants are conceptualized in the collective consciousness of white America. This conceptualization of immigrants in the white collective consciousness affects how they are portrayed in the media and creates a self-sustaining system of white logic and white supremacy. While other chapters in this volume address the criminalization of Latino immigrants, this chapter addresses how concepts of race and citizenship undergird the factors that shape the discourse on immigrant Latinos and the actions taken against Latino immigrants.

Immigration discourse in the United States is in fact a complex web of racist American ideology (Feagin 2014). I interpret the disdain many white Americans feel for immigrants as rooted in the discursive logics of white supremacy imbibed via social institutions such as educational systems, the U.S. government, and the American media. In their everyday lives, white Americans are talking about Latino immigrants based on histories and institutional discourse (Gubrium and Holstein 2001). This discourse *props up* the power and privilege afforded by the ternary U.S. racial caste system consisting of whites, honorary whites, and the collective black population (Bonilla-Silva 2002). By addressing the geographies of this discourse I connect the roots of mythmaking to the present-day perpetuation of these myths. I highlight the logics of white supremacy that specifically undergird five myths about Latinos and show how these racist myths are central to maintaining the myth of white Americans as virtuous (Feagin 2013). My ultimate goal is to clarify how the myths about Latino immigrants not only oppress immigrants via age-old stereotypes, but fundamentally and systematically support white supremacist thought, ideology, and discourse.

CONCEPTUALIZING MYTHS ABOUT LATINO IMMIGRANTS AND RACE

There are two sides to mythmaking about immigration: myths about Latinos as a problem and myths about white Americans as virtuous. Much of the literature focuses on how myths are directed at immigrants, but little has focused on how this mythmaking is also about white Americans. Implicit in the arguments about Latino immigrants as a problem is that white people are virtuous. This white virtuousness is exemplified in the discourse of "legal" and/or "illegal." The European ancestors of many whites came here through means that today would be considered "illegal," or they entered under special circumstances that no longer exist. This discourse enables whites to stand in a place of virtue as descendants of "legal" immigrants (compared to current immigrants and those descended from Latino immigrants), and, as scholars have noted, it also enables "American citizens" to become synonymous with "white," as the category of legality comes to be associated only with previous largely European immigrant waves (Feagin and Cobas 2014; Theiss-Morse 2009; Vallejo 2012). At the root of these issues is recognizing the historical context of how whiteness came to be seen as virtuous and what this racialization process means for whites today.

MYTHMAKING AND ITS ROOTS IN WHITE EUROPEAN COLONIALISM

Whiteness and white supremacy did not arise out of nothing—both have been constructed over time. Scholars such as Troy Duster (2001) argue that whiteness has a unique quality that allows it to morph and change as context and circumstances change. For the ancestors of many white Americans, whiteness became solidified soon after their arrival in the Americas. Ronald Takaki (1992) documents that the myth of savagery had a significant impact on the processes of racialization that shaped white Europeans' views and treatment of the slaves and indigenous people they raped, killed, and abducted in their quests for gold, land, and power in the Americas. Their primary understanding of indigenous people was located in the fictions of these groups as godless people, which justified their violence against and genocide of existing civilizations in the Americas.

This belief about a godless savage eventually came to be conflated with the interpretation of indigenous and African people as racially distinct through a discursive sleight of hand known as civilization. It's important to note that these discursive distancing practices are useful as they supersede and justify violence, rape, and murder. The supposed realization that the indigenous people of the Americas were actually not civilized and in many ways not worth the same considerations as other humans enabled the Spanish colonizers to interpret them as animalistic, ultimately permitting them to act against these groups as if they were a distinct subspecies.

The "proof" of a distinction lies in their use of the *requerimiento*. According to David Stannard (1992), the requerimiento was a document that was read to indigenous people by European Spanish colonizers in the early 1500s demanding they swear immediate allegiance to the Pope, Christianity, and Spanish Crown or face death. Knowing that the indigenous people would not understand their words, the colonizers would immediately kill or shackle the people they encountered. The requerimiento was the discursive justification for genocide; it drew the line between civilized and uncivilized. Without the ability to comprehend the Spanish language, indigenous people were deemed uncivilized and beastly. Stannard (1992, 66) points out that "the [requerimiento] was merely a legalistic rationale for a fanatically religious and fanatically juridical and fanatically brutal people to justify a holocaust." Supported by nonsecular legalese, European colonizers were able to justify genocide through claims of divine entitlement. They believed their actions were guided and supported by their Christian god and that those who were equally attuned to this god would understand the requerimiento.

Some scholars argue that language often plays a significant role in the processes of racialization (Hill 2008; Matsuda et al. 1993; Santa Ana 2002). In this instance, it was the primary step toward the formation of the racial Other. White European colonizers set in motion the future of the colonial subject embodied by Latinos today. Their early claims of superiority and civility and their claims that indigenous people were uncivilized and animalistic laid the groundwork for current interpretations of Latinos. The formation of the racial Other was a consequence of this colonization, as the vast majority of indigenous peoples were phenotypically different from white European colonizers. Even as Africans, Europeans, and indigenous people had offspring together, these children were never treated as equal to white children, which highlights a long history of mixed race peoples' subjugation (Rockquemore and Brunsma 2002). For Europeans, these perceived racial differences became conflated with beliefs of divinized superiority and ultimately became markers for interpreting people of color not as non-Christians but as subhumans.

If we move from the early colonization of the 1500s to the later colonial period of the 1700s, we see that these narratives are solidified in social practice with larger institutions such as the political and educational systems (Acuña 2014; Hernández 2012; Urbina and Álvarez 2015, 2016, 2017; Urbina and Smith 2007). The U.S. nation-state relied on these ideological conceptualizations of people of color in framing the U.S. Constitution and other foundational systems of the government. Renowned scholar Joe R. Feagin (2014) claims that the formation of the United States was predicated on the maintenance of slavery and the eradication of indigenous populations. I would add that it was also predicated on the colonization of what is now referred to as the U.S. Southwest (see Acuña 2014; Gómez 2007; Hernández 2012). What began two hundred fifty years earlier by the first European colonizers had, by the end of the 1770s, become entrenched in the U.S. nation-state's institutions, ideologies, laws, and constitution. White supremacy and the racial Other have become ideological underpinnings guiding the nation's systems, beliefs, and practices.

By 1848 white belief in *Manifest Destiny*, coupled with legislative justification in the Treaty of Guadalupe Hidalgo, led to expansion of what was termed "the American Frontier," as documented by Martin Guevara Urbina and colleagues in *Ethnic Realities of Mexican Americans: From Colonialism to 21st Century Globalization* (2014). The expansionism of whites in the Americas drew on centuries of white colonial approaches to the space of the Americas (Acuña 2014; Almaguer 2008; De León 1983; De León and Del Castillo 2012; Hernández 2012). Whites viewed the land as free for the taking, though it was clearly occupied by millions of indigenous people (Acuña 2014; McWilliams 1990). Stannard (1992) cites, as a conservative estimate, well over 100 million people living in the Americas prior to Christopher Columbus—during the so-called discovery of America. Yet, even the language of "frontier" imbues the space with a sense of the unknown and emptiness. The colonial views of what constitutes occupied space have lasted into the twenty-first century, with many high school and college students being taught the same myths about the "frontier." The formation of the United States depended on colonial interpretations of divine rights of land ownership and the belief that indigenous, black, and Latino people lacked civilizations, myths created about these people to justify European colonizers' violence and genocide.

The discursive binaries of civilized/uncivilized and human/animal were crucial to the European colonial process. Such language has persisted for centuries in order to justify racialized genocide throughout the Americas and enable these practices to become normative (Acuña 2014; Almaguer 2008; De León 1983; De León and Del Castillo 2012; McWilliams 1990; Urbina, Vela, and Sánchez 2014). Throughout colonization, white Europeans *implemented a variety of racial projects* that decimated indigenous populations, kept the descendants of African people in chains and prisons, and kept Latinos equally under their control (Acuña 2014; Almaguer 2008; De León 1983; De León and Del Castillo 2012; Hernández 2012; McWilliams 1990; Mirandé

1987; Omi and Winant 1994; Reclamation Project 2014; Urbina, Vela, and Sánchez 2014). Legacies of colonialism have shaped the racial hierarchies of all countries in South, Central, and North America to the present day (Acuña 2014; Gómez 2007; Hernández 2012; Urbina and Smith 2007).

The segregation, detainment, and oppression of Latinos in American cities today represent a continuation of these systems of oppression (Acuña 2014; Feagin and Cobas 2008, 2014; Gonzales 2014; Urbina 2014; Urbina and Álvarez 2015, 2017; Urbina, Vela, and Sánchez 2014), as recently documented by Lupe S. Salinas in *U.S. Latinos and Criminal Injustice* (2015). Conceptualizing immigrants as the racial Other is structural, institutional, and systemic, and it plays out every day in the United States. White people in the United States are socialized to interpret incoming Latinos through these racist systems (Urbina and Wright 2016), which is a major reason why many white Americans for whom these systems were built question the presence of Latinos in the United States. Typically, whites cannot and do not want to understand the realities of racial oppression because it comes at a cost to them in the form of structural, systemic, and institutional change.

MYTHMAKING AS CLAIMS OF WHITE VIRTUOUSNESS

Feagin (2013) argues that undergirding the systemic and ideological practices of racism is a white racial frame. This frame shapes the way white Americans see people of color and their own racial identities every day. For Feagin (2013, 94), this frame organizes how many whites interpret the social spaces in which they exist and participate; he states: "Commonplace white narratives of U.S. historical development still accent whites' superiority and courage over centuries. Implicitly or explicitly, the contemporary white frame accents continuing aspects of this superiority—that is, that whites are typically more American, moral, intelligent, rational, attractive, and/ or hardworking than other racial groups, and especially than African Americans and other dark-skinned Americans." Mythmaking works both ways under white supremacist colonialism: as whites create negative myths about people of color, they must also create positive myths about themselves and their ancestors—as virtuous. Accounts of extreme heroism pervade U.S. history and shape the way Americans and immigrants understand the roles America has played in history.

One example of white virtuousness is the perceived virtue of white Texas Rangers during the late 1800s and early 1900s (Urbina and Álvarez 2015; Urbina, Vela, and Sánchez 2014). The most famous (though fictional) was the Lone Ranger, whose story has been told time and again as that of a selfless former Texas Ranger who saves the day. However, we can also look at larger, historical narratives that portray the Texas Rangers as heroic. In a recent ethnographic study, I found that a state museum explicitly and incorrectly stated that the Texas Rangers "never killed or lynched Mexicans" (Delgado 2014). Various scholars and researchers have shown otherwise with their historical research, archival data, and interview materials (Acuña 2014; Navarro 2005; Paredes 2006; Urbina and Álvarez 2015). Today, the Texas Rangers police force is an active state-sanctioned law enforcement institution that employs 150 officers in spite of their well-documented role in lynching, raping, and violently attacking Mexicans and Mexican Americans (Delgado 2009; Gonzales-Day 2006), as recently documented by Urbina and Álvarez in *Latino Police Officers in the United States: An Examination of Emerging Trends and Issues* (2015). Despite this history, they continue to be seen as virtuous in a predominantly white institution.

In Arizona, myths of white virtuousness have justified white supremacy and racial profiling of immigrant Latinos by Arizona Maricopa County Sheriff Joe Arpaio and the Maricopa County Sheriff's Office (MCSO). The sheriff has been reelected six times despite being found guilty of racial profiling by the U.S. Department of Justice, as documented in *Melendres v. Arpaio* (2013). Despite Arpaio's guilt, this white sheriff's practices continued to be widely seen as virtuous, lawful, and justified (Hensley and Dempsey 2012). In the "Findings of Fact and Conclusions of Law" written by U.S. District Judge G. Murray Snow addressing *Melendres v. Arpaio* (2013), Snow outlines the manner in which the sheriff and his office disproportionately policed, arrested, and harassed Latinos and Latino immigrants, though the MCSO's numerous press releases on the MCSO website and through local media attempted to mask this racism by using a rhetoric of color blindness, stating that they are an equal opportunity police agency that arrests "anyone who breaks the law" (Arpaio 2011). The narratives of the MCSO press releases are largely attempts to obfuscate the fact, made clear by Judge Snow, that the majority of their arrests on immigration issues targeted Latino people. The myth of a virtuous white sheriff, like the Texas Rangers and the aforementioned Border Patrol, is solidified through the narrative of color blindness and equal opportunity policing and arrests.

Mythmaking in general has come to shape the way whites and immigrant Latinos are perceived. The myths of white virtuousness work to maintain the racial order and specific racial hierarchies wherein whites are on top and all other racial categories are in the middle or on the bottom (Acuña 2014; Almaguer 2008; Bonilla-Silva 2002; Feagin 2012). Crucial to understanding mythmaking about immigrants is how these myths serve to maintain the racial order of the United States. As the Texas Rangers and Sheriff Arpaio regulate the lives of Latinos, immigrant and citizen alike, the narratives of their virtuousness enable their actions of racism and racial profiling to continue unabated and seldom questioned. As detailed below, myths about immigrants are directly tied to myths of white supremacy and virtuousness. I unpack the narratives of five myths about Latino immigrants to highlight this connection.

MYTHS THAT WHITE SUPREMACY BUILT

Numerous scholars have outlined myths encountered by immigrant Latinos in their daily lives. Leo Chávez (2013a) outlines how much of the myth about Latinos and Latino immigrants is organized by a discursive logic of "Latinos as a threat." This Latino threat narrative organizes the discourse on how documented and undocumented Latinos are interpreted. However, Chávez's arguments do not explicitly address the white supremacist logic of this narrative. Similarly, Aviva Chomsky (2007) provides a detailed discussion of many of these myths, with a thorough problematizing of each myth relative to the social realities that shape its viability. Her analysis provides a critical framework from which to look at the discourse that shapes the experiences of Latino immigrants. Yet, she too fails to dig deeply into the logics of white supremacy that underscore all the myths or narratives of immigrant Latinos. Other scholars have also talked about how larger systems of inequality shape the structures of these mythologies (Inda 2000; Martinez et al. 2014; Santa Ana 2002). These arguments highlight how the formation of the discourse is rooted in questions of who constitutes a citizen of the United States. This scholarship recognizes that it's not enough to examine the problems with these myths; we must also recognize that these myths are totalizing in their ability to oppress immigrants. In particular, this scholarship argues that race and citizenship are uniquely intertwined. I build on this scholarship by focusing on the ways in which race has become the guiding factor in the mythologizing of immigrants and immigration, while centering this chapter on how discourses focused on immigrants as "illegal" or "criminal" are racialized attempts to maintain systems of white supremacy in the context of growing white fears of, as Santa Ana (2002) reports, "a brown tide rising."

While there are scholars who have centered their discussion of immigration on race, much of the scholarship on immigration focuses on how this issue is about several factors other than racism (Kivisto and Faist 2010). This scholarship is guided by past interpretations of immigration from those scholars who focused on white immigration to interpret the experiences of Latino immigration. This scholarship is exemplified by the research completed at the Chicago School (University of Chicago) in the mid-1900s (Kivisto and Faist 2010). Scholars such as Milton Gordon (1964) argued for a model that accounted for the ways in which white European immigrants would assimilate into white American life. An assimilation framework for analyzing immigrant experiences arose from this model, and how this assimilation was operating became key in how the social sciences interpreted immigrants (Alba and Nee 2003; Park 1950; Portes and Rumbaut 2001; Portes and Zhou 1993). But the assimilation model largely failed to account for racial structures built into the fabric of the nation. The white immigrants studied by the Chicago School, though not always considered white upon their arrival (Goldstein 2006), were phenotypically closer to whiteness than many Latino immigrants. While many factors, from the economy to gender status, impact all immigrants, race is a central component for Latino immigration and is a "key dimension of immigration policies" (Saenz and Douglas 2015, 178).

Drawing on scholarship addressing these myths and discourse (Chomsky 2007; Martinez et al. 2014; Santa Ana 2002), I interpret how several myths should be seen as focally problematic with regard to race. Ultimately, my goal is to highlight how racism is a significant and guiding factor in immigration discourse and mythmaking. Following significant U.S. media coverage regarding immigration, several sources have created lists that problematize the top five (Fernández 2015), seven (Martinez et al. 2014), ten (Teaching Tolerance 2011), or even twenty (Chomsky 2007) myths about immigrants. While informative, most of these lists do not deeply interrogate how white supremacy is a significant factor impacting this discourse. Drawing on these lists, this section outlines how the myths should be interpreted with regard to racism and white virtuousness. I have organized these discourses into five myths, addressing law, criminality, the economy, immigrant racial demographics, and immigrants' social impacts on the United States.

MYTH 1: VIOLATION OF EXISTING U.S. IMMIGRATION LAW GUIDES EXCLUSION FROM U.S. CITIZENSHIP

One myth is rooted in the premise that national and state-level immigration law is color-blind. As race scholars have shown, color blindness is rarely the case in the U.S. legal system (Bonilla-Silva 2001, 2006; López 2003, 2006; Urbina and Álvarez 2015, 2016, 2017). Instead, people of color are more often targets of police agencies and are more likely than whites to be impacted by the legal system (Alexander 2012; Bell 1987; Delgado 1995; Rios 2011; Salinas 2015; Urbina 2012, 2014, 2018; Urbina and Álvarez 2015, 2016, 2017). Feagin (2014, 14) argues that the U.S. Constitution, the basis for the U.S. legal system, "was created to maintain separation and oppression at the time and for the foreseeable future. The framers reinforced and legitimated a system of racist oppression that they thought would ensure that whites, especially white men of means, would rule for centuries to come." For Feagin and various other scholars (see Gotanda 1995; Reclamation Project 2014; Urbina, Vela, and Sánchez 2014), the true intentions of this document were to make people of color easy targets of the legal system, support white supremacy, and maintain total white dominance in all facets of social life. The Constitution directly impacts Latino immigrants as it is a foundational document for determining citizen rights versus noncitizen rights (Gonzales 2014; Salinas 2015; Urbina 2014, 2018; Urbina, Vela, and Sánchez 2014).

Broadly speaking, under constitutional law, race is not considered a factor for discrimination unless one can prove intent to discriminate. Barbara Flagg (1993, 961) reports that "the rule [of discriminatory intent] owes its longevity, at least in part, to its conformity with distinctively white ways of thinking about race discrimination." This white way of thinking has at its heart understandings of whites as virtuous, and it fails to recognize that intentionality is always subject to social context and is therefore malleable. This means that narratives regarding intent can be shifted to reflect current racial hierarchies, structures, and attitudes; in the United States these current realities are such that Latino immigrants are understood as the racial Other. In *Racism Without Racists: Color-Blind Racism and the Persistence of Racial Inequality in the United States* (2006), Eduardo Bonilla-Silva documents that this shifting of intent constitutes a "colorblind discursive move" wherein whites are able to practice racism without being overtly racist. Narrating these practices as nonracist masks a white supremacist logic, eliding a racist practice by interpreting such practice as non-overt, accidental, or unintentional and at worst as normative. The logic of white supremacy normalizes the practices of racial discrimination in the U.S. legal system, and "white ways of thinking" shape how racial discrimination is interpreted by legislatures, courts, and police officers (Bonilla-Silva 2001, 2006; López 2003, 2006; Moore 2007; Urbina 2003; Urbina and Álvarez 2015, 2016, 2017; Zuberi and Bonilla-Silva 2008). Further, decades of data show the realities of racial discrimination, both intentional and unintentional, against immigrants and Americans of color and prove that little has changed despite claims of racial progress in the United States (Alexander 2012; Durán 2014; Posadas and Medina 2012), as documented by Alfonso Gonzales in *Reform Without Justice* (2014).

The systemic and structural factors shaping race in the United States and its legal system have led to the disproportionate imprisonment of many people of color (Alexander 2012; Salinas 2015; Urbina 2018; Urbina and Álvarez 2015, 2016, 2017) and immigrants (Aranda and Vaquera 2015; Urbina 2014). Race scholarship on social interaction between people of color and whites clearly shows that the distribution of social power is consistently asymmetrical and favors whites of European ancestry (Bonilla-Silva 2006; Feagin 2012, 2014; Moore 2007; Pizarro 2005). This means that immigrants' everyday encounters with the Border Patrol are inherently racialized because embedded in historically unjust structural factors. Irrespective of the race of the officer, these interactions will always be dictated by racial categories and racial hierarchies of the nation-state (Correa and Thomas 2015; Urbina and Álvarez 2015) because the law enforced by the Border Patrol is a white way of thinking (Flagg 1993), or to be more specific, codified white supremacy—which is propagated by the educational system, as well as by the media, numerous politicians, and some government officials (Acuña 1998, 2011; Boyer and Davis 2013; Mirandé 2005; Noboa 2005; Urbina and Wright 2016; Zuberi and Bonilla-Silva 2008), as illustrated by Wendy Leo Moore in *Reproducing Racism: White Space, Elite Law Schools, and Racial Inequality* (2007).

Arizona's law (S.B. 1070) regarding reasonable suspicion about who constitutes an immigrant is a perfect contemporary example of how white supremacy is codified law practiced at the micro-interactional level. The original version of S.B. 1070 argued for wide latitude for state police officers regarding the search and detainment of immigrants. The linchpin for this wide scope given to the police was the wording of *reasonable suspicion*, which allows officers to request documentation and stop anyone based on what they determine to be reasonable suspicion of violating U.S. criminal codes.

Closer examination, though, reveals that because reasonable suspicion laws are reliant on the decision making of police officers, they are "necessarily" imbued with racist practice (Salinas 2015; Urbina and Álvarez 2015, 2017). In effect, as reported by Urbina and Peña in a forthcoming piece, "Policing Borders," these laws were designed with the intent to organize police action through racial categories. The S.B. 1070 law gave police the latitude of reasonable suspicion with the realization that race would be instrumental in its implementation. This is largely due to the fact that officers are trained to quickly identify who may be a criminal (Urbina and Álvarez 2015). Much of police work is based on intuition and largely relies on physical features, bodily comportment, social context, and a "gut feeling" by the officer in a given situation. While police must, of course, find evidence to arrest, convict, or imprison, the "white thinking" undergirding constitutional law comes into play (Flagg 1993), with Latino immigrants being suspect because of their perceived lack of white phenotype and other factors such as bodily comportment, clothing, or lack of knowledge of English. Codified white supremacy opens the door for officers to investigate and find evidence for conviction (Álvarez 2012; Morín 2009; Salinas 2015).

Belief in the virtuousness of white police officers and predominantly white politicians and other government officials guides law based on white supremacist U.S. legal structures that were historically constructed to maintain in-group or out-group status (Feagin 2012; Reclamation Project 2014; Urbina and Álvarez 2015, 2016, 2017; Urbina, Vela, and Sánchez 2014). This legal system, though touted as color-blind (Gotanda 1995), reflects significant racial asymmetry favoring whites that ultimately guides legal decisions in the criminal justice system and in the creation of both immigration and criminal laws (Álvarez 2012; Gonzales 2014; Posadas and Medina 2012; Salinas 2015). In effect, whiteness under the U.S. legal system carries assumed virtuousness, and as the legal system determines in-groups and out-groups, whiteness becomes synonymous with in-group status, thereby requiring all to achieve whiteness to access in-group status or, more specifically, citizenship.

The law itself, despite its verbose and sometimes passionate or aggressive claims, is not color-blind, but composed of the same racial hierarchies to which humans are subject. Every day, enforcement of immigration law is meted out by police trained to protect the interests of a white supremacist nation-state (Feagin 2014; Omi and Winant 1994; Urbina and Álvarez 2015, 2017; Walker 1998). On the macro-level, legislation is organized by various state and national constitutional measures historically and presently designed to protect and maintain white supremacy, supported by strategically structured institutions (Bender et al. 2008; Bonilla-Silva 2006; Chávez 2013a; Cobas, Duany, and Feagin 2009; Feagin 2012; López 2003, 2006; Mirandé 2005; Moore 2007; Reclamation Project 2014; Urbina 2014, 2018; Urbina and Álvarez 2015, 2016, 2017; Urbina and Wright 2016; Urbina, Vela, and Sánchez 2014; Zuberi and Bonilla-Silva 2008). Latino immigrant *violations* at either level, micro or macro, will be structured not by merely a lack of U.S.-citizenship documents, but first and foremost by how the people creating and enforcing the law conceptualize Latino immigrants' race and associated characteristics. Therefore, Myth 1 should be understood as racism that is deeply ingrained in the U.S. legal system, with a primary goal—the maintenance of white supremacy and white virtuousness.

MYTH 2: MOST LATINO IMMIGRANTS ARE IN THE UNITED STATES ILLEGALLY

Myth 2, that most Latino immigrants are in the United States illegally, is factually untrue: the vast majority of immigrants, more than 30 million of 40 million total, are authorized to be in the United States (Pew Research Center 2013). However, statistical data rarely triumph over the ideology of white supremacy. This myth draws on decades of discourse regarding the immigration of Latinos to the United States and on discourse that focuses on whites' fear of and anxiety about an invasion by Latino people (Chávez 2013a; Inda 2000; Santa Ana 2002). White fears of invasion are largely a fear of loss of resources, power, control, and dominance (Acuña 2011, 2014; Reclamation Project 2014; Urbina and Álvarez 2015, 2016, 2017). Centuries of de facto and de jure segregation from people of color has led many white Americans to believe that any presence of people of color contaminates their living space (Bonilla-Silva 2006; Meyerhoffer 2015; Urbina, Vela, and Sánchez 2014). This was reflected in whites' purposeful attempts to segregate Latinos during the Jim Crow era, and is currently reflected in the significant levels of segregation Latinos experience in almost every major U.S. city (Logan and Turner 2013). As the historical record plainly reveals, one easy way to facilitate segregationist ideology and practice is to maintain systems of racial and economic oppression. The binary discourse of *illegal/legal* citizenship works to maintain polarity regarding immigration. Illegality requires a benchmark to be understood, and the benchmark is documented U.S. citizenship.

Therefore, one must understand that the language of *illegal* or *legal* regarding status is an important aspect of this myth. This distinction immediately organizes Latino people such that they are presumed to be illegal until they prove otherwise. Proof of citizenship can be determined only by police and the criminal justice system, which both historically and as presently constructed maintains white supremacy (Acuña 2014; Durán 2014; Gonzales 2014; Salinas 2015). The presumption of illegal status carries with it very specific consequences in a nation-state engaged in numerous racial projects (Álvarez 2012; Gonzales 2014; Omi and Winant 1994) regarding Latino immigrants (Posadas and Medina 2012; Provine and Doty 2011). These racial projects lead to perceiving immigration as crime, or "crimmigration" (Stumpf 2013). Under crimmigration law, merely being present, that is, merely existing *sin papeles* ("without papers"), constitutes a crime. When we look at what is foundational to the interpretations of legality, we see that only on its face is race irrelevant for how one acquires the *proper* documentation for citizenship.

Rather than being a color-blind process, citizenship and its benefits hinge on racial identity, and a fundamental aspect of belonging in the United States is that one must be white. A person's status as legal is dependent on the recognition of equality within the criminal justice system, and illegality and legality can only be understood in relation to each other. Legality under U.S. liberal ideologies requires a realization of the equality of opportunity and the equality of access to citizenship; that is, *anyone* can become a citizen if they just apply through the proper channels (see Myth 5 below). Under the white logics of legality, a person need only apply for citizenship, and it will be granted irrespective of race. In truth, not everyone can apply or be granted citizenship because of the interconnectedness of citizenship and race. The process of naturalization has changed significantly in the last century and has become intertwined with law since many European immigrants came to the United States. Post–Ellis Island immigration law has been fundamentally about keeping people of color out of the United States (Saenz and Douglas 2015). Legality is not a simple matter of a person having the proper documentation; rather, it is about whether or not a person comes from a white European nation.

Some scholars argue that when Latino immigrants are determined to be illegal, their existence constitutes an invading body and, implicitly, a body that is nonhuman (Inda 2000). Building on Jonathan Inda (2000), I argue that it is not just about Latinos being an invading body, but also about Latino immigrants being interpreted as having an existence that is the antithesis to U.S. citizenship. That is, Latino immigrants become the negation, the totalized opposite of a U.S. citizen, not merely an invasion of this social status. Under white conceptualizations of legality, whites are the embodiment of a U.S. citizen and rarely fall within the domain of illegality. (For instance, how often do we see the Border Patrol searching for "illegal" Canadians,

English, Germans, Russians, or some other white "illegals" along the U.S.-Canada border or in cities where high concentrations of white illegals reside?) This does not mean that Latinos have always been conceptualized as illegal, but it does mean that what constitutes a legal citizen has been historically amended to fit with the needs of whiteness and white-controlled institutions, including the economic, political, and educational systems (Cobas and Feagin 2008; Feagin 2012; Moore 2007; Urbina and Álvarez 2015, 2016, 2017; Urbina and Wright 2016; Zuberi and Bonilla-Silva 2008).

Whiteness and citizenship are necessarily tied to the presumption that Latinos are immigrants and therefore illegal. Chávez (2013a) documents that Latinos, irrespective of citizenship, are always interpreted as a "threat." For Chávez this threat has led many Latino Americans to be seen as noncitizen immigrants, with corresponding implications and ramifications. This has been discussed in relation to the growing Latino middle class, many of whom are mistaken for immigrants despite being successful in their respective fields and disciplines (Delgado 2014). Race underlies Latinos' citizenship status in their everyday interactions with whites and in all facets of social life. In effect, illegality or legality is dependent on racial phenotype for many Latinos, and the myth of a majority illegal Latino immigrant population in the United States depends primarily on this association between race and legality. Thus, Latino immigrants are normally conceptualized as illegal criminals by whites and the white-controlled media (Cobas and Feagin 2008), situating immigrant "illegality" within a national and international sphere, as we witnessed after President Obama announced immigration reform and later Donald Trump's derogatory comments about Mexican immigrants.

This myth maintains *binary* interpretations of crime (illegality) and citizenship— that is, either one is criminal and illegal or one is law-abiding and a citizen. Conceptualizing immigrants in this manner leads to understanding all Latino immigrants *sin papeles* as criminal, thus spiking reports of immigrants as contributing to crime. This logic directs attention away from the problems with the U.S. criminal justice system—a system that preys on poor whites, Latinos, and blacks—and from how whites commit all types of crimes (Pickett et al. 2012; Salinas 2015; Urbina 2007, 2012, 2014, 2018; Urbina and Álvarez 2015, 2016, 2017), as illustrated by Jeffrey Reiman and Paul Leighton in *The Rich Get Richer and the Poor Get Prison* (2013). Of course, beyond the political rhetoric, concerns about immigrant criminality are based not on the actual crimes committed by Latino immigrants, but rather panic over a supposed Latino invasion of the United States (Dowling and Inda 2013).

According to some of the discourse on immigration (Camarota and Vaughn 2009), immigrants commit a significant portion of crime in the United States; however, understanding what constitutes crime with regard to immigration will help clarify why such claims are inaccurate. Criminality for immigrants happens the moment their documents expire and, for some, the moment they enter the country without the required documentation. The scholarship in this area shows that this has led to a rise in crimmigration (Stumpf 2013), which involves individuals having to "earn" citizenship through a difficult and long process of documentation while being perceived and treated as subjects (criminals) throughout the process. It may seem as though immigrant criminality and crimes are on the rise. However, when we understand that the vast majority of these crimes fall into the category of "unlawful entry," the story of immigrant crime changes (Light, López, and Gonzalez-Barrera 2014). Michael Light, Mark Hugo López, and Ana Gonzalez-Barrera (2014) point out that while immigrant crime accounts for 30 percent of all federal crimes, 26 percent have to do with "unlawful entry." Therefore, the vast majority of these immigrant offenders (68 percent) were convicted of unlawful entry, while the remaining were sentenced for drug offenses, other immigration-related offenses, or miscellaneous crimes (Light, López, and Gonzalez-Barrera 2014). The overwhelming factor in immigrant crimes is a lack of access to residence and citizenship. So the panic over immigrant crime stems not from an actual danger to the lives of American people, but rather from a fear of Latino immigrant presence and equality, underscored by racism and white supremacist ideology.

Once we recognize that immigrants commit a small percentage of crimes relative to people in all other ethnic/racial categories in the United States (Light, López, and Gonzalez-Barrera 2014), our real concern should be with those who have historically been immune from criminalization, namely white men, particularly wealthy white men, who have been in the position of power in America's main institutions—the decision-makers. As the saying goes, "crime in the suites, not in the streets." As the great recession of the late 2000s and early 2010s has shown, the most egregious crimes have been committed by white men. Given the role whites played in the decline of the economy in 2008, and their representation in a significant portion of crimes committed in the United States, logic dictates that they should be among our greatest concerns. However, the discourse is focused squarely on Latino immigrants, whose illegality, as illustrated herein, is spurious at best and at worst has far-reaching implications for the arrest, prosecution, incarceration, and deaths of many Latinos coming to the United States (Castañeda 2007; Gutiérrez 1997; Romero and Sánchez 2012).

The failure to focus on the crimes and social issues that most affect the nation is largely due to the way in which white virtuousness operates. White men running the financial system of the United States, for instance, were instrumental in the great recession, yet few were held directly accountable for their crimes. Few were penalized, many were given promotions, and most continue to work in the financial sector. As another saying has it, "the best way to rob a bank is to own one" (Black 2013). Using immigrant Latinos as the criminal foil props up white virtuousness and distracts from the realities of white supremacy. Donald Trump's racist comments during the 2016 presidential campaign is a case in point, as he used Mexican immigrants as a means to reinforce conservative white voters' beliefs in their own virtuousness (Sakuma 2015). Trump strategically drew on age-old stereotypes about Latino (specifically Mexican) immigrants as drug dealers, rapists, and killers, generally as criminals, to demonize Latinos while supporting ideas of whites as virtuous. Like many other politicians before him (Urbina, Vela, and Sánchez 2014), he asserted that Latinos are the problem, the "Mexican problem" we often hear about, not white Americans such as himself or the large white conservative voting population. Focusing on Latino immigrants as a significant source of criminality continues to direct attention away from the real social problems that arise from asymmetrical white supremacist power relations that enable whites to continue filling the nation's most powerful positions. It provides whites with a discursive logic to support their racist dichotomy of U.S. citizens as white and racial Others as noncitizens. Clearly, in the twenty-first century, the perpetuation of the myth of Latino immigrants as overwhelmingly illegal undergirds the notion of white virtuousness and maintains white supremacy by treating Latino immigrants as permanent criminals.

MYTH 3: MOST IMMIGRANTS COME FROM LATIN AMERICA

While the majority of immigrants living in the United States are from Central or South American nations, currently the largest immigrant flows are from Asian countries (Pew Research Center 2013). According to a 2013 report, "the modern immigration wave from Asia is nearly a half century old and has pushed the total population of Asian Americans—foreign born and U.S born, adults and children—to a record 18.2 million in 2011, or 5.8% percent of the total U.S. population, up from less than 1 percent in 1965" (Pew Research Center 2013, 2). According to this report, Latino immigration from 2000 to 2010 declined almost 30 percent, while Asian immigration increased by almost 20 percent. The trends in these populations crossed in 2009 when their rates of immigration were similar, and by 2010 Asian immigrants were arriving in the United States at greater rates than Latino immigrants. Yet eight years later, at the time of this writing, the myth continues that a majority of immigrants come from Latin America. Why? Looking at how Asians are racialized versus how Latinos are racialized, we once again see how assumptions about ethnicities shape these perceptions. Rosalind Chou and Joe Feagin (2008) highlight how Asian Americans are assumed to be a model minority, which leads whites to assume that Asian Americans are successful and therefore threatening in ways that are different from those in other racial categories. Specifically, Asian Americans are stereotyped as scientists and engineers rather than criminals and drug dealers. This is not to say that Asian immigrants are perceived and treated as "equals," only that the processes of racialization are different for different racial categories but nonetheless detrimental to both groups.

Underscoring this myth is the assumption that some "selected" bodies are illegal. While Asian Americans are often seen by white Americans and portrayed in white media sources as immigrants, rarely are they conceptualized as undocumented or illegal (though their identification as immigrants is often implicit rather than explicit like it is for Latinos). While the majority of immigration following the waves of white immigration through Ellis Island is Latino, this fact is misleading in our current immigration environment. Unlike most other immigrants of color, Asian Americans have the highest levels of education and the highest incomes, and are most recently the fastest growing minority population in the United States. Latinos are also a fast-growing population, but they do not have incomes or education comparable to Asian Americans. In fact, there is a significant decline in educational achievement among people of Mexican ancestry, who constitute the largest majority of Latinos living in the United States, after the third-plus generation (Telles and Ortiz 2009).

Asian immigrants (see Portes and Rumbaut 2001) often carry the assumption of high achievement. This assumption is evident in their demographics, but these assumptions also shape how white Americans perceive, react to, and treat Asians' presence in the United States. For example, Asian Americans have high achievement in school, representing 15 to 25 percent of Ivy League enrollment, and thus are regarded as a "model minority." Further, Asians are among the most likely to have romantic relationships outside their racial categories (Sassler and Joyner 2011), and their general acceptability as peers in white spaces is more commonplace than for Latinos. Latinos must negotiate previously discussed racial stereotypes from a centuries-old discourse characterizing them as lazy, dangerous criminals, violent, and in a sense nonhuman.

After analyzing the twists and turns of racial stereotypes and scapegoating over the years, it seems evident that the myth of a predominantly Latino immigrant population has persisted because it supports white supremacist beliefs in a superior white immigration wave (see Myth 5). The myth of a horde of Latino immigrants crossing the border reinforces the notion of a white population under attack. In many ways, this myth supports other myths by putting the focus on Latino immigrants. It enables a sustained interpretation of a clear racial Other who can be juxtaposed against white virtuousness. Centering the discussion on Latino immigration redirects attention from more acceptable immigrant populations (Asians) and the larger issues in U.S. society such as the impact that corporate crime has on the U.S. economy (Prechel and Morris 2010). Further, it enables a stratified system in which Latino immigrants are scapegoats for working-class and poor whites while Asian immigrants are scapegoats when middle- and upper-class whites have difficulty accessing jobs and resources.

Bonilla-Silva (2006) reports that there is an honorary white buffer between whites and "the collective black" racial category. Similarly, Asian and Latino immigrants act as a buffer for many white Americans. They become the face to blame when white supremacy and virtuousness are questioned or confounded. When white middle-class Americans, for example, are not able to access higher education, the scapegoats are Asian Americans, and when working-class whites are unable to access blue-collar sectors of the labor market, Latinos are the scapegoat. Whites are rarely in direct contact with "the collective black," and because many job sectors overtly discriminate against individuals in this category, blacks cannot function as a scapegoat for many whites.

Therefore, the myth that most immigrants come from Latin America supports buffering and scapegoating. It also supports the myth of white virtuousness by backing white claims of a Latino invasion. Central to Myth 3 is a white fear of invasion that implicitly differentiates Latino immigrants from earlier white European immigrant waves. This distinction between invader immigrants and law-abiding immigrants revolves around racialization. Latinos come to be seen as the invaders, while white Europeans are celebrated and perceived as virtuous.

MYTH 4: LATINO IMMIGRANTS HURT THE U.S. ECONOMY BECAUSE THEY TAKE JOBS AWAY FROM AMERICAN CITIZENS AND DRAIN SOCIAL SERVICES

Much like the previous myths, the myth that Latino immigrants hurt the U.S. economy by taking away jobs from American citizens and draining social services may seem to be devoid of any racial language or intent. The key to interpreting how this myth is racialized is understanding how economics (labor market, wealth, social services) is racialized (Acuña 1998, 2014; Almaguer 2008; Bender 2003; Chávez 2013a, 2013b; Chávez 2011; Cobas, Duany, and Feagin 2009; De León 1983; Mirandé 1987; Urbina and Álvarez 2015, 2017), as recently illustrated in *How White Folks Got So Rich: The Untold Story of American White Supremacy* (Reclamation Project 2014) and Urbina and Álvarez in "Neoliberalism, Criminal Justice, and Latinos: The Contours of Neoliberal Economic Thought and Policy on Criminalization" (2016). Crucial to this myth is the idea that Western economies function without human intervention, when in fact the opposite is true. Economies are fundamentally the product of, maintained by, and controlled by people. Historically, the U.S. economy was dependent not just on immigrant labor but also cheap, easily exploited labor, a labor population that has always been people of color. African slaves and their black American descendants were *originally* the primary sources for cheap labor. Many Latinos have African ancestry; so many of the people who were enslaved by white colonizers were the ancestors of Latinos (Jimenez and Flores 2010). In fact, Latinos have a long history of being enslaved and forced to labor for little or no payment (Gonzales 2014; Gutiérrez 1997; Kubrin, Zatz, and Martínez 2012). While toiling in the fields, for instance, these Latinos built the agricultural economies that now flourish in the southwestern United States (Navarro 2005).

The legacy of cheap Latino labor shifted to immigrants as the old forms of exploitation such as de jure slavery and segregation were legally curtailed. Scholars have pointed to the various waves of Latinos lured to the United States as American farm subsidies and other U.S. economic practices and policies wreaked havoc on Mexico's economy throughout the nineteenth and twentieth centuries and into the twenty-first (Castañeda 2007; Kubrin, Zatz, and Martínez 2012). These immigrant waves became a new source of cheap (nearly slave) labor for white agriculturalists and industry owners (Gonzales 2014; Gutiérrez 1997). The U.S. government used initiatives, such as the Bracero Program (1942–67), to bring in such cheap and easily exploited labor. The program ended with the implementation of Operation Wetback, a federally sanctioned program that racially profiled people of Mexican ancestry and deported an estimated 1.3 million to Mexico (Mize and Swords 2010).

Various scholars note that immigrant labor rarely hurts the U.S. economy, and in the case of the Bracero Program, immigration helped make up for a significantly depleted U.S. labor force by providing a seemingly limitless number of workers from Mexico. Today, immigrant labor is completing the same task. As the white baby boomer generation ages out of the labor market but continues to drain Social Security funds, a new population of laborers must fill this gap. Latino immigrants are once again rescuing the United States as they did during World War II with the Bracero Program, but instead they are conceptualized as the primary drain on the U.S. welfare state despite the fact that the majority of individuals who draw on state welfare programs are white; that is, *the vast majority of people on welfare are not Latino*.[1] Much as in the discourse created by the Reagan administration about welfare queens, Latino immigrants have become the scapegoat for a staggering American economy.

The reality of the U.S. economic decline that began in 2007, now referred to as the Great Recession (2007–9), is that it was created by U.S. corporations and, in particular, corporate banks. Obviously, mostly white Americans and no undocumented immigrants operate these banks; especially since ownership would require citizenship status or an equivalency for employment. So the individuals who were responsible for these economic downturns were white American citizens, not immigrants from Central or South America. In fact, as in all American institutions, the vast majority of the individuals who were in decision-making positions in these banks were white men. More importantly, this economic decline had significantly greater effects on the lives of immigrants and people of color living in the United States than on the white people who caused them. Certainly, poor and working-class whites, even some middle-class whites, were impacted, but the fallout disproportionately impacted black and Latino communities (Oliver 2008). During 2008, many large banks preyed on the desire of Americans of color to live the American dream. They pulled them into subprime loans through various predatory practices, loans that were disproportionately directed at and given to people of color. These loans were extremely volatile, with adjustable interest rates, ballooning payments, and terms that were impossible to renegotiate. Consequently, a significant portion of those who defaulted on their home loans were people of color (Oliver 2008). Melvin Oliver (2008) found that this was particularly devastating for black Americans and will have long-term effects on the building of black wealth in the United States as black homeownership rates decline. Similarly, Mark Hugo López, Gretchen Livingston, and Rakesh Kochhar (2009) illustrate how these economic downturns had a significant impact on Latino communities and immigrants, with 75 percent of Latinos stating that their finances were in "poor or fair shape" because of the recession.

Pragmatically, then, when it comes to the U.S. economy, the focus should be on the sectors controlled by very powerful white corporate interests that dealt a heavy blow to the United States and world economies through their economic practices—in other words, not the people who are cleaning the windows, but the decision-makers sitting inside. Latino immigrants should instead be understood as providing an important service to the United States, as they account for a significant portion of labor in a society with a declining white birth rate and an increasingly aged population. As white populations age out of various labor sectors, Latino immigrants will fill positions and prop up an economy through their payment of wage taxes.

Therefore, as with the other myths noted herein, the myth of immigrant job theft and economic drains largely supports the narrative of white supremacy and virtuousness as it elides the proportion of whites who use social services relative to people of color and the devastation wrought upon the U.S. economy by mostly white men who perpetrated malicious banking practices. This myth blames immigrants for multiple problems in the United States, even though this country has a history of state welfare programs that benefited only whites for many years following World War II (Katznelson 2005) and today has a welfare system that is used largely by whites. Globally, this mythology of a social-service abusing, economy-destroying, and job-stealing Latino immigrant supports ideas of whites as virtuous bootstrappers and redirects attention from the historical and present populations that rely on U.S. welfare systems. It also distracts from the reality that white men, not Latino immigrants, created many of the problems in the U.S. economy. Latino immigrants provide a significant boost to the American economy, but the white supremacy that guides Myth 4 masks how their work significantly benefits the United States.

MYTH 5: PREVIOUS IMMIGRANTS (WHITE EUROPEANS) CAME TO THE UNITED STATES PROPERLY AND SHOULD BE UNDERSTOOD AS A MODEL FOR ALL IMMIGRANTS

Like the preceding myths, Myth 5 draws on clearly defined narratives that have racial tones. For those who invoke this myth, the "previous immigrants" are white Europeans, who supposedly discovered America, built America, and made America great. Many are the ancestors of today's Jewish Americans, Irish Americans, Polish Americans, and other European-descended Americans. A crucial point that typically goes unmentioned is that all of these groups became white or resembled whiteness phenotypically enough to access citizenship immediately on arriving or very quickly after arriving in the United States. Further, the laws that governed these groups' access were significantly different from the rules that now govern access to U.S. citizenship. This is significant as it established whether or not immigration was possible during the periods when Europeans were emigrating to the United States.

The primary point of entry for many European immigrants was at Ellis Island in New York. They took ships from Europe and landed on the shores of the United States. They were greeted with a processing station designed to allow individuals a relatively quick and easy way to enter the country. The processing station helped millions of white immigrants get citizenship, and the museum itself discusses how easy it was for individuals to gain citizenship; many became U.S. citizens in less than one day (Statue of Liberty 2015). In fact, millions of white people gained citizenship just by showing up on Ellis Island, being a self-reported noncriminal, being found free of disease after a six-second medical exam, and filling out the proper paperwork. Legality took a matter of hours and less than 2 percent were denied citizenship on arrival to the island. Ellis Island is now a museum celebrating white immigration and the proper way to become a citizen. The island is on the National Register of Historic Places and since 1966 has been part of the Statue of Liberty monument. It has also become a source of pride for many white Americans and illustrates a clear narrative and collective memory for how one should become a citizen. As a shrine and the primary source for white collective memories about immigration, it illustrates who constitutes the deserving (and legal) immigrant.

Gaining citizenship today requires hundreds of hours spent dealing with bureaucracies, years of permanent residency, background checks, and complex paperwork. Contrary to popular belief, whites never had to follow rules as they exist today. In fact, many of the white Americans who claim citizenship might find that their family members who passed through Ellis Island would be denied legal citizenship under today's arduous standards. Conveniently, Ellis Island and Myth 5 stand as props for the white supremacist ideology of whites as virtuous by masking how many European immigrants became citizens through the supposed proper channels. It obscures how the "proper channels" were in fact designed to "process" many people in a short period of time. U.S. citizenship was freely given to Europeans without any real process or problem relative to today's standards. Historically, immigration for Europeans was treated not as a privilege to be earned, as many conservative political pundits and immigrant hawks describe it today, but as a hand reaching out to help the poor and huddled masses needed to build a nation, in a newly "conquered" territory.

On the contrary, with the "Cuban exception," Latino immigrants are rarely seen as worthy of similar treatment because they are conceptualized as the racial Other. For whiteness to operate, that is, to justify previous white Europeans' unobstructed immigration to the United States, a binary is created in which white actions appear more favorable. As noted earlier, this is accomplished by creating a nonhuman, savage, and demonized race of people. Myth 5 maintains the racial Other narrative by comparing the past actions of European immigrants, actions supported as virtuous by the Ellis Island monument, with those of Latino immigrants. This comparison is built on the collective memories of two racial categories that are conceptualized very differently. Many Latino immigrants are the racial Other, while white Europeans have historically carried with them a perceived refugee status. Juxtaposing these groups under such interpretations leads to the white supremacist logic of treating Latinos as undeserving of a comparable road to citizenship.

LINKING WHITE SUPREMACY, LEGISLATION, AND LATINO IMMIGRANT LIVES

In the maintenance of these myths and the discourse about Latino immigrants, white people, and in particular white Americans of European decent, will be conceptualized as citizens. However, citizenship is finally not about having the proper documentation, but rather whether one fits the racial category that constitutes *citizen*. Whiteness shapes boundaries of such citizenship, and previous immigrants, like those from southern and eastern Europe, while not always treated the same as northern Europeans, had significant access to citizenship in ways never available to Latino immigrants. Subsequently, racial rules and hierarchies set the tone for how Latino immigrants access America.

Beyond keeping this hold over citizenship, these myths validate the general conceptualization of whites as deserving, hardworking, and, of course, virtuous and superior. The myth of white immigrants' ability to triumph against all odds, also known as the Horatio Alger story, is imbued with racial tones of white virtue and superiority. Ellis Island is a monument to this collective memory of white supremacy and triumph over impossible odds. Latino immigrants are conceptualized in relation to such mythologies, and despite their difficult, arduous, and sometimes deadly paths taken to citizenship, they are considered the problem—as we often hear, "the Mexican problem." White immigrant stories have become internalized and have become the narratives that shape the ideologies of America as a whole. American liberal ideologies of independence and success are represented in such narratives. The interconnectedness of collective memory, ideology, and mythmaking has consolidated to form our current racial structures and hierarchies. Invariably, these hierarchies and the related discourse have shaped and will continue to shape the experiences of Latino immigrants.

Arizona has been a prime example of how anti-Latino immigrant discourse can shape policy, legislation, and practice, as the Maricopa County Sheriff's Office (MCSO) and Sheriff Arpaio disproportionately policed, arrested, and imprisoned Latino people under suspicion of not being citizens. A letter to Maricopa County Attorney Bill Montgomery from U.S. Assistant Attorney General Thomas Perez clearly states that Maricopa County was found to practice racial profiling. Perez (2011) wrote, "Based upon our extensive investigation, we find reasonable cause to believe that MCSO engages in a pattern or practice of unconstitutional policing. Specifically, we find that MCSO, through the actions of its deputies, supervisory staff, and command staff, engages in racial profiling of Latinos; unlawfully stops, detains, and arrests Latinos; and unlawfully retaliates against individuals who complain about or criticize MCSO's policies or practices." Crucial to the maintenance of Arpaio's white virtuousness was an understanding of who constituted a reasonably suspicious person. Under Arizona's S.B. 1070 law, the provisions for reasonable suspicion were loose and covered any individual considered by the officer to be in the United States "illegally." The U.S. Department of Justice found that this policing practice was a violation of the U.S. Constitution; yet until he lost reelection in November 2016 very little was done to remove the sheriff or the MCSO from power in Arizona. Consider, for instance, if a Mexican American sheriff was profiling white people; he would most likely be removed right away using whatever means necessary. Myths of Latino immigrants continue to drive racist discourse, ideology, and practice in Arizona. These discourses continue to influence the way in which immigration laws are developed at the state level in other states. (On July 31, 2017, Arpaio was found guilty of criminal contempt by a federal judge for violating a court order in a racial profiling case targeting Latino immigrants. Arpaio was scheduled for sentencing on October 5, 2017, but on August 25, President Trump formally pardoned Arpaio. At the time of this writing legal challenges have been mounted to that pardon.)

The implementation of other immigration legislation at the national level has been colored by this same discourse. The United States continues to close avenues of citizenship for immigrants. President Obama's immigration reform plan released in early 2015 made little change in the realities of immigrant deaths in the borderlands, and it did not allow immigrants to become citizens of the United States. Instead, national-level policies continue to reinforce existing structures of white supremacy. Beyond citizenship, these policies continue to deny immigrants feasible access to education and jobs, all while exploiting their labor. Further, most of President Obama's 2014 initiatives worked to feed into the myths discussed above, with "four principles" guiding his policies: increased border security, earned citizenship, penalizing employers who hired undocumented workers, and streamlining legal immigration (Oleaga 2014). These principles aligned the president's goals with the fears presented in the five myths while ultimately reinforcing narratives of white supremacy. Each principle has its corresponding myth that has driven the creation of the principle. Principle one described as *increased border security* drew on myths of out-of-control "illegal" immigration and an invasion of Latino immigrants (Myths 2, 3, and 4). Principle two, *citizenship must be earned*, drew on myths of the illegality and criminality of Latino immigrants (Myths 2, 4, and 5). Principle three, *penalizing of employers*, drew on myths of immigrants taking jobs away from American citizens (Myth 4). The last principle of the Obama administration was *streamlining legal immigration*, which drew on assumptions that all immigrants are here illegally (Myth 2).

Each principle was put forth by the Obama administration to fix a "broken immigration system" (Oleaga 2014). Yet each principle meant to guide the U.S. government's approach was oriented by white supremacy. To be clear, the Obama administration's commonsense plan for immigration was only different in name from those of past presidents. However, this plan illustrated a larger trend among administrations to structure and organize immigration reforms that address white fears of loss of power. White supremacy is a means for whites to maintain power and control over resources and people of color, and thus immigration laws are fundamentally about maintaining power and control. These myths mask the power white people and white supremacy gain from the implementation of immigration reform policies, laws, and practices.

These myths facilitate fear of Latino citizens and immigrants, particularly during economic hardships and at election time. Challenging these myths requires a clear understanding of their roots in white supremacy and of how these roots have come to shape our present conditions. Ignoring this background leads to a system where young Latinos are targets of law enforcement agencies rather than the new tired, poor, huddled masses, wretched and homeless, that Emma Lazarus's poem welcomed. The future of Latino immigrants and their children in the United States is tenuous despite the Latino population growing exponentially across the nation (Ennis, Rios-Vargas, and Albert 2011). Failure to understand the racial identities and contexts experienced by Latinos, immigrants and citizens alike, will be a significant hindrance for a nation that must keep up with a changing world. Latinos are providing the growth needed by the U.S. economy, educational system, labor market, and other crucial social institutions that are already faltering without an adequate labor force to fill the baby boomers' shoes. The processes of racialization that organize U.S. social systems must change to accommodate the new Latino presence, and the ways these changes occur will ultimately determine whether Latinos play the vital role they deserve in the future of the United States.

CONCLUSION

There are many myths about Latino immigrants circulating in the United States. These discourses are too numerous to capture in their entirety in this chapter, but the five myths I highlight are most prevalent and important for thinking about how immigration and citizenship are conceptualized by many U.S. citizens. Most importantly, these myths do not always look as they have been exposed herein. There are many iterations, but they all have similar arguments. The overall purpose of this chapter is to highlight how these myths are linked by the ideology of white supremacy and the myth of white virtuousness. Showing the details of each myth's logic as white supremacy illustrates the need to interpret these myths as fundamentally shaping the racial climate experienced by Latino immigrants on their arrival in the United States. Moving beyond political rhetoric to equitable and just reform, we must first acknowledge that at no point are Latinos *con papeles o sin papeles* going to be conceptualized as full U.S. citizens, given the racial histories and racial hierarchies that pervade all levels of social interaction between Latinos and whites. Ultimately, no amount of assimilation, as some critics charge, is going to make them "white."

NOTE

1. For instance, for decades blacks and Latinos have been demonized for supposedly being lazy and not wanting work, while "milking" the welfare state. Yet, in truth, welfare (e.g., food stamps) has been a well-orchestrated and manipulated *white secret*, as welfare was in fact originally created for whites, has remained a white program for white people, and the majority of people benefiting from welfare have been, from its inception, white people. According to 2013 data from the U.S. Department of Agriculture, which runs the Supplemental Nutrition Assistance Program, 40.2 percent of all recipients are white, 25.7 percent are black, and 10.3 percent are Latino—illustrating that about 90 percent of all people on welfare are non-Latino. It is time that we look a little closer at who is "milking" the welfare state.

REFERENCES

Acuña, R. 1998. *Sometimes There Is No Other Side: Chicanos and the Myth of Equality.* Notre Dame, Ind.: University of Notre Dame Press.

———. 2011. *The Making of Chicana/o Studies: In the Trenches of Academe.* Piscataway, N.J.: Rutgers University Press.

———. 2014. *Occupied America: A History of Chicanos.* 8th ed. Boston: Pearson.

Alba, R., and V. Nee. 2003. *Remaking the American Mainstream: Assimilation and Contemporary Immigration.* Cambridge, Mass.: Harvard University Press.

Alexander, M. 2012. *The New Jim Crow: Mass Incarceration in the Age of Colorblindness.* New York: New Press.

Almaguer, T. 2008. *Racial Fault Lines: The Historical Origins of White Supremacy in California.* Berkeley: University of California Press.

Álvarez, S. E. 2012. "Latinas and Latinos in the U.S.: The Road to Prison." In *Hispanics in the U.S. Criminal Justice System: The New American Demography*, edited by M. G. Urbina, 203–24. Springfield, Ill.: Charles C Thomas.

Aranda, E., and E. Vaquera. 2015. "Racism, the Immigration Enforcement Regime, and the Implications for Racial Inequality in the Lives of Undocumented Young Adults." *Sociology of Race and Ethnicity* 1: 88–104.

Arpaio, J. 2011. Maricopa County Sheriff's Office press release, January 31. http://www.mcso .org/PressRelease/Default.aspx.

Bell, D. 1987. *And We Are Not Saved: The Elusive Quest for Racial Justice.* New York: Perseus Group Press.

Bender, S. W. 2003. *Greasers and Gringos: Latinos, Law, and the American Imagination.* New York: New York University Press.

Bender, S. W., R. Aldana, G. P. Carrasco, and J. G. Ávila. 2008. *Everyday Law for Latino/as.* Boulder, Colo.: Paradigm.

Black, W. K. 2013. *The Best Way to Rob a Bank Is to Own One: How Corporate Executives and Politicians Looted the S&L Industry.* Austin: University of Texas Press.

Bonilla-Silva, E. 2001. *White Supremacy and Racism in the Post–Civil Rights Era.* Boulder, Colo.: Lynne Rienner.

———. 2002. "We Are All Americans: Toward a New System of Racial Stratification in the U.S.A." *Race and Society* 5: 85–101.

———. 2006. *Racism Without Racists: Color-Blind Racism and the Persistence of Racial Inequality in the United States.* Lanham, Md.: Rowman and Littlefield.

Boyer, P. G., and D. J. Davis, eds. 2013. *Social Justice Issues and Racism in the College Classroom: Perspectives from Different Voices.* Bingley, UK: Emerald.

Camarota, S. A., and J. Vaughn. 2009. *Immigration and Crime: Assessing a Conflicted Issue.* A Report for the Center for Immigration Studies. http://cis.org/ImmigrantCrime.

Castañeda, J. 2007. *Ex Mex: From Migrants to Immigrants*. New York: New Press.

Chávez, L. R. 2013a. *The Latino Threat: Constructing Immigrants, Citizens, and the Nation*. Stanford, Calif.: Stanford University Press.

———. 2013b. *Shadowed Lives: Undocumented Immigrants in American Society*. Belmont, Calif.: Wadsworth.

Chávez, M. 2011. *Everyday Injustice: Latino Professionals and Racism*. Lanham, Md.: Rowman and Littlefield.

Chomsky, A. 2007. *"They Take Our Jobs!": And 20 Other Myths About Immigration*. Boston: Beacon Press.

Chou, R., and J. R. Feagin. 2008. *The Myth of the Model Minority: Asians Americans Facing Racism*. Boulder, Colo.: Paradigm.

Cobas, J., J. Duany, and J. Feagin. 2009. *How the United States Racializes Latinos: White Hegemony and Its Consequences*. Boulder, Colo.: Paradigm.

Cobas, J., and J. R. Feagin. 2008. "Language Oppression and Resistance: The Case of Middle Class Latinos in the United States. *Ethnic and Racial Studies* 31: 390–410.

Correa, J. G., and J. Thomas. 2015. "The Rebirth of the U.S.-Mexico Border: Latina/o Enforcement Agents and the Changing Politics of Racial Power." *Sociology of Race and Ethnicity* 1: 239–54.

De León, A. 1983. *They Called Them Greasers: Anglo Attitudes Toward Mexicans in Texas, 1821–1900*. Austin: University of Texas Press.

De León, A., and R. Del Castillo. 2012. *North to Aztlán: A History of Mexican Americans in the United States*. 2nd ed. Hoboken, N.J.: Wiley-Blackwell.

Delgado, D. J. 2014. "'And You Need Me to Be the Token Mexican?': Examining Racial Hierarchies and the Complexities of Racial Identities for Middle Class Mexican Americans." *Critical Sociology* 42: 1–20.

Delgado, R. 1995. "The Imperial Scholar: Reflections on a Review of Civil Rights Literature." In *Critical Race Theory: The Key Writings That Formed the Movement*, edited by K. Crenshaw, N. Gotanda, G. Peller, and K. Thomas, 46–57. New York: New Press.

———. 2009. "The Law of the Noose: A History of Latino Lynching." *Harvard Civil Rights–Civil Liberties Law Review* 44: 297–312.

Dowling, J. A., and J. X. Inda, eds. 2013. *Governing Immigration Through Crime: A Reader*. Stanford, Calif.: Stanford University Press.

Durán, R. 2014. "Borders, Immigration, and Citizenship: The Latino Experience with Gringo Justice." In Urbina, *Twenty-First Century Dynamics of Multiculturalism*, 59–80.

Duster, T. 2001. "The Morphing Properties of Whiteness." In *The Making and Unmaking of Whiteness*, edited by B. B. Rasmussen, E. Klinenburg, I. J. Nexica, and M. Wray, 113–37. Durham, N.C.: Duke University Press.

Ennis, S. R., M. Rios-Vargas, and N. G. Albert. 2011. "The Hispanic Population: 2010." *U.S. Census Bureau*, May 2011. https://www.census.gov/prod/cen2010/briefs/c2010br-04.pdf.

Feagin, J. R. 2012. *White Party, White Government: Race, Class, and U.S. Politics*. New York: Routledge.

———. 2013. *The White Racial Frame: Centuries of Racial Framing and Counter-Framing*. 2nd ed. New York: Routledge.

———. 2014. *Racist America: Roots, Current Realities, and Future Reparations*. New York: Routledge.

Feagin, J. R., and J. A. Cobas. 2008. "Latino/as and the White Racial Frame: Procrustean Bed of Assimilation." *Sociological Inquiry* 78: 39–53.

———. 2014. *Latinos Facing Racism: Discrimination, Resistance, and Endurance*: Boulder, Colo.: Paradigm.

Fernández, C. 2015. "Watch: These Are the Top 5 Immigration Myths." *Latina*, May 5. https://www.latina.com/lifestyle/news/watch-these-are-top-5-immigration-myths.

Flagg, B. 1993. " 'Was Blind but Now I See': White Race Consciousness and the Requirement of Discriminatory Intent." *Michigan Law Review* 91: 953–1017.

Goldstein, E. L. 2006. *The Price of Whiteness: Jews, Race, and American Identity*. Princeton, N.J.: Princeton University Press.

Gómez, L. E. 2007. *Manifest Destinies: The Making of the Mexican American Race*. New York: New York University Press.

Gonzales, A. 2014. *Reform Without Justice: Latino Migrant Politics and the Homeland Security State*. New York: Oxford University Press.

Gonzales-Day, K. 2006. *Lynching in the West, 1850–1935*. Durham, N.C.: Duke University Press.

Gordon, M. 1964. *Assimilation in American Life: The Role of Race, Religion, and National Origins*. New York: Oxford University Press.

Gotanda, N. 1995. "A Critique of 'Our Constitution Is Colorblind.' " In *Critical Race Theory: The Key Writings That Formed the Movement*, edited by K. Crenshaw, N. Gotanda, G. Peller, and K. Thomas, 257–75. New York: New Press.

Gubrium, J., and J. Holstein. 2001. *Institutional Selves: Troubled Identities in a Postmodern World*. New York: Oxford University Press.

Gutiérrez, D., ed. 1997. *Between Two Worlds: Mexican Immigrants in the United States*. Wilmington, Del.: Jaguar Books.

Hensley, J. J., and M. Dempsey. 2012. "Sheriff Joe Arpaio Has Raised More Money Than Ever." *ALIPAC*, January 28. https://www.alipac.us/f12/sheriff-joe-arpaio-has-raised-more-money-than-ever-249640/.

Hernández, C. C. G. 2012. "Immigrant Outsider, Alien Invader: Immigration Policing Today." *California Western Law Review* 48: 231–44.

Hill, J. 2008. *The Everyday Language of White Racism*. Malden, Mass.: Blackwell.

Inda, J. X. 2000. "Foreign Bodies: Migrants, Parasites, and the Pathological Nation." *Discourse* 22: 46–62.

Jimenez, M., and J. Flores. 2010. *The Afro-Latin@ Reader: History and Culture in the United States*. Durham, N.C.: Duke University Press.

Katznelson, I. 2005. *When Affirmative Action Was White: An Untold History of Racial Inequality in Twentieth-Century America*. New York: W. W. Norton.

Kivisto, P., and T. Faist. 2010. *Beyond a Border: The Causes and Consequences of Contemporary Immigration*. Thousand Oaks, Calif.: Pine Forge Press.

Kubrin, C. E., M. S. Zatz, and R. Martinez, eds. 2012. *Punishing Immigrants: Policy, Politics, and Injustice*. New York: New York University Press.

Light, M., M. López, and A. Gonzalez-Barrera. 2014. *The Rise of Federal Immigration Crimes: Unlawful Reentry Drives Growth*. Washington, D.C.: Pew Research Center. http://www.pewhispanic.org/2014/03/18/the-rise-of-federal-immigration-crimes/.

Logan, J., and R. Turner. 2013. *Hispanics in the United States: Not Only Mexicans*. Report for Russell Sage Foundation. http://www.s4.brown.edu/us2010/Data/Report/report03202013.pdf.

López, I. F. H. 2003. *Racism on Trial: The Chicano Fight for Justice*. Cambridge, Mass.: Belknap Press of Harvard University Press.

———. 2006. *White by Law: The Legal Construction of Race*. New York: New York University Press.

López, M. H., G. Livingston, and R. Kochhar. 2009. *Hispanics and the Economic Downturn: Housing Woes and Remittance Cuts*. Washington, D.C.: Pew Research Center. http://www.pewhispanic.org/2009/01/08/hispanics-and-the-economic-downturn-housing-woes-and-remittance-cuts/.

Martinez, J., A. Unterreiner, A. Aragon, and P. Kellerman. 2014. "Immigration Reform and Education: Demystifying Mythologies About Latina/o Students." *Multicultural Teaching and Learning* 9: 115–218.

Matsuda, M., C. R. Lawrence, R. Delgado, and K. W. Crenshaw. 1993. *Words That Wound: Critical Race Theory, Assaultive Speech, and the First Amendment*. Boulder, Colo.: Westview Press.

McWilliams, C. 1990. *North from Mexico: The Spanish-Speaking People of the United States*. New York: Praeger.

Meyerhoffer, C. 2015. "'I Have More in Common with Americans Than I Do with Illegal Aliens': Culture, Perceived Threat, and Neighborhood Preferences. *Sociology of Race and Ethnicity* 1: 378–93.

Mirandé, A. 1987. *Gringo Justice*. Notre Dame, Ind.: University of Notre Dame Press.

———. 2005. *The Stanford Law Chronicles: Doin' Time on the Farm*. Notre Dame, Ind.: University of Notre Dame Press.

Mize, R., and A. Swords. 2010. *Consuming Mexican Labor: From the Bracero Program to NAFTA*. Toronto: University of Toronto Press.

Moore, W. L. 2007. *Reproducing Racism: White Space, Elite Law Schools, and Racial Inequality*. Lanham, Md.: Rowman and Littlefield.

Morín, J. L. 2009. *Latino/a Rights and Justice in the United States: Perspectives and Approaches.* 2nd ed. Durham, N.C.: Carolina Academic Press.

Navarro, A. 2005. *Mexicano Political Experience in Occupied Aztlan: Struggles and Change.* Walnut Creek, Calif.: Alta Mira Press.

Noboa, J. 2005. *Leaving Latinos Out of History: Teaching U.S. History in Texas.* New York: Routledge.

Oleaga, M. 2014. "White House Promotes Obama's Four Principles for 'Common Sense' Immigration Reform Proposal." http://www.latinpost.com/articles/21110/20140910/white -house-promotes-obamas-four-principles-common-sense-immigration-reform.htm.

Oliver, M. 2008. "Subprime as Black Catastrophe." *American Prospect*, September 20. http:// prospect.org/article/sub-prime-black-catastrophe.

Omi, M., and H. Winant. 1994. *Racial Formation in the United States: From the 1960s to the 1990s.* New York: Routledge.

Paredes, A. 2006. *With His Pistol in His Hand: A Border Ballad and Its Hero.* Austin: University of Texas Press.

Park, R. 1950. *Race and Culture.* Glencoe, Ill.: Free Press.

Pérez, T. 2011. Letter Regarding United States' Investigation of the Maricopa County Sheriff's Office. U.S. Department of Justice, December 15. http://www.justice.gov/crt/about/spl/ documents/mcso_findletter_12-15-11.pdf.

Pew Research Center. 2013. *The Rise of Asian Americans.* Washington, D.C.: Pew Research Center. http://www.pewsocialtrends.org/files/2013/04/Asian-Americans-new-full-report -04-2013.pdf.

Pickett, J. T., T. Chiricos, K. M. Golden, and M. Gertz. 2012. "Reconsidering the Relationship Between Perceived Neighborhood Racial Composition and Whites' Perceptions of Victimization Risk: Do Racial Stereotypes Matter?" *Criminology* 50: 145–86.

Pizarro, M. 2005. *Chicanas and Chicanos in School: Racial Profiling, Identity Battles, and Empowerment.* Austin: University of Texas Press.

Portes, A., and R. Rumbaut. 2001. *Legacies: The Story of the Immigrant Second Generation.* Berkeley, Calif.: University of California Press.

Portes, A., and M. Zhou. 1993. "The New Second Generation: Segmented Assimilation and Its Variants." *Annals of the American Academy of Political and Social Science* 530: 74–96.

Posadas, C., and C. Medina. 2012. "Immigration Lockdown: The Exclusion of Mexican Immigrants Through Legislation." In *Hispanics in the U.S. Criminal Justice System: The New American Demography*, edited by M. G. Urbina, 80–93. Springfield, Ill.: Charles C Thomas.

Prechel, H., and T. Morris. 2010. "The Effects of Organizational and Political Embeddedness on Financial Malfeasance in the Largest U.S. Corporations: Dependence, Incentives, and Opportunities." *American Sociological Review* 75: 331–54.

Provine, D. M., and R. L. Doty. 2011. "The Criminalization of Immigrants as a Racial Project." *Journal of Contemporary Criminal Justice* 27: 261–77.

Reclamation Project. 2014. *How White Folks Got So Rich: The Untold Story of American White Supremacy*. U.S.: Reclamation Project.

Reiman, J., and P. Leighton. 2013. *The Rich Get Richer and the Poor Get Prison: Ideology, Class, and Criminal Justice*. 10th ed. Eaglewood Cliffs, N.J.: Prentice Hall.

Rios, V. 2011. *Punished: Policing the Lives of Black and Latino Boys*. New York: New York University Press.

Rockquemore, K., and D. Brunsma. 2002. *Beyond Black: Biracial Identity in America*. Thousand Oaks, Calif.: Sage.

Romero, M., and G. Sánchez. 2012. "Critical Issues Facing Hispanic Defendants: From Detection to Arrest." In *Hispanics in the U.S. Criminal Justice System: The New American Demography*, edited by M. G. Urbina, 63–79. Springfield, Ill.: Charles C Thomas.

Saenz, R., and K. M. Douglas. 2015. "A Call for the Racialization of Immigration Studies: On the Transition of Ethnic Immigrants to Racialized Immigrants." *Sociology of Race and Ethnicity* 1: 166–80.

Saenz, R., C. Menjivar, and S. J. García. 2013. "Arizona's SB 1070: Setting Conditions for Violations of Human Rights Here and Beyond." In Dowling and Inda, *Governing Immigration Through Crime*, 165–80.

Sakuma, A. 2015. "Why Donald Trump's Racist Remarks Matter." *MSNBC*, July 1. http://www.msnbc.com/msnbc/why-donald-trumps-racist-remarks-matter.

Salinas, L. S. 2015. *U.S. Latinos and Criminal Injustice*. East Lansing: Michigan State University Press.

Santa Ana, O. 2002. *Brown Tide Rising: Metaphors of Latinos in Contemporary American Public Discourse*. Austin: University of Texas Press.

Sassler, S., and K. Joyner. 2011. "Social Exchange and the Progression of Sexual Relationships in Emerging Adulthood." *Social Forces* 90: 223–46.

Skoloff, B. 2013. "Border Patrol Shot Mexican Teen Jose Antonio Elena Rodriguez 8 Times: Autopsy." *Associated Press*, February 8. http://www.huffingtonpost.com/2013/02/08/border-patrol-shot-mexican-teen-jose-antonio-elena-rodriguez-autopsy_n_2646191.html.

Stannard, D. 1992. *American Holocaust: The Conquest of the New World*. New York: Oxford University Press.

Statue of Liberty. 2015. "Ellis Island History." https://www.libertyellisfoundation.org/ellis-island-history.

Stumpf, J. P. 2013. "The Crimmigration Crisis: Immigrants, Crime, and Sovereign Power." In Dowling and Inda, *Governing Immigration Through Crime*, 59–76.

Takaki, R. 1992. "The Tempest in the Wilderness: The Racialization of Savagery." *Journal of American History* 79: 892–912.

Teaching Tolerance. 2011. "10 Myths About Immigration." *Teaching Tolerance*. http://www.tolerance.org/immigration-myths.

Telles, E., and V. Ortiz. 2009. *Generations of Exclusion: Mexican Americans, Assimilation, and Race*. New York: Russell Sage Foundation.

Theiss-Morse, E. 2009. *Who Counts as an American?: The Boundaries of National Identity*. New York: Cambridge University Press.

Urbina, M. G. 2003. "The Quest and Application of Historical Knowledge in Modern Times: A Critical View." *Criminal Justice Studies: A Critical Journal of Crime, Law and Society* 16: 113–29.

———. 2007. "Latinas/os in the Criminal and Juvenile Justice Systems." *Critical Criminology: An International Journal* 15: 41–99.

———. 2012. *Capital Punishment in America: Race and the Death Penalty over Time*. El Paso, Tex.: LFB Scholarly Publishing.

———, ed. 2012. *Hispanics in the U.S. Criminal Justice System: Ethnicity, Ideology, and Social Control*. 2nd ed. Springfield, Ill.: Charles C Thomas. (2nd ed. forthcoming, 2018.)

———, ed. 2014. *Twenty-First Century Dynamics of Multiculturalism: Beyond Post-racial America*. Springfield, Ill.: Charles C Thomas.

Urbina, M. G., and S. E. Álvarez, eds. 2015. *Latino Police Officers in the United States: An Examination of Emerging Trends and Issues*. Springfield, Ill.: Charles C Thomas.

———. 2016. "Neoliberalism, Criminal Justice, and Latinos: The Contours of Neoliberal Economic Thought and Policy on Criminalization." *Latino Studies* 14: 33–58.

———. 2017. *Ethnicity and Criminal Justice in the Era of Mass Incarceration: A Critical Reader on the Latino Experience*. Springfield, Ill.: Charles C Thomas.

Urbina, M. G., and I. A. Peña. 2018. "Policing Borders: Immigration, Criminalization, and Militarization in the Era of Social Control Profitability." In *Spatial Policing: The Influence of Time, Space, and Geography on Law Enforcement Practices*, edited by C. Crawford. Durham, N.C.: Carolina Academic Press.

Urbina, M. G., and L. Smith. 2007. "Colonialism and Its Impact on Mexicans' Experience of Punishment in the United States." In *Race, Gender, and Punishment: From Colonialism to the War on Terror*, edited by M. Bosworth and J. Flavin, 49–61. Piscataway, N.J.: Rutgers University Press.

Urbina, M. G., J. E. Vela, and J. O. Sánchez. 2014. *Ethnic Realities of Mexican Americans: From Colonialism to 21st Century Globalization*. Springfield, Ill.: Charles C Thomas.

Urbina, M. G., and C. R. Wright. 2016. *Latino Access to Higher Education: Ethnic Realities and New Directions for the Twenty-First Century*. Springfield, Ill.: Charles C Thomas.

U.S. Border Patrol. 2014. "U.S. Border Patrol Fiscal Year Southwest Border Sector Deaths (FY 1998—FY 2014)." *U.S. Customs and Border Protection*.

Vallejo, J. A. 2012. *Barrios to Burbs: The Making of the Mexican American Middle Class*. Stanford, Calif.: Stanford University Press.

Walker, S. 1998. *Popular Justice: A History of American Criminal Justice*. 2nd ed. New York: Oxford University Press.

Zuberi, T., and E. Bonilla-Silva, eds. 2008. *White Logic, White Methods: Racism and Methodology*. Lanham, Md.: Rowman and Littlefield.

Chapter 10

COVERING THE IMMIGRANT STORY

Immigration Through the Lens of the American Media

PETER LAUFER

No tengo que asimilarme a nada. Tengo mi propia historia.

(I don't have to assimilate to anything. I have my own story.)

—CARLOS FUENTES

SMILING THEIR USUAL wide and happy smiles despite the baking summer sun, the Rodriguez family gathered in 2015 for a quick iPhone snapshot in front of their home—a weary and worn double-wide, parked, as it's been for a couple decades, adjacent to a feedlot on a California cattle ranch. They are a typical American family: The father crossed the border from Mexico over two dozen years ago, intent on making a better life for his young family stateside than he figured he could back home in Jalisco. His wife followed not long after, equally intent to keep the family together. Their infant son was in her arms as she strode across a Rio Grande/Río Bravo bridge, her *gringada* disguise making her invisible to La Migra. Soon a second son was born to the new Californians, of course a U.S. citizen by birth, and later another Yankee, a daughter.

Juana María, the mother, is missing from the 2015 family photograph. She succumbed to cancer, but not before she lived to see her dreams for her family's legal future about to turn from *sueños* into *realidad*.

IMMIGRATION AND THE LAW: AND THEN COMES THE FAMILY

The relationship between immigration and the law is, *por supuesto*, more than a question for police, lawyers, scholars, and populists seeking scapegoats—like a Donald Trump on the campaign trail. Immigration and the law collide at our most human place: the family. Love for our families exacerbates our vulnerabilities, and that same love fuels our perseverance and strength. Migration, border, and identity disappear and immediately are reinvented when our families are at stake.

That is why I appreciate the license I received from this book's editors to tell Juana María Rodriguez's story (obviously not her real name) as a grassroots example of the emotional costs—along with the lovely successes—that can occur when individuals take immigration law into their own hands.

JUANA MARÍA: AN AMERICAN DREAMER

With that preamble, please meet an American dreamer—of course a distinct individual, but an American dreamer with a life like so many millions of others. Juana María was a bright and bubbly woman in her late thirties when I sat down with her in that double-wide to hear her immigration rite of passage, both a unique and a typical migrant's tale that I first recounted in my book *Wetback Nation: The Case for Opening the Mexican-American Border.*

Juana María's toddler daughter is in the living room learning English from a television program when we sit down in her kitchen to talk about her trip across the border over thirteen years before. Her two boys are in school. She offers me a cup of tea.

"Do you have anything decaffeinated?" I ask.

She does. Her bicultural kitchen cupboards include mola, tortillas, and caffeine-free mint tea. I've heard Juana María's border-crossing story often, but in bits and pieces. This day she's taking time out of her schedule to recount it from start to finish.

It was 1990 when Juana María first came north. She had waited patiently in line at the U.S. Consulate in Guadalajara and applied for a tourist visa, which she received. Eight months prior her husband had crossed into California without a visa, looking for work. A hardworking mechanic, he found a job easily—on a ranch where his pay included living quarters.

She remembers all the dates precisely. "I came on May 27 in 1990—that's the first time I came to the United States." Juana María speaks English with a thick Mexican accent, and only rarely drops a Spanish word into the conversation. Her English vocabulary is more than adequate for her story. She's spent the last several years studying English, working with a volunteer tutor, and her boys bring English home from school and into the household. (My wife, the writer Sheila Swan Laufer, was that tutor; through their work together our families became friends.) "I flew from Guadalajara here to California." In addition to her three-month-old first son, she traveled north with her mother-in-law and her thirteen-year-old brother. She was twenty-three. Stamped into her Mexican passport was her prized tourist visa.

When she reached the immigration officer at the airport she faced a few key questions. "He asked, 'How much money do you have to spend in the United States?' I had only five hundred dollars. My mother-in-law didn't have anything. He said, 'That is not enough money for three people to visit the United States for two months.'" The officer asked the next crucial question, and she now knows her honest answer doomed her trip. "He asked, 'Why are you coming here?' And I told the truth: 'I come to visit my husband. I want to stay with my husband and I want my child to grow up with his father.'" Despite the valid visa, Juana María and her family were refused entry. It was obvious she was no tourist. She was a migrant.

"We stayed all night, like we were arrested. We didn't go to jail because we had two little boys. But we stayed all night in one room in the airport."

The officer was Latino, she says, and told her, "Oh, I'm so sorry. I feel so bad about what I'm doing." She says she remembers the moment vividly when he took her cash. "He bought a ticket. The next day we flew back to Mexico on another airplane. One officer went with us into the airplane and made sure we were sitting down in the airplane. And he never gave me my money back. He bought that ticket with my money."

JUANA MARÍA, A COYOTE, AND THE DREAM OF EL NORTE

A month later Juana María was shopping for a coyote. "I didn't want to stay in Mexico. My husband was here." Her older brother convinced her to avoid the Tijuana crossing into San Diego, scaring her with stories of rape, robbery, abandonment, and murder in the hills along *la frontera*. She chose a Ciudad Juárez-into-El Paso bridge for her crossing point. With her baby bundled up, and once again accompanied by her mother-in-law, she flew from Guadalajara to Juárez. This time she didn't tell her husband of her travel plans. She smiles at the memory. "I didn't tell him because if something happened he would have worried about me and my boy. I wanted to give him a surprise." She laughs.

Juana María's brother confirmed arrangements with the coyote, and secured an address of a house for the rendezvous with the guide. Juana María grabbed a cab at the Juárez airport, but when the three travelers arrived at the Juárez house, they were unable to find their contact. And they quickly realized that they had left a suitcase in the long-gone taxicab. "We were missing in the big city," she says. "In the suitcase we had diapers and the baby's formula." They told their story to whomever they could find around the address and who would listen. *Suerte* was with the trio. A mechanic knew their coyote by a different name, but didn't know how to find him. The taxi company insisted on buying formula for the baby, and when it found the missing baggage and delivered it to their hotel, the driver refused a tip, and instead apologized that he neglected to check the trunk for her bag. She laughs again as she relives the Mexico-side-of-the-border crisis and its happy ending.

Juana María called her brother. He contacted the coyote and sent him to the hotel, and there they made their border-crossing plans. "I was nervous, but the coyote told me to relax." In those pre-9/11 days, Mexicans routinely crossed the bridge into El Paso to shop. The crowds were so great and the traffic so important to the local economy on the U.S. side that immigration officers only spot-checked border crossers walking north. Juana María was told to dress like a typical Mexican housewife, carry a shopping bag, and act confident. "We looked like people from Mexico who are shopping and going back home." They agreed to make the crossing during the noon rush hour. The coyote figured inspectors would be eating lunch and that the throngs crossing the bridge would camouflage his clients.

The next morning a car came to the hotel for Juana María. She was dropped near the border and walked north. "We crossed, walking." Juana María, the baby, her mother-in-law, and the coyote. "I was wearing a dress to look like a Mexican woman. We crossed at the border and we didn't go too far. We walked for maybe ten or fifteen minutes into El Paso." As the migrants walked north, homeless people living on the street kept the coyote informed that the street was free of La Migra; they each were tipped a dollar for the intelligence. "Finally we stopped at a McDonald's, because it was 104 degrees." Again she laughs as she recalls the moment from the comfort of her California home.

She ate her first U.S. meal in the air-conditioned cool of the McDonald's, a hamburger of course, while the coyote called a taxi. They drove to a house where a friend of her brother lived, and there they spent the night. The easy part of the journey was complete. Now the job was to get Juana María out of the borderlands and up into the Texas interior and on to her husband in California. A further masquerade was required. She no longer needed to look like a Mexican housewife; her next camouflage was to look Mexican American. "That's when they made me look like a teenager. They put me in shorts with a lot of flowers. They put me in a blouse—phosphorescent orange—a bright color. And they put my hair up," she's laughing again, "like a chola! They colored my eyes black, and red lipstick! Oh, my goodness." Juana María was a pretty woman, but she dressed conservatively and wore only minimal makeup. Nonetheless she was happy to play dress-up, "because I needed to look like the girls from El Paso, Texas. The teenagers in El Paso, Texas, look different from the teenagers in Mexico. That's why they changed my looks."

The migrating group flew to Dallas with no trouble, the baby disguised as an El Paso infant, sporting a Hawaiian shirt. Her mother-in-law was still with them, not worried in "a dress like a North American girl" because her hair is blonde. "I felt nervous," Juana María admits, but more than just nervous. "I felt embarrassed to look like that. When I looked at myself in the mirror I said, 'Oh, my God. No!' But I needed to relax and look normal, like all the other people in the airport."

When they arrived at the Dallas–Fort Worth airport they waited for another brother to pick them up. "He passed me three times, and he didn't recognize me." Finally she said to him, "Hi, honey! I'm Juana María." He was shocked at her appearance. "Well, I looked like a chola! He told me, 'If your husband sees you looking like that, immediately he will divorce you.' We left the airport, and the first stop was Sears to buy makeup and a dress, to wash my face and change everything. We went to my brother's house and then we called up my husband and I said, 'Honey, I'm here!' He said, 'No, you are joking.' I told him I was serious and that I had another surprise, I had his mother with me."

The mother-in-law had told her husband she would only go as far as Ciudad Juárez, but she went across into the United States, says María Juana, on a lark. "The coyote said, 'It's fun. You can cross. It's not dangerous.' So she crossed to have one more adventure in her life. My brother paid only five hundred dollars for all three people. Very cheap." Juana María is enjoying telling her story; she continues to laugh at the memories of her escapade.

BETWEEN TWO WORLDS: PITFALLS AND NEW BEGINNINGS

The date of her second arrival in El Norte also is fixed in her mind. "I crossed the border June 24, 1990." After a week visiting her brother, she flew to California for a reunion with her husband. It was July 1, just in time for the Fourth of July festivities at the ranch where he worked. "My husband told me I needed to buy clothes for the celebrations. I got blue jeans and a red and white blouse, because those are the three colors of the American flag. I felt comfortable with that."

We were talking more than thirteen years later. Juana María's parrot is chirping, and her daughter takes a break from the television to listen, eat some corn chips, and make a mess on the counter trying to pour some 7 Up into a glass. Outside, cattle are feeding at the trough. Her dogs periodically bark. Through her kitchen windows I see the bucolic California hills that surround her home. "I haven't been back to Mexico for thirteen years." She looks pensive when I ask her why. "Because I don't have a green card and now I am worried about crossing the border. I hear a lot of bad stories."

Living without proper documentation for thirteen years was nothing much more than an annoyance for Juana María. "I don't do anything illegal. I live a good life and take care of my kids. The only effect of not having a green card is that we cannot have a driver's license." Juana María did carry an official California identification card. (Until 1996, these were available from the Department of Motor Vehicles with no questions asked, based only on a birth certificate. The law changed that year, and those without green cards were no longer eligible for either driver's licenses or the official identification cards. The law changed again in 2015, and as of this writing California residents can obtain licenses no matter their immigration status.) Immigration officers rarely showed up in Juana María's rural neighborhood, and when they do patrol places she frequents in the nearby urban district, she told me she's warned and just avoids them. "When the Migra is around, the radio station (one of several broadcasting to her locale in Spanish) says, Don't go out to Walmart or Sears or whatever shopping center because the Migra is around. So I don't go there. I don't go. After one or two days, they're gone."

I ask Juana María what she would do if an immigration agent approached her at Walmart or Sears. "If he asks me for a green card, I can't do anything," she says about this perpetual threat to her domestic tranquility. "If you don't have the green card, they only arrest. They say, 'You have a right to call a relative, but you're going to jail.' If I don't have a green card, they'll deport me to my country, to Mexico. That's what they do. They don't ask for identification, they ask for a green card, or your permission to stay in the United States, like a passport. If I don't have anything with me, they'll arrest me, and they'll take me out to the border. It makes me nervous," she acknowledges.

But life was more uncertain for her when Pete Wilson was governor of California and rallied voters to pass Proposition 187, the referendum that limited the rights of undocumented migrants but which was ultimately struck down by the courts. During the anti-immigrant climate of those years in the mid-1990s, just picking up the children at school was cause for concern. "The Migra came to the schools and they arrested parents. The Migra didn't care if they needed to pick up their kids at the kindergarten. They arrested them. For more than a week, we didn't send our boy to the school, when I heard that the Migra was here in my county." Juana María figures about 70 percent of her Latino friends in California are in the state without government authorization.

Juana María held out hope for legalizing her status in the United States. Perhaps there would be another amnesty for immigrants who came into the country without documentation. Perhaps when her second son, who was born in the United States and is an American citizen, became an adult he would be able to establish legal residency for his parents and older Mexican-citizen brother. Meanwhile, she and her family thrived. She worked hard at the local PTA, organizing fund-raising dinners of rich Mexican food to pay for the renovation of the playground. Her daughter was christened at the local Catholic church in a Spanish-language ceremony, followed by a block party crowded with friends and relatives, food, and music. Her husband went off to work each day; she worked cleaning houses. They paid their taxes. She was an American by every definition except for her paperwork.

There she was at the local elementary school a few days after we talked at her home on the ranch. It was Mexican Lunch Day. Juana María brought together a group of the Latino mothers to fix burritos. The women were lined up in the kitchen, the first ladling out the rice, the next passing out a tortilla, the third the beans. The burritos were topped off with lettuce and cream and salsa. Juana María was proud of the healthy ingredients, far from her Mexican roots. "I didn't use lard in the beans," she told the other mothers. The money raised was used to provide childcare for the children of Latino mothers taking classes to earn a high school equivalency certificate.

There was one important imposition on her life that Juana María suffered because of her illegal status in the United States. "I feel sad because I cannot go to Mexico and come back again. I cannot visit my relatives. My friends who have green cards, they do that every year or every other year. I want to go to Mexico. But how can I cross? Maybe I'd be lucky, and not have any problems, like the first time. Or maybe I'd have a lot of problems." She had reason to worry; she'd heard the horror stories. "I have friends who came two months after I came here to the United States. Two years later they went to Mexico." The return trip was a disaster. "One of the ladies," she says it with a combination of sadness and a staccato matter-of-fact reporting of the news. "The coyote killed her. With a screwdriver. In Tijuana. I say no. I'm not going. I love my relatives. But I don't want to put my life in between. My life is first, and my kids too."

When Juana María's father-in-law was dying, her husband chose to take the chance on a trip back to Mexico. He crossed back into California with a false green card. Not a counterfeit green card, but a stolen one. Coyotes prowl border nightclubs, Juana María explained, looking for drunk Latinos with legitimate identification papers. They steal their green cards. Her husband sat down at a table with a coyote who displayed a stack of stolen green cards. Together they searched through the cards, seeking a picture of a Mexican who looked enough like her husband to satisfy a border guard. He crossed the border with someone else's green card.

The use-another's-ID system isn't perfect. He crossed successfully three times. "But the last time," Juana María tells me, "the officer said, 'You don't look like him!' They arrested him and sent him back to Mexico. He called me from Rosarito and said, 'I am here because they caught me and sent me back to Mexico.' I called the coyote and said, 'You promised me my husband would come to California safely. If my husband is not here in my house, I will not pay you anything.' The coyote went to get my husband at Rosarito, and he crossed again at Tijuana with the same stolen green card. That day was lucky." She smiles and says, "Sometimes the coyotes have business with the immigration officer, and they give him money under the table. That's what we call it: under the table." We call it the same thing, I tell her, and she smiles. That's her theory, that the coyote bribed the guard. It's hard to imagine a U.S. immigration officer jeopardizing his career and pension—not to mention risking prison time—for a cut of a coyote fee. Hard to imagine, but certainly possible. U.S. officials along the border have been arrested for conspiring with smugglers. Corruption is not limited to the Mexican side of the border. "He flew home from San Diego. When he was on the airplane, I sent the money by Western Union to the coyote."

Juana María and her family have been model citizens since they migrated to California. Model citizens except, of course, for the fact that when she and her husband migrated, they broke the law. What is the solution for Juana María and the millions of others living without documentation in the United States? "Amnesty for good persons," she says. "So many persons come here for work, to have the best life."

I interrupt her and remind her that the argument against another amnesty is that good people such as her family did, in fact, violate the law when they crossed the border and came to the United States illegally. Why should someone who broke the law be given amnesty and the opportunity legally to pursue the American dream? Her answer comes immediately and without hesitation. "Because we work hard and we are important to the country, to help the country grow. And we grow too, because we have the best life."

What about the long-term solution, I ask. Any determined Mexican who wants to come to the United States can figure out a path.

"No problem," she agrees, "they can come."

But if it is an illegal crossing north, they must perpetually fear deportation. Does she favor an open border?

"Yes. Open the border."

Her reasons are clear and come from personal experience.

"No business for the coyote. No people dead along the border. Then people in Mexico can come here and work, and the United States has cheap workers. That's simple. Open the border and you won't have any problems. Then Mexican people can feel free to come here, like the Americans go to Mexico."

If the border were open, where would Juana María prefer to live, Mexico or California?

"I love the life in California, but I miss my family."

Her voice slows down and she sounds a little dreamy. "Especially Christmas time, or New Year, when we make family parties. The traditions are so different comparing here to there. In Mexico we can eat beans and cheese and tortillas, but every family is together. Here we have turkeys with everything, but I don't feel happy." This time the laugh is caustic. Then she corrects herself. "I feel happy because my kids have the best school, and we stay together with my husband. But I have a heart, and my heart is in Mexico."

THE FINAL TRIP Y EL ULTIMO ADIOS

Juana María did make one more trip south. Her father was dying and she decided to take the risk despite the toughened post-9/11 border. She flew from Oakland to Guadalajara. But the return trip was a disaster. The Border Patrol caught her as she was running north across the desert. She was arrested, photographed, fingerprinted, and deported. And that paper trail, she knew, compromised her chances of obtaining legal status in her adopted hometown on the north side.

Determined woman that she was, she headed north again following her arrest, made it across *la frontera* and back to the ranch she called home where she and her family were reunited until her death a few years later.

IMMIGRATION, THE MEDIA, AND THE DREAM OF DIGNITY

How to characterize La Familia Rodriguez vis-à-vis immigration and the law? "What part of illegal don't you understand?" chant the sealed border absolutists. Juana María's own words offer a credible response: "We work hard and we are important to the country, to help the country grow. And we grow too, because we have the best life." We all break laws, if only something as seemingly inconsequential as exceeding the speed limit on the freeway. Should the infraction of crossing into the country without proper documentation sentence an otherwise law-abiding family to lives perpetually at risk of disruption while they feed cattle and clean houses? That is an easy question to answer.

The simplistic chant, "What part of illegal don't you understand?" is the type of language that's led many journalists to change the terminology used in their dispatches about migration. The Associated Press and some other news purveyors no longer identify people as illegal. Rather, they refer to acts people commit—such as crossing the border without proper documentation—as illegal acts.

Disaster metaphors are easy and appropriate devices for news reporter shorthand. But when such words are chosen for migration, borders, and identity news stories, they can be dehumanizing and fuel xenophobic paranoia. Consider the not-so-subtle subtext of phrases that use dangerous weather, military, and pollution metaphors to describe migrants and migration issues. Endless waves, torrents, and floods of migrants equate to threatening and dangerous weather. When those waves and floods are termed "invasions," the perceived threat from the Other is exacerbated to wartime. And when migration is identified as a mess that needs to be cleaned up, squalor is the imagery painted in news consumers' minds even if the news story is about bureaucratic and legal complexities.

Often these types of metaphoric references to migrants and immigration are undoubtedly not malicious. Years ago I used the term "illegal aliens" for my own reporting shorthand before I thought through the negative connotations and incorrect usage. How easy it is for a journalist on deadline to slip unthinkingly into clichés no matter the story. Forest fires blaze in rugged terrain. Police cars become emergency vehicles. Legislators borrow from Peter to pay Paul. The lazy list goes on. But that said, there are, of course, news media demagogues who revel in building audiences by spreading fear and paranoia, hate and xenophobia through their warped reporting on immigration and the law.

Lou Dobbs during his long stay on CNN repeatedly broadcast about the invasion of disease-carrying criminal illegal aliens into the United States from Mexico. Nationally syndicated radio talk show host Michael Savage offers plenty of examples, such as this offensive exchange with an anonymous caller about what Savage suggests is a typical undocumented immigrant family: "If the man is working as a waiter or a gardener do you think his wife is also working? Or is she home making as many anchor babies as she can as quickly as she can?" To which the caller, following Savage's prompt, answers, "I think that's true." And his radio compatriot Rush Limbaugh announced, "Mexico is getting rid of people they don't want. They're sending them here." Limbaugh takes full advantage of the intimacy of radio as a mass medium when he talks to his millions of listeners. "Folks," he added, "we're making a mistake referring to this as immigration. This is an invasion."

The *New York Daily News* freely uses the identifier "illegal immigrant," as does the *Washington Times*. And the *Times* deploys the slang term "illegals," a word that reeks of disparaging dismissive connotations. In the pages of the *National Review* are references to "criminal illegal immigrants" and "illegal immigrant criminals," along with that insult to the U.S. Constitution, "anchor babies."

Such journalistic prejudice fuels abuse, whether on a day-to-day basis in our public spaces or at the supposedly lofty bully pulpit of presidential campaigns. Witness Donald Trump and the news media exposure he enjoyed when he called Mexicans traveling north without the proper U.S. government documents "criminals, drug dealers, rapists, etc.," comments he not only refused to apologize for, but amplified on. "When Mexico sends its people," he crowed with insipid sarcasm, "they're not sending their best. They're sending people that have lots of problems, and they're bringing those problems. They're bringing drugs. They're bringing crime. They're rapists. And some, I assume, are good people."

No question there are news reporters and news outlets sympathetic to the plight of migrants making life-or-death decisions to leave their homelands in search of peace and progress. Consider that it was reporters who documented the unbelievable image of the Hungarian news videographer tripping a running Syrian refugee who was cradling a child in his arms. If sympathetic news coverage had been absent, politicians and aid workers, volunteers and the Pope may have been even slower than they were to respond to the escalating disaster for Everyman of imploding civil societies in the early twenty-first-century Middle East and Africa.

LIVING IN AMERICA: REMEMBERING JUANA MARÍA

Come with me now from those European borders back to California and that iPhone portrait of the Rodriguez family (absent the late Juana María) posing in front of their home on the cattle ranch. I stopped by to deliver a present for the daughter's *quinceañera*, the fifteenth-birthday party that celebrates a Mexican girl becoming a woman. We went inside their home to get out of the hot sun and to drink some water. We swapped stories. I saw the daughter's satin quinceañera dress and heard about her typical American experiences at the local rural high school.

The oldest son told me about his job driving heavy equipment. "I have a health plan and a retirement plan," he announced, so happy to be working legally despite the fact that when he crossed the border in Juana María's arms his passage was clandestine. After over twenty-one years of living without papers he was the proud holder of a California driver's license, a Social Security card, and a work permit because of President Obama's Deferred Action for Childhood Arrivals executive order. "I have a two-year work permit," he said with a confidence I never heard before from him. His body language was that of a young man no longer worried about the consequences of living as an outlaw. "My record is clean. I'll get my work permit renewed for another two years." After the second two-year term he's convinced there will a route for him to obtain permanent legal residency and eventually U.S. citizenship.

The second son is studying at a junior college (his school spirit shows on his school regalia-festooned shirt with cutoff sleeves), intent on a career in veterinary medicine. He's looking forward to a transfer to a four-year California state university. But he's also looking forward to helping his father. He's turned twenty-one, and, as a U.S. citizen by birth, he can petition for legal status for his father. He is shopping for an immigration lawyer he can trust.

As for the father, he was listening contentedly to our conversations, smiling about his children's success. But when his son finished explaining how he intended to regularize his father's immigration status, the father pointed to an adjacent room. "Juana María's ashes are in a box in there." He explained that he wanted his U.S. residency to be legal so that he can travel to Mexico and return to his job and family in California without risking another illegal border crossing. His motivation for the trip speaks to the heart of migration, border, and identity. "I want the family to take her ashes back home to Mexico."

The friendship between the Rodriguez family and my own is an intimate one. We share holidays, birthdays, picnics, and intriguing intercultural chats conducted, naturally, in Spanglish—one of so many American languages. Our quinceañera visit coincided with one of Donald Trump's outbursts against Mexico and Mexicans. The contrast of Trump's arrogance with the elegance of the Rodriguez family motivated me to pen an op-ed for the Portland *Oregonian*, an essay that seems appropriate as a coda for this chapter.

ONCE IN AMERICA, "SPEAK AMERICAN!"

"Speak American!" Sarah Palin counseled Jeb Bush recently, echoing Donald Trump's criticism of Bush's frequent fluent Spanish while speaking on the presidential campaign trail. Although Palin quickly clarified her advice by adding, "Let's speak English . . . a unifying aspect of a nation is the language that is understood by all," her admonition to "speak American" resonated with me. It reminded me that here in the States we do speak a loose and always-changing American English that reflects the reality of our melting pot.

Years ago, when I returned home from grammar school with muddy shoes, my father would call out—I think only half in jest—that I should wipe my feet before coming in the house and not be a *Schweinehund*. Born in Budapest, his English was flawless, but he peppered it—as all Americans do theirs—with words borrowed from other languages. I grew up in Sausalito listening to my father's typical Middle European easy use of a half-dozen languages. He greeted the Italian bakers in North Beach with a hearty "*Buon giorno*"; he heard "*Danke schön*" from appreciative German visitors who needed directions to San Francisco tourist attractions; and he tolerated my aunt when she insisted on still speaking to him in Hungarian decades after they passed through Ellis Island.

I'm sure the linguistic potpourri at home influenced my career choices: first as an NBC News correspondent reporting from all over the world and now as an academic researching migration, border, and identity. At the University of Oregon I teach journalism students techniques for reporting and interviewing across language barriers. One of the first lessons they learn is how welcoming American English is to the influence of other tongues.

An ultimate example of linguistic borrowing facilitates communication along our southern border. The potent mix of Spanish and English creates the uniquely American (geographic America, not just the United States of) argot spoken throughout the borderlands. Spanglish thrives there and stretches north—a rich third patois that also can be called an American language.

As Americans we should celebrate speaking Mixmaster variations of English. They provide us entrée into other cultures, and they help open the United States to immigrants who come to our shores without the language skills my father enjoyed.

There's a sobering joke told around the world: What do you call someone who speaks three languages? Trilingual. What do you call someone who speaks two languages? Bilingual. And what do you call someone who speaks one language? The worrisome answer is, of course, American.

Borders are fluid. Walls never stop migration. We create our own identities. Language use cannot be controlled at national frontiers. So with the hope that we all find the tools we need to keep talking with each other, I offer this open letter of support to Sarah Palin as a reminder, to use her words, of what unifies our country.

AN OPEN LETTER: UNA ULTIMA CARTA

¡Hola, Sarah Palin!

What *chutzpah* you showed when you joined the *brouhaha* about language, responding to that *bon vivant* Donald Trump's suggestion that Jeb Bush stop speaking Spanish with your call that we *gringos* should all "speak American." It was a typical *bon mot* on your part, reminiscent of your "how's that hopey-changey stuff working out" remark. But this time you caught the *Zeitgeist*. I say *basta* to the *dilettante* English-only crowd too as I wander this great country from *Sault Ste. Marie*, Michigan, to New *Braunfels*, Texas, from *Cairo*, Illinois, to my own *San Francisco*. We've been speaking, writing, and reading American here in these United States since the *Pennsylvanischer Staatsbote* editor thought *carpe diem* and his became the first newspaper to publish the Declaration of Independence on the fifth of July, 1776—in German.

Ciao, Peter Laufer

Chapter 11

IMMIGRATION, CRIMINALIZATION, AND MILITARIZATION IN THE AGE OF GLOBALIZATION

SOFÍA ESPINOZA ÁLVAREZ AND MARTIN GUEVARA URBINA

> I mean, your society's broken, so who should we blame? Should we blame the rich powerful people who caused it? No, let's blame the people with no power and no money and these immigrants who don't even have the vote, yeah, it must be their fucking fault.
>
> —IAIN BANKS

FOR ALMOST TWO decades, critics, from all walks of life, have passionately and sometimes aggressively charged that the U.S.-Mexico border is porous, unsafe, a safe haven for "illegal aliens," drug traffickers, narco-terrorists, and international terrorists, and that additional federal agents and military personnel are needed to secure the borders, along with high-tech military equipment for national security. In 2014, for instance, various lawmakers and other government officials connected the increase of unaccompanied children arriving at the U.S.-Mexico border trying to cross into the United States to an insecure border and grave lack of border enforcement. Some politicians even suggested that Central American children could be disease carriers or terrorists. During the second GOP presidential candidate debate in September 2015, Carly Fiorina charged, "The border's been insecure for 25 years," Donald Trump declared the need to "build a wall, a wall that works," and Ben Carson proclaimed that "if we don't seal the border, the rest of this stuff clearly doesn't matter."

Reality, however, is far from highly charged political rhetoric, which is propagated and sensationalized by conservative media. In actuality, the two-thousand-mile U.S.-Mexico border is not only heavily guarded but already a testing region for domestic militarization. Wartime technologies are not just stockpiled in warehouses in case of a foreign invasion, but are being deployed on immigrants and people like you and us. The militarization of the southern border has been unfolding for years (Dunn 1996; Kraska and Kappeler 1997), but drastically escalated after September 11, 2001 (Balko 2013; Golash-Boza 2012a, 2012b; Miller 2014; Welch 2002, 2006, 2009), vividly captured by Michael Welch in "Immigration Lockdown Before and After 9/11: Ethnic Constructions and Their Consequences" (2007). The Department of Homeland Security constructed 649 miles of high-tech fencing along the U.S.-Mexico border in 2011, adding federal agents, radio towers, flood lighting, mobile surveillance, and other advanced military technology. By 2012, there were 21,370 Customs and Border Protection agents, targeting "high-risk areas and flows" and prepared to act on any given *threat*, including the apprehension of children from Central America. Ironically, lawmakers and other anti-immigrant critics "missed" the connection that border agents detained around 66,115 children at the border in 2014, revealing that the border is perhaps more secure than ever before.

By some accounts, the United States already has sixty thousand border guards, more than double the size of Ecuador's army, illustrating that the U.S. government has strategically militarized the U.S.-Mexico border, funneling $17.9 billion into more "boots on the ground" and infrastructure by fiscal year 2012. Yet, net migration from Mexico has zeroed out or could even be negative, meaning that more people left the United States between 2005 and 2010, and the country's undocumented population has remained constant in recent years, leveling off at about 11.3 million during the past five years. Americans tend to see walls, fences, and war zones around the world with indignation, but what is going on in America, in our own backyard? After all, we tend to envision war in foreign lands, but not in America and certainly not in our neighborhoods.

GAZA IN THE LAND OF THE FREE: THE MILITARIZATION OF THE U.S.-MEXICO BORDER

As vividly detailed by Radley Balko in *Rise of the Warrior Cop: The Militarization of America's Police Forces* (2013) and Todd Miller in *Border Patrol Nation: Dispatches from the Front Lines of Homeland Security* (2014), American police departments are looking more like an occupying army than a "protect and serve" law enforcement agency. While the army metaphor might seem far-fetched, the border region is in fact looking more and more like a war zone. Consider, for instance, how about seven hundred miles of wall have *marked* the landscape of the borderlands, backed by sophisticated surveillance equipment, like cameras, towers, and more than twelve thousand motion sensors.

THE RIO GRANDE UNDER SIEGE: BEYOND THE DESERT

Customs and Border Protection (part of the Department of Homeland Security) has its own air and marine forces, a special operations branch, and a separate tactical unit, with rapid-response teams of five hundred federal agents ready for deployment within forty-eight hours, anywhere. The federal agency also has armored personnel carriers and uses operating bases like those used in U.S.-involved wars to secure positions in remote areas along the border. In fact, its Blackhawk helicopters and Predator B drones have been patrolling areas of the border region as if they were in a war zone, like Afghanistan. For decades government spending has increased astronomically (Urbina and Álvarez 2016), but since 9/11 the government has funneled $100 billion into border armament and high-tech surveillance systems. In the words of Drew Dodds, a salesperson trying to cash in on the border security gold rush at the 2012 Border Security Expo, "We are bringing the battlefield to the border," now that U.S. intervention in Afghanistan, Iraq, and other places is winding down (Miller 2014, 129).

Parallel to agents of Customs and Border Protection, U.S. Border Patrol agents (also part of the Department of Homeland Security) are also increasingly being up-armored with a combination of military hardware, assault rifles, helicopters, drones, and surveillance technologies. The once somewhat "open" border region is being transformed into what Timothy Dunn, in *The Militarization of the U.S.-Mexico Border* (1996), characterizes as a state of "low-intensity warfare." The new warfare is not, as some argue, restricted to the desert or the Arizona border, but exists all along the river. In the Rio Grande valley of Texas, for instance, federal agents are using surplus military aircraft once used to safeguard U.S. soldiers in Afghanistan from Taliban attacks or other targets. Stationed on the U.S. side of the international divide, the aerostat (moored balloon) is an unmanned, high-altitude sentinel carrying sophisticated cameras that enable Customs and Border Protection to look deep into Mexican territory and "spot" people from twelve miles away in the darkness of the night, allowing immigration officials to detect movement and mobilize forces.

With less U.S. involvement in Iraq and Afghanistan, more than seventy Defense Department aerostats are now available for use along the U.S.-Mexico border. Reportedly, along the Rio Grande Valley, four balloons are currently patrolling the skies over the Mexican state of Tamaulipas. According to Ryan Baggett, an Eastern Kentucky University professor who has worked as a Department of Homeland Security contractor, "It's an exciting time with regards to the use of technology.... When you combine the boots on the ground with this type of technology, it becomes a force multiplier" (Black 2015, 1). The aircraft is doing so well that the agency is asking for more balloons (Black 2015). The balloon by Lockheed Martin Corporation is the biggest, 117 feet long, able to hover at five thousand feet, and, lifted by inert helium, can stay aloft for thirty days. Ronald Brown, a director for Lockheed states, "Being with the troops in forward operating bases was a very good fit, and now looking at large reaches of the border is a very good fit" (Black 2015, 2). Reportedly, monthly expenses for each balloon being tested run from $300,000 to $350,000, about one-tenth the expense of a drone (Black 2015). The program had $24 million in annual funding in early 2015, and the Obama administration budget plan unveiled on February 2, 2015, asked for and received an additional $8.5 million to add another aerostat to the Texas airborne. Texas Republican Michael McCaul, who leads the House Committee on Homeland Security, has proposed further expanding aerostats in Texas as well as Arizona and California.

THE SOUTHERN BORDER SURGE: IMMIGRATION, CITIZENSHIP, AND SOCIAL CONTROL

On November 20, 2014, President Obama announced a series of immigration reform executive orders to resolve the issue of "illegal" immigration, while securing the border. Speaking before the American public, Obama referenced the bipartisan immigration legislation passed by the U.S. Senate in June 2013 that would further up-armor the border region, which has been characterized as a "border surge," reflective of action in U.S. war zones. The commander in chief lamented that the bill had been stalled in the House of Representatives. According to Obama, the bill was a "compromise" that "reflected common sense." The bill, according to the president, would "have doubled the number of Border Patrol agents, while giving undocumented immigrants a pathway to citizenship." His announcement, which included executive actions that would shelter five to six million immigrants from future deportation, quickly stirred national debate, portrayed as conflict between Democrats and Republicans.

In the *war of words*, however, the initial executive action that Obama had announced, which involved an increased militarization of the U.S.-Mexico border supported by both parties, went unnoticed. "First," the president declared, "we'll build on our progress at the border with additional resources for our law enforcement personnel so that they can stem the flow of illegal crossings and speed the return of those who do cross over." However, as noted by some observers, the "common sense" of the border-surge bill could add more than $40 billion dollars in funding for immigration agents, walls, fences, technology, and other border enforcement equipment to an already unparalleled border enforcement apparatus (Miller and Schivone 2015). Not to mention magnifying what Martin Guevara Urbina and Sofia Espinoza Álvarez (2016) characterize as the "driving force" of social control, the *profitability* of criminalization. The private sector directly signaled (as the trade magazine *Homeland Secu-*

rity Today put it) another "treasure trove" of profit for a border enforcement market already experiencing an "unprecedented boom period."

THE PALESTINE-MEXICO BORDER: AMERICA'S CONSTITUTION-FREE ZONE

Until recently, war zones, airstrikes, police-community confrontations or riots, and even police brutality have been associated with so-called Third World countries lacking democracy and civility and in terrorist countries. However, in the twenty-first century, no foreign travel or television set is required to witness the frontline of warfare, dividing, intimidating, and sometimes brutalizing communities, in operations that resemble testing grounds for federal agents, military personnel, and tech companies. The American Civil Liberties Union, for instance, reports that like the Gaza Strip for the Israelis, the U.S.-Mexico border region has been transformed into a "constitution-free zone," an open-laboratory for exploration, exploitation, and profit.

Under the new border regime, almost any type of security, surveillance, and equipment can be developed, tested, and showcased, like in a *militarized shopping mall*, for politicians, law enforcement officials, and other nations to see and buy. In fact, border security is increasingly becoming a globalized industry, where corporate venders like Israel's Elkabetz are revolutionizing transnational boundaries. In February 2014, before Donald Trump's Great Mexican Wall idea, Customs and Border Protection (CBP), in charge of policing U.S. borders, contracted with Israel's giant private military manufacturer Elbit Systems to build a "virtual wall," a highly technologically advanced physical divide set back from the actual international boundary in the Arizona desert. The Israeli company (through Elbit Systems of America), whose U.S.-traded stock increased by 6 percent during Israel's massive military operation against Gaza in the summer of 2014, will utilize the same databank of advanced technology used in Israel's border region (Gaza and the West Bank) in Arizona (Miller 2014; Miller and Schivone 2015). With possibly up to $1 billion at its disposal, CBP has tasked Elbit with building a "wall" of "integrated fixed towers" utilizing the latest and most advanced equipment, including radars, cameras, motion sensors, and control rooms, making Arizona the mecca of border enforcement, for other states to follow. Wall construction will begin in the rugged, desert canyons around Nogales, Arizona. Once the DHS determines that part of the multimillion-dollar wall project is effective, the rest of the wall will be built to monitor and patrol the state's entire border with Mexico.

To be sure, these towers are only part of a much broader border operation, the Arizona Border Surveillance Technology Plan. The Arizona wall project is simply a *blueprint* for a historically unprecedented infrastructure of high-tech border battlements, which has attracted various companies and the attention of lawmakers and other government officials for several years. In fact, this is not the first time Israeli corporations have been involved in border buildup in the United States. Soon after 9/11, in 2004, Elbit's Hermes drones were the first so-called unmanned aerial crafts to patrol the U.S.-Mexico border. Then in April 2007, as detailed by Naomi Klein in *The Shock Doctrine: The Rise of Disaster Capitalism* (2007, 438), another Israeli consulting company (Golan Group) composed of former officers of Israeli Defense Forces (IDF) Special Forces, provided an intensive eight-day course for special DHS immigration agents working along the Mexican border, covering "everything from hand-to-hand combat to target practice to 'getting proactive with their SUV.'" Beyond federal immigration agencies, the Israeli company NICE Systems also supplied "America's toughest sheriff," Joe Arpaio, with a surveillance system to monitor one of his "famous" Arizona jails. Exploring America's transformation of the southern region, journalist Jimmy Johnson (2012) characterized the border as the new "Palestine-Mexico border," America's new *constitution-free zone*, where law becomes illusive and law enforcement practice highly questionable.

AMERICA'S NEW BATTLEFIELD: THE U.S.-MEXICO BORDER REGION

Pointing to the surveillance industry "synergy" between two distant places, Naomi Weiner, project coordinator for the Israel Business Initiative, proclaims, "We've chosen areas where Israel is very strong and Southern Arizona is very strong," further suggesting that Arizona possesses the "complete package" for Israeli companies (Miller and Schivone 2015, 5). Her language is quite telling: "We're sitting right on the border, close to Fort Huachuca," a nearby U.S. military base where technicians maneuver the drones surveilling the U.S.-Mexico borderlands, and "We have the relationship with Customs and Border Protection, so there's a lot going on here. And we're also the Center of Excellence on Homeland Security" (Miller and Schivone 2015, 5). Along the way, as an additional layer of "legitimacy," the DHS designated the University of Arizona the lead university for the Center of Excellence on Border Security and Immigration in 2008, incorporating selected universities into the global border security enterprise and enabling schools to receive millions of dollars in federal grants. Conducting research, while developing border-policing technologies and related equipment, engineers in the Center of Excellence are analyzing locust wings in order to develop miniature drones equipped with high-tech cameras that can move into the tiniest areas near ground level, while large military drones (like the Predator B) continue to patrol over the U.S.-Mexico border region at thirty thousand feet. With growing interest in the Arizona-Israeli border security and economic venture, officials from Tech Parks Arizona see Global Advantage (a partnership between the Tech Parks and the Offshore Group) as the ideal collaboration to strengthen the U.S.-Israel "special relationship," visible in military operations around the world.

As reported by Todd Miller and Gabriel Schivone (2015, 6), "That mammoth security firm is ever more involved in finding 'civilian applications' for its war technologies," aggressively pushing to bring the battlefield to borderlands around the world, where the notion of *national security* serves as a prime justification for increased border enforcement, neutralizing laws while redefining borders and justice systems (Golash-Boza 2012a, 2012b, 2015; Welch 2002, 2007), as documented by Michael Welch in *Crimes of Power and States of Impunity: The U.S. Response to Terror* (2009) and *Scapegoats of September 11th: Hate Crimes and State Crimes in the War on Terror* (2006). In "Scenes from an Occupation" (2011), demographer Joseph Nevins documents that although there are multiple differences between the political, economic, and social situations of the United States and Israel, Israel-Palestine and Arizona *share* the common target of keeping out "those deemed permanent outsiders," including Palestinians, undocumented Mexicans, unauthorized Latinos from Central or South America, indigenous people from remote areas of the world, or black people from unwanted countries.

The notion of national security, however, tends to bypass the human element—with violations of international law and human rights, along with ethnic/racial profiling and brutality by immigration agents and local law enforcement (Golash-Boza 2012a, 2012b; Urbina and Álvarez 2015, 2017; Welch 2006, 2007, 2009; Whitehead 2013). Of course, as the saying goes, *Blood is thicker than water and money is thicker than both.* Violations seem to matter little when there is great profit to be made, as Brigadier General Elkabetz indicated in a 2012 border technology conference. As described by Miller and Schivone (2015, 6), in considering the aggressive move that the United States and Israel are taking in "securing" borders and patrolling borderlands, "The deals being brokered at the University of Arizona look increasingly like matches made in heaven (or perhaps in hell)." Or, as characterized by journalist Dan Cohen and colleagues, "Arizona is the Israel of the United States," and with great profits to be made, borders are being redefined to maximize profitability (Urbina and Álvarez 2016), not only in Arizona but in other border states that are likely to follow suit.

REDEFINING BORDERS: NATIONAL SECURITY OR DIVIDING COMMUNITIES?

In this new era of border security, where borders are being redefined to further expand "border enforcement," we must also question if the ultimate mission of the new regime is in fact for national security. Or is the goal to create an environment of fear, instilling a mentality of us versus them (the enemy), which then calls for even more security? If we spend a little time along the U.S.-Mexico border, we soon realize that "in the name of safeguarding the nation" (Fernández 2014, 2) the border has expanded far beyond the river, where militarized immigration enforcement is exacerbating a climate of fear and impunity. Officially, for instance, the jurisdiction of Custom and Border Protection (CBP) extends a hundred miles inward from the U.S.-Mexico border, covering a substantial segment of the nation's population along the two-thousand-mile international boundary. In fact, 197.4 million people live within the specified zone; that is, 66 percent of Americans live in areas where they are, essentially, stripped of basic constitutional rights (Kagel 2014). A closer look shows that constitution-free zones are not just at the U.S.-Mexico border, given that the zone, where CBP and Border Patrol agents patrol, extends a hundred miles inland. In fact, CBP jurisdiction envelops the entire perimeter of the United States, reaching one hundred miles inland along both coasts, the two-thousand-mile southern border, and the four-thousand-mile-long northern border.

Miller (2014) uses the 2010 Super Bowl at Sun Life Stadium in Miami, Florida, as an example of the rapidly expanding operations of border enforcement. The event used the security service of the Border Patrol, and showed how the agency can quickly "mobilize international boundaries . . . to any part of the homeland for any given reason" (Miller 2014, 19). Similarly, in *Lockdown America: Police and Prisons in the Age of Crisis* (1999, 141), Christian Parenti details how "militarized immigration enforcement . . . has been repatriated, piece by piece, to the U.S. interior." Working with local law enforcement agencies across the country, Border Patrol anti-immigrant sweeps often involve "heavily armed tactical raiding parties backed up by helicopters and dogs" (Parenti 1999, 141; Urbina and Álvarez 2015), intimidating and harassing both undocumented and documented citizens, as shown by John Whitehead in *A Government of Wolves: The Emerging American Police State* (2013).

Clearly, militarized border security functions, including surveillance and operations, are strategically designed for *mass* social control (Urbina and Álvarez 2015, 2017), as a governing mechanism to not only easily manage the population but maintain total control and dominance, while pressing and silencing the poor and minorities (Urbina and Álvarez 2016, 2017). Parenti (1999, 159), for instance, reports that racialized law enforcement practices (like the profiling of *brown* people, "Mexican"-looking people, or the harassment of anyone who looks Latino) have fueled a system of "apartheid by other means," a "de facto criminalization and political marginalization of documented and undocumented immigrants alike." Miller (2014, 260) documents how mass surveillance, intimidation, and aggressive operations amount to a "process of self-segregation" that "results in a white monopoly on public space" (Fernández 2014, 2), and, subsequently, "cleansing" to ensure that "public space—parks, libraries, streets, and hospitals—will be largely reserved for those privileged by citizenship, wealth, and, most important, whiteness" (Golash-Boza 2012a, 2015; McDowell and Wonders 2010, 68; Romero 2006).

David Lyon (1994, 2015) illustrates how the design and implementation of surveillance and social control technologies always start by targeting society's most disadvantaged population, the weakest and most marginalized groups, which normally tend to be the poor and people of color. From international boundaries and side margins, high-tech technologies, along with militarized immigration enforcement officers, move inward across the country. Beyond selected segments of society, report Craig Whitlock and Craig Timberg (2014, 1), law enforcement agencies are "increasingly borrowing border-patrol drones for domestic surveillance operations," creating "novel privacy challenges" (Finn 2011) for all citizens. In truth, as charged by some critics, "whether it's gunning down rock throwers on Mexico's side of the border or racially profiling residents of Arizona, you don't need a video-equipped drone to see that the Border Patrol is overstepping its bounds" (Fernández 2014, 3).

Since militarized immigration officials are *free* to patrol in the border zone and far into the county's interior, with the right to violate the Fourth Amendment, agents use the hundred-mile zone to enter private property, search vehicles and private possessions, and randomly or arbitrarily stop people without a warrant or probable cause (Golash-Boza 2012a, 2012b; McDowell and Wonders 2010; Michalowski 2007; Romero 2006; Stephen 2004). In 2009, for example, U.S. Senator Patrick Leahy was forced out of his vehicle 125 miles from the New York State's border, and in 2012, former Arizona governor Raul Castro, who was ninety-six years old at the time, was detained by CBP agents, who forced him out of his vehicle and to stand in ninety-degree heat for about half an hour because the immigration agents detected radiation from his pacemaker. In a recent case, Shena Gutiérrez (U.S. citizen) was detained for five hours, in a traumatizing encounter, as CBP agents interrogated her and searched through her possessions. Reportedly, agents trampled her and cuffed her so tight that Gutiérrez was left with bruises (Kagel 2014). As immigration reform is being debated and borders redefined in the name of national security, with civil liberties being pushed to the margins, U.S. militarized zones reveal that human rights violations are becoming the challenge of our times, in our own backyard.

THE PROFITABILITY OF BORDER SECURITY: THE NEW CAPITALISM

Illustrating the profitability of social control (Urbina and Álvarez 2016), in the post-9/11 era, sales of Israeli "security exports" increased from $2 billion to $7 billion annually. The equipment of Elbit Systems is now in use from Europe to America to Australia, forming a transatlantic operation in security systems. Sensing economic profits, in 2012 Arizona legislators declared their state and Israel to be natural "trade partners . . . a relationship we seek to enhance." Using Arizona as testing grounds for technology and revenue, Israel and the United States joined forces to maximize profits, deploying mechanisms to expand the "laboratory" along the U.S.-Mexico borderlands and beyond the border region. Orchestrated through Global Advantage partnership, corporate enterprises and scientists, along with others vested in the new "gold fields" of border security, exploiting Mexican low-wage manufacturing, are collaborating with Israel's homeland security companies. Global Advantage is a joint project between the University of Arizona's Tech Parks Arizona, which has scholars, lawyers, and accountants to help any foreign company set up business in the state, and Offshore Group, a business advisory and housing firm (located across the border in Mexico), offering "nearshore solutions for manufacturers of any size."

As reported by Miller and Schivone (2015, 3), the unfolding romance between Israel's high-tech companies and Arizona has been acknowledged by Tucson mayor Jonathan Rothschild: "If you go to Israel and you come to Southern Arizona and close your eyes and spin yourself a few times . . . you might not be able to tell the difference." While Arizona and Israel are separated by thousands of miles, Rothschild charges that in "economics, there are no borders" (Miller and Schivone 2015, 4). In an ironic twist on future social control, in these global developments of boundary-busting partnerships, the factories that are producing the border fortresses designed by U.S.-Israeli high-tech firms, including Elbit, will be located in Mexico, where poorly paid Mexican workers will manufacture the parts of a rapidly expanding surveillance regime, "which may well help locate, detain, arrest, incarcerate, and expel some of them if they try to cross into the United States" (Miller and Schivone 2015, 4). The optimism and success of Global Advantage's Israel Business Initiative is evident, as already ten to twenty Israeli companies are in discussion about joining the transatlantic homeland security and border program, whose operation resembles a multinational assembly line.

Talking from a conference room in the 1,345-acre park on the southern outskirts of Tucson, Bruce Wright, CEO of Tech Parks Arizona, predicted that the Homeland Security market would grow from a $51 billion annual business in 2012 to $81 billion in the United States alone by 2020, and $544 billion worldwide by 2018 (Miller and Schivone 2015, 4), clearly illustrating the profitability of social control on the global scale, as recently documented by Urbina and Álvarez in "Neoliberalism, Criminal Justice, and Latinos: The Contours of Neoliberal Economic Thought and Policy on Criminalization" (2016). Some critics charge that this unprecedented growth is being fueled by an "unheralded shift" to strategic and aggressive use of drone surveillance in the U.S.-Mexico border region (Associated Press 2014; Urbina and Álvarez 2015;

see also Golash-Boza 2012a, 2015). Reportedly, more than ten thousand drone flights were launched in the border region air space between March 2013 and November 2014, with flights to drastically increase, particularly after the Border Patrol doubles its aerial fleet (Miller and Schivone 2015). Obviously all who are invested are well aware that the Arizona laboratory *park* is sitting atop a twenty-first-century gold mine. In another ironic twist, the ocean-to-ocean Mexican border is simply replacing the highly marketed Palestinian testing border region, and Mexicans, now characterized as "terrorists," will be the twenty-first-century precious (low-cost) laborers for the multibillion dollar American-Israeli empire. According to Wright, "If we're going to be in bed with the border on a day-to-day basis, with all of its problems and issues, and there's a solution to it . . . why shouldn't we be the place where the issue is solved and we get the commercial benefit from it" (Miller and Schivone 2015, 5).

IMMIGRANTS IN THE NEW LABOR FORCE: THE NEW SLAVES OF AMERICA

While private corporations, government officials investing in private companies, government agencies (federal funds), and employees (payroll) are benefiting, *immigrants are being transformed into the new slaves of America* (Urbina and Álvarez 2016), as recently documented by Julia O'Connell Davidson in *Modern Slavery: The Margins of Freedom* (2015). In "Using Jailed Migrants as a Pool of Cheap Labor," Ian Urbina (2014) reports that U.S. Immigration and Customs Enforcement (ICE) and its subcontractors relied on the labor of more than sixty thousand immigrant workers in 2013 alone to clean, cook, do laundry, and prepare meals for other government institutions while being kept behind locked doors and barbed-wire fences and walls. Immigrants working in the federal government's detention centers across the country were paid one dollar per day, and in some cases, ICE simply "compensated" immigrant laborers with sodas and candy bars. Worse, as reported by Carl Takei of the American Civil Liberties Union, "the U.S. government treats detained immigrants like slaves" (2014). In one facility, people who organized a hunger strike to stop the exploitation and brutality were "thrown into solitary confinement" (Takei 2014, 1).

As with the financial benefits for Arizona by providing testing grounds for border security systems, imprisonment profits are obvious. According to some figures, when immigrants in labor detention centers are paid thirteen cents an hour (others work for free or are paid with sodas or candy bars), the U.S. government and partnering private companies save over $40 million a year, and avoid having to pay outside contractors the federal minimum wage of $7.25 (Davidson 2015; Urbina 2014). On any given day, around 5,500 immigrant detainees (of the 30,000-plus average daily immigrant population) work for one dollar in 55 of the approximately 250 facilities, with local governments operating 21 of the programs and for-profit private companies operating the remaining detention centers. Other figures show that more than 135,000 immigrants a year may be involved in prison labor (to some degree), and thus the U.S. government and for-profit private prison companies may be avoiding paying more than $200 million in wages (Urbina 2014). The two largest for-profit companies reveal the profitability of prison labor. Some figures show that the revenue of Corrections Corporation of America (CCA) increased more than 60 percent between 2000 and 2010, with its stock price climbing to more than thirty dollars from less than three dollars, and in 2013 CCA made $301 million in net revenue, while GEO Group made $115 million (Urbina 2014).

Unlike state or federal inmates convicted of some type of crime, who often voluntarily participate in prison work programs (and forfeit their rights to wage protections), detained immigrants are civil detainees placed in immigration facilities, with the majority awaiting deportation or a hearing before an immigration judge to determine their legal status, a process that may take months or years. Reportedly, about half of the people who appear before an immigration court are ultimately allowed to remain in the United States, typically because they were in the country legally, they provide a compelling humanitarian argument, or immigration authorities decide not to pursue their case, by which point, though, immigrants have served time in detention centers.

The federal government and the private prison companies that run many of the facilities are bending or manipulating the rules to convert a captive population into a self-contained low-paid labor force, where immigrant workers are simply administrative detainees in the agency's growing network of approximately 250 immigration detention facilities across the country. They perform the labor that keeps immigration detention facilities operating, at minimal cost, while maximizing profits of social control (Urbina and Álvarez 2016, 2017). While lawmakers and other anti-immigrant critics rail against immigrants and immigration authorities target undocumented immigrants, prohibiting them from working elsewhere and forbidding businesses to hire them, the U.S. government is relying on thousands of immigrants each year to provide cheap labor (usually for one dollar a day or less) at facilities where they are being held after their capture by authorities, making the U.S. government, ironically, the largest employer of undocumented immigrants in the country (Urbina 2014; Urbina and Álvarez 2016).

According to government officials, detainees working in facilities are not officially employees, as their payments are stipends, not wages, and no one is forced to work. However, a 2012 report by the American Civil Liberties Union described immigrants being threatened with solitary confinement if they refused to work. According to

Jacqueline Stevens, professor at Northwestern University, the program is violating the Thirteenth Amendment, which abolished slavery and involuntary servitude (except when applied as punishment for crimes), declaring that "by law, firms contracting with the federal government are supposed to match or increase local wages, not commit wage theft" (Urbina 2014, 4). Clayton J. Mosher, professor at Washington State University, who specializes in the economics of the prison industry, adds that immigration detention centers are low-margin businesses, where every cent counts to maximize profits (Urbina 2014), reminiscent of the historical profitability of slave labor and the convict labor system. In fact, the "convict lease" system is the historical antecedent of the modern private prison industry and the ICE detainee labor program. Like the "freed" slaves arrested for supposedly violating newly created vagrancy laws (or, in another twist, even for seeking better jobs) after the Civil War, in the twenty-first century many of the more than 400,000 people swept into immigration facilities each year are locked behind bars for one justifiable reason—lack of documentation—under exploitive conditions and often without due process (Bosworth and Kaufman 2011; Golash-Boza 2012b; Takei 2014; Urbina 2014), as explained by Donna Selma and Paul Leighton in *Punishment for Sale: Private Prisons, Big Business, and the Incarceration Binge* (2010).

IMMIGRANT LABORERS OUTSIDE DETENTION CENTERS: THE QUESTION OF TAXES—WHO'S MAKING THE PROFIT?

For documented immigrants who manage to avoid apprehension and detention and are able to find employment, a central argument is about taxes, with anti-immigrant critics passionately arguing that "illegals don't pay taxes." The Federation for American Immigration Reform (FAIR), a conservative anti-immigrants group, has reported that the 2010 cost of undocumented immigration at the local, state, and federal level was about $113 billion, with nearly $29 billion at the federal level and $84 billion at the state and local level, and charged that taxes paid by undocumented immigrants "do not come close to the level of expenditures" by the U.S. government for undocumented workers. Multiple studies, though, show that undocumented workers not only pay their "share" of taxes, but are economically exploited, along with the physical exploitation of working in low-paying jobs under oppressive conditions (Chomsky 2007; Gomberg-Muñoz 2011; Lipman 2006; Negi et al. 2013). For instance, a recent nationwide study on the fiscal implications of undocumented immigration concludes that millions of undocumented immigrants are paying billions of dollars in taxes into state and local reserves, and that substantially more would be generated if President

Obama's executive orders preventing many workers from being deported had not been undone by President Trump (Gardner, Johnson, and Wiehe 2015). Even if FAIR's numbers are correct, one can argue that with immigration reform not only would state and local tax contributions increase, but billions less would need to be spent on border security and immigration enforcement in general.

The fifty-state analysis by the Institute on Taxation and Economic Policy (ITEP), a nonprofit, nonpartisan research organization that works on local, state, and federal tax policy issues, found that about 8.1 million of 11.4 million undocumented immigrants paid more than $11.8 billion in local and state taxes in 2012 (not including paid federal taxes), which includes $1.1 billion in personal income taxes, $3.6 billion in property taxes, and $7 billion in sales and excise taxes. The study shows that undocumented immigrants paid an average local and state tax rate of 8 percent in 2012, higher than the 5.4 percent paid by the top one percent of taxpayers. Tax contributions from undocumented immigrants ranged from less than $3.2 million in the state of Montana (with an estimated undocumented population of six thousand) to more than $3.2 billion in California, with more than 3.1 million undocumented immigrants. Nationally, according to the researchers, "The reality is the 11.4 million undocumented immigrants living in the United States pay billions of dollars in local, state, and federal taxes, and their tax contributions would increase under immigration policy reform" (Gardner, Johnson, and Wiehe 2015, 1). Further, the authors of the study estimate that undocumented immigrants' combined nationwide local and state tax contributions would increase by $845 million under Obama's 2012 and 2014 executive orders and by $2.2 billion under broad comprehensive immigration reform (Gardner, Johnson, and Wiehe 2015). Emphasizing the economic benefits of reforming the country's immigration laws, President Obama has noted that low-skilled immigrant workers in agriculture also boost the economy by increasing work for U.S. citizens in other labor sectors, such as transportation and marketing. For the executive director of ITEP, Matthew Gardner, "The numbers alone make a compelling case for reform. . . . This analysis shows that undocumented immigrants already are paying billions in taxes to state and local governments, and if they are allowed to work in the country legally, their state and local tax contributions would considerably increase" (Gardner, Johnson, and Wiehe 2015; Pianin 2015, 1).

To be sure, the government itself admits the substantial economic contributions of undocumented people. Stephen Goss of the U.S. Social Security Administration estimates that 3.1 million undocumented workers pay into Social Security each year (Goodkind 2013). In 2010 alone, undocumented immigrants (and their employers) paid $15 billion into Social Security, while undocumented workers received only $1 billion back in 2010. Goss estimates that about $150 billion in undocumented workers' money has been funneled into the Social Security trust fund, constituting about 8 percent of the total $1.7 trillion that Social Security has in reserves. In fact, according to Goss, if it was not for the millions of undocumented workers paying into Social Security in 2010 alone, the Social Security system would have "entered persistent shortfall of tax revenue to cover [payouts] starting [in] 2009" (Goodkind 2013, 1). For those who wonder how undocumented workers pay or collect Social Security, some immigrants are issued Social Security numbers with their student visa (or some other type of temporary visa), others forge documents issued by Social Security before the screening process was tightened after 9/11, some steal numbers, others pay people who specialize in fabricating Social Security numbers, and some simply fabricate the numbers themselves.

Some critics, however, argue that legalizing undocumented immigrants will not enhance Social Security. For instance, Mark Krikorian, executive director of the Center for Immigration Studies (a conservative anti-immigrants organization), charges that "if they're legalized then they can collect Social Security and guess what? People with low incomes get more out of Social Security, generally speaking, than they pay in. So the Social Security argument is actually an argument for keeping illegal immigrants illegal because that way they won't ever collect Social Security" (Goodkind 2013, 2). Of course, the exploitation of immigrant workers is well documented, as undocumented immigrants typically earn lower wages, with some figures showing that the average undocumented immigrant earns about $17,000 less a year than their documented counterparts. Others, however, argue that documenting immigrants (via working permits or amnesty) should not be viewed as an opportunity to continue with labor exploitation, as suggested by Krikorian and others, but as an opportunity to train and educate workers, while securing better working conditions and higher wages for individual workers and their young children, who often work side by side with them (Urbina and Álvarez 2015; Urbina and Wright 2016). As reported by Edward Alden of the Council on Foreign Relations, with properly situated mechanisms, granting amnesty would actually lead to higher wages, allowing undocumented workers to pay more toward Social Security. Further exposing the daily realities of undocumented workers, Alden declares, "You have people who are often working in very low wage jobs [and] because they're uncertain about their status they're scared.... So these people generally, the analysis shows their wages will go up, they're going to pay more into the Social Security system. The CBO has run these numbers, in the short-run there's a big boost for the Social Security system" (Goodkind 2013, 3). Increased revenue from immigrants, according to Alden, will help rescue Social Security. As for possible "rescue" figures, in 2007 the Congressional Budget Office projected that granting amnesty to undocumented immigrants would actually increase Social Security funds $57 billion by 2017, and, as noted above, Stephen Goss of the Social Security Administration has also stated that amnesty would more than double the number of immigrants paying into Social Security. All in all, if Social Security has been going through grave crises and is likely to collapse in the future, immigrants might be the salvation to possible bankruptcy, and with thousands of baby boomers entering retirement and thousands approaching retirement, Latino immigrants (undocumented and documented) will be the *driving engine in the U.S. labor force* (Urbina and Álvarez 2015; Urbina and Wright 2016).

CONCLUSION

As U.S. intervention abroad in places like Afghanistan and Iraq winds down, the federal government in multimillion-dollar joint ventures with transnational corporations are bringing the battlefield to the American border—conveniently and strategically, the U.S.-Mexico border. In the context of immigration and social control, U.S. public policies that have historically driven anti-immigrant movements, enforcement, sentiment, and discourse have been politically driven and financially motivated, with targeted motives underneath it all, as explained in the conclusion to this volume. Additionally, in the twists and turns of immigration, undocumented (and documented) immigrants have historically been scapegoated for the country's problems, particularly during economic crises and during elections. Worse, using highly charged anti-immigrants rhetoric, in an effort to rally mainstream America and obtain votes, politicians present myths as facts in order to instill public fears, while persuading lawmakers and the American society that the U.S.-Mexico border needs heightened surveillance and enforcement—resulting in redefined borders and divided communities.

Borders and accompanying walls or fences between people, whether in a neighborhood, city, state, city, or at an international boundary, emanate from society's internalization of an us-versus-them mentality that justifies increased border enforcement, a militarized U.S.-Mexico border region, violations of civil liberties, ethnic/racial profiling, displacement of immigrants, state repression, exploitation of immigrants, and the perpetuation of political, academic, military, and corporate power structures. While American attitudes about the security of the U.S.-Mexico border may not have changed much over the past several years, according to the Pew Research Center (2015), there is one grave figure that has significantly increased in response to the government's increased border protection since 1994, escalating after 9/11. Militarized urban areas where immigrants traditionally crossed has resulted a "funnel effect," forcing immigrants to use more dangerous terrain, often guided by coyotes who sometimes exploit, abuse, rape, or murder them. For instance, there was an average of twelve deaths annually between 1990 and 1999 in southern Arizona alone, but after 9/11 (between 2000 and 2014) more than six thousand people died trying to cross the *dream* border (or perhaps the *nightmare* border), an average of about 163 deaths annually (Orduna 2014).

The influx of federal immigration agents and high-tech surveillance systems, with their aggressive national security mission, will not be limited to the U.S.-Mexico border, where the Homeland Security presence is becoming an occupying army, stretching inland on both sides of the international boundary. As immigration laws become more *illusive* along the border, the federal government is strategically bringing the battlefield to our states, our cities, our neighborhoods. Anti-immigrant critics and those vested in economic profits or public office, try to justify their proposed actions by using sensational terms, like *illegals, wetbacks, criminal aliens, terrorists, narco-terrorists, they take our jobs,* and *they don't pay taxes,* charges that are further sensationalized by the media. In fact, as the current transatlantic joint border security operations indicate, along with the unprecedented number of deportations, the militarization of the southern border is rapidly advancing into the country interior. Yet, in another ironic twist, since everything indicates that Americans will never be satisfied with increased levels of security along the U.S.-Mexico border region, the security empire will continue to grow, like a well-grounded organism, swallowing anything and everything that gets in the way. Already occurring in Arizona and other areas along the border (and even in the interior), if you are, or simply appear, foreign, watch out for La Migra. As the saying goes, when all you have is a hammer, everything looks like a nail.

REFERENCES

Associated Press. 2014. "Drones Patrol Nearly Half of US-Mexico Border in Shift Targeting Remote Areas." *Fox News U.S.,* November 12. http://www.foxnews.com/us/2014/11/12/ap -exclusive-drones-patrol-nearly-half-us-mexico-border-in-shift-targeting.html.

Balko, R. 2013. *Rise of the Warrior Cop: The Militarization of America's Police Forces.* New York: PublicAffairs.

Black, T. 2015. "The Latest Border Control: Iraq War Blimps." *Bloomberg,* February 10. http:// www.bloomberg.com/news/articles/2015-02-10/blimps-from-taliban-watch-now-block-u -s-mexico-border-smugglers.

Bosworth, M., and E. Kaufman. 2011. "Foreigners in a Carceral Age: Immigration and Imprisonment in the U.S." *Stanford Law and Policy Review* 22, pt. 2 (2011): 429–54.

Chomsky, A. 2007. *"They Take Our Jobs!": And 20 Other Myths About Immigration.* Boston: Beacon Press.

Davidson, J. O. 2015. *Modern Slavery: The Margins of Freedom.* London: Palgrave Macmillan.

Dunn, T. J. 1996. *The Militarization of the U.S.-Mexico Border 1978–1992: Low-Intensity Conflict Doctrine Comes Home.* Austin: University of Texas Press.

Fernández, B. 2014. "The Creeping Expansion of the Border Patrol." *Al Jazerra America*, May 7. http://america.aljazeera.com/opinions/2014/5/border-patrol-immigrationmilitarizationhomelandsecurity.html.

Finn, P. 2011. "Domestic Use of Aerial Drones by Law Enforcement Likely to Prompt Privacy Debate." *Washington Post*, January 22. http://www.washingtonpost.com/wp-dyn/content/article/2011/01/22/AR2011012204111.html.

Gardner, M., S. Johnson, and M. Wiehe. 2015. "Undocumented Immigrants' State and Local Tax Contributions." Washington, D.C.: Institute on Taxation and Economic Policy.

Golash-Boza, T. M. 2012a. *Immigration Nation: Raids, Detentions, and Deportations in Post-9/11 America*. New York: Routledge.

———. 2012b. *Due Process Denied: Detentions and Deportations in the United States*. New York: Routledge.

———. 2015. *Deported: Policing Immigrants, Disposable Labor and Global Capitalism*. New York: New York University Press.

Gomberg-Muñoz, R. 2011. *Labor and Legality: An Ethnography of a Mexican Immigrant Network*. New York: Oxford University Press.

Goodkind, N. 2013. "Immigration Reform Could Cost Social Security Billions." *Yahoo! Finance*, March 14. http://finance.yahoo.com/blogs/daily-ticker/social-security-risk-impact-immigration-reform-124712696.html.

Johnson, J. 2012. "A Palestine-Mexico Border." *NACLA*, June 29. https://nacla.org/blog/2012/6/29/palestine-mexico-border.

Kagel, J. 2014. "There's Something Scary Happening on the Left Side of This Picture." *Mic*, July 20. http://mic.com/articles/94032/there-s-something-scary-happening-on-the-left-side-of-this-picture#.paI2MbnMb.

Klein, N. 2007. *The Shock Doctrine: The Rise of Disaster Capitalism*. New York: Picador.

Kraska, P. B., and V. E. Kappeler. 1997. "Militarizing American Police: The Rise and Normalization of Paramilitary Units." *Social Problems* 44: 1–18.

Lipman, F. 2006. "The Taxation of Undocumented Immigrants: Separate, Unequal, and Without Representation." *Harvard Latino Law Review* 9: 1–58.

Lyon, D. 1994. *The Electronic Eye: The Rise of Surveillance Society*. Minneapolis: University of Minnesota Press.

McDowell, M., and N. A. Wonders. 2010. "Keeping Migrants in Their Place: Technologies of Control and Racialized Public Space in Arizona." *Social Justice* 36: 54–72.

Michalowski, R. J. 2007. "Border Militarization and Migrant Suffering: A Case of Transnational Inquiry." *Social Justice* 34: 60–72.

Miller, T. 2014. *Border Patrol Nation: Dispatches from the Front Lines of Homeland Security*. San Francisco, Calif.: City Lights.

Miller, T., and G. Schivone. 2015. "Gaza in Arizona: The Secret Militarization of the U.S.-Mexico Border." *Salon*, February 1. http://www.salon.com/2015/02/01/gaza_in_arizona_the_secret_militarization_of_the_u_s_mexico_border_partner/.

Negi, N. J., L. Michalopoulos, J. Boyas, and A. Overdorff. 2013. "Social Networks That Promote Well-Being Among Latino Migrant Day Laborers." *Advances in Social Work* 14: 247–59.

Nevins, J. 2011. "Scenes from an Occupation." *Dissident Voice*, May 20. http://dissidentvoice.org/2011/05/scenes-from-an-occupation/.

Orduna, J. 2014. "Tasers, Drones, and Cold Chicken: Inside the Multibillion-Dollar Business of Keeping Me Out of America." *BuzzFeed*, December 18. http://www.buzzfeed.com/josemorduna/inside-the-multibillion-dollar-business-of-keeping-me-out-of#.htD4d65wb.

Parenti, C. 1999. *Lockdown America: Police and Prisons in the Age of Crisis*. New York: Verso.

Pew Research Center. 2015. "On Immigration Policy, Wider Partisan Divide over Border Fence Than Path to Legal Status." *Pew Research Center*, October 18. http://www.people-press.org/2015/10/08/on-immigration-policy-wider-partisan-divide-over-border-fence-than-path-to-legal-status/.

Pianin, E. 2015. "Study Finds Illegal Immigrants Pay $11.8b in Taxes." *Fiscal Times*, April 16. http://www.thefiscaltimes.com/2015/04/16/Study-Finds-Illegal-Immigrants-Pay-118B-Taxes.

Romero, M. 2006. "Racial Profiling and Immigration Enforcement: Rounding Up of Usual Suspects in the Latino Community." *Critical Sociology* 32: 447–72.

Selma, D., and P. Leighton. 2010. *Punishment for Sale: Private Prisons, Big Business, and the Incarceration Binge*. Lanham, Md.: Rowman and Littlefield.

Stephen, L. 2004. "The Gaze of Surveillance in the Lives of Mexican Immigrant Workers." *Development* 47: 97–102.

Takei, C. 2014. "The U.S. Government Treats Detained Immigrants Like Slaves." *ACLU*, May 28. https://www.aclu.org/blog/us-government-treats-detained-immigrants-slaves.

Urbina, I. 2014. "Using Jailed Migrants as a Pool of Cheap Labor." *New York Times*, May 25. http://www.nytimes.com/2014/05/25/us/using-jailed-migrants-as-a-pool-of-cheap-labor.html?_r=0.

Urbina, M. G., and S. E. Álvarez, eds. 2015. *Latino Police Officers in the United States: An Examination of Emerging Trends and Issues*. Springfield, Ill.: Charles C Thomas.

———. 2016. "Neoliberalism, Criminal Justice, and Latinos: The Contours of Neoliberal Economic Thought and Policy on Criminalization." *Latino Studies* 14: 33–58.

———. 2017. *Ethnicity and Criminal Justice in the Era of Mass Incarceration: A Critical Reader on the Latino Experience*. Springfield, Ill.: Charles C Thomas.

Urbina, M. G., and C. R. Wright. 2016. *Latino Access to Higher Education: Ethnic Realities and New Directions for the Twenty-First Century*. Springfield, Ill.: Charles C Thomas.

Welch, M. 2002. *Detained: Immigration Laws and the Expanding I.N.S. Jail Complex*. Philadelphia: Temple University Press.

———. 2006. *Scapegoats of September 11th: Hate Crimes and State Crimes in the War on Terror.* New Brunswick, N.J.: Rutgers University Press.

———. 2007. "Immigration Lockdown Before and After 9/11: Ethnic Constructions and Their Consequences." In *Race, Gender, and Punishment: From Colonialism to the War on Terror,* edited by M. Bosworth and J. Flavin, 149–63. Piscataway, N.J.: Rutgers University Press.

———. 2009. *Crimes of Power and States of Impunity: The U.S. Response to Terror.* New Brunswick, N.J.: Rutgers University Press.

Whitehead, J. 2013. *A Government of Wolves: The Emerging American Police State.* New York: SelectBooks.

Whitlock, C., and C. Timberg. 2014. "Border-Patrol Drones Being Borrowed by Other Agencies More Often Than Previously Known." *Washington Post,* January 14. https://www.washingtonpost.com/world/national-security/border-patrol-drones-being-borrowed-by-other-agencies-more-often-than-previously-known/2014/01/14/5f987af0-7d49-11e3-9556-4a4bf7bcbd84_story.html.

Conclusion

IMMIGRATION LAWS AND SOCIAL CONTROL MOVEMENTS

Situating the Realities of Immigration in the Twenty-First Century

MARTIN GUEVARA URBINA AND SOFÍA ESPINOZA ÁLVAREZ

> They came first for the Communists, and I didn't speak up
> because I wasn't a Communist. Then they came for the Jews, and
> I didn't speak up because I wasn't a Jew. Then they came for the
> trade unionists, and I didn't speak up because I wasn't a trade
> unionist. Then they came for me and by that time no one was left
> to speak up.
>
> —PASTOR MARTIN NIEMÖLLER

IN FEBRUARY 2013, captured on video, a Native American man forcibly expressed his emotions and thoughts on the highly controversial dilemma of immigration by criticizing protesters at an Arizona anti-immigrants rally. He called Europeans the real "illegals" for invading his country, manipulating and killing Native Americans as they settled in the territory and tried to gain total control of the native population. "You're all fucking illegal. You're all illegal," the Native American man yelled at protesters, who had gathered in Tucson, Arizona, to express their opposition to undocumented immigration. "We didn't invite none of you here. We're the only Native Americans here.... Get on with your bogus arguments. We're the only legal ones here," he shouted. One protestor who was carrying a small American flag and an anti-immigrants sign became the target of the Native American's scolding. "We should have put that sign up when you sons-of-bitches came," the counterprotestor declared. Pointing toward the American flag held by one protester, the Native American charged that it [the colors] "represents blood spilled by Native Americans, protecting this land from the invaders. You don't want to hear the God damn truth! Get on, bitch! All the Native Americans you killed, you plant your houses here. That's the truth. That's what [the American] flag stands for—all the Native Americans you killed to plant your houses here. . . . That's the truth."

As detailed in the preceding chapters, immigration predates the U.S. Constitution, and immigration laws, enforcement, and discourse have been swinging back and forth, like a pendulum, propelled by the interactions of multiple forces, from politics to economics to racism to control and dominance. During the last several years, particularly during election time, immigration has been the *litmus test* for lawmakers and other anti-immigrant critics who aggressively charge that undocumented people are "taking over America." With shifts in demographics, of course, there are more immigrants living in the United States than in previous decades; however, the percentage of new immigrants in the overall population is proportionate to historical waves of immigrants from the 1850s to 1880s and from the 1900s to 1930s. Today, in the early part of the twenty-first century, there are an estimated ten to twelve million undocumented immigrants in the country, accounting for approximately 3 percent of the U.S. population.

This 3 percent, though, have been profiled, stereotyped, demonized, criminalized, and sanctioned. The undocumented are accused of being not only an economic threat but a security one, and thus posing a serious threat in all facets of social life. In truth, the many myths about undocumented people tend to clash with reality. Consider the criminality thesis, a central element of immigration discourse. In truth, U.S. citizens are more likely to commit crimes than both undocumented and documented immigrants (Bailey and Hayes 2006; Butcher and Piehl 2007; Morín 2009; Rumbaut and Ewing 2007). As for the severity of criminality, studies also show that undocumented immigrants are less likely than native-born citizens to commit both nonviolent and violent crime. According to Leo Anchondo (2010), recently arrived immigrants focus on securing employment and are cautious to avoid illegal activities and encounters with law enforcement; therefore, they are unlikely to be involved in crime, and teenage immigrants are less likely than native-born teens to be involved in drug use, violence, or other delinquent behavior. A lingering question, then, becomes even more pressing: Why is the United States, supposedly the most powerful country in the world, declaring a multibillion-dollar war to ward off 3 percent of the population, the undocumented laborers who are among the most vulnerable, exploited, oppressed, and marginalized segments of society?

SOCIAL CONTROL MOVEMENTS AND THEIR CONSEQUENCES

A comprehensive analysis of the immigration discourse also requires an appreciation of how global structural, political, cultural, and ideological forces govern immigration laws, deportations, the criminalization process, and punishment. As documented by Sofía Espinoza Álvarez (2012), starting in the early 1980s, a series of punitive social control movements, like *the war on drugs, the war on immigrants, and the war on terrorism*, not only significantly influenced the nature of social control, but situated it on a global scale, while redefining the legal, political, and social parameters of social control.

Toward the end of the twentieth century, Jonathan Simon (1997, 173) proposed that advanced industrial societies were actually "governed through crime," with the overdeveloped societies of the West and North Atlantic "experiencing not a crisis of crime and punishment but a crisis of governance that has led [them] to prioritize crime and punishment as the preferred contexts of governance," redefining the limits of criminal and immigration laws, while socially reconstructing the confines of race and ethnicity. Then, at the turn of the century, Tony Fitzpatrick (2001, 220) argued that as "global capital becomes apparently unmanageable" and "as the polity and the economic detached after a century of alignment," the state must give itself, particularly its agents, something to do, and so the state "socially and discursively constructs threats that only it can address through . . . punitive responses to the chaos it has [helped facilitate]," as in the case of the war on drugs, the war on terrorism, and the war on immigrants. With crime and criminal justice systems becoming increasingly transnational, assisted by advanced technological innovations and a highly charged American media, "at once totalizing and individualizing," such strategies coalesce in appealing political formations that can govern "all and each" with stealthy precision (Gordon 1991, 3), giving the state of the appearance of absolute control, legitimacy, and justice, and to a fearful and mal-informed society an appearance of global power and solidarity.

These social control movements, though, have been driven just as much by a historical desire for revenge, conquest, control, dominance, and global expansion as by a defined mission for unity, safety, equality, and justice, with grave consequences for certain segments of society. As documented by various scholars, social control movements fuel border militarization, ethnic/racial profiling, intimidation, harassment, and violence against immigrants, violation of civil rights, widespread deportations and detentions, and intrusive government surveillance on both the undocumented and U.S. citizens. In fact, both the war on terror and the war on drugs have increasingly become a war against immigrant and minority communities. Kelly Lytle (2003, 5), for instance, reports that the war on drugs led to the militarization of the U.S.-Mexico border, and a change in focus from *wetbacks* to *border violators*: "the day of the Wetback was over . . . the day of the border violator, a fugitive in a foreign country had arrived . . . the beginnings of rhetoric within the U.S.-Mexico borderlands that criminalized undocumented Mexican immigrants." According to law professor David Cole

(2001, 248), "Racial profiling studies . . . make clear that the war on drugs has largely been a war on minorities. It is, after all, drug enforcement that motivates most racial profiling." As for the war on terrorism, the American Civil Liberties Union reports that "the war on terror has quickly turned into a war on immigrants."

The resulting implications and consequences, however, are often brushed aside as unavoidable "side effects" or the price of doing business for keeping "illegals" out to secure our borders. Comprehensive immigration reform, though, requires a critical examination of the most consequential outcomes of social control movements. What follows then, is a brief analysis of three crucial consequences of the latest anti-immigrants movement: criminalization, the Border Patrol's use of deadly force, and lack of law enforcement accountability.

CRIMINALIZATION: IMMIGRATION, CONVICTIONS, AND DEPORTATIONS

To begin, as documented in previous chapters, like the war on drugs and the war on terrorism, the war on immigrants drives not only mass deportations but also criminalization and subsequently mass incarceration (Álvarez 2012; Robelo 2014; Urbina 2018; Urbina and Álvarez 2016, 2017; Welch 2002, 2006, 2009). Among the many questions is, What actually becomes of the immigrants who are deported to their country of origin? Of course, in their long journey to and from the United States, they are first disappeared in the growing for-profit detention and prison systems, with many awaiting a court hearing, then sent back to their countries of origin, where they may no longer have any ties to family, friends, or community, may lack survival necessities (like food, housing, education opportunities, and health services), and face serious threats to their security as they try to settle and reintegrate into their communities. As for immigrants who are removed from the country, they are usually barred from reentry, sometimes for life, no matter if they have decades-long ties to their communities of residence in the States or family members (including children) who are U.S. citizens, resulting in thousands of broken families and fragmented communities every single year.

A major feature of criminalization has been the mass convictions of immigrants, further fueling deportations. A 2014 study by the Transactional Records Access Clearinghouse at Syracuse University found that every year from 2008 to 2013 about 40,000 people were deported for drug law violations (TRAC Immigration). By these figures, nearly 250,000 people were deported for nonviolent drug offenses in just six years. In another study, "The Rise of Federal Immigration Crimes: Unlawful Reentry Drives Growth," Michael Light, Mark Hugo López, and Ana Gonzalez-Barrera (2014) report that between 1992 and 2012, the number of *reentry* convictions increased by a factor of twenty-eight (twenty-eight-fold), rising from 690 to 19,463 cases and accounting for nearly half (48 percent) of the growth in the total number of people sentenced in federal courts. The second highest increase in convictions was for drug offenses, accounting for 22 percent of the growth, and of those sentenced, "nearly all" were given a prison sentence. In fact, according to Grace Meng of Human Rights Watch in *A Price Too High: US Families Torn Apart by Deportations for Drug Offenses* (2015, 6–7), more than 260,000 foreign nationals convicted for drug offenses were deported from 2007 to 2012: "Deportations of non-citizens whose most serious conviction was for a drug offense increased 22 percent from 2007 to 2012, totaling more than 260,000 deportations over the same period. Deportations for non-citizens with convictions for drug possession increased 43 percent. ICE claims that it does not keep track of whether these individuals were lawful permanent residents or undocumented immigrants. But, as detailed in this report, the U.S. is deporting a significant number of both permanent residents and undocumented individuals with strong family and community ties to the U.S., often for minor or old drug offenses."

Clearly, given the devastating effects on these vulnerable offenders, comprehensive reform in both immigration and drug policies is long overdue. As reported by Armando Gudino, policy manager for the California Drug Policy Alliance: "The failures of drug policy disproportionately affect communities of color, including immigrants. . . . The broader movement to reform the sentencing and prosecution of minor drug crimes must include efforts to end mass deportations for such offenses" (Chardy 2015, 2). Indeed, sensing the harm to thousands of people who are being swept into the net, in 2015 (and again in 2017), the U.S. Department of Justice announced new initiatives and reforms to partially address drug convictions; half of the more than 200,000 people in federal prisons are incarcerated for drug charges. Similarly, several states are enacting broad reforms, providing judges with more discretion in sentencing drug offenders and decriminalizing and even legalizing possession of marijuana (Chardy 2015; Meng 2015).

THE BORDER PATROL'S USE OF DEADLY FORCE

Until recently, Americans tended to associate police harassment, brutality, or deadly force with police forces in foreign counties, like our neighbor to the south. In truth, police brutality and deadly force have been routine practices since the advent of law enforcement organizations in America (Alpert and Dunham 2004; Bayley and Mendelsohn 1969; Escobar 1999; Fyfe 1981; Morales 1972; Skolnick and Fyfe 1993), as historically documented by Samuel Walker in *Popular Justice: A History of American*

Criminal Justice (1998) and Jerome Skolnick in *Justice Without Trial: Law Enforcement in Democratic Society* (2011). Some critics, though, charge that not only are we hearing more about police practice nowadays owing to technological advances, including the social media, but that police violence has increased against certain segments of society and in some cases has grown out of control (Aguirre-Molina 2014; Applebome 2012; Balko 2006; Barlow and Barlow 2012; Durán 2009; Holmes 1998, 2000; Human Rights Watch 1998; Jacobs and O'Brien 1998; Kane and White 2013; Pew Research Center 2014; Russell 1998; Smith and Holmes 2003; Urbina and Álvarez 2015, 2017; Whitehead 2013).

As for immigration law enforcement officers, the Border Patrol has been criticized for a series of killings of Mexican nationals, which in fact has been going on for years (Urbina and Álvarez 2015). In an effort to expose the nature of border policing, in 2012 the American Civil Liberties Union presented a list of alleged human rights violations in the U.S.-Mexico border region before the U.N. General Assembly, citing eighteen people who died from alleged excessive force by Border Patrol agents since 2010. According to multiple accounts, agents have deliberately stepped in the path of moving vehicles to justify shooting drivers, and they have fired at people for throwing rocks from the Mexican side of the border. For instance, in one recent independent review of sixty-seven cases that resulted in nineteen deaths, from January 2010 to October 2012, law enforcement experts criticized the Border Patrol for "lack of diligence" in investigating immigration agents who had fired their weapons and that it was unclear whether the agency "consistently and thoroughly reviews" use-of-deadly-force incidents, which are appearing more and more like routine behavior and not isolated accidental incidents (Police Executive Research Forum 2013, 4).

A Homeland Security Office of Inspector General report shows that border agents opened fire on Mexican rock throwers twenty-two times in fiscal year 2012; it was not reported how many people were injured by the "rock assaults" or "returning" gunfire. Among the multiple incidents, on October 2012, Jose Antonio Elena Rodriguez, sixteen, was shot and killed near Nogales, Mexico, by a Border Patrol agent who fired through a fence. The agency reported that the immigration agent was hit with rocks when he was responding to reports of drug smugglers climbing the border fence, but the autopsy revealed that Rodriguez was shot eight times in the back (Bennett 2014). Lawyers for the mother of the Mexican teenager filed a U.S. federal civil rights lawsuit on July 2014, calling the killing "brazen and lawless" and one of the many examples of agents using excessive force. The lawsuit filed in U.S. District Court in Tucson by the American Civil Liberties Union states that U.S. Border Patrol agents unjustifiably fired fourteen shots, violating the constitutional rights of the juvenile. The lawsuit asked for a jury trial and unspecified damages against an undetermined number of agents. In an atypical case, on September 2015, the agent, Lonnie Swartz, was indicted by a federal grand jury for second-degree murder, while the federal civil rights lawsuit is still pending. The trial was originally slated for November 2015, but the trial was delayed five times throughout 2016 and 2017.

For years, civil rights activists, police reformers, Mexican authorities, and others vested in social justice have complained that U.S. immigration agents who intimidate, harass, rape, or kill Mexican immigrants on U.S. soil or Mexicans across the border are rarely disciplined, with investigation results often not being made public for years. More abuses, violence, and deaths are inevitable unless stricter polices are designed, imposed, and monitored to limit the use of lethal force along the two-thousand-mile U.S.-Mexico border (Urbina and Álvarez 2015). According to Christopher Wilson, an expert on U.S.-Mexico relations at the Woodrow Wilson Center, a think tank in Washington, "There needs to be a level of accountability if you want to change the culture and the pattern.... People are being killed that don't need to be killed" (Bennett 2014, 1).

ABUSE OF IMMIGRANTS—NO ACTION TAKEN: A CALL FOR ACCOUNTABILITY

Beyond their use of deadly force, immigration law enforcement officers have engaged in a wide array of misconduct, often with total *immunity*. For years it has been reported that CBP and Border Patrol agents constantly ignore the constitutional rights of both undocumented and documented people. In fact, immigration agents are known for regularly overstepping their authority by engaging in unlawful searches and seizures, making racially or ethnically motivated stops and arrests, detaining people without probable cause or under inhumane conditions, removing people from the country with unjustified coercion, excessive force, and manipulation of information (Martinez, Cantor, and Ewing 2014). For instance, in a recent study, *Bordering on Criminal: The Routine Abuse of Migrants in the Removal System* (2013), Daniel Martinez, Jeremy Slack, and Josiah Heyman found that verbal and physical mistreatment of immigrants while in U.S. custody is not a random occurrence but a systemic and continued pattern of abuse. While the situation is currently getting more public attention and scrutiny, immigration agents still enjoy almost total immunity and lack of accountability (Phillips, Hagan, and Rodriguez 2006; Phillips, Rodriguez, and Hagan 2002).

In analyzing the nature of police misconduct and thus the urgency for well-defined police accountability policies, the American Immigration Council (Martinez, Cantor, and Ewing 2014) obtained data that reveal the lack of transparency and accountability afflicting both Customs and Border Protection and the Border Patrol. A review of 809 complaints of alleged abuse by Border Patrol agents between January 2009 and

January 2012, where cases included verbal, sexual, and physical abuse of immigrants, showed continual abuse. Astonishingly, among cases in which a formal decision was issued, 97 percent resulted in "No Action Taken," revealing a longstanding pattern of abuse, inaction, and unaccountability. The situation is further complicated by the fact that only a very small fraction of individuals who are victims of abuse actually file a formal complaint with the proper authorities, with approximately one in ten immigrants reporting having experienced physical abuse while in U.S. custody.

Clearly, as reported in "No Action Taken: Lack of CBP Accountability in Responding to Complaints of Abuse," the lack of action taken by CBP officials in response to complaints received indicates not only how CBP handles complaints, but also the operations of the agency (Martinez, Cantor, and Ewing 2014). Therefore, as recently delineated by Urbina and Álvarez in *Latino Police Officers in the United States: An Examination of Emerging Trends and Issues* (2015), if police brutality is going to decrease, accountability must be made a priority by lawmakers, police administrators, and police officers. To begin, as asserted by the authors of "No Action Taken," the complaint process should be centralized, and complaints need to be carefully and thoroughly reviewed and be processed more quickly to avoid further victimization. Also, considering the seriousness of the issues involved, external review of complaints filed against immigration agents is essential for authenticity and legitimacy, and it is important for the CBP and Border Patrol to become more transparent. To have a clearer understanding of filed complaints, process, and outcomes, it is also essential for DHS to streamline complaint processes into a unified well-defined procedure, which would then allow DHS to readily review complaints filed with the Joint Intake Center, Office of Inspector General, Civil Rights and Civil Liberties, and local sector offices and ports of entry for CBP. Similarly, it is imperative that communication regarding filed complaints be streamlined, avoiding unnecessary confusion or delay. Further, individuals or organizations who file complaints should be informed of the complaint's status throughout the review process.

To remedy the situation and reduce the possibility of recurrence, specific sanctions adopted during the process or after the review is finalized must be enforced and monitored, and finalized reports should be made available to supervisors, allowing police administrators to strategically design and implement adequate performance plans for improvement. However, complaints should be used by the agency not as an opportunity to demoralize personnel, but as an opportunity to educate and train employees to improve the performance of all personnel. That is, as recommended by Daniel Martinez, Guillermo Cantor, and Walter Ewing (2014, 9), "the lessons from the complaints review should be actively shared with key CBP personnel in order to foster a change of culture within the agency." Finally, as proposed by Martinez, Cantor, and Ewing (2014), a stronger system of incentives (both positive and negative) for all immigration agents (CBP and the Border Patrol) to obey the law, respect constitutional rights, and refrain from misconduct must be implemented and monitored. Along the way, we must be mindful that while well-defined policies, transparency, monitoring, and accountability are essential for eliminating unjustified behavior, essential elements must be incorporated to avoid behavior displacement or even a backlash (Urbina and Álvarez 2015).

THE CONTOURS OF IMMIGRATION: UNDERNEATH IT ALL

Created in 1924 to secure U.S. borders, the Border Patrol, now part of the Department of Homeland Security's Customs and Border Protection agency, has been active in its defined mission for almost a hundred years, with its agents, as the frontline agents of border enforcement, the most visible upholders of national security, patrolling the two-thousand-mile southern border. According to the department's website, its "priority mission" is "preventing terrorists and terrorists [sic] weapons, including weapons of mass destruction, from entering the United States." Its "primary mission," though, is "to detect and prevent the illegal entry of aliens" into the country. Critics, however, charge that the formally defined objectives, mission, and vision of some institutions are often more a reflection of political rhetoric and manipulation than of the realities of life, often serving as a smoke screen for what Urbina and Álvarez (2016) characterize as *underneath it all*—the hidden motives of social control. So, in this section we discuss two central forces governing immigration laws, enforcement, and discourse, which intertwine with the historical demon of racism: the political dynamics of immigration and the profitability of anti-immigrant movements. From an economic standpoint, though we are concerned with a *comparatively* small percentage of undocumented people, about $12 billion is spent annually on border security, more than for all other federal security agencies (apart from the Pentagon) combined (Tirman 2015a; Urbina and Álvarez 2015, 2016), under the hysterical argument that we are under attack by dangerous immigrants, narco-terrorists, international terrorists, even children from Central America, and most recently Syrian refugees. In fiscal year 2012, 364,000 "aliens" were reported to have been arrested, but not a single international terrorist (Fernández 2014). At all political levels, from local politicians to presidential candidates, immigrants have been demonized through highly charged media-propagated myths, in a despicable effort to win office, including the White House. Among the long list of political pundits and bigots, Donald Trump and his supporters (including Ted Cruz, Rick Santorum, Carly Fiorina, and Ben Carson), along with commentators like Bill O'Reilly and Ann Coulter, have voiced their anti-immigrant racism and xenophobia in seeking the winning ticket to the Capitol—like a political lottery.

THE POLITICAL DYNAMICS OF IMMIGRATION: IMMIGRATION AS THE NEW POLITICAL LOTTERY

To further appreciate the political dynamics of the current anti-immigrants movement, we must seriously consider the highly consequential accusations by some politicians, lawmakers, media commentators, intellectual racists, and other anti-immigrants critics. While some people tend to view anti-immigrant slogans as merely political rhetoric, when voiced by highly influential and powerful individuals and widely propagated by conservative media, such statements can influence the public, who then take "action" by voting for politicians with similar anti-immigrant views, without truly comprehending the realities of immigration and brushing aside the key issues facing the American society. Consider, for instance, the following series of statements by various individuals, who are currently in positions of power or are seeking elected positions, where they will be making decisions affecting not only immigrants but the entire community.

"When Mexico sends its people, they're not sending the best. . . . They're not sending you. They're sending people that have lots of problems and they're bringing those problems. . . . They're bringing drugs. They're bringing crime. They're rapists. And some, I assume, are good people, but I speak to border guards and they're telling us what we're getting. . . . I would build a Great Wall, and nobody builds walls better than me, believe me, and I'll build them very inexpensively. I will build a great, great wall on our southern border and I will have Mexico pay for that wall, mark my words." This from Republican candidate Donald Trump, who declared his presidential bid on June 16, 2015. Trump promised to build a Great Wall on the nation's southern border and vowed to end Obama's immigration executive actions.[1] "I believe that Mr. Trump is kind of telling it like it really, truly is," Republican Jan Brewer, former governor of Arizona, told CNN's Don Lemon on July 8, 2015, exposing her continued immigrant hatred.

On July 6, 2015, Bill O'Reilly told his audience that Donald Trump's immigration analysis was correct, asserting that there are "big problems stemming from Mexican illegal immigration. . . . ISIS has nothing on these drug cartels. . . . They are both savage enterprises. . . . So Trump is correct in saying that only a massive wall will stop the chaos and even then drugs and people will get through although not to the extent they do now."

Rush Limbaugh, popular radio talk show host and conservative political commentator, was quick to embrace Trump and give him kudos for his inflammatory anti-immigrant accusations.

Former Texas governor and presidential candidate Rick Perry said in a televised interview that illegal immigration is "like a disease," implying that immigrants are deadly.

In 2010, state representative Debbie Riddle, a Texas Republican, famously warned of immigrant mothers in the United States giving birth to "terror babies," charging that "anchor babies are little terrorists"; and some Republican lawmakers continue to characterize U.S. citizen children of undocumented immigrants as "anchor babies."

In 2014, Texas Republican Chris Mapp, a U.S. Senate candidate, charged that ranchers should be allowed to shoot on sight anyone illegally crossing the border onto their land, referred to immigrants as "wetbacks," and called the president (Obama) a "socialist son of a bitch," while claiming that the use of racial epithets is as "normal as breathing air in South Texas." "We can't have illegal immigrants, drug cartels, human traffickers or terrorists coming across our border," declared Mapp. (Reilly 2014, 1)

In 2013, Steve Krieser, a top official in Wisconsin's Department of Transportation, wrote on Facebook that he sees undocumented immigrants as none other than the devil, stating, "You may see Jesus when you look at them. I see Satan."

Since 2013, Iowa Republican representative Steve King has received great attention for his anti-immigrants rhetoric, claiming that an electrified fence could be used to deter "illegal" border crossings, similar to those used to contain livestock, and that some young immigrants have calves the size of cantaloupes because of their continual hauling of marijuana across the desert.

In 2015, Brandon Judd, the National Border Patrol Council (NBPC) president, declared, "We ask that everyone keep our agents in their thoughts and prayers as we continue to prevent drugs, crime, and individuals intending to do harm to our citizens from crossing our border."

To top it all off, some intellectual racists (like Samuel P. Huntington) have also been quick to demonize undocumented immigrants, particularly Mexican immigrants, and some scholars (like Cuban American George Borjas, professor at Harvard University), rely on their high-status positions to advocate for immigration reduction. Politician, law professor, and legal scholar Kris Kobach, for example, has filed numerous cases across the country (including in Kansas and Nebraska) seeking to restrict the rights of immigrants, expel them, or make life so difficult that they will leave or deport themselves. Having become an "intellectual authority" for the right-wing anti-immigrants movement, Kobach, who was the chief drafter of Arizona's anti-immigrants law, was elected in 2010 to serve as secretary of state in Kansas. Others have proclaimed themselves immigration experts in their attempt to influence the media, public opinion, and immigration laws by demonizing immigrants. Consider, for instance, conservative commentator Ann Coulter, who took on immigration reform in her recent book *Adios America: The Left's Plan to Turn Our Country into a Third World Hellhole* (2015). Lawmakers and other conservatives celebrated her new work, described as an exposé uncovering "the left's plan to turn our country into a third-world hellhole." In it she jokes, "I'd run immigration policy 'like Tinder.'" In June 2015, Representatives Mo Brooks and Steve King, two firm opponents of Obama's immigration reforms, praised the firebrand pundit, with Brooks stating, "I think she's spot on.... She's definitely a long-term thinker, but unfortunately, we have too many short-term thinkers on Capitol Hill" (Hardiman 2015).

Clearly, the demonization and criminalization of immigrants has become a political ticket to get recognized, elected, reelected, or appointed. In contrast, advocating for humane comprehensive immigration reform is perceived as political suicide and, in a sense, academic suicide, as some academic administrators, faculties, students, and readers in general seem to be fascinated with anti-immigrant stories and modern-day *super-heroes*, like Donald Trump, promising to "make America great again." Of course, there has been many *Donalds* over the centuries, and thus his anti-Mexican and anti-immigrant hatred should not come as a surprise. What is a little surprising, though, is the thousands and thousands of people who support him and like-minded candidates, revealing the inner core (emotions, mentality, and ideology) of hundreds of thousands or perhaps even millions of Americans. After centuries of supposed transformation, the question remains: How far have we really come?

THE PROFITABILITY OF IMMIGRATION: THE NEW CAPITALISM

As documented by the contributors to this volume, immigration laws, enforcement, and discourse have historically been shaped by the interaction of historical and contemporary forces—though often highly subjective, manipulated, skewed, and sometimes plagued by outright lies. While the immigration debate tends to revolve around national security, along with provocative charges like "they take our jobs," a quieter force is the profitability of social control movements. The anti-immigrant movement has become a major capitalist component of the U.S. economic system (Urbina and Álvarez 2016). In this section, we highlight some crucial findings about the political economy of immigration, which obviously interact with the historical demon of racism. As noted in the introductory story, Arizona has become the rallying point of the anti-immigrants movement, and thus we utilize Arizona as an illustration of what is unfolding throughout the country.

ARIZONA IMMIGRATION LAWS: TESTING THE LIMITS OF SOCIAL CONTROL AND ECONOMIC PROFITABILITY

Understanding final outcomes in their totality, from deportation to incarceration, requires that we gain insight into the *law-making process*, which allows us to deconstruct myths, political rhetoric, and even some supposed academic findings. In "Prison Economics Help Drive Arizona Immigration Law," Laura Sullivan (2010) vividly illustrates the behind-the-scenes efforts to draft immigration laws, pass the laws, and shape existing state laws quickly and with little scrutiny, as in the case of Arizona's Support Our Law Enforcement and Safe Neighborhoods Act, which has served as a baseline law model for other states to follow. Let us venture into the behind-the-scenes effort to draft and pass Arizona Senate Bill 1070 by a highly political multimillion dollar industry that stands to benefit from immigration laws—the private prison industry.

It started on December 2009 at the Grand Hyatt in Washington, D.C., in a business meeting of a secretive group known as the American Legislative Exchange Council or, as called by insiders, ALEC. The selective membership organization includes state legislators and powerful associations and corporations, like tobacco company Reynolds American Incorporated, ExxonMobil, the National Rifle Association, and the billion-dollar Corrections Corporation of America (CCA), the largest private prison company in the country. "ALEC is the conservative, free-market orientated, limited-government group," reported Michael Hough, staff director of the meeting. When asked if private companies usually get to draft and propose *model bills* for legislators, Hough replied, "Yeah, that's the way it's set up. It's a public-private partnership. We believe both sides, businesses and lawmakers, should be at the same table, together" (Sullivan 2010, 4). Revealing the symbiotic relationship between politicians and the business sector, Arizona state senator Russell Pearce admitted that the bill was his idea and that he was instrumental in drafting the state's immigration law. In fact, most of the language of the bill had been written as model legislation at a December 2009 meeting of the American Legislative Exchange Council, where Pearce was joined as an attendee by officials of Corrections Corporation of America. By April 2010, the finalized bill was on Governor Jan Brewer's desk to be signed into law. Later a vocal supporter and cheerleader for Donald Trump, Brewer has her own connections to private prison companies (Sullivan 2010).

As designed, the law could have sent thousands of undocumented immigrants to prison in ways never done before, while generating millions of dollars in profit for private prison companies. Fortunately for immigrants, most key provisions of S.B. 1070 have been declared unconstitutional, though the Supreme Court upheld the "show me your papers" provision, allowing local police officers to check for immigration status if they have "reasonable suspicion" that individuals are in the country without documentation—obviously opening the door for ethnic/racial profiling of *brown* people. Civil rights activists, immigration advocates, and other critics have long reported that Arizona police officers racially profile Latinos (undocumented and documented), but now the "show me your papers" law functions as the ideal justification to pull over "undocumented-looking people," or, more precisely, "Mexican-looking people," and brown people in general. Teodulo Sánchez, as one example, was driving home when an Arizona police officer pulled him over and threatened to "kill" or "shoot" him if he moved. In the video that captured the incident on October 2014, the officer tells Sánchez in Spanish to show his license and threatens, "If you do something, I will kill you right here. Do you understand me?" The officer repeated, "If you move, I will shoot you right here. Do you understand me?" (Lee 2014).

BEYOND ARIZONA: AMERICA'S POLITICAL AND ECONOMIC SYMBIOTIC RELATIONSHIP

Fueled by the proliferation of punitive laws, covering a wide spectrum of offenses, social control movements that predate the 9/11 border buildup, and the anti-immigrants movement (Álvarez 2012), immigration enforcement and social control in general has become a booming multibillion-dollar business. In fact, since local, state, and federal governments adopted a strategy of concentrated border enforcement along the U.S.-Mexico border region characterized as "prevention through deterrence" in the early 1990s, the annual budget for the Border Patrol alone has increased tenfold, from $363 million in 1993 to $3.5 billion in 2013 (Ewing 2014; Urbina and Álvarez, 2016). After 9/11, the government created the Department of Homeland Security (DHS) in 2002, with the annual budget of Customs and Border Protections (CBP), which includes the Border Patrol, quickly increasing from $5.9 billion in 2003 to $11.9 billion in 2013. Similarly, funding for Immigration and Customs Enforcement (ICE), the interior-enforcement counterpart to CBP within DHS, increased 73 percent, from $3.3 billion in 2003 to $5.9 billion in 2013. The budget of Enforcement and Removal Operations (ERO) has also increased, from $1.2 billion in 2005 to $2.9 billion in 2012 (Ewing 2014; Urbina and Álvarez 2016).

Almost two decades into the twenty-first century, government officials, along with political pundits, immigration hawks, anti-immigrant bigots, and intellectual racists, continue railing against immigrants, with slogans like "national security," "protecting our sovereignty," or "securing our freedom." Anti-immigrant critics argue that "Mexico's violence" is constantly threatening to spill across the border into the United States. In truth, most border cities on the U.S. side have lower crime rates than the national average. For example, El Paso, Texas, across from Juárez is consistently ranked among the safest cities in the country. Critics further charge that drugs are currently the best way for Mexican drug cartels and other transnational criminal organizations to make money, but that if drugs are legalized criminals will "go to the next level," which could be the transportation of weapons of mass destruction into the United States. Yet, despite the fact that America's most violent cities are not along the border, with Mexican immigration to the United States now hovering around net zero, the government continues to increase enforcement funding. In 2012 alone, the government reportedly spent $18 billion on immigration enforcement, which is more than all other criminal law enforcement spending combined, revealing a *fascination* for pursuing immigrants.

While many believe that government spending is being consumed by immigrants and criminals, budgets are tied to government personnel, politicians, multimillion-dollar private companies, and multibillion-dollar corporations who build, maintain, and supply all equipment and supplies, from police badges to hats to drones to facilities (Urbina and Álvarez 2016). As for immigration enforcement payroll, the number of Border Patrol agents doubled from 10,717 in 2003 to 21,394 in 2012, the number of CBP officers increased from 17,279 to 21,423, and the number of ICE agents more than doubled from 2,710 to 6,338 during the same time frame (Urbina and Álvarez 2015).

THE CRIMINALIZATION OF IMMIGRANTS: EXPANDING CRIME AND EXPANDING PROFIT?

With the advent of various social control movements, intensified by the September 11, 2001, terrorist attacks on the United States, apprehending immigrants quickly turned into a wide-scale criminalization movement, with billions of dollars for unprecedented border enforcement; which in turn fueled the criminalization process and by extension increased spending. For instance, the fascination with criminalizing immigrants, supported by billions in government funding, has fueled programs like the Criminal Alien Program (CAP), Secure Communities, and 287(g), allowing immigration officers to reach into every corner of the country, blurring the line between border and interior enforcement (Ewing 2014). Rapidly, with billions of dollars available and the feeling of *let's use it now or the government will take it back*, officials have been pushing for construction, expansion, and conversion of jail space to house immigrants. Seeking to establish a long-term foundation for the prison enterprise, government agencies and prison companies have been collaborating to maximize expansion, sometimes leading to clashes between states with rival facilities for immigrant detainees, such as the reported spat between lawmakers from Alabama and Georgia in 2010–11.

In fact, while some states and the federal government are seeking avenues to reduce the nation's prison population, particularly for minor offenses, immigration detention has become such a commodity that it is now protected by Congress, with a "bed mandate" that forced immigration officials under President Barack Obama to fill a *minimum* of 34,000 prison spaces a day. The expansion of the immigrant detention system began in 2004, when the Intelligence Reform and Terrorism Prevention Act, in response to 9/11, directed Homeland Security to add 8,000 beds a year, with Congress increasing funds for 18,500 beds in 2005 and 33,400 beds by 2009. Since 2005, the number of beds to house undocumented immigrants has increased 84 percent, according to the Congressional Research Service. In 2009 a de facto immigrant detention quota was further formalized when Senator Robert Byrd inserted specific language into Immigration and Customs Enforcement's detention budget: "funding made available under this heading shall maintain a level of not less than 33,400 detention beds." Arguing that the bed quota forces U.S. immigration officials to apprehend, detain, and deport undocumented people, keeping America safe, Congress has pressed to ensure the beds are full. It is revealing that no other law-enforcement agency has a quota for the number of people that they must keep in jail or prison to keep American safe. Thus, the immigration detention quota mandated by Congress has been an unprecedented *driver* of an increasingly aggressive immigration enforcement operation. However, one has to ask: Does mandating ICE to detain 34,000 individuals a day actually make our border or us safer?

THE MONEY LINE: FEEDING THE CRIMINAL OR FEEDING THE SYSTEM?

Whether we are actually safer remains to be seen, but there is one fact that is quite clear—*the money line*. Immigration enforcement has been boosting revenue for commercial prison companies and local and state governments, as companies and lawmakers with detention centers and jails in their districts have been pushing for a greater share of a growing multibillion-dollar enterprise. Some lawmakers have made no secret of the economic benefits of supporting the anti-immigrants movement, including the quota mandate, acknowledging that it funnels money to their districts, providing jobs for U.S. citizens in private prisons and those built and maintained by local governments—and, of course, jobs for federal employees. The profitability of jailing immigrants was displayed at a March 2013 hearing, when lawmakers grilled John Morton (ICE director who later resigned) for releasing immigrant detainees because of supposed budget constraints. During the hearing, Representative Tom Marino, a Pennsylvania Republican, chastised Morton for not detaining enough inmates to fill immigrant detention beds in his district, asking, "Why not take advantage—more advantage—of facilities like this?" (Selway and Newkirk 2013, 7). Along with the reported struggles of government officials (like Robert Aderholt and Richard Shelby) to increase the number of immigrant arrests and keep immigrant detainees and ICE dollars in their state, released information suggests that officials have proposed going through old probation lists to find foreigners who had committed minor offenses, searching driver's license databases for undocumented people, setting higher bail to keep people in detention centers, and participating in roadblocks organized by local police to round people up (Selway and Newkirk 2013).

Detention has grown astronomically, from holding seven thousand inmates in 1994 to thirty-four thousand in 2013 (Kirkham 2014), *creating a highly profitable market for private companies to compete in and expand.* By 2013, Corrections Corporation of America (CCA), the GEO Group, and other for-profit prison companies were holding almost two-thirds of all immigrants detained in federally funded prisons as they awaited deportation (Selway and Newkirk 2013). In 2015, 62 percent of all ICE beds were run by private prison companies; that is, for-profit prison companies operate nine of the ten largest immigrant facilities in the country, with eight of the ten being run by CCA or GEO (Barajas 2015). While most immigrants are housed in for-profit prisons, ICE data show that the rest are scattered around the country in jails run by local governments paid to hold immigrants. Clearly, as immigrant detentions have increased, so have profits, with some figures showing that U.S. immigration agencies spend about $2 billion annually on detention. For instance, federal contracts accounted for about 43 percent ($752 million) of CCA's 2012 revenue, up from 23 percent in 2000, including $206 million from ICE in 2012. In 2013, CCA, the biggest contractor of private prisons in the United States, generated nearly $1.7 billion in revenues (Orduna 2014). CCA's profits went from $133 million in 2007 to $195 million in 2014, and GEO's profits increased by 244 percent during the same time period, from $41.8 million to $143.8 million, with both companies having more than doubled their revenues from immigration detention since 2005. Of course, profit is not limited to immigration facilities, as CCA, GEO, and other for-profit companies have also benefited from increased border enforcement and punitive immigration policies, which have resulted in criminal convictions and prison sentences for thousands of immigrants captured while crossing into the United States. Since normally their only "crime" is having entered the country without documentation, most apprehended immigrants end up in low-security, privately managed federal facilities.

The criminalization and incarceration of immigrants have become so profitable that the two leading private companies actively lobby Congress. CCA has spent more than $13 million on lobbyists since 2005, among them past appropriations-committee members, and GEO has spent more than $2.8 million lobbying during the same time frame (Selway and Newkirk 2013). Some figures show that since the 2008 elections, CCA, GEO, and Management and Training Corporation (the three biggest private prison contractors) have donated about $132,500 to the campaigns of members of congressional subcommittees who appropriate funds for ICE and other federal agencies and determine how much money is spent on immigrant detention (Selway and Newkirk 2013). In fact, serving as a "jailer" for the federal government has been a great success on Wall Street, as CCA and GEO have doubled their values since mid-2010. Illustrating the aggressive and expanding incarceration market, in a May 2010 conference call with investors, GEO's president declared, "I can only believe the opportunities at the federal level are going to continue apace as a result of what's happening. Those people coming across the border and getting caught are going to have to be detained and that for me, at least I think, there's going to be enhanced opportunities for what we do" (Sullivan 2010, 5). Evidently, as the industry continues to boom, there is a huge private interest involved in border enforcement, criminalization, and incarceration of immigrants. Republicans continue to defend the bed-quota system, while promoting more enforcement, which in turn drives demand for more beds and, ultimately, more immigration facilities, which will then further accelerate enforcement to fill empty beds. In fact, while the government is already providing around $4.5 billion for private contractors over the next half decade to *secure the border* (Orduna 2014), all proposed immigration reforms include increases in so-called border enforcement and security spending. While some social control advocates argue that the government is spending too much feeding inmates ("criminals"), in reality very little money goes to inmates' food. States like Texas, for example, are required to spend only 33 cents per meal, less than a dollar a day for an inmate. So is the government feeding the "criminal" or feeding the system, along with America's multibillion-dollar corporations?

MANAGEMENT UNDER PRIVATE FOR-PROFIT COMPANIES

As border enforcement, criminalization, and incarceration of immigrants continue to increase, immigration security discourse has been revolving around funding for federal agencies and private corporations, with little attention paid to the realities of detention. Civil and human rights groups, for instance, have reported multiple problems in privatized federal facilities. At GEO-operated Reeves County Detention Center in West Texas there were two major riots in a single month in late 2008 and early 2009, following a series of suicides and inmate deaths in the facility. In 2014, GEO opened the Karnes County Residential Center southeast of San Antonio, Texas, where six hundred women and children are being held, and with people continuing to flee violence in Central America, GEO plans to expand capacity to twelve hundred detainees. CCA's Eloy Detention Center in Arizona has also had suicides. In less than six months in 2012 and 2013, there were three. According to information released by ICE, ten detainees died between 2003 and 2012 at Eloy (Kirkham 2014).

Immigrant advocates and critics of privatized detention charge that by giving so much responsibility to for-profit private companies, the federal government now lacks the *will* to implement needed reform to the largest and most profitable detention network in the world. As noted by Bob Libal, executive director of Grassroots Leadership, "They've abdicated a lot of responsibility, because it's quicker and easier this way.... The result is what's largely a captured agency. I don't see how [the immigration agency] makes major moves without consultation from the private prison corporations, and that's not an effective immigration policy" (Kirkham 2014, 3).

As a first step for reform, though, Congress needs to eliminate the immigrant detention quota to reduce ICE's reliance on for-profit prison companies, and instead fund a well-designed program to replace large-scale detention with less costly community supervision programs, managed by immigration officials to avoid the continued race for maximizing profit, as grave abuse continues.

THE UNSPOKEN REALITIES OF THE IMMIGRATION DEBATE

For some people, the anti-immigrants movement and social control movements in general might appear to make sense, be justified, and be legally, politically, economically, and socially legitimate. For those with anti-immigrant views and those who are politically and economically benefiting from the multibillion-dollar social control market, immigration enforcement and detention are the new gold mines of American capitalism, which need to be further exploited and expanded using whatever means necessary to make profits and reach unspoken goals of social control (Urbina and Álvarez 2016, 2017). For instance, beyond federal immigration policies and enforcement, even though the U.S. Supreme Court has overturned key parts of Arizona's anti-immigrants law S.B. 1070 (June 15, 2012), states such as Alabama, Georgia, Indiana, and Utah have passed laws to further criminalize immigrants for their undocumented status. Among the many justifications noted throughout this book, six often cited rationales underlie federal and state punitive immigration policies, enforcement, and detention: (1) anti-immigrant sentiment by legislators and the public; (2) local police departments trained by federal U.S. officials seek out individuals suspected of being in the country without documentation; (3) undocumented people driving without a license; (4) immigrants are committing crimes; (5) undocumented people do not pay taxes; and (6) immigrants are taking advantage of government resources. In truth, these rationales are simply the smoke screen to avoid confronting the realities of immigration and disguise the unspoken motives underlying anti-immigrant actions.

In *Dream Chasers: Immigration and the American Backlash* (2015b), MIT research scientist John Tirman reports that right-wing hostility toward undocumented immigrants is not really about legality, but about cultural shifts that are currently "remaking" America as never seen before, as illustrated by Urbina in *Twenty-First Century Dynamics of Multiculturalism: Beyond Post-Racial America* (2014). While the general public tends to see immigrants as an economic necessity and are welcoming (or tolerant) of the benefits and diversity they bring, the *base* is primarily defined and mobilized by cultural issues. Unlike in previous generations, American cultural issues revolve around the Spanish language, which for years was prohibited from being used in schools, and the erroneous idea that Latinos, most of whom are Mexican, do not wish to "assimilate" as did immigrants in past generations—creating, supposedly, an un-American and even anti-American climate and culture and posing a grave danger to the American society.

In truth, with some geographical exceptions, Latinos do adopt English as previous immigrants did, doing so gradually so that by the third generation they speak English almost exclusively. According to recent studies, more than 80 percent of U.S. immigrants study to learn English and 75 percent of Spanish-speaking immigrants speak English after fifteen years, and an overwhelming percentage of immigrants encourage their children and grandchildren to be fluent English speakers, while maintaining Spanish fluency at home (Immigration Compliance Group 2008; Roach 2012; Teaching Tolerance 2011). However, in a country that is now experiencing widespread diversity, including biracial couples, same-sex couples, biracial children, extended religious freedom, feminism, women's empowerment, and multicultural influence in most facets of social life, immigrant assimilation is definitely not going to resemble the *rigid conformity of the past*—when wealthy white men dictated all aspects of everyday life. Adding to the white anxiety over these combined *cultural revolutions* is the fact that the Latino culture has been rooted in the United States for centuries, a long historical "connection," and people with family origins in Cuba, Mexico, Puerto Rico, and Central and South America can continue to engage with their extended family. In fact, Latinos were some of the first immigrants in the United States, and thus Mexican Americans and other Latinos have been in the United States for centuries. Before the English came to America in 1609, there was a Latino presence in the Southwest, including Texas, and they have been in the present-day United States since 1565 in Florida and 1598 in New Mexico, centuries before the Treaty of Guadalupe Hidalgo that ended the Mexican-American War in 1848 (De León and Del Castillo 2012; Urbina, Vela, and Sánchez 2014).

With shifting trends in demographics, immigration critics, including political pundits, bigots, intellectual racists, and other immigration hawks, seem to be panicking and aggressively reacting to what they characterize as an immigrant invasion. As documented by Tirman (2015a, 2), conservatives "simply can't wrap their heads around this steady shift away from their 'deport them all' mentality." As noted above, right-wing immigration critics, from high-ranking politicians (like Donald Trump and Ted Cruz) to entertainers (like Laura Ingraham and Michelle Malkin) to talk show hosts (like Mark Levin and Rush Limbaugh), and practically the entire Republican caucus in Congress, regard Latinos, especially Mexicans, as embodying the characteristics that weaken America; that is, they are the face of cultural diversity and multiculturalism—rather than the "American Way"—and represent job stealing, welfare dependency, lazy work habits, drug traffickers, narco-terrorists, criminals, and lack of respect for U.S. laws. Entertainer Ingraham (2014, 2), for instance, recently charged that "among immigrants today, it is increasingly fashionable to reject American exceptionalism in favor of multiculturalism. To pretend that this isn't happening isn't optimism; it's sheer fantasy." Tirman (2015a, 2) believes that the "specter of America becoming a bilingual nation is probably the most hot button issue of all." Scholars Jack Citrin, Beth Reingold, Evelyn Walters, and Donald Green (1990, 536) report that language is indeed a driving force, as "English proficiency is a highly resonant symbol of American nationality. The evidence strongly suggests that an important reason for the popularity of 'official English' is the pervasive public desire to reaffirm an attachment to a traditional image of Americanism that now seems vulnerable." In the late twentieth century Harvard's leading political scientist, Samuel P. Huntington (1996, 204), joined the anti-Mexican immigration debate by loudly commenting about the growing Latino population and therefore the inevitable "clash of civilizations," charging that "while Muslims pose the immediate problem to Europe, Mexicans pose the problem for the United States." Several years later, Professor Huntington (2004, 32) argued that "the single and most immediate and most serious challenge to America's traditional identity comes from the immense and continuing immigration from Latin America, especially from Mexico. . . . [The] transformation into two peoples with two cultures (Anglo and Hispanic) and two languages (English and Spanish) [represent] a major potential threat to the country's cultural and political integrity."

While the forces of multiculturalism have reset the boundaries of language in the United States, it has been documented that English is the preferred language of third-generation Latinos, and that "Americanness" unfolds similarly to how it did in previous generations of immigrants. For instance, by the third generation, a majority of Latinos consider themselves "Americans." Further, as argued by Tirman (2015a, 2), while there are provoking claims about the *legality* of immigration—"what part of illegal immigrants don't you understand?"—coming into the United States without documentation is unauthorized, but is not criminal, and has historically not been handled as a criminal offense. Essentially, unauthorized entry into the country is a civil infraction, "entry without inspection" to verify documentation. This has been a major reason pro-immigrant activists have been so horrified and outraged by the draconian immigration policies, border enforcement, detention, and deportation system; that is, the response to unauthorized immigration is grossly out of proportion to the infractions—exposing the false front of the "rationality and legitimacy of legality" and the confused nature of the immigration discourse and its impact on both undocumented and documented people.

The immigrant myths that many of us learned as children and the myths and stereotypes we continue to hear as adults, which are widely propagated by the conservative media, are probably *weaker* than ever due to the endless railing about "illegal" immigrants (Tirman 2015b). However, the consequences of these myths and stereotypes are more serious than ever, as delineated by the contributors to this volume (see also Urbina 2014; Urbina and Álvarez 2015, 2016). Along with the grave implications and ramifications discussed throughout this book, consider the following two incidents. In June 2013, eleven-year-old Mexican American Sebastien de la Cruz, a San Antonio native, who sang the national anthem during game three of the NBA finals in San Antonio, Texas, sparked racist comments in the social media, with comments like, "there should be an AMERICAN singing the national anthem not this illegal," "this lil Mexican snuck in the country like 4 hours ago now he singing the anthem," "why an illegal alien," "why was he dressed like a little Mexican," and "a Mexican kid singing the national anthem makes it un-American." More recently, in June 2015, a week after graduating from Thurgood Marshall College at the University of California, San Diego, Indira Esparza, a twenty-two-year-old undocumented immigrant, was still getting plenty of criticism for proudly waving a Mexican flag on stage as she received her college diploma. A photo of her waving the Mexican flag sparked sharp reactions by offended viewers/readers who wrote angry letters and statements, with comments like, "Send her undocumented ass home to her precious Mexico" and "Ignorant waste of a news feed."

Of course, the acceptance or tolerance of immigrants has always been uncertain, highly influenced by multiple factors, particularly the person's national origin or, more precisely, skin color. To be sure, resistance to immigration is not only cultural but generational, as opponents tend to be much older than people who welcome diversity and multiculturalism (Tirman 2015b; Urbina 2014). Testing for the influence of race and ethnicity, Ted Brader, Nicholas Valentino, and Elizabeth Suhay (2008) found that with shifting demographics, Americans are now thinking of immigration in an *ethnically* specific way. In effect, Americans now think of immigrants as Latino; that is, Latinos are now being *equated* with immigrants. Unsurprisingly, the authors found that Latinos trigger an anxiety in some white people that other ethnic or racial groups simply do not trigger. Such anxiety then incites fear, which then affects their attitudes and behavior in regard to immigration policies, enforcement, incarceration, and deportation. The researchers, for instance, found that negative news featuring Latino immigrants raises whites' worries and anxieties about increasing immigration, seeing it as a threat, but news about immigrants from Russia, a supposed international "enemy and threat," does not create the same anxiety. Broadly, media frenzies about immigration and negative news about Latinos make white Americans anxious, heightening opposition to immigration and increasing anti-immigrant activism, revealing the powerful influence of race, ethnicity, national origin, skin color, and, logically, culture.

While contributors to this volume delineate the contours of immigration, showing how out of touch some people are with the realities of immigration laws and enforcement, *underneath it all* there has been a much more strategically orchestrated motive, with a well-defined mission, that goes far beyond *culture* (Urbina 2012, 2014, 2018; Urbina and Álvarez 2015, 2017; Urbina, Vela, and Sánchez 2014; Urbina and Wright 2016). In "Neoliberalism, Criminal Justice and Latinos: The Contours of Neoliberal Economic Thought and Policy on Criminalization" (2016), Urbina and Álvarez illustrate that by examining the combined forces of neoliberal economic policies, which are tied to immigration laws, *the identification, categorization, and criminalization of immigrants and other dispossessed segments of society, the affirmation of salient borders, and control of marginalized populations*, we can get beyond investigations couched in the language of *legality* and law and order. We can trace how the criminal justice system and its institutional tentacles, like policing, courts, probation, parole, jails, prisons, and criminal databases, have provoked discourse about immigration, crime, national security, and public disdain for undocumented (and documented) immigrants and offenders in general. "Resonating with the historical White supremacy ideology, acting like a *supreme* and *active* God, as illustrated by Manifest Destiny, conquest, slavery, colonialism, and other imperialist movements," the authors charge, *anti-social* control movements, through ethnic identity formation, categorization, criminalization, and penalization, are more a reflection of control, expansion, power, and dominance than of the realities of immigration, public safety, or national security—that is, are an effort to maintain a monopoly of wealth, power, and control for whites in the United States.

With shifting demographic trends, the uncontrolled and expanding penal system is being fueled by the identification, classification, criminalization, and reactivation of the stigma of *brownness* as dangerousness. With Latinos now being perceived as a possible political, economic, cultural, and social threat to white America, "the racist and essentialist ideologies that permeate Americans are once again being manifested in the very fabric of the criminal justice system: American criminal law. At the end, as in colonial times, race and now ethnic minorities have become *the grease that keeps the wheels of justice turning*, and the 'fuel' that keeps the criminal justice system expanding, controlling, and silencing *los de abajo*, the ones at the bottom" (Álvarez 2012, 224).

HUMANIZING IMMIGRATION IN THE TWENTY-FIRST CENTURY: THE CHALLENGE OF OUR TIMES

While immigrants have historically confronted a wide array of obstacles in their pursuit of the American dream, today's immigrants (undocumented and documented), particularly Latinos, are experiencing unprecedented barriers in their quest *por el Sueño Americano*—an experience that for many is no longer a dream but an illusion and worse, an illusion that is turning into grave injustices in all facets of social life. As illustrated by the contributors to this book, the current state of immigration, in all dimensions, calls for immediate comprehensive reform, along with social change, justice, and human dignity. In this section, therefore, we briefly revisit a series of essential factors that must be considered if the United States is going to be reflective of a democratic society and situate itself as the country of the future.

THE SIGNIFICANCE OF EDUCATION FOR UNDOCUMENTED STUDENTS AND THE FUTURE OF AMERICA

Access to education has always been a major challenge to segments of society, but while the challenge continues to be detrimental to ethnic/racial minorities and poor whites, undocumented people are the most disadvantaged, from having access to education to receiving needed resources to being able use their degrees upon graduation (Johnson 2013; Urbina and Wright 2016). Undocumented immigrants in Florida, for instance, cannot obtain a license to practice law, according to a state supreme court ruling in 2014. Jose Godinez-Samperio, who moved to Florida from Mexico at the age of nine, applied for a license but was denied by the Florida high court, which claimed that federal law prohibits undocumented people from obtaining professional licenses.

The court's justices acknowledged that state law can override the federal ban, but Florida has not taken action to resolve the matter; so the expectation that immigrants will educate and improve themselves is contradicted by not providing opportunities for advancement upon graduation (Urbina and Wright 2016). Justice Jorge Labarga expressed disappointment with the decision, characterized the situation an injustice, and noted that Godinez-Samperio was an Eagle Scout and the valedictorian of his high school; yet he agreed with the court's decision. Sounding more like a colonial oppressor than a crusader for justice, Labarga, the first Cuban American to hold the post of chief justice in Florida, said that he and his family were welcomed with open arms when they arrived from Cuba because they were perceived as fleeing a tyrannical communist government, but Godinez-Samperio is perceived as a defector from poverty in Mexico and thus "viewed negatively." The powerful gatekeeper added that Godinez-Samperio was "the type of exemplary individual the Florida Bar should strive to add to its membership" (Al Jazeera 2014, 1). There have been similar cases in other states. In 2014, the California Supreme Court granted a law license to Sergio García, who came to the United States from Mexico as a child to pick almonds with his father. However, the ruling came after the state approved a law that allows undocumented immigrants the right to obtain licenses.

Promoting the importance of education for immigrants, in Laurene Powell Jobs's first interview after the death of her husband, Steve Jobs (Apple cofounder), with NBC's anchor Brian Williams, she pledged her support for DREAMers and comprehensive immigration reform. Then, voicing her concerns to the *Wall Street Journal*, Powell Jobs explained why this issue caused her to break her silence. It began in 1995, when she started tutoring low-income students and soon witnessed that those who were in the country without documentation were unable to secure financial aid or other financial resources to go to college. Powell Jobs declared, "Year after year we saw potential wasted" (Lessin and Jordan 2013, 3), and in her interview with Brian Williams on April 12, 2013, she explained, "I started getting more and more active around immigration reform because this was such a waste of lives, such a waste of potential, such a waste for our country not to have the human capital that we developed—geared towards improving our entire society." She soon teamed up with filmmaker Davis Guggenheim to promote immigration reform and awareness through a new film, *The Dream Is Now*, showing the significance of the DREAM Act (Development, Relief, and Education for Alien Minors), which would provide high school graduates, those who have served in the military, and other students a pathway toward legal status.

In California, a minority-majority state, University of California President Janet Napolitano, former U.S. secretary of Homeland Security and former Arizona governor, confronted the highly controversial issue by announcing in 2013 that she would authorize $5 million in university funds to help undocumented students who do not qualify for federal financial aid (about 900 of UC's 230,000 students are thought to be DREAMers), declaring that "UC will continue to be a vehicle for social mobility. We teach for California; we research for the world. . . . Graduate students and post-docs are the essential links between teaching for California and researching for the world. They are our future faculty members. They are our future innovators. They are our future Nobel laureates" (Gordon 2013, 1–2).

Speaking about immigration reform and the significance of education to our country, U.S. CEO Linda Hudson declared, "I cannot help but wonder if hobbling our ability to hire top scientists, mathematicians, programmers, and engineers who happen to have been born on foreign soil doesn't carry national security risks of its own" (Shapiro 2014, 1). In our now highly technological world, we must encourage foreign students getting STEM graduate degrees from our universities to stay in the United States, and provide them a quick pathway to citizenship, enabling them to contribute to our economy and enrich our culture. In *Latino Access to Higher Education: Ethnic Realities and New Directions for the Twenty-First Century* (2016), Urbina and Wright report that with the advent of globalization, including the globalization of knowledge, education has become a central force enabling "survival and success" not only for individuals, but also for communities and essentially the entire country. Thus, we must acknowledge the significance of education and it must be made a priority; the educational system is essential for balancing other American institutions, from the economic system to America's military forces.

AMNESTY AND CITIZENSHIP

As illustrated throughout this volume, without amnesty or citizenship, the American experience for undocumented students is extremely limited, oppressing for immigrant workers, and complicated and costly for legal residents to have a voice in our supposed democratic society. While eleven to twelve million people in the United States are currently waiting for Congress to pass laws that will enable them to qualify for legal status (residence) and citizenship, another 8.8 million people in the country are already eligible for citizenship but have not applied, in part because of the high cost. In 2000, the beginning of the George W. Bush administration, the cost of applying for citizenship was $225, but increased to $675 by 2008, the final year of Bush's administration (Gamboa 2015). Naturalization fees remained unchanged under President Barack Obama's administration, and fee waivers exist for applicants who have household incomes of 150 percent of poverty level and can meet a means test (Gamboa 2015), but the complicated process, which often forces applications to hire an attorney, discourages or prevents people from applying.

In fact, citizenship application costs rose so high during the Bush administration that naturalizations dropped dramatically, especially for poor legal residents, the less educated, and residents of Mexican origin. According to Joshua Hoyt, co-chair of the National Partnership for New Americans, "Right now, cost has become such a barrier for the working poor that citizenship is becoming a privilege that is limited to wealthy immigrants, and the working poor, especially Mexican immigrants, are being excluded from the benefits of citizenship" (Gamboa 2015, 1). In 2013, researchers reported that nearly two-thirds of legal Mexican immigrants had not become citizens (Gonzalez-Barrera et al. 2013), showing that of the 5.4 million legal Mexican nationals, only 36 percent were naturalized in 2011. Comparatively, nearly twice as many non-Mexican immigrants (69 percent) began the naturalization process, and compared to immigrants from Latin America and the Caribbean, Mexicans had the lowest rate of naturalization (Gonzalez-Barrera et al. 2013). More broadly, figures show that while legal residents of Mexican heritage constitute 29 percent of the 8.8 million legal residents eligible to naturalize, they constitute 40 percent of the working poor eligible to naturalize with household incomes below 150 percent of poverty and 37 percent of those with household incomes between 150 percent and 250 percent of poverty, for families of four (Gamboa 2015). Not surprisingly, after a 2007 surge, the share of legal residents of Mexican origin who naturalized dropped from 19.8 percent in 2008 to 12.7 percent in 2010 (Gamboa 2015).

Those opposed to easing the means of immigration argue that providing some type of amnesty and a path to citizenship for the eleven to twelve million undocumented immigrants currently residing in the United States will attract more undocumented immigrants, and subsequently a demand for more citizenship. Other observers, though, claim that neither amnesty nor citizenship will encourage wide-scale immigration, especially since Mexican immigration has been hovering around zero during last few years. David Koelsch, director of the Immigration Law Clinic at the University of Detroit Mercy School of Law, for instance, reports that proposed reforms will not encourage unauthorized immigration in the future for three main reasons: (1) since the proposed pathways to legal status will be long and expensive, any reward for future undocumented immigration is distant; (2) the birth rate in Mexico has been in rapid decline; and (3) Mexico is now providing more opportunities for their workers and their domestic industry wages are rising, "making the U.S. less attractive"; and all things considered in both Mexico and the United States, "there is not a strong draw for illegal immigration" from Mexico (Goodale 2013, 1), as illustrated by recent demographic trends.

No obstacle to citizenship is more critical than the denial of birth certificates and thus citizenship to U.S.-born children. For nearly 150 years, the United States (under the Fourteenth Amendment) has recognized people born in the country as citizens, regardless of the legal status of their parents. Since 2014, though, Texas has been refusing to issue birth certificates to children of undocumented parents who were born in the United States.[2] According to James Harrington, an attorney with the Texas Civil Rights Project, "Even in the darkest hours of Texas' history of discrimination, officials never denied birth certificates to Hispanic children of immigrants. Everyone born in the United States is entitled to the full rights of citizenship" (del Bosque 2015, 1). Jennifer Harbury, a lawyer with Texas RioGrande Legal Aid, reports that the sudden refusal to provide U.S.-born children with birth certificates is linked to the influx of children from Central America who crossed the border in the summer of 2014 seeking asylum. According to Harbury, "They are targeting the undocumented population, but immigration is a federal function and not the job of the Department of State Health Services. It causes all kinds of problems. How is a woman going to prove she's the child's parent without a birth certificate" (del Bosque 2015, 1)? Without a birth certificate, women are unable to enroll their children in daycare or school, and worse, to authorize their children to be treated in medical emergencies, which are extremely crucial after birth. To be sure, denying citizenship to U.S.-born children goes beyond Central American children; it's obviously part of the broader anti-immigrants movement, which includes the denial of amnesty to undocumented people who are already in the country and the various barriers hindering citizenship for legal residents, particularly Mexican immigrants.

In sum, poverty, lack of financial assistance, and administrative barriers have been identified as the main issues, but various other personal barriers hinder legal immigrants from pursuing citizenship. To begin, since Mexico is adjacent to the United States, Mexican immigrants tend to maintain close ties with their families and friends in Mexico, with some of them wishing to return one day, and so they are unsure whether to apply for dual or U.S. citizenship. Further, besides lacking English language and reading and writing skills, many Mexicans are not aware that they can hold dual citizenship, in part because up until 1998 Mexico did not allow its citizens that option. Given the significance of citizenship, which includes the ability to vote, we must make a stronger commitment to educate people about the importance of citizenship, encourage citizenship, and provide resources to facilitate the process, including English classes, reading and writing classes, civics classes, legal counsel, and community outreach. President Obama's 2014 executive action included a directive allowing families to pay naturalization fees in installments with credit cards, and his administration was planning to launch a national campaign to promote and encourage citizenship, focusing on ten states where a high concentration of legal residents reside: Arizona, California, Florida, Illinois, Massachusetts, New Jersey, New York, Texas, Virginia, and Washington (Gamboa 2015). However, with Obama's term coming to an end, the campaign was not carried out.

DRIVER'S LICENSES

Another situation drastically hindering the mobility, security, and well-being of undocumented people is their inability to obtain an official driver's license in the great majority of states, an issue that some states are finally addressing. For instance, highly influenced by the demands of the workforce, ten states (and the District of Columbia), including New Mexico, Utah, and Washington, now allow undocumented people to drive. Illinois started issuing Temporary Visitor Driver's Licenses for undocumented people in 2013, and that same year the California legislature passed a bill (A.B. 60) that would give undocumented immigrants the ability to apply for driver's licenses. As a minority-majority state and home to the largest population of undocumented people in the country, California has approximately 2.6 million documented immigrants, who constitute nearly 10 percent of the state's workforce. Signaling a *positive reaction* to shifting demographic trends and a *move* toward incorporating the state's immigrant population into mainstream society, A.B. 60 passed with bipartisan support in the California legislature. Or, perhaps, California's lawmakers, other politicians, and the public are coming to the realization that *it's a new world*.

WHAT'S IN A WORD?

Further fueling the anti-immigration discourse is anti-immigrant terminology, prop-agated by conservative media as a means of arousing anti-immigrant passion, moral panics, and hate, and influencing public opinion. As a first step, we must change the tone and rhetoric surrounding the country's continuous and tedious debate on com-prehensive immigration reform. The widely used terms of "wetbacks," "illegal immi-grants," or "illegals" not only carry *negative* and *criminal* connotations, but they have become code words for ethnic minorities, or more precisely, these terms are equated with "criminality," "Mexicans," and "Latinos" in general. Further, these labels demon-ize, dehumanize, and, in a sense, brutalize undocumented people. For instance, those who use such terms continue to perpetuate the perception that immigration enforce-ment is about national security, which includes rounding up Mexican and other Latino *criminals*, when in reality the central issue is not criminality. While we have the most secure border in over four decades, a highly militarized border, the highest number of deportations ever, and Mexican immigration hovering around zero in the last few years, the immigration discourse revolves around myths about immigrants, antagonizing taxpayers and voters while doing little to properly address the realities of immigration or to acknowledge that the vast majority of immigrants who enter the United States do so in search of a better life—and help the American economy by filling the lower strata of our demand for cheap labor and jobs that have been characterized as "Mexican jobs" or "Latino labor."

THE FUTURE OF IMMIGRATION: THINKING AHEAD

Considering the wide array of issues surrounding immigration laws, enforcement, deportation, incarceration, and discourse, it is difficult to predict the future of immigration, particularly now with the current aggressive anti-immigrants movement and other social control movements, like the war on drugs and the war on terrorism, which are all tied to a multibillion-dollar enterprise. Thinking ahead, though, we must be mindful of a series of pressing issues, as we strive for comprehensive immigration reform and to humanize immigration and *difference* in the American society. To begin, for decades immigration has been "equated" with Latinos, particularly Mexicans, and thus the anti-immigration discourse, in all dimensions, has revolved around Latinos. However, Asians have surpassed Latinos as the largest group of new immigrants to the United States, they are now the fastest-growing *racial* group in the country, and they are projected to surpass Latinos as the largest group of immigrants by 2065.

As noted herein, while people of Mexican heritage have constituted the majority of Latino immigrants (according to some figures), the net migration from Mexico has fallen to zero, and is likely to fall even more with Donald Trump as president. While the storyline continues to use a negative image of Mexico and its people, for Mexican immigrants, employment prospects, income, education, healthcare, and life in general is getting better in Mexico, making the dangerous journey *a el norte* less appealing. Besides the demographic shifts and longer-term economic trends in Mexico, recent economic reforms by the Mexican government may produce a smaller cohort of undocumented immigrants to the United States in the coming years. To be sure, two influential factors alone, a much lower birth rate and rising economic opportunities in Mexico, are likely to reshape the landscape in both countries. For instance, Mexico's income and per capita gross domestic product have both risen 45 percent since 2000, as the average birth rate continues to fall, now standing at about two children per family (Cave 2011).

Meanwhile, even though the American economy seems to be slowly recovering, the U.S. recession has reduced the gap between what undocumented workers can earn in the United States and what they can earn by staying in Mexico. Therefore, as life in Mexico improves, some Mexicans are staying home because their families are smaller, legal visas are easier to obtain to travel north for shopping or to visit relatives residing in the United States, and, of course, the dangers of the journey remain deadly on both sides of the border. In addition, the highly militarized border, which includes increased enforcement, fencing, and surveillance, is another reason for Mexicans to stay in their home country. From a cost-benefit analysis, border crossing for many Mexicans is no longer advantageous, making their homeland look more beneficial, while enabling them to be with their families. As noted above, undocumented Mexican immigration has leveled out at zero; that is, the number of Mexicans leaving the United States (deported or for other reasons) has been about equal to the number of new immigrants who cross into the country. In fact, according to a recent study by the Pew Research Center, more Mexican immigrants are leaving the United States than entering, and most Mexicans leaving the United States are doing so voluntarily to reunite with their families or to start a family and a new life. The report, "More Mexicans Leaving Than Coming to the U.S.," released on November 19, 2015, shows that from 2009 to 2014, more than one million Mexicans and their families left the United States for Mexico, compared to about 865,000 who entered. Reportedly, more than sixteen million Mexican immigrants have migrated to the United States in the last fifty years, more than from any other country, with unauthorized immigrants from Mexico accounting for about half of all U.S. unauthorized immigrants. However, according to Ana Gonzalez-Barrera (2015), author of the report, the overall flow of Mexican immigrants between the two countries is at its lowest since the 1990s. Therefore, instead of jumping on the anti-immigrants bandwagon, as many are currently doing, we should use this era to finally design and implement comprehensive immigration reforms. However, the mentality of some people continues to revolve around exploitation, like "who will work the fields," "who will do the Mexican labor," or "who will tend our gardens?" Worse, even as we witness an ongoing historical exploitation of undocumented people, racial profiling, criminalization, and incarceration of immigrants intensify.

Advocates of immigration reform and other activists are confronting and fighting against the profiling, criminalization, and incarceration of Latino immigrants, particularly immigrant children, simply because of their national origin or color of their skin by emphasizing the significant contributions of immigrants to the United States, exposing the cruelties of immigration enforcement and detention, and defending the rights of innocent children and their safe integration into the educational system. As asserted by Hinda Seif (2009, 3–4), while the human rights of immigrant children (particularly those migrating from Central America) have sparked heated discourse in the current debates over immigration legislation, enforcement, deportation, and detention, what cannot be contested is the increased "growth and dispersal of Latina/o youth" in schools and communities. Thus, "there are strong arguments for incorporating all immigrant children into the U.S. society and not penalizing their parents' circumstances and 'choices.'"

As for other Latino immigrants, especially migrants from Central America, while the majority are being detained along the Mexico-Guatemala border or the U.S.-

Mexico border, there is little indication that immigrants will stop trying to make the journey north. The grave economic, political, and social conditions in Central America continue to encourage "north migration." Early in 2015, the Obama administration asked Congress for $1 billion to help reduce the problems in El Salvador, Honduras, and Guatemala, the countries where most of the child and adult immigrants come from (*New York Times* 2015). Soon after, congressional appropriators in the House of Representatives in charge of allocating foreign aid set aside less than $300 million for Central America, with the lion's share of the aid being approved for security initiatives. Clearly, this amount will do little, if anything, to improve the lives of potential Central American immigrants. As a country that presents itself as *the saver and peacekeeper of the world*, the United States can be much more strategic and constructive in helping Central American countries. Allowing economic and social problems to fester will result in more people migrating north to seek safety and a better life. This will lead to yet another so-called immigration crisis and ultimately complicate the issues discussed in previous chapters, along with the multibillion-dollar anti-immigration and social control movements. And according to recent figures and projections, the majority of new immigrants and future immigrants will not be Mexican or even Latinos from Central or South America, but non-Latino immigrants, most of all Asians.

CONCLUSION

Looking at the profile of the estimated eleven to twelve million undocumented people residing in the United States, it's obvious that most of these people are not single men who recently arrived, with no connection to mainstream society. As delineated by of the contributors to this volume, the great majority are men, women, and children who are already part of the American society. The Department of Homeland Security, for instance, estimates that nearly three-fifths of undocumented immigrants have lived in the United States for more than a decade (Ewing 2014). As for Mexican immigrants, who have constituted the majority of Latino immigrants, their migration to the United States has not only come to a standstill but recently started an unprecedented shift—reverse migration, marking a dramatic change in the history of Mexican migration, particularly over the last four decades. As for Mexicans who continue to migrate north, according to a recent study, "A Transformation in Mexican Migration to the United States," by Rogelio Sáenz (2015), Mexicans migrating to the United States today tend to be older, are more likely to be women, hold higher socioeconomic status, have greater English-language fluency, and are less likely to be connected to the workforce than Mexicans who migrated in the early to middle 2000s.

Still, the intention of the anti-immigrants movement is to make immigrant life so difficult that they will deport themselves, which has contributed to thousands of Mexicans migrating south, while also creating many barriers for people migrating north and making life a nightmare for those who manage to cross into the United States. On September 4, 2015, for instance, U.S. District Judge Susan Bolton upheld part of Arizona's controversial immigration law, rejecting claims that the so-called "show your papers" provision of the law discriminates against Latino immigrants and Latinos in general. Thus, the law allows police in Arizona to check the immigration status of anyone they stop. The federal judge also upheld a provision that allows police to check the legal status of detainees in the United States. Ironically, Judge Bolton's ruling came two days after a federal judge approved a deal between the U.S. Department of Justice and Maricopa County to resolve accusations of civil rights violations and dismissed the department's lawsuit against Arizona Sheriff Joe Arpaio and his deputies.

Looked at in the context of a highly globalized social control movement, the root causes of migration have not been addressed. For instance, employment, violence, and poverty continue in Central America, and thus no law or level of enforcement or even deportations will deter people from migrating north. In fact, economic and social conditions are not improving in Central America. If the United States, which relies heavily on allies to maintain world dominance, is not willing to do everything possible to assist its closest neighbors and allies, then how can it have a credible foreign policy? We should also consider U.S. policy from a moral standpoint. "Protection of the children is not a priority in the allocation of U.S. government funds to the region," charges Megan McKenna, of the KIND children's assistance organization, which collaborated with a project to reintegrate repatriated children to Guatemala (EFE 2015, 1). As a way of establishing solidarity, the United States needs to collaborate with El Salvador, Guatemala, Honduras, and Mexico to strategically, effectively, and humanely reform immigration laws and develop a regional response in the countries of origin, transit, and destination.

Nationally, we have been seeing a xenophobic hysteria—illegals, Mexicans, terrorists, ISIS, border crisis, child immigrant crisis, Syrian refugees, and Ebola mashed together to instill public fear, provoke public sentiment, and influence public opinion. The reality is that our highly militarized border is more secure than ever before, and Mexican immigration has leveled out at zero. Regarding the current call for mass deportation of immigrants residing in the United States, even if undocumented immigrants could simply be "rounded up" and deported back to their native countries, neither the immigration dilemma nor related issues would be resolved, as we have learned from prior mass deportations. Instead, we should approach these trends as an opportunity to design and implement comprehensive immigration, economic, and social reform.

To begin, let's bring undocumented people out of the shadows so that they can be integrated into mainstream society, allowing them access to essential things, like training and education (Gershwin et al. 2007; Johnson 2013), which in turn will enable them to further contribute to the rebirth of the U.S. economy. According to a recent study by the Migration Policy Institute (2015), Mexican immigrants are the most disadvantaged immigrant group, and thus resources for the most disadvantaged must be a priority to allow them to actualize their full potential in all facets of social life as we strive for a better America.

Second, we need to confront the prejudice, racism, and discrimination against immigrants (undocumented and documented). To be sure, while some critics vehemently deny that ethnicity/race is a significant factor (or even a factor) in immigration laws, enforcement, criminalization, incarceration, or discourse, ethnic and racial minorities are already "wearing" a *racial uniform*—skin color—which itself has become the mark of illegality; ultimately, illegality is equated with *brownness* and *brownness* is equated with illegality. In essence, immigrants are "guilty" of being undocumented, they are "guilty" of being *brown* people, they are "guilty" of being Mexican immigrants, and, in a sense, they are "guilty" for simply existing or having been born. Of course, underneath it all, there is a more devastating motive—the continued exploitation, oppression, and marginalization of society's most vulnerable people, while seeking to maintain total control, dominance, and silencing of immigrants, the poor, and ethnic/racial minorities.

Third, we need to ensure that agencies address not only the racial profiling, brutality, and violence against immigrants, but the injustices during arrest and incarceration. However, with the political economy of the criminal justice system now being a major component of the U.S. economic system, reform will be the challenge of our times, as it may harm the criminal justice system's multibillion-dollar enterprise and the billions of dollars in revenue for private corporations. In fact, even the so-called liberal reform proposed by Democrats in 2017 increased funding for border enforcement and spending for private prison companies. As illustrated in previous chapters, for those who are benefiting from the multibillion-dollar criminal justice enterprise, reform has the lowest priority. Or, as the saying goes, reform is like taking the bone away from a dog.

Fourth, to humanize immigration and *difference*, we need to deconstruct immigrant myths and stereotypes and promote immigrant stories through positive ads, sharing their stories of how they give back to the community and contribute to the American economy and society. Further, as illustrated by Urbina in *Twenty-First Century Dynamics of Multiculturalism: Beyond Post-racial America* (2014), we need to teach immigrants to take pride in their own heritage. Additionally, we need to educate, mentor, and empower them to not feel ashamed about being immigrant minorities, allowing them to have pride and develop their capabilities and exercise their full potential.

Finally, as recently documented in *Latino Access to Higher Education: Ethnic Realities and New Directions for the Twenty-First Century* (Urbina and Wright 2016), the message must be clear: it's a new world. Of course, the challenges of living in an increasingly diverse society where ethnicity/race remains interwoven in our every-day lives, where whites and nonwhites remain worlds apart, require us to be active participants if we are to achieve positive social transformation. Solutions for many of the issues detailed herein require innovation, strategy, cooperation, courage, and a strong voice—a big task. A movement of this magnitude will also require endurance, a focused mission, and a well-defined vision, as engaging with the established social structure is like wrestling with alligators—slippery and dangerous. As a community, "After centuries of marginalization and neglect, we need to cast our own movements, projects, and ideas as a battle for relevancy in the face of historical manipulation, exploitation, and oppression. We need to fight, tooth and nail, for equity in all areas of social life. One point to make clear, ethnic and racial minorities are not looking for scraps or a handout from the old paternalistic system but an equitable, stable, and leveled playing field" (Urbina 2014, 276). As for the ultimate challenge of achieving positive social transformation in the new millennium, *si se puede*, we have to march forward *creating our own post-racial society—a multiperspective for the twenty-first century*. Ultimately, people of all races and ethnicities must unite and work together with a unified mission and inclusive vision if the United States wishes to situate itself as the country of the future.

NOTES

1. On January 2011, the Obama administration ended a high-tech border fence project that cost taxpayers nearly $1 billion, but did little to improve security. Congress ordered the high-tech fence along the U.S.-Mexico border in 2006 in response to arguments of a porous border. Initiated in 2005, it yielded only fifty-three miles of "virtual fence" (known as SBInet) in Arizona at a cost of at least $15 million a mile. The Bush administration awarded Boeing a three-year, $67 million contract, but Homeland Security Secretary Janet Napolitano used $50 million originally assigned for the fence to buy other technology and Border Patrol vehicles (Gamboa 2011).

2. The Department of Homeland Security has also used a supposed Mexican law that denied U.S. citizenship to individual adults, citing "Article 314" of the Mexican Constitution, which they said required out-of-wedlock births to be "legitimated" under Mexican law. However, no such provision exists in the Mexican Constitution. The U.S.

government's use of this fictitious law extends back to 1978; however, since immigration cases are not open to the public, no one can determine how many times "Article 314" has been cited, according to a 2013 brief by the Fifth U.S. Circuit Court of Appeals.

REFERENCES

Aguirre-Molina, M. 2014. "Police Aggression: A Social Determinant of Health (and Death)." *Informaciónal Denudes*, September 17. http://informacionaldesnudo.com/police-aggression-a-social-determinant-of-health-and-death/.

Al Jazeera. 2014. "Undocumented Immigrant Denied Law License in Florida." *Al Jazerra America*, March 7. http://america.aljazeera.com/articles/2014/3/7/illegal-immigrantdeniedlawlicenseinflorida.html.

Alpert, G., and R. Dunham. 2004. *Understanding Police Use of Force: Officers, Suspects, and Reciprocity*. Cambridge: Cambridge University Press.

Álvarez, S. E. 2012. "Latinas and Latinos in the U.S.: The Road to Prison." In *Hispanics in the U.S. Criminal Justice System: The New American Demography*, edited by M. G. Urbina, 203–24. Springfield, Ill.: Charles C Thomas.

Anchondo, L. 2010. "Top 10 Myths About Immigration." *Immigration Policy Center*. https://static1.squarespace.com/static/56948ad40e4c11c98e2e1871/t/56d47e4286db4336abda7fa4/1456766532004/Top+10+Myths+About+Immigration+-+Leo+Anchondo+of+Justice+for+Immigrants.pdf.

Applebome, P. 2012. "Police Gang Tyrannized Latinos, Indictment Says." *New York Times*, January 24. http://www.nytimes.com/2012/01/25/nyregion/connecticut-police-officers-accused-of-mistreating-latinos.html?mcubz=0.

Bailey, A., and J. M. Hayes. 2006. "Who's in Prisons? The Changing Demographics of Incarceration." *California Counts: Population Trends and Profiles* 8: 1–27.

Balko, R. 2006. "Overkill: The Rise of Paramilitary Police Raids in America." *Cato Institute*, July 17. http://object.cato.org/sites/cato.org/files/pubs/pdf/balko_whitepaper_2006.pdf.

Barajas, M. 2015. "Private Prison Companies Grow Fat Off Immigrant Detention." *Houston Press*, April 16. http://www.houstonpress.com/news/private-prison-companies-grow-fat-off-immigrant-detention-7372966.

Barlow, D., and M. Barlow. 2012. "Myth: The Core Mission of the Police Is to Fight Crime." In *Demystifying Crime and Criminal Justice*, 2nd ed., edited by R. M. Bohm and J. T. Walker, 73–80. Los Angeles, Calif.: Roxbury.

Bayley, D., and H. Mendelsohn. 1969. *Minorities and the Police: Confrontation in America*. New York: Free Press.

Bennett, B. 2014. "Border Patrol's Use of Deadly Force Criticized in Report." *Los Angeles Times*, February 27. http://articles.latimes.com/2014/feb/27/nation/la-na-border-killings-20140227.

Brader, T., N. A. Valentino, and E. Suhay. 2008. "What Triggers Public Opposition to Immigration? Anxiety, Group Cues, and Immigration Threat." *American Journal of Political Science* 52: 959–78.

Butcher, K. F., and A. M. Piehl. 2007. "Why Are Immigrants' Incarceration Rates So Low? Evidence on Selective Immigration, Deterrence, and Deportation." National Bureau of Economic Research. Working Paper No. 13229. Cambridge, Mass.

Cave, D. 2011. "For Mexicans Looking North, a New Calculus Favors Home." *New York Times*, July 6. http://www.nytimes.com/interactive/2011/07/06/world/americas/immigration.html.

Chardy, A. 2015. "Authorities Deport Hundreds of Thousands of Immigrants Convicted of Drug Offenses." *Miami Herald*, June 19. http://www.miamiherald.com/news/local/immigration/article24995425.html.

Citrin, J., B. Reingold, E. Walters, and D. Green. 1990. "The 'Official English' Movement and the Symbolic Politics of Language in the United States." *Western Political Quarterly* 43: 535–59.

Cole, D. 2001. "Formalism, Realism, and the War on Drugs." *Suffolk University Law Review* 35: 241–55.

Coulter, A. 2015. *Adios America: The Left's Plan to Turn Our Country into a Third World Hellhole*. Washington, D.C.: Regnery.

De León, A., and R. Del Castillo. 2012. *North to Aztlán: A History of Mexican Americans in the United States*. 2nd ed. Hoboken, N.J.: Wiley-Blackwell.

Del Bosque, M. 2015. "Children of Immigrants Denied Citizenship." *Texas Observer*, July 13. http://www.texasobserver.org/children-of-immigrants-denied-citizenship/.

Durán, R. 2009. "Legitimated Oppression: Inner-City Mexican American Experiences with Police Gang Enforcement." *Journal of Contemporary Ethnography* 38: 143–68.

EFE. 2015. "Study: Migrant Minors' Rights Systematically Violated in CentAm, U.S., Mexico." *EFE*, February 12. http://www.efe.com/efe/english/world/study-migrant-minors-rights-systematically-violated-in-centam-u-s-mexico/50000262-2534950.

Escobar, E. 1999. *Race, Police, and the Making of a Political Identity: Mexican Americans and the Los Angeles Police Department, 1900–1945*. Los Angeles: University of California Press.

Ewing, W. A. 2014. "The Growth of the U.S. Deportation Machine." *Immigration Impact*. http://www.immigrationpolicy.org/just-facts/growth-us-deportation-machine.

Fernández, B. 2014. "The Creeping Expansion of the Border Patrol." *Al Jazeera America*, May 7. http://america.aljazeera.com/opinions/2014/5/border-patrol-immigrationmilitarization homelandsecurity.html.

Fitzpatrick, T. 2001. "New Agenda for Social Policy and Criminology: Globalization, Urbanization, and the Emerging Post-Social Security State." *Social Policy and Administration* 35: 212–29.

Fyfe, J. 1981. "Who Shoots? A Look at Officer Race and Police Shooting." *Journal of Police Science and Administration* 9: 367–82.

Gamboa, S. 2011. "Obama Administration Ends High-Tech Border Fence." *Deseret News*, January 14. http://www.deseretnews.com/article/700100813/Obama-administration-ends-high-tech-border-fence.html.

———. 2015. "High Fees Limiting U.S. Citizenship to Wealthy, Non-Mexicans." *NBC News*, January 11. http://www.nbcnews.com/news/latino/high-fees-limiting-u-s-citizenship -wealthy-non-mexicans-n283061.

Gershwin, M., T. Coxen, B. Kelley, and G. Yakimov. 2007. "Building Tomorrow's Workforce: Promoting the Education and Advancement of Hispanic Immigrant Workers in America." Ann Arbor, Mich.: Corporation for a Skilled Workforce.

Gonzalez-Barrera, A. 2015. *More Mexicans Leaving Than Coming to the U.S. Pew Research Center*, November 19. http://www.pewhispanic.org/2015/11/19/more-mexicans-leaving-than -coming-to-the-u-s/.

Gonzalez-Barrera, A., M. H. López, J. S. Passel, and P. Taylor. 2013. *The Path Not Taken: Two-Thirds of Legal Mexican Immigrants Are Not U.S. Citizens. Pew Research Center*, February 4. http://www.pewhispanic.org/2013/02/04/the-path-not-taken/.

Goodale, G. 2013. "Immigration Reform: Will 'Amnesty' Produce More Illegal Immigration?" *Christian Science Monitor*, January 28. http://www.csmonitor.com/USA/2013/0128/ Immigration-reform-Will-amnesty-produce-more-illegal-immigration.

Gordon, C. 1991. "Governmental Rationality: An Introduction." In *The Foucault Effect: Studies in Governmentality*, edited by G. Burchell, C. Gordon, and P. Miller, 1–52. Chicago: University of Chicago Press.

Gordon, L. 2013. "Napolitano Commits Funds to Aid UC Students Who Entered U.S. Illegally." *Los Angeles Times*, October 30. http://articles.latimes.com/2013/oct/30/local/la-me -uc-napolitano-20131031.

Hardiman, K. 2015. "Ann Coulter: I'd Run Immigration Policy 'Like Tinder.'" *The Hill*, June 17. http://thehill.com/blogs/in-the-know/245249-ann-coulter-id-run-immigration-policy -like-tinder.

Holmes, M. 1998. "Perceptions of Abusive Police Practices in a U.S.-Mexico Border Community." *Social Science Journal* 35: 107–18.

———. 2000. "Minority Threat and Police Brutality: Determinants of Civil Rights Criminal Complaints in U.S. Municipalities." *Criminology* 38: 343–67.

Human Rights Watch. 1998. *Shielded from Justice: Police Brutality and Accountability in the United States. Human Rights Watch*. http://www.hrw.org/legacy/reports98/police/index.htm.

Huntington, S. 1996. *The Clash of Civilizations? The Debate*. New York: Foreign Affairs.

———. 2004. "The Hispanic Challenge." *Foreign Policy*, March/April: 30–45.

Immigration Compliance Group. 2008. "Top 5 Immigrant Myths of the Campaign Season." *Immigration Compliance Group*, March 13. http://www.immigrationcompliancegroup .com/immigration-compliance-blog/tag/2008-presidential-race/.

Ingraham, L. 2014. "Laura Ingraham: Why Conservatives Should Say No to Immigration Reform." *Washington Post*, February 19. https://www.washingtonpost.com/opinions/ laura-ingraham-why-conservatives-should-say-no-to-immigration-reform/2014/02/19/ 85ae3438-98f0-11e3-b931-0204122c514b_story.html.

Jacobs, D., and R. O'Brien. 1998. "The Determinants of Deadly Force: A Structural Analysis of Police Violence." *American Journal of Sociology* 103: 837–62.

Johnson, K. R. 2013. "The Keys to the Nation's Education Future: The Latina/o Struggle for Educational Equity." *Denver University Law Review* 90: 1231–49.

Kane, R., and M. White. 2013. *Bad Cops, Police Misconduct, and the New York City Police Department.* New York: New York University Press.

Kirkham, C. 2014. "How Corporations Are Cashing In on the Worldwide Immigration Crackdown." *Huffington Post,* January 23. http://www.huffingtonpost.com/2014/01/23/private -prisons-immigration_n_4603448.html.

Lee, E. 2014. "Cop to Immigrant During Traffic Stop: 'If You Do Something, I Will Kill You Right Here.'" *ThinkProgress,* October 14. https://thinkprogress.org/cop-to-immigrant -during-traffic-stop-if-you-do-something-i-will-kill-you-right-here-6a7202543455.

Lessin, J., and M. Jordan. 2013. "Laurene Powell Jobs Goes Public to Promote Dream Act." *Wall Street Journal,* May 16. http://www.wsj.com/articles/SB10001424127887323582904 578487263583009532.

Light, M., M. López, and A. Gonzalez-Barrera. 2014. *The Rise of Federal Immigration Crimes: Unlawful Reentry Drives Growth. Pew Research Center,* March 18. http://www.pewhispanic .org/2014/03/18/the-rise-of-federal-immigration-crimes/.

Lytle, K. 2003. "Constructing the Criminal Alien: A Historical Framework for Analyzing Border Vigilantes at the Turn of the 21st Century." Working Paper 83. University of California San Diego, Center for Comparative Immigration Studies.

Martinez, D. E., G. Cantor, and W. A. Ewing. 2014. "No Action Taken: Lack of CBP Accountability in Responding to Complaints of Abuse." American Immigration Council, May 4. http://www.americanimmigrationcouncil.org/sites/default/files/No%20Action%20Taken _Final.pdf.

Martinez, D. E., J. Slack, and J. Heyman. 2013. *Bordering on Criminal: The Routine Abuse of Migrants in the Removal System. American Immigration Council,* December. https://www .americanimmigrationcouncil.org/sites/default/files/research/bordering_on_criminal.pdf.

Meng, G. 2015. *A Price Too High: US Families Torn Apart by Deportations for Drug Offense. Human Rights Watch,* June 16. https://www.hrw.org/report/2015/06/16/price-too-high/ us-families-torn-apart-deportations-drug-offenses.

Migration Policy Institute. 2015. "The Mexican Diaspora in the United States." *Migration Policy Institute,* June. http://www.migrationpolicy.org/research/select-diaspora-populations -united-states.

Morales, A. 1972. *Ando Sangrando: A Study of Mexican American-Police Conflict.* La Puente, Calif.: Perspectiva.

Morín, J. L. 2009. *Latino/a Rights and Justice in the United States: Perspectives and Approaches.* 2nd ed. Durham, N.C.: Carolina Academic Press.

New York Times. 2015. "Central America's Unresolved Migrant Crisis." *New York Times*, June 16. http://www.nytimes.com/2015/06/16/opinion/central-americas-unresolved-migrant -crisis.html?_r=0.

Orduna, J. 2014. "Tasers, Drones, and Cold Chicken: Inside the Multibillion-Dollar Business of Keeping Me Out of America." *BuzzFeed*, December 18. http://www.buzzfeed.com/ josemorduna/inside-the-multibillion-dollar-business-of-keeping-me-out-of#.htD4d65wb.

Pew Research Center. 2014. "Stark Racial Divisions in Reactions to Ferguson Police Shoot- ing." *Pew Research Center*, August 18. http://www.people-press.org/2014/08/18/stark-racial -divisions-in-reactions-to-ferguson-police-shooting/.

Phillips, S., J. Hagan, and N. Rodriguez. 2006. "Brutal Borders?: Examining the Treatment of Deportees During Arrest and Detention." *Social Forces* 85: 93–109.

Phillips, S., N. Rodriguez, and J. Hagan. 2002. "Brutality at the Border: Use of Force in the Arrest of Immigrants in the United States." *International Journal of the Sociology of Law* 30: 285–306.

Police Executive Research Forum. 2013. *Use of Force Review: Cases and Policies*. U.S. Customs and Border Protection. Washington, D.C.: U.S. Customs and Border Protection. https:// www.cbp.gov/sites/default/files/documents/PERFReport.pdf.

Reilly, M. 2014. "GOP Senate Candidate Defends Use of 'Wetback' Slur as 'Normal as Breath- ing Air.'" *Huffington Post*, February 24. http://www.huffingtonpost.com/2014/02/24/chris -mapp-wetbacks_n_4849184.html.

Roach, D. 2012. "Don Roach: An Equitable Solution to Illegal Immigration." *GoLocalProv*, June 20. http://www.golocalprov.com/politics/don-roach8.

Robelo, D. 2014. "The Drug War = Mass Deportation: 250,000 Deported for Drug Offenses in Last 6 Years." *Drug Policy Alliance*, April 10. http://www.drugpolicy.org/blog/drug-war -mass-deportation-250000-deported-drug-offenses-last-6-years.

Rumbaut, R. G., and W. Ewing. 2007. "The Myth of Immigrant Criminality and the Paradox of Assimilation: Incarceration Rates Among Native and Foreign-Born Men." Immigration Policy Center, January. https://www.researchgate.net/publication/237563250_The_Myth _of_Immigrant_Criminality_and_the_Paradox_of_Assimilation_Incarceration_Rates _Among_Native_and_Foreign-Born_Men.

Russell, K. 1998. *The Color of Crime: Racial Hoaxes, White Fear, Black Protectionism, Police Harassment, and Other Macroaggressions*. New York: New York University Press.

Saenz, R. 2015. *A Transformation in Mexican Migration to the United States*. Carsey Research, National Issue Brief #86. Summer. http://scholars.unh.edu/cgi/viewcontent.cgi?article= 1246&context=carsey.

Seif, H. 2009. "The Civic Education and Engagement of Latina/o Immigrant Youth: Challeng- ing Boundaries and Creating Safe Spaces." Research Paper Series on Latino Immigrant Civic and Political Participation, No. 5. June. Woodrow Wilson International Center for Scholars.

https://www.wilsoncenter.org/sites/default/files/Seif%20%20Challenging%20Boundaries
%20and%20Creating%20Safe%20Spaces.pdf.

Selway, W., and M. Newkirk. 2013. "Congress Mandates Jail Beds for 34,000 Immigrants as Private Prisons Profit." *Bloomberg*, September 24. http://www.bloomberg.com/news/articles/
2013-09-24/congress-fuels-private-jails-detaining-34-000-immigrants.

Shapiro, G. 2014. "How Immigration Reform Could Boost Our National Defense." *Washington Post*, March 21. https://www.washingtonpost.com/news/innovations/wp/2014/03/21/how
-immigration-reform-could-boost-our-national-defense/.

Simon, J. 1997. "Governing Through Crime." In *The Crime Conundrum*, edited by L. Friedman and G. Fisher, 171–90. Oxford: Oxford University Press.

Skolnick, J. 2011. *Justice Without Trial: Law Enforcement in Democratic Society*. New Orleans, La.: Quid Pro Books.

Skolnick, J., and J. Fyfe. 1993. *Above the Law: Police and the Excessive Use of Force*. New York: Free Press.

Smith, B., and M. Holmes. 2003. "Community Accountability, Minority Threat, and Police Brutality: An Examination of Civil Rights Criminal Complaints." *Criminology* 41: 1035–64.

Sullivan, L. 2010. "Prison Economics Help Drive Ariz. Immigration Law." *NPR*, October 28. http://www.npr.org/2010/10/28/130833741/prison-economics-help-drive-ariz
-immigration-law.

Teaching Tolerance. 2011. "10 Myths About Immigration." *Teaching Tolerance*. http://www
.tolerance.org/immigration-myths.

Tirman, J. 2015ba. "The Immigration Debate Is Not About Legality, It's About Culture." *Huffington Post*, March 16. http://www.huffingtonpost.com/john-tirman/the-immigration
-debate-is-not-about-legality_b_6876910.html.

———. 2015b. *Dream Chasers: Immigration and the American Backlash*. Cambridge, Mass.: MIT Press.

TRAC Immigration. 2014. "Secure Communities and ICE Deportations: A Failed Program?" http://trac.syr.edu/immigration/reports/349/.

Urbina, M. G. 2012. *Capital Punishment in America: Race and the Death Penalty over Time*. El Paso, Tex.: LFB Scholarly Publishing.

———, ed. 2014. *Twenty-First Century Dynamics of Multiculturalism: Beyond Post-racial America*. Springfield, Ill.: Charles C Thomas.

———, ed. 2018. *Hispanics in the U.S. Criminal Justice System: Ethnicity, Ideology, and Social control*. 2nd ed. Springfield, Ill.: Charles C Thomas.

Urbina, M. G., and S. E. Álvarez, eds. 2015. *Latino Police Officers in the United States: An Examination of Emerging Trends and Issues*. Springfield, Ill.: Charles C Thomas.

———. 2016. "Neoliberalism, Criminal Justice, and Latinos: The Contours of Neoliberal Economic Thought and Policy on Criminalization." *Latino Studies* 14: 33–58.

————. 2017. *Ethnicity and Criminal Justice in the Era of Mass Incarceration: A Critical Reader on the Latino Experience*. Springfield, Ill.: Charles C Thomas.

Urbina, M. G., J. E. Vela, and J. O. Sánchez. 2014. *Ethnic Realities of Mexican Americans: From Colonialism to 21st Century Globalization*. Springfield, Ill.: Charles C Thomas.

Urbina, M. G., and C. R. Wright. 2016. *Latino Access to Higher Education: Ethnic Realities and New Directions for the Twenty-First Century*. Springfield, Ill.: Charles C Thomas.

Walker, S. 1998. *Popular Justice: A History of American Criminal Justice*. 2nd ed. New York: Oxford University Press.

Welch, M. 2002. *Detained: Immigration Laws and the Expanding I.N.S. Jail Complex*. Philadelphia: Temple University Press.

————. 2006. *Scapegoats of September 11th: Hate Crimes and State Crimes in the War on Terror*. New Brunswick, N.J.: Rutgers University Press.

————. 2009. *Crimes of Power and States of Impunity: The U.S. Response to Terror*. New Brunswick, N.J.: Rutgers University Press.

Whitehead, J. 2013. *A Government of Wolves: The Emerging American Police State*. New York: SelectBooks.

CONTRIBUTORS

Sofía Espinoza Álvarez is an author, researcher, legist, social advocate, and philanthropist. She received a law degree from Universidad de León, San Miguel de Allende, Guanajuato, Mexico, and holds a bachelor of science degree in criminal justice (Sul Ross State University–Rio Grande College). Her areas of interest include Mexican and U.S. jurisprudence, the philosophy of law, constitutional law, immigration law, law and society, and penology. Her research has been published in national and international peer-reviewed journals, including "Capital Punishment on Trial: Who Lives, Who Dies, Who Decides—A Question of Justice?" (*Criminal Law Bulletin*, 2014) and "Neoliberalism, Criminal Justice, and Latinos: The Contours of Neoliberal Economic Thought and Policy on Criminalization" (*Latino Studies*, 2016). Her books include *Latino Police Officers in the United States: An Examination of Emerging Trends and Issues* (2015) and *Ethnicity and Criminal Justice in the Era of Mass Incarceration: A Critical Reader on the Latino Experience* (2017). Since 2013, Álvarez has been working with migrant children, women, and men traveling to the United States through Mexico, seeing firsthand the global dynamics of immigration, prompting her to start a nonprofit organization—Empower Global Foundation (https://globalempower.org/). With a global mission, Empower Global is focused on empowering, habilitating, and creating awareness and seeking equality, justice, respect, and human dignity. In addition to her work as a legal scholar and her academic endeavors, Álvarez assists people with immigration-related issues, including visa requirements. Her website is http://sofiaalva.com/.

Steven W. Bender, JD, is professor of law and associate dean for research and faculty development at Seattle University School of Law, joining the Seattle faculty in 2011 after twenty years of teaching at the University of Oregon School of Law. He is former copresident of the Society of American Law Teachers (SALT) and of Latina and Latino Critical Legal Theory (LatCrit). Bender's writing reflects his experiences growing up in East Los Angeles as the son of a Mexican mother. Bender is author of many law review articles addressing law, culture, politics, and history, and several books, including *Greasers and Gringos: Latinos, Law, and the American Imagination* (2003); *One Night in America: Robert Kennedy, César Chávez, and the Dream of Dignity* (2008); *Comprende?: The Significance of Spanish in English-Only Times* (2008); *Tierra y Libertad: Land, Liberty, and Latino Housing* (2010); *Everyday Law for Latino/as* (2008); and *Run for the Border: Vice and Virtue in U.S.-Mexico Border Crossings* (2012). His latest book is *Mea Culpa: Lessons on Law and Regret from U.S. History* (2015). Many of his published articles address the need and potential sources for compassionate immigration reform, including "Compassionate Immigration Reform" (*Fordham Urban Law Journal*, 2010). He is recipient of the 2008 Oregon Book Award for general nonfiction.

Leo R. Chávez, PhD, received his PhD from Stanford University and currently teaches in the Department of Anthropology at the University of California, Irvine. In addition to scores of academic articles, Chávez is author of *Shadowed Lives: Undocumented Immigrants in American Society* (3rd ed., 2013), *Covering Immigration: Popular Images and the Politics of the Nation* (2001), and *The Latino Threat: Constructing Immigrants, Citizens, and the Nation* (2nd ed., 2013). Chávez received the Margaret Mead Award in 1993, the Association of Latina and Latino Anthropologists Book Award for *The Latino Threat* in 2009, and the Society for the Anthropology of North America award for Distinguished Achievement in the Critical Study of North America in 2009.

Arnoldo De León, PhD, is distinguished professor of history emeritus, Angelo State University, San Angelo, Texas. He has authored and edited several books and articles on the history of Mexican Americans. They include *The Tejano Community: 1836–1900* (1982, 1997); *The Mexican Image in Nineteenth-Century Texas* (1983); *They Called Them Greasers: Anglo Attitudes Toward Mexicans in Texas, 1821–1900* (1983); *Tejanos and the Numbers Game* (1989); *Not Enough Room: Mexicans, Anglos, and Socio-Economic Change in Texas, 1850–1990* (1993); *Mexican Americans in Texas: A Brief History* (1993, 1999, 2009); *North to Aztlán: A History of Mexican Americans in the United States* (1997, 2006); *Ethnicity in the Sun Belt* (2001); *Racial Frontiers: Africans, Chinese, and Mexicans in Western America, 1848–1890* (2002); *Tejano Epic:*

Essays in Honor of Felix D. Almaraz, Jr. (2005); *Beyond Texas Through Time: Breaking Away from Past Interpretations* (2011); *War Along the Border: The Mexican Revolution and Tejano Communities* (2012); *A History of Texas* (2014); and *Tejano West Texas* (2015). De León is a fellow of the Texas State Historical Association and the West Texas Historical Association. In 2013, the Tejas Foco of the National Association of Chicana and Chicano Studies bestowed on De León the Premio Estrella de Aztlán Lifetime Achievement Award.

Daniel Justino Delgado, PhD, is an assistant professor of sociology at Texas A&M University at San Antonio. His research focuses on the processes of racialization experienced by Latinos and other racialized groups in the United States. Professor Delgado has published various academic articles in diverse journals, including, most recently (with David Brunsma and Kerry Ann Rockquemore), "Liminality in the Multiracial Experience: Towards a Concept of Identity Matrix" (2013) in *Identities: Global Studies in Culture and Power* and " 'And You Need Me to Be the Token Mexican?': Examining Racial Hierarchies and the Complexities of Racial Identities for Middle-Class Mexican Americans" in *Critical Sociology.* His current project explores the discourse used by the Maricopa County Sheriff's Office regarding Latinos living in Arizona.

Roxanne Lynn Doty, PhD, is associate professor in the School of Politics and Global Studies at Arizona State University. Her book *The Law into Their Own Hands: Immigration and the Politics of Exceptionalism* (2009) was awarded the Silver Book Award in 2010 by the Association of Borderland Studies. Dr. Doty is also author of *Anti-Immigrantism in Western Democracies: Statecraft, Desire, and the Politics of Exclusion* (2003) and *Imperial Encounters: The Politics of Representation in North-South Relations* (1996). She has published in *International Studies Quarterly*; *Millennium: European Journal of International Relations*; *Review of International Studies*; *Alternatives*; and *International Political Sociology*. Doty teaches courses on ethics and human rights in global politics, global inequality, and critical international relations theory. She serves on the editorial boards of *International Political Sociology*; *Environment and Planning D: Society and Space*; and *Journal of Narrative Politics*.

Brenda I. Gill, PhD (formerly Marshall) is a mixed-methods prepared family sociologist and an associate professor of sociology in the Department of Criminal Justice and Social Sciences at Alabama State University (ASU) in Montgomery, Alabama. She received her doctorate from Wayne State University. Her research is mostly international in scope and includes the areas of immigration, multiculturalism, diversity, family, media, and violence (family and school). Dr. Gill's work includes publications on immigration, multiculturalism, and culture from an international perspective, exploring the experiences, challenges, similarities, and differences among several countries. Presently she is compiling research findings into a report for dissemination to the Guyana government. Her study, entitled "Developing Evidence-Based Intervention Strategies for Caribbean at Risk Youth: Risks and Protective Behaviors" (EBISCRY), is projected as a longitudinal study of adolescent trends in the Caribbean. Recently, Dr. Gill was contracted to supervise a large study that assesses students' knowledge, attitudes, perceptions, and experiences relative to federally mandated Sexual, Domestic, Dating, and Stalking (SDDS) violence services.

Ruth Gomberg-Muñoz, PhD, is an assistant professor of anthropology at Loyola University, Chicago. Her research explores how undocumented people and their family members navigate the political and socioeconomic landscape of the United States. Results from Dr. Gomberg-Muñoz's ethnographic research studies have been published in various academic journals, including *American Ethnologist, American Anthropologist, Human Organization, Journal of Ethnic and Migration Studies*, and *DuBois Review*. In 2011, Oxford University Press published her book on immigration, *Labor and Legality: An Ethnography of a Mexican Immigrant Network*. In her recent book, *Becoming Legal: Immigration Law and Mixed Status Families* (2016), she follows undocumented people over a three-year period as they attempt to change their status under U.S. immigration laws.

Peter Laufer, PhD, is the James Wallace Chair Professor in Journalism at the University of Oregon School of Journalism and Communication. Dr. Laufer is author of more than a dozen books that deal with social and political issues, from borders and identity to human relationships with other animals. They include *Wetback Nation: The Case for Opening the Mexican-American Border* (2004) and *Calexico: True Lives of the Borderlands* (2011). More about his books, documentary films, and broadcasts, which have won the George Polk, Robert F. Kennedy, Edward R. Murrow, and other awards, can be found at http://peterlaufer.com.

Lupe S. Salinas, JD, is the Eugene Harrington Professor of Law at Texas Southern University's Thurgood Marshall School of Law in Houston. The Honorable Lupe S. Salinas, retired judge of the 351st Criminal District Court of Harris County, Texas, has served in various professional and academic capacities. Early in his career, in addition to his work as a civil rights attorney and federal prosecutor in Houston, Salinas served as special assistant to the U.S. attorney general in Washington, D.C., where he assisted in the 1980 hearings that resulted in the Final Report of the Select Commission on Immigration and Refugee Policy (SCIRP) and the 1986 IRCA legislation. Professor Salinas is also a prolific academic researcher and author. His research interests focus on criminal procedure and Latino civil rights issues. Recently, Salinas published *U.S. Latinos and Criminal Injustice* (2015), delineating the Latino experience with the U.S. criminal justice system. In 2010, the Mexican government honored Salinas with the Ohtli Award, presented to an individual who has opened doors of opportunity for Mexican immigrants and for the Mexican American community in the United States.

Mary C. Sengstock, PhD, was professor of sociology at Wayne State University in Detroit, Michigan. (She passed away as this project was being finalized.) She received a PhD from Washington University in St. Louis, Missouri. Her major focus of research was in the area of immigration and ethnicity in the United States. Dr. Sengstock worked collecting and analyzing data on the Chaldeans, a Detroit-based community of Christian immigrants from Iraq, for over fifty years. Her research resulted in two books on this particular minority community: *Chaldean-Americans: Changing Conceptions of Ethnic Identity* (2nd ed., 1999); and *Chaldeans in Michigan* (2005). Dr. Sengstock's book on immigration and multiculturalism, *Voices of Diversity: Multi-Culturalism in America* (2009), analyzes the socialization experiences of persons from mixed ethnic and racial backgrounds. Dr. Sengstock also conducted research in social gerontology and family violence, with a special focus on abuse of the elderly, and she often conducted training programs for health professionals on the importance of cultural sensitivity in providing medical and social services.

Martin Guevara Urbina, PhD, a native of San Miguel de Allende, Guanajuato, Mexico, is a Mexican American author, writer, researcher, professor, and speaker who, as a sociologist and criminologist, has engaged in an intensive academic research, publication, and discourse agenda, with an emphasis on the exploration of the Latino experience and a focus on the Mexican American experience. Dr. Urbina is professor of criminal justice in the Department of Natural and Behavioral Sciences at Sul Ross State University–Rio Grande College, and an adjunct instructor of sociology for Southwest Texas Junior College. He is author, coauthor, or editor of over sixty scholarly publications on a wide range of topics. His most recent books are *Ethnic Realities of Mexican Americans: From Colonialism to 21st Century Globalization* (2014); *Twenty-First Century Dynamics of Multiculturalism: Beyond Post-Racial America* (2014); *Latino Police Officers in the United States: An Examination of Emerging Trends and Issues* (2015); *Latino Access to Higher Education: Ethnic Realities and New Directions for the Twenty-First Century* (2016); *Ethnicity and Criminal Justice in the Era of Mass Incarceration: A Critical Reader on the Latino Experience* (2017); and *Hispanics in the U.S. Criminal Justice System: Ethnicity, Ideology, and Social Control* (2nd ed., 2018). In the United States, Professor Urbina appears frequently on primetime evening news for Telemundo, where he has discussed historical, existing, and emerging social, economic, and political issues—like immigration, deportations, excessive/deadly force in policing, imprisonment of children, the school-to-prison pipeline, and national security. For a complete list of Urbina's research and publications, visit his website (http://martinguevaraurbina.com) and his author page on Amazon.

Claudio G. Vera Sánchez, PhD, is an assistant professor in the Criminal Justice Department at Roosevelt University, Chicago. His areas of research center on youth justice, policing, and ethnic/racial minorities in the United States. His studies have explored the experiences of young minorities (e.g., Latinos and African Americans) with the police, the perceived legitimacy of the police in underprivileged neighborhoods, and how officers negotiate police work within inner-city neighborhoods. His recent publications analyze diverse topics and include "Sacrificed on the Altar of Public Safety: The Policing of Latino and African American Youth" (2011); "Racialized Policing: Officers' Voices on Policing Latino and African American Neighborhoods" (2011); and "Latino Officers, Policy, and Practice" (2015). Professor Vera Sánchez is also committed to transformative learning, and he has worked collaboratively with university students to redirect students with previous involvement with the legal system from a "path of prison" to college.

INDEX

1882 Chinese Exclusion Act, 46, 58, 102, 106, 211

1986 Select Commission on Immigration and Refugee Policy (SCIRP), 131

2016 DHS Appropriations Bill, 137

287G program, 63–64, 75, 88–89, 93, 144–46, 315

9/11, 22, 70, 123, 186, 219, 271, 276, 282–83, 286, 289, 295–96, 314, 316

AB 540, 195

abuse, xv, 147, 178, 277, 296, 307–8, 319

accountability, 304, 307–9

Aderholt, Robert, 317

aerostats, 283–84

affirmative action, 218, 220, 222

Affordable Care Act, 110, 195

Africa, 227, 278

Agamben, Giorgio, 70

AGIF, 36–37, 39

Aguirre, Adalberto, 18

Al Qaeda, 5, 55

Alabama HB 56, xvii–xviii, 88

Alabama, xvii–xviii, 9, 316, 319

Alden, Edward, 295

ALEC, 313

Alfred P. Murrah Federal Building, 68

Algers, Horatio, 257

Alien Absconder Initiative, 57

American Civil Liberties Union (ACLU), xviii, 125, 152, 285, 291–92, 304, 306

American Dream, 14, 17, 255, 275, 324

American G.I. Forum, 36

American Legislative Exchange Council, 313

American Protective Association, 213

American Protestant Union, 213

American Revolution, 101, 213

Americans for Immigrant Justice, 155

Amish, 206

Anchondo, Leo, 302

Anderson, E.N., 172

Anglicans, 205

Anglo Saxon, xvi, 30, 207, 216

Antiterrorism and Effective Death Penalty
　Act of 1996 (AEDP), 68, 133, 159
Apple, 86
Arab, 57
Aranda, Luis, 141
Arcega, Cristian, 141
Arizona Border Surveillance Technology
　Plan, 285
Arkansas, 89
Army, 128, 142
Ashcroft, John, 64
Asia, 52, 227, 251
Austria, 206
Austria-Hungry, 50

Baby Boomers, 158–59, 259, 296
Bacon, David, 68
Baggett, Ryan, 283
Bakke (1978), 220
Balibar, Etienne, 68
Balko, Radley, 282
Banks, Iain, 281
Barker, Martin, 68
Barnett, Roger, 35, 37
Bath Riots, 18
Battle of San Jacinto, 209
Bean, Frank D., 197
Beckett, Katherine, 91
Bejarano, Cynthia, 19
Berlin Wall, 14, 122, 134
bifocal lens, 19
bilingualism, 5, 186
birth certificates, 151, 273, 328
Bizzell, Steve, 146
Black Hawk helicopters, 89
Bolton, Susan, 333
Bonilla-Silva, Eduardo, 68, 245
border crisis, 271, 333

Border Security Expo, 283
Borjas, George, 311
Bosniak, Linda, 127
Box, John, 126, 146
Brader, Ted, 323
Brazil, 213
Brewer, Jan, 310, 314
British, 206, 215
Brooks, Mo, 312
Brown, Ronald, 284
Brown, Susan K., 197
Buddha, 217
Bureau of Immigration, 104
Bush, George W., 10, 67, 135–36, 326
Byrd, Robert, 136, 316

Cain, Herman, 55
Calhoun, John C., 145
California Drug Policy Alliance, 305
California Supreme Court, 47, 325
California the National Alliance for
　Human Rights, 37
Cameron, Allan, 141–42
Canada, 53, 111, 132, 249
Cantor, Guillermo, 308
Capitol Hill, 5, 9, 312
Caraballo, Eduardo, 151
Caribbean, 121, 215–16, 227, 327
Carlos Frey, John, 135
Carnegie, Andrew, 102
Carson, Ben, 281, 309
Carter, Jimmy, 34, 37, 130
*Casas-Castrillon v. Department of Home-
　land Security* (2008), 139, 160
Casey, William, 130
Castro, Raul, 289
Center for Immigration Studies, 8, 69,
　295

Center of Excellence on Homeland Security, 286

Central American children, xv, 4, 14, 281, 328

Chacon, Jennifer, 83

Chae Chan Ping v. United States (1889), 58

Chapin, Violeta, 89

Chapman, Leonard, 67

Chavez, Cesar, 127

Chávez, Leo R., 22, 31, 168, 197, 243, 344

Chicago School, 243–44

Chicano Movement, 37

child immigrant crisis, 14, 333

Chinese Exclusion Act of 1882, 46, 58, 102, 160, 211

Chomsky, Aviva, 80, 243

Chou, Rosalind, 251

Christopher Columbus, 240

Citrin, Jack, 321

Ciudad Juárez, 270, 272

civil rights activists, 307, 314

Civil War, 101–2, 131, 211, 293

Civiletti, Benjamin R., 131

Clinton, William Bill, 54, 64, 87, 133, 135, 159, 169

Coe, Barbara, 83

Cohen, Dan, 287

Colby, William, 67

Cold War, 57

Cole, David, xviii, 303

Colombia, 122

Colorado, 46, 51, 209

Communists, 46, 56, 301

Confucius, 217

Congregationalists, 205

Congressional Budget Office, 295

Congressional Research Service, 316

Conner, Roger, 146

Constitution's Bill of Rights, 139

Constitution-free zone, 285–86

contract detention facilities, 71

Corbett, Nicholas, 150

Corrections Corporation of America (CCA), 71–73, 137, 139, 154, 292, 313–14, 317–18

corruption, 69, 112, 124, 275

Cortes, Patricia, 85

Coulter, Ann, 217, 309, 312,

Council on Foreign Relations, 295

Criminal Alien Program (CAP), 72, 315

Crow, Jim, xvii, 9, 211, 247

Cruz, Ted, 217, 309, 321

Cuba, 19, 227, 320, 325

Cubans, 19, 223–24

Czech Republic, 100, 113

De la Cruz, Sebastien, 322

de la Garza, Eligio, 227

Declaration of Independence, xvi, 3, 280

Defense of Marriage Act, 57

Deferred Action for Childhood Arrivals (DACA), 56, 140–41, 171, 196, 278

Deferred Action for Parents of Americans and Lawful Permanent Residents, 56

Delgado, Luis Alberto, 151

Department of Motor Vehicles, 273

Department of State Health Services, 328

Depression era, 33, 51–52, 129, 156

DeSipio, Louis, 197

Detention and Removal Operations, 70, 121

Development, Relief, and Education for Alien Minors (DREAM) Act, 41, 140, 325

DHS Appropriations Act of 2010, 136

Dillingham, William, 215–16, 218

District of Columbia, 329

Dobkin, Donald, 65
Dodds, Drew, 283
Dominican Republic, 19
Dunn, Timothy, 283
Durbin, Richard, 140
Duster, Troy, 238

E. Pluribus Unum, 171
Earned Income Tax Credit, 110
Earnings Suspense File, 86
Eastern Europe, 7, 103–4, 147, 214, 257
Eastern Hemisphere, 52
Eastern Kentucky University, 283
Ebola, 333
Edkins, Jenny, 61
educational system, 81, 259, 326, 331
Elbit Systems, 285, 290
Elkabetz, 285, 287
Ellis and Angel Islands, 103, 248, 252,
    256–57, 279
Eloy Detention Center, 319
Emancipation Proclamation, 211
Endangered Species Act, 135
Enforcement and Removal Operations
    (ERO), 70, 75, 315
England, 102, 205
Esparza, Indira, 322
Eugenics Research Association, 103
Evans, Heather, 91
E-Verify, 110
Ewing, Walter, 308

Feagin, Joe, xvi, 215, 240, 251
Federal Bureau of Prisons, 72
Federal housing programs, 110
Federation for American Immigration
    Reform (FAIR), 146, 293
Federation of Organized Trades and
    Labor Unions, 113

Fernández-Armesto, Felipe, 3
Fifth Amendment, 91, 150, 154
Fifth U.S. Circuit Court of Appeals, 149,
    336
Finland, 207
Finnish Lutherans, 207
Fiorina, Carly, 281, 309
Fisher, Mike, 14
Fitzpatrick, Tony, xvii, 303
Flagg, Barbara, 245
Florence Service Processing Center, 75
Florida Bar, 325
food stamps, 5, 110, 260
Ford, Henry, 102
for-profit detention and prison systems,
    204
Fourteenth Amendment, 42, 115, 139, 154,
    161, 327
Fourth Amendment, 18, 139, 143, 150, 157,
    299
Franklin, Benjamin, 48, 206
Fuentes, Carlos, 268
fumigation, 18

Gadsden Purchase, 209
Garcia Hinojosa de Salinas, Dolores, 125
Garcia, Gus C., 127
García, Sergio, 325
Gardner, Matthew, 294
GATT, 108
Gaza and the West Bank, 285
Gaza Strip, 285
Geo Group, 71, 112, 137, 139, 154, 292, 317
Georgia, xvii, 72, 316, 319
German, 48, 100, 103, 113, 206–7, 214,
    279–80
Germanic, 206–7
Gilded Age, 102
Gingrich, Newt, 133

Giroux, Henry, 80

Global Advantage, 287, 290

Godinez-Samperio, Jose, 324

Golan Group, 286

Gold Rush, 47, 283

Gonzales, Alfonso, xvi, 245

Gonzalez-Barrera, Ana, 250, 304, 331

Google, 86

Gorbachev, Mikhail, 122, 134

Gordon, Milton, 243

Grassroots Leadership, 73, 319

Great Britain, 49

Great Depression, 46, 50–51, 105, 111, 128–29, 156

Great Recession, 8, 250, 254

Greeks, 49, 215

green card, 134, 272–74

Green, Donald, 321

Greenstone, Michael, 85

Griswold, Daniel, 83

Gross, Stephen, 294, 294

Guadalajara, Mexico, 269–70, 276

Guam, 48

Guatemala, 14–17, 19, 69, 121, 130–31, 173, 331–33

Gudino, Armando, 305

Guerrero, Mario, 153

Guggenheim, Davis, 325

Gutiérrez, David G., 36

Gutiérrez, Shena, 289

Guzman, Pedro, 154

Habeas Corpus, 91

Hall, Stuart, 171

Hamilton Project, 83

Hannity, Sean, 217

Harbury, Jennifer, 328

Harrington, James, 328

Hart, Jim, 67

Hart-Celler Act, 11, 33

Harty, Allison, 89

Harvard University, xix, 311

Hatch, Orrin, 89

Hawaiian, 48, 271

Haymarket Rally, 113

Haymarket Square, 113

health care, 9, 56, 81, 84, 87, 110, 219, 226

Hedges, Chris, 83

Henry, Patrick, 3

Heritage Foundation, 63

Hernandez v. Texas (1954), 127

Heyman, Josiah, 307

high skill workers (H1-B), 111

Hinojosa, Rosendo, 8

Holland, 206

homicide, 82

Honduras, 15–17, 19, 73, 121, 332–33

Hoover, Herbert, 128

Hoyt, Joshua, 327

HR4437, 35, 37–38, 42

Huachuca, Fort, 286

Hudson, Linda, 326

Human Rights Watch, 305

human trafficking, 335–36

Huntington, Samuel P., xix, 311, 321

ideological forces, xxi, 4, 93, 224, 302

IDF Special Forces, 286

Illegal Immigration Reform and Immigrant Responsibility Act IIRIRA (1996), 54, 63–64, 69, 86, 88, 108, 133, 144, 159

Illinois, 140, 142, 173, 280, 328–29

Immigration Act of 1917, 57, 103

Immigration and Intergenerational Mobility in Metropolitan Los Angeles (IIMMLA), 173, 197

Immigration and Nationality Act (INA) of 1965, 52, 66, 107, 216

Immigration and Nationality Act of 1952 (INA), 57, 133, 159

Immigration and Naturalization Service (INS), 33–34, 37, 39, 54, 63, 120, 129–30, 132

Immigration Law Clinic, 327

Immigration Policy Center, 12, 158

immigration raids, xvii, xxi, 5, 16, 22, 40, 54, 69, 93, 123, 128, 132, 156

Immigration Reform and Control Act (IRCA) of 1986, 12, 34, 54, 63, 84, 108, 131–32, 155, 171

imperialist movements, xiv, 323

Independent Republic of Texas, 227

India, 6–7, 48, 111, 169

Indiana, 319

indigenous people, 203, 238–40, 287

Ingraham, Laura, 321

Institute on Taxation and Economic Policy (ITEP), 86, 110, 294

intellectual racists, xiii, 8, 52, 219, 310–11, 315, 321

Intelligence Reform and Terrorism Prevention Act of 2004 (IRTPA), 136, 316

Inter-American Commission on Human Rights, 148

international terrorists, 121, 132, 281, 309

inverted double jeopardy, 72, 91

Iraq, 42, 89, 283, 296, 347

Ireland, 113, 212

IRS, 86,

Isacson, Adam, 82

ISIS, 310, 333

Israel Business Initiative, 286, 290

Israeli, 285–87, 289–91

Israelis, 285

Issa, Darrell, 141

Italian, 48–49, 114, 212–13, 279

Italy, 49, 103

Jalisco, Mexico, 268

Jamestown, 101

Japan, 7, 48

Javed, Arifa, 222

Jefferson, Thomas, 3, 101

Jewish, 48, 114, 213–14, 256

Jobs, Steve, 325

Johnson, Jeh, 74, 138, 140

Johnson, Jimmy, 286

Johnson, Terry, 146

Johnson-Reed Act of 1924, 103

Johnston, Albert, 103

Judaism, 214

Judd, Brandon, 311

Kansas, 312

Karnes County Residential Center, 319

Kennedy, John F., 52, 100, 203

Kennedy, Robert, 53

Kholoptseva, Jenya, 172

King, Desmond, 65

King, Steve, 311–12

Klein, Naomi, 286

Known-Nothing Party, 213

Kobach, Kris, 312

Kochhar, Rakesh, 255

Koelsch, David, 237

Krieser, Steve, 311

Krikorian, Mark, 69, 295

Ku Klux Klan (KKK), 66–67, 213–14

La Bestia, 16

La Raza, 225

Labarga, Jorge, 325

labor market, 21, 81, 84, 92, 111, 253–54, 259

Lajvardi, Faridodin, 141

Latin America, xix, 7, 52–53, 108, 122, 251, 253, 321, 327

Latino threat, 243

LatinoJustice, 125, 148

Laufer, Peter, 23, 268, 280

Lazarus, Emma, 122, 259

League of United Latin American Citizens (LULAC), 36–37, 39, 126

Leahy, Patrick, 289

Lee, Jennifer, 197

Legal Arizona Workers ACT (LAWA), 87, 90

Leighton, Paul, 249, 293

Lemon, Don, 310

Levin, Mark, 321

Libal, Bob, 319

Light, Michael, 304

Limbaugh, Rush, 217, 277, 310, 321

Livingston, Gretchen, 255

Lockheed Martin Corporation, 283

Lone Ranger, 241

Looney, Adam, 85

López, David, 209

López, Mark Hugo, 250, 255, 304

Lutheran Immigration and Refugee Service and the Women's Refugee Commission, 73–74

lynching, 50, 67, 242

Lyon, David, 289

Lytle, Kelly, 35, 85, 303

Malkin, Michelle, 321

Management Training Corporation, 73, 318

Manges Douglas, Karen, 173

Manifest Destiny, xiv, xvi, 30, 124, 127, 145, 209, 240, 323

manipulation, xvi, xxi, 4, 50, 307, 309, 335

Mapp, Chris, 311

marginalization, xvi, 4, 36, 288, 334–35

Maricopa County, 89, 144, 242, 258, 333

marijuana, 149, 305, 311

Marino, Tom, 317

Martinez, Daniel, 307–8

mass incarceration, 304

Massachusetts Institute of Technology (MIT), 141

Massachusetts, 69, 328

Mazzio, Mary, 142

McCarran-Walter Act, 36

McCaul, Michael, 284

McKenna, Megan, 333

Medicaid services, 110

Medicare, 86–87, 110, 158

Melendres v. Arpaio (2013), 161, 242

Menjívar, Cecilia, 19

Mennonites, 206

Merida Initiative, 10

Methodists, 206

Mexican American Legal Defense and Educational Fund (MALDEF), 125, 143

Mexican Constitution, 335

Mexican Revolution, 31, 49, 125, 128

Mexican-American War in 1848, xvi, 321

Mexico's National Immigration Institute, 16–17

Mexico-Guatemala border, 15, 331

Meyer, Maureen, 82

Michigan, 280

Microsoft, 86

Middle Easterners, 174, 225

migrant agricultural workers (H2-A), 111

Miller, Todd, 282, 287

Minuteman Project, 40

Miranda, 19, 91

Mirandé, Alfredo, 18

Missouri Synod Lutheran denomination, 206

Moderna Museet, 75

Molina, Natalia, 31, 33

Montana, 294

Montgomery, Bill, 258

Moore, Joan, 210

Moore, Wendy Leo, 215, 246

Morales, Daniel, 88

Morton, John, 317

Mosher, Clayton, J., 293

Movimiento Pro-Migrante, 37–38

multicultural society, 8, 19–20, 92, 221

multiethnic, 8, 20, 92, 197, 221, 227

multiracial, 8, 20, 92, 197, 221, 227

Muslims, xix, 42, 57, 217, 221, 225, 321

NAFTA, 108

Napolitano, Janet, 325, 335

narco-terrorists, 5, 17, 20, 281, 297, 309, 321

National Alliance, 37, 66

National Border Patrol Council (NBPC), 311

National Chicano/Latino Conference on Immigration and Public Policy, 37

National Council of La Raza, 39, 69

National Criminal Information Center, 65

National Environmental Policy Act, 135

National Guard, 51

National Labor Relations Board, 100, 114

national origin, 21, 47, 49–50, 52–53, 56–57, 66, 113, 143, 152–53, 206, 225, 322–23, 331

National Origins Act, 31–33, 49

National Partnership for New Americans, 327

National Register of Historic Places, 256

National Rifle Association, 313

nationalism, 66, 83, 93, 94

Native American Graves Protection and Repatriation Act, 135

Native Americans, xvii, 4, 31, 104, 127, 145, 204–5, 209–10, 227, 301

naturalization, 248, 326–28

Navarro, Armando, 37, 41

Nazi concentration camps, 147

Nazi German, 18, 93, 149

Nebraska, xvii, 312

Neo-racism, 68

Nevada, 57

Nevins, Joseph, 287

New Amsterdam, xiii

New Mexico, 31, 38, 46, 51, 57, 64, 73, 124, 209, 321, 329

new racism, 68

Ngai, Mae M., 31

Nicaraguans, 130

NICE Systems, 286

Niemoller, Martin, 301

Ninth Circuit Court of Appeals, 87, 135, 138–39, 144

No Child Left Behind Act of 2001, 219

Noel, Linda C., 35

Noonan, John T., 87

North Carolina, 67, 146

Northwestern University, 292

Norway, 207

Nuevo Leon, Mexico, 125

O'Connell Davidson, Julia, 291

O'Reilly, Bill, 309–10

Oakland, 276

Office of Enforcement and Removal (ERO), 70, 75, 315

Office of Immigration Statistics (OIS), 121

Office of Investigations Alien Criminal Apprehension Program, 75

Office of the Inspector General, 137

Offshore Group, 287, 290

Oklahoma, 50, 68, 132

Oliver, Melvin, 255

Omi, Michael, 65

Operation Gatekeeper, xviii, 34, 37, 55, 64, 132

Operation Hold the Line, xviii, 34, 64

Operation Jobs, xviii, 132

Operation Repatriation, xviii, 128

Operation Return to Sender, xviii, 135

Operation Safeguard, xviii, 34, 37, 64

Operation Streamline, xviii, 72–73, 75, 135

Operation Wetback, xviii, 18, 33, 39, 52, 106, 111, 128, 254

Oppression, xvi, xxi, 4, 43, 50, 124, 216, 224, 227, 241, 244, 247, 334–35

Organization of American States (OAS), 148

Pacific Islands, 215

Padilla v. Kentucky (2010), 91, 159

Palestine, 285–87

Palin, Sarah, 279–80

parole, 112, 323

Pearce, Russell, 313

Pearl Harbor, 211

Peña Nieto, Enrique, 15–16

Pennsylvania, 48, 87, 206, 317

Pentagon, 120, 309

People v. Hall (1854), 58

Perales, Cesar, 148

Pérez Molina, Otto, 16

Perez, Thomas, 258

Perry, Rick, 311

Personal Responsibility and Work Opportunity Reconciliation Act, 87

Philippines, xiv, 7, 106, 111, 122, 173

Plan Frontera Sur, 15–16

Plan of the Alliance for Prosperity in the Northern Triangle, 17

Poland, 103

police brutality, 285, 305, 308

policing, 15, 19, 196, 236, 242, 246, 253, 258, 285–86, 306, 323

Polish, 212–13, 224–25, 256

Political Association of California, 37

political pundits, 14, 52, 219, 257, 309, 315, 321

Pope, 239, 278

Portuguese, 213

Post-Civil War, 102

post-racial society, 335

poverty, 17, 58, 109, 112, 122, 124, 132, 325–28, 333

Powell, Laurene, 325

Prado, Edward, 150

Predator B drones, 283

Presbyterians, 206

probation, 112, 217, 323

profitability of social control, xviii, 14, 71–72, 109, 111–12, 139, 154, 284–85, 287, 289–90, 292–93, 304, 309, 312–15, 319

Proposition 187, 9, 34, 39–40, 56, 64, 83, 86, 219, 273

protectionism, 83

Protestant Reformation Society, 213

Protestant religion, 205, 207

Protestantism, 206

Protestants, 206–7, 212, 214, 221, 224

Puerto Rican Legal Defense and Educational Fund, 125

Puerto Ricans, xvii, 55, 223–25

Puerto Rico, xiv, 122, 150, 227, 320

racial stereotypes, 18, 23, 252

Raher, Stephen, 72

Reagan, Ronald, 54, 122, 131–32, 134, 150, 154

Reeves County Detention Center, 319

reform school, 182

Reiman, Jeffrey, 249

Reingold, Beth, 321
repatriations, 52
repression, 35, 296
Requerimiento, 239
Revolutionary Period, 102
Reynolds American Incorporated, 313
Rhode Island, 214
Riddle, Debbie, 311
Rio Bravo (Grande), 8, 268–69, 283
Rio Grande Valley of Texas, 8, 283
riots, 18, 285, 319
Rockefeller, John D., 102
Rodino, Peter, 34, 37, 39
Rodriguez v. Robbins (2015), 118
Rodriguez, Jose Antonio Elena, 235–36, 306
Romania, 52
Roosevelt, Eleanor, 147, 152
Roosevelt, Franklin D., 130, 147
Roosevelt, Theodore, 208
Rothschild, Jonathan, 290
Rumbaut, Rubén G., 197
Russell Sage Foundation, 173
Russia, 103, 323
Russian Empire, 50
Rutgers University, 84

Sáenz, Rogelio, 173, 332
Salazar, Ken, 30
Salinas López, Reyes, 125
Salinas, Lupe S., 22, 120, 241
San Diego, 64, 132, 155, 187, 270, 275, 322
Sánchez, Teodulo, 314
Santillan, Lorenzo, 141
Santorum, Rick, 309
SB 1070, xviii, 46, 56, 83, 87–90, 93, 236, 246, 258, 313–14, 319
SBInet, 335
Scandinavian, 103, 207

scapegoats, 128, 252–53, 268
Schivone, Gabriel, 287
Schmidt, Carl, 70
Scotland, 102
Scots-Irish, 206–7, 212
seasonal nonagricultural workers (H2-B), 111
Secure Communities, 140, 315
Secure Fence Act of 2006, 42, 55, 140, 159
SEDENA, 16
Seif, Hinda, 331
Selma, Donna, 293
Senate Appropriations Committee, 136–37
Senders, Bernie, 137
Sengstock, Mary C., 22, 203, 225
Service Employees International Union (SEIU), 114
Service Processing Centers (SPC), 71, 75
Shanhani, Aarti, 91
Shelby, Richard, 317
silencing minorities, xvi, xix, 288, 324, 334
Simon, Jonathan, xvi, 303
Sixth Amendment, 91
skin color, xviii, 56–57, 210, 213, 226, 323, 334
Skolnick, Jerome, 306
Slack, Jeremy, 307
slavery, xvii, xx, 23, 51, 101–2, 115, 152, 154, 210, 240, 254, 293, 323
Slavs, 49, 215
Smith, Rogers, 65
Snow, G. Murray, 242
social control movement, xvi, 92, 333
Social Security, 86–87, 110, 151, 158, 254, 278, 294–95
social services, 21, 50, 63, 81, 85, 92, 253, 255
soldiers, 105, 134, 283
South Carolina, xvi, 67

South Korea, 7, 111

South Texas Family Residential Center, 73

Southern Border Plan, 14–16

Soviet Union, 67, 147

Spaniards, 127

Stannard, David, 239

Stanton-Salazar, Ricardo, 209

Statue of Liberty, xv, 46, 122, 256

stereotypes, 18, 23, 35, 238, 251–52, 322, 334

Stevens, Jacqueline, 153, 155, 292

stigma, 58, 324

Stockholm, Sweden, 75

Stormfront, 66

Suhay, Elizabeth, 223

Sullivan, Laura, 313

Supplemental Nutrition Assistance Program, 260

Supplemental Security Income, 110

surveillance, xvii, 21, 33, 81, 93, 150, 282–83, 285–86, 288–90, 296–97, 303, 331

Swain, Carol, 66

Swartz, Lonnie, 306

Sweden, 75, 207

Switzerland, 206

Syracuse University, 304

Syrian refugees, xiv, 309, 333

Takaki, Ronald, 238

Takao Ozawa v. United States (1922), 58

Takei, Carl, 291

Taliban, 283

Tamaulipas, Mexico, 283

Tanton, John, 146

Taxpayer Identification Number (ITIN), 110

Taylor, Paul S., 125

Tea Party, 9, 83, 141

Tech Parks Arizona, 287, 290

Temporary Assistance for Needy Families, 110

Terrorism Prevention Act, 136, 316

terrorism, xiv, xvii, xviii, 5, 24, 67–68, 133, 136, 303–4, 330

Terry v. Ohio (1968), 143, 159

Texas Civil Rights Project, 328

Texas Rangers, 241–42

Texas rebellion, 209

Texas Rio Grande Legal Aid, 328

Thailand, 48

The 800 Mile Wall, 135

Thirteenth Amendment, 154–55, 293

Thurgood Marshall College, 322

Timberg, Craig, 289

Tirman, John, 6, 320

Transactional Records Access Clearinghouse, 304

Treaty of Guadalupe Hidalgo, xiii, xvi, 240, 321

Triangle Shirtwaist factory, 114

Truman, Harry, 147

Trump, Donald, 8, 42, 74, 80–81, 92–93, 112, 122, 124, 146, 156, 169, 196, 217, 219, 225, 251, 258, 268, 277, 281, 294, 309–10, 312, 314, 321, 330

Turner, Jonathan, 18

Twin Towers, 120

U.N. Declaration of Human Rights, 22, 123, 147, 151

U.N. General Assembly, 306

U.N. Member States, 151

U.S. Court of Appeals for the 9th Circuit, 87, 138

U.S. Declaration of Independence, xvi, 3, 280

U.S. Department of Labor, 50, 104, 106, 127

U.S. Supreme Court, xv, 3, 18, 48, 55–56, 87, 90–91, 127, 138, 143, 145, 314, 319

United Farm Workers Union, 37

United Farmworkers, 37, 114

United Nations, 147–48, 151

United States v. Brignoni-Ponce (1975), 18, 59, 143–44, 155–60

United States v. Martínez-Fuerte (1976), 18

United States v. Montero-Camargo (1999), 144, 160

Universal Declaration of Human Rights (UDHR), 147, 151

University of Arizona, 286–87

University of California, xviii, 37, 170, 187, 322, 325

University of Chicago, 243

University of Detroit, 327

Urban Institute, 69

Urbina, Ian, 291

Utah, 57, 319, 329

Valentine, Nicholas, 323

Vazquez, Oscar, 141

Vela, Filemon, 127

Vermont, 215

vigilantes, 50, 55

Vikings, 207

violations of civil liberties, xv, 296

Virginia, 205, 328

Virtual Fence, 335

Walker, Samuel, 305

Walters, Evelyn, 321

war on drugs, xiv, xvi–xviii, 5, 10, 24, 303–4, 330

war on immigrants, xiv–xviii, 303–4

war on terrorism, xiv, xvii–xviii, 5, 24, 303–4, 330

war zone, 282–83

warfare, 283, 285

Warhol, Andy, 75

Warnshius, Paul, 18

Washington State University, 293

Washington, George, 101

Waterloo, 9

Weiner, Naomi 286

Welch, Michael, 55, 282, 287

welfare state, 254, 260

West Indies, 111, 216

Western Europe, 7, 103

Western Hemisphere, 11, 32, 50, 52–53, 66, 101, 129, 216, 218, 223

White House, 136, 208, 309

White Revolution, 66

White supremacy, 22–23, 40, 203, 218, 235, 237–38, 240, 242–48, 250–51, 253, 255, 257, 259–60, 323

Whitehead, John, 288

Whitlock, Craig, 289

Wilson, Christopher, 307

Wilson, Woodrow, 213

Winant, Howard, 65

Wisconsin's Department of Transportation, 311

Wong Wing v. United States (1896), 91

Woodrow Wilson Center, 307

World Trade Center, 54, 132

World War I, 31, 49, 103, 106

World War II, xiii, 33, 36, 48, 51, 58, 105, 122, 124, 129, 134, 212, 225, 254–55

Wright, Bruce, 290

Yoshikawa, Hirokazu, 172

Yuval-Davis, Nira, 172, 186

Zadvydas v. Davis (2001), 138

Zhou, Min, 197

Zuckerberg, Mark, 61

Zyklon B, 18